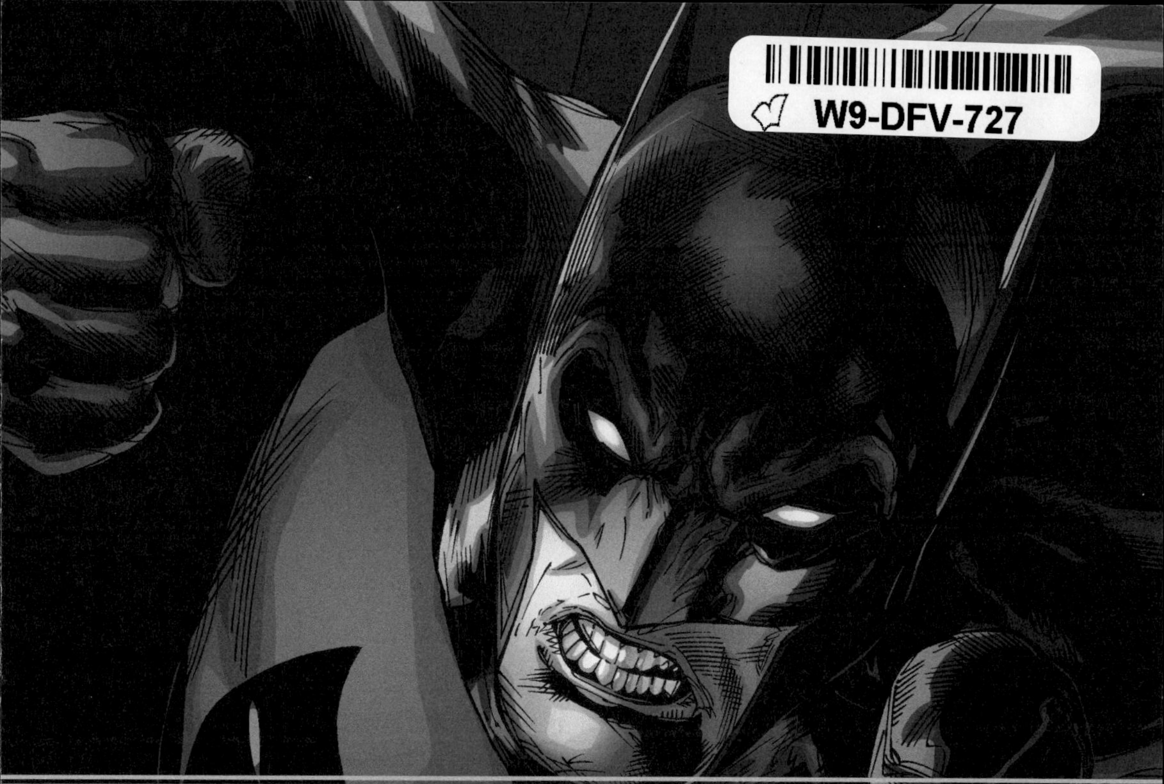

BATMAN
DETECTIVE COMICS

VOL. 4:
COLD VENGEANCE

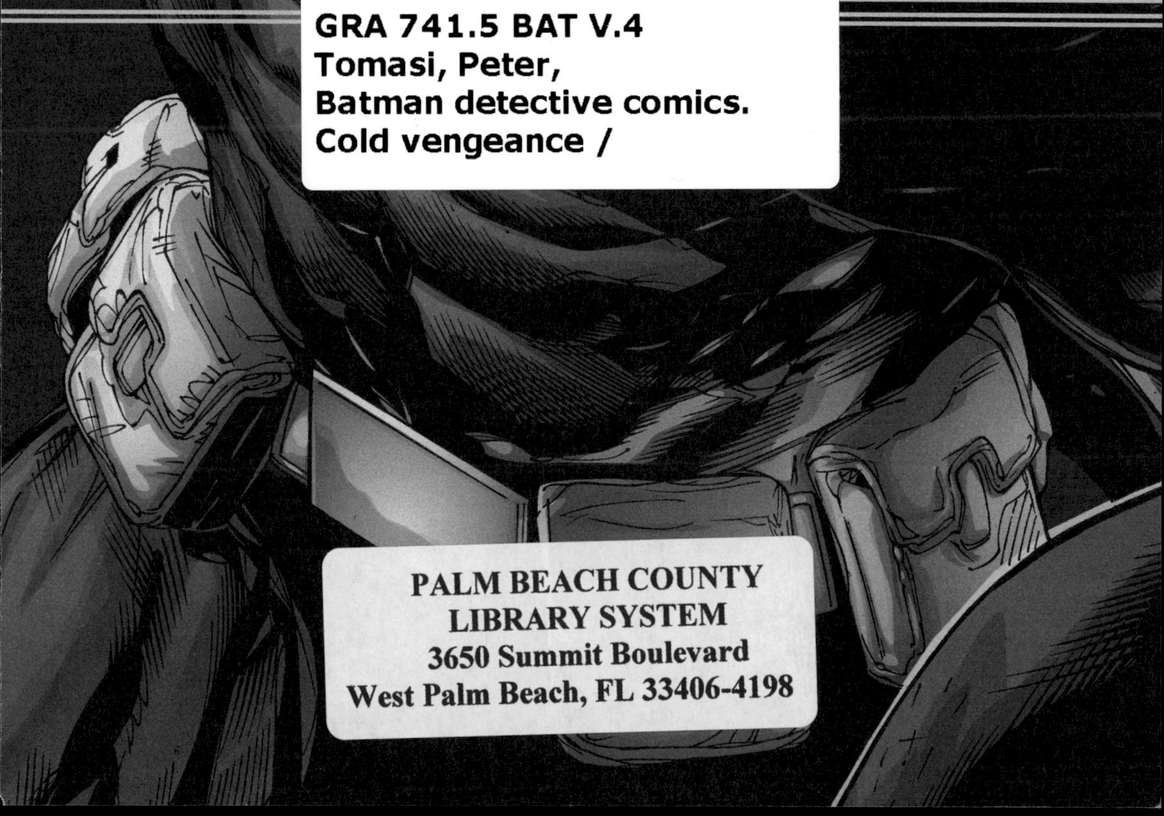

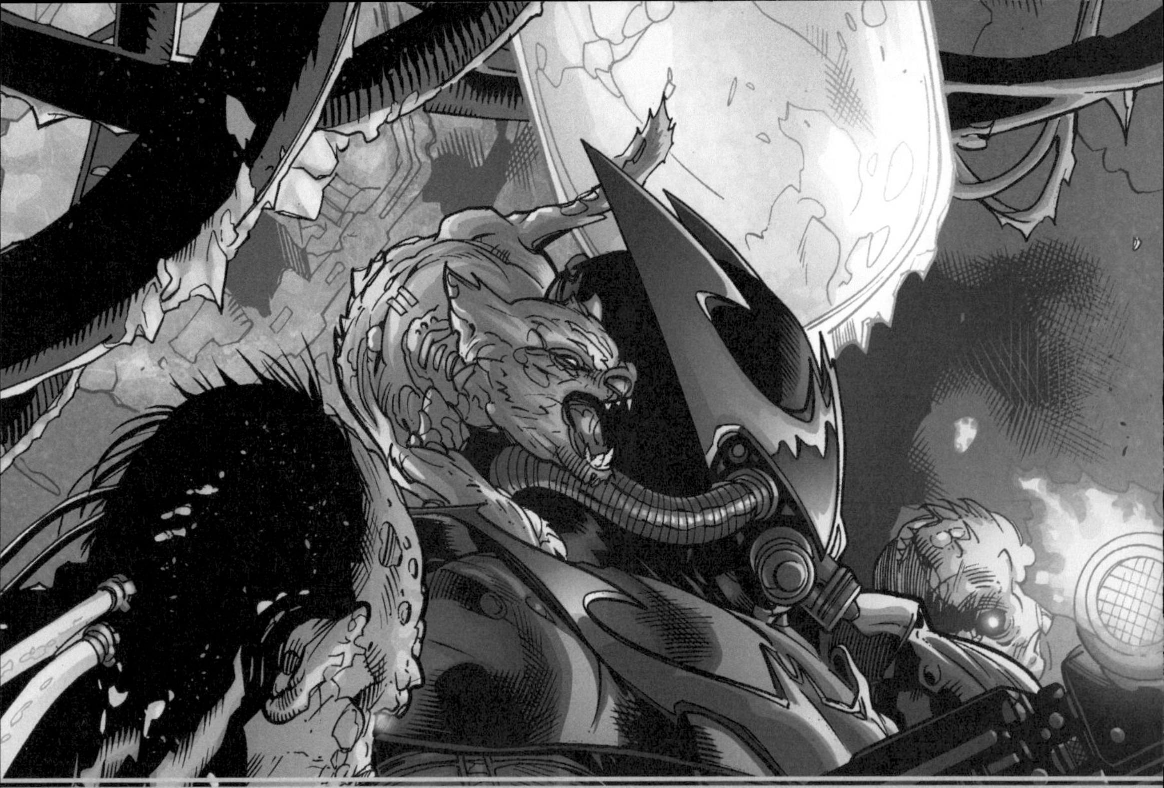

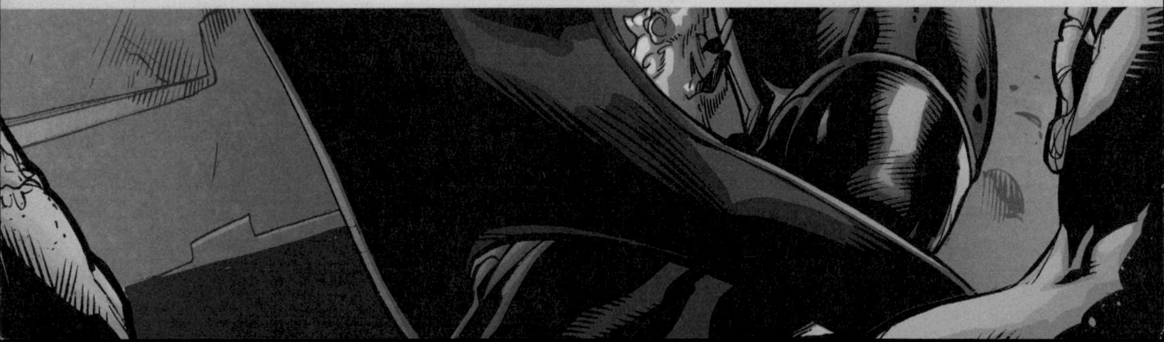

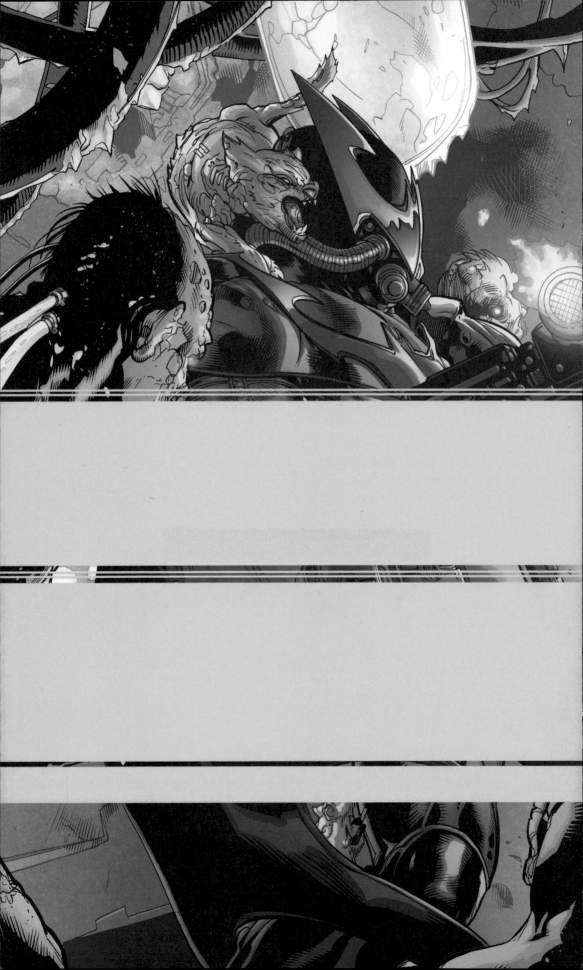

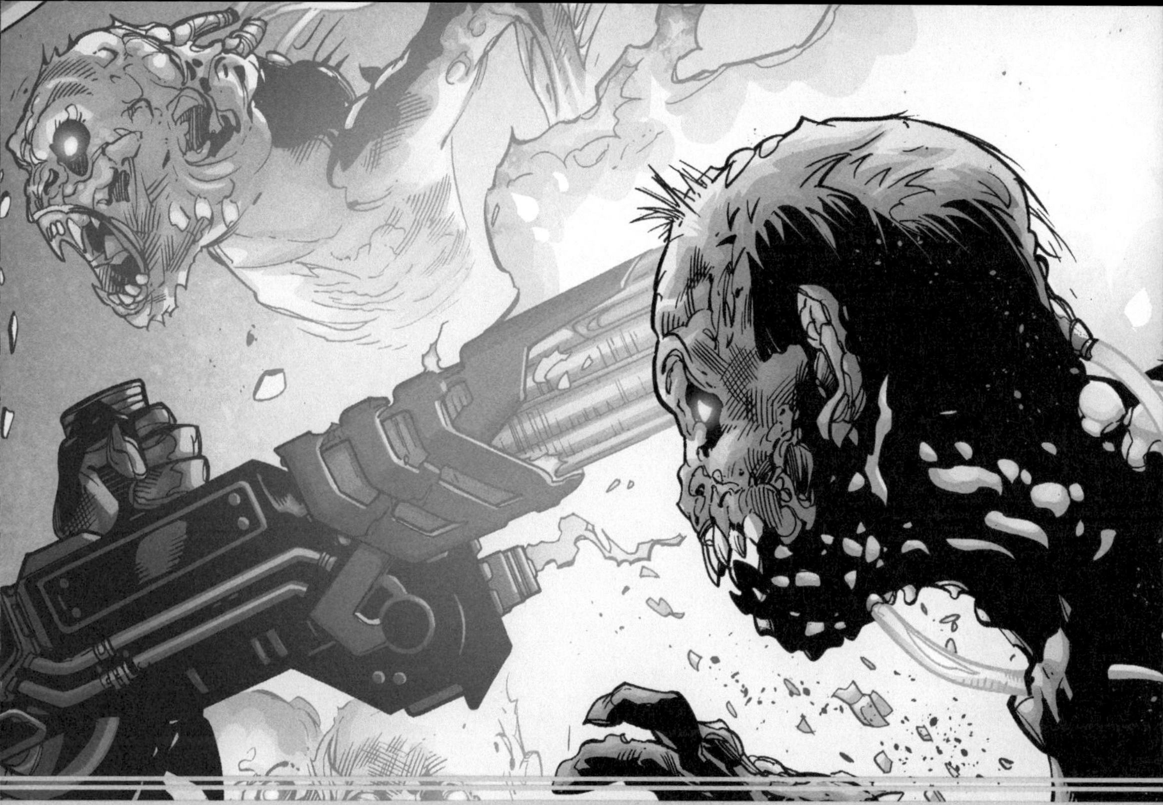

BATMAN
DETECTIVE COMICS
VOL. 4:
COLD VENGEANCE

PETER J. TOMASI
TOM TAYLOR
WRITERS

DOUG MAHNKE
SCOTT GODLEWSKI, TYLER KIRKHAM
CHRISTIAN ALAMY, JOSÉ LUÍS
JAIME MENDOZA, MATT SANTORELLI
KEITH CHAMPAGNE, MARK IRWIN
FERNANDO BLANCO
ARTISTS

DAVID BARON
JOHN KALISZ
COLORISTS

ROB LEIGH
TRAVIS LANHAM
LETTERERS

DOUG MAHNKE
and DAVID BARON
COLLECTION COVER ARTISTS

BATMAN CREATED BY **BOB KANE** WITH **BILL FINGER**

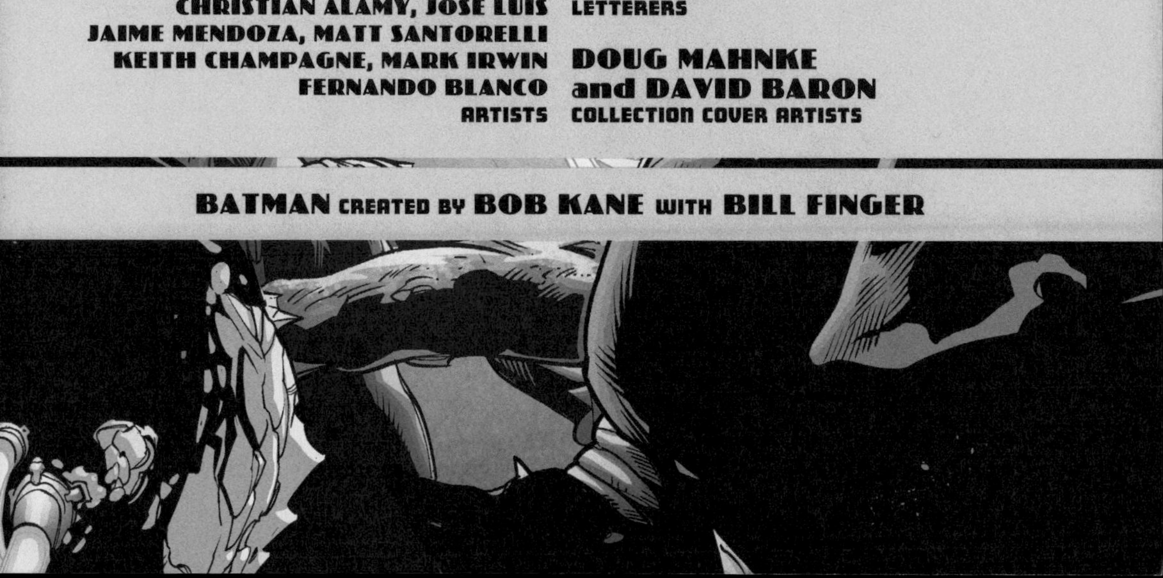

PAUL KAMINSKI
MOLLY MAHAN Editors – Original Series
BRITTANY HOLZHERR
DAVE WIELGOSZ Associate Editors – Original Series
JEB WOODARD Group Editor – Collected Editions
ROBIN WILDMAN Editor – Collected Edition
STEVE COOK Design Director – Books
DAMIAN RYLAND Publication Design
SUZANNAH ROWNTREE Publication Production

BOB HARRAS Senior VP – Editor-in-Chief, DC Comics

JIM LEE Publisher & Chief Creative Officer
BOBBIE CHASE VP – Global Publishing Initiatives & Digital Strategy
DON FALLETTI VP – Manufacturing Operations & Workflow Management
LAWRENCE GANEM VP – Talent Services
ALISON GILL Senior VP – Manufacturing & Operations
HANK KANALZ Senior VP – Publishing Strategy & Support Services
DAN MIRON VP – Publishing Operations
NICK J. NAPOLITANO VP – Manufacturing Administration & Design
NANCY SPEARS VP – Sales
JONAH WEILAND VP – Marketing & Creative Services
MICHELE R. WELLS VP & Executive Editor, Young Reader

BATMAN: DETECTIVE COMICS VOL. 4: COLD VENGEANCE

DC Comics, 2900 West Alameda Ave., Burbank, CA 91505
Printed by LSC Communications, Owensville, MO, USA. 11/20/20. First Printing.
ISBN: 978-1-77950-455-5

Library of Congress Cataloging-in-Publication Data is available.

PEFC Certified

This product is from
sustainably managed
forests and controlled
sources

PEFC/29-31-337   www.pefc.org

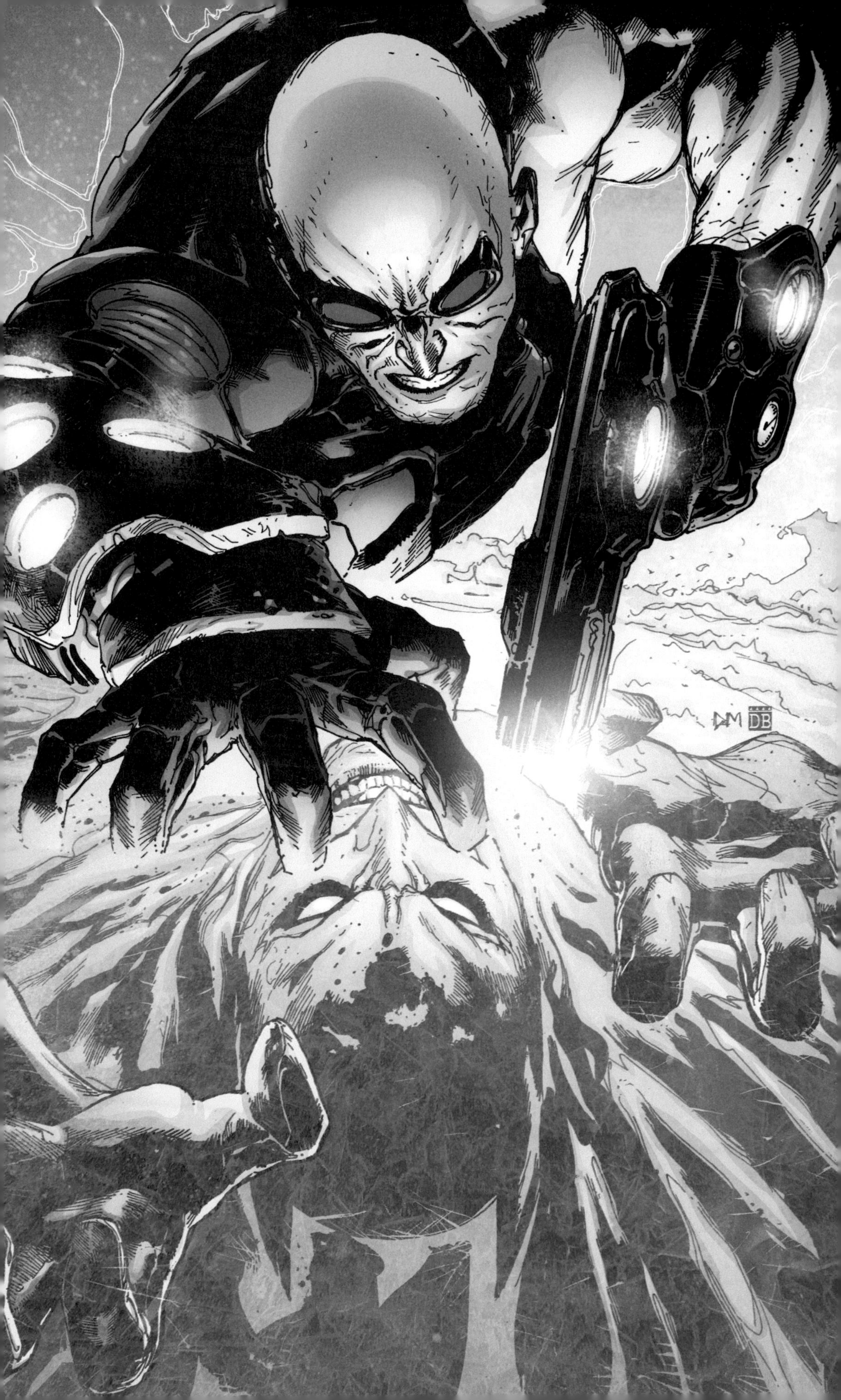

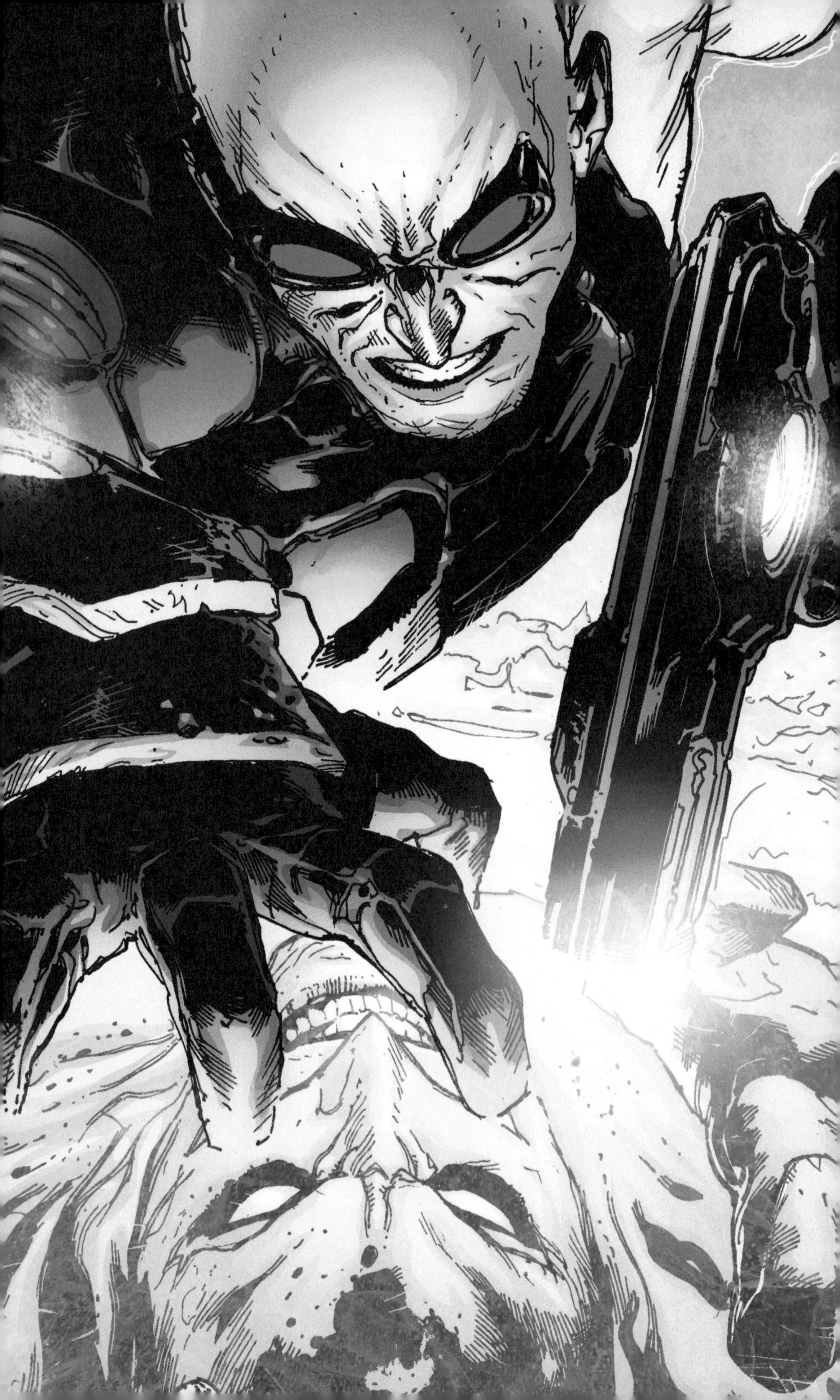

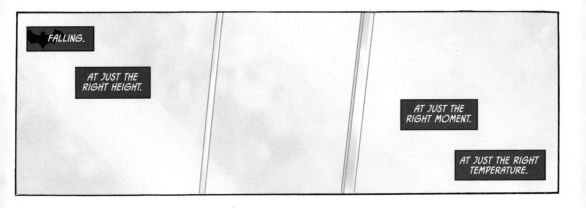

FALLING.

AT JUST THE RIGHT HEIGHT.

AT JUST THE RIGHT MOMENT.

AT JUST THE RIGHT TEMPERATURE.

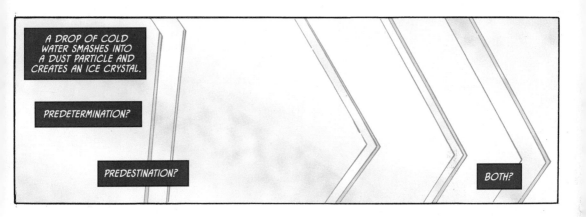

A DROP OF COLD WATER SMASHES INTO A DUST PARTICLE AND CREATES AN ICE CRYSTAL.

PREDETERMINATION?

PREDESTINATION?

BOTH?

THEY'VE EACH TAKEN TWO DIFFERENT PATHS.

TWO DIFFERENT ANGLES.

BUT STILL MANAGE TO ATTRACT EACH OTHER.

AND FOR A SHORT TIME, THEY DANCE IN THE SKY.

UNIQUE.

DISTINCT.

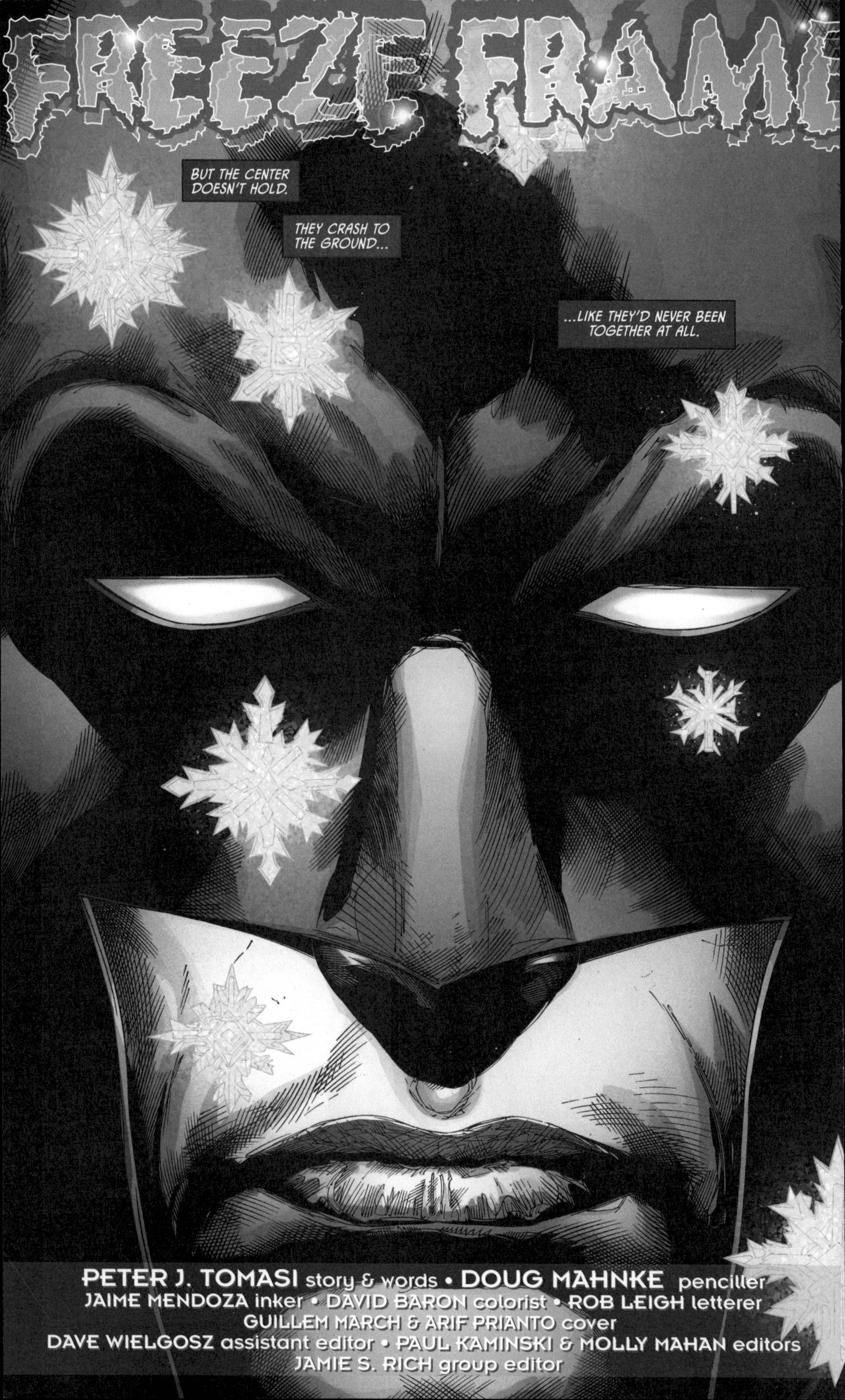
FREEZE FRAME
BUT THE CENTER DOESN'T HOLD.
THEY CRASH TO THE GROUND...
...LIKE THEY'D NEVER BEEN TOGETHER AT ALL.
PETER J. TOMASI story & words • DOUG MAHNKE penciller
JAIME MENDOZA inker • DAVID BARON colorist • ROB LEIGH letterer
GUILLEM MARCH & ARIF PRIANTO cover
DAVE WIELGOSZ assistant editor • PAUL KAMINSKI & MOLLY MAHAN editors
JAMIE S. RICH group editor

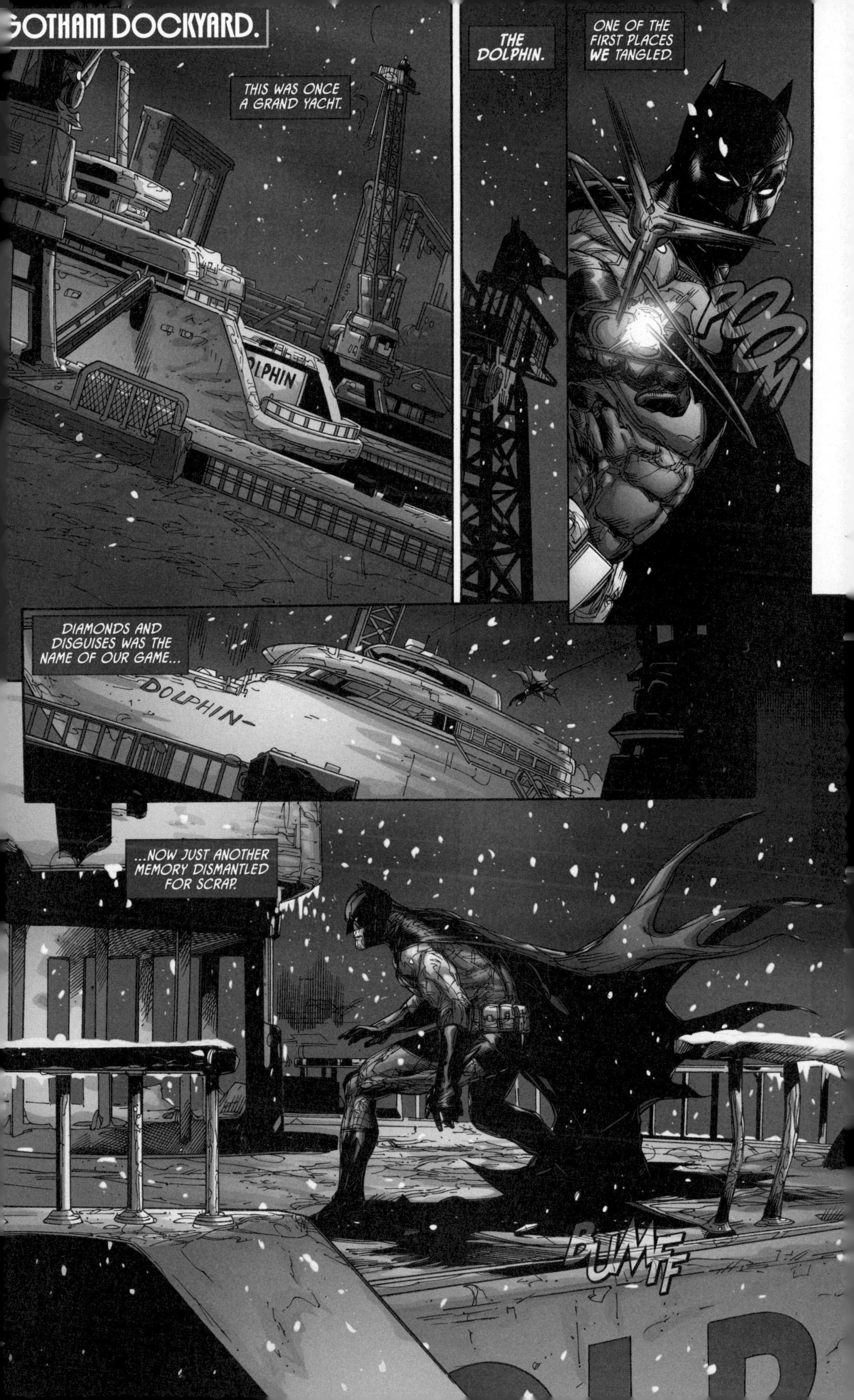
GOTHAM DOCKYARD.
THIS WAS ONCE A GRAND YACHT.
DOLPHIN
THE DOLPHIN.
ONE OF THE FIRST PLACES WE TANGLED.
BOOM
DIAMONDS AND DISGUISES WAS THE NAME OF OUR GAME...
DOLPHIN
...NOW JUST ANOTHER MEMORY DISMANTLED FOR SCRAP.
BUMF

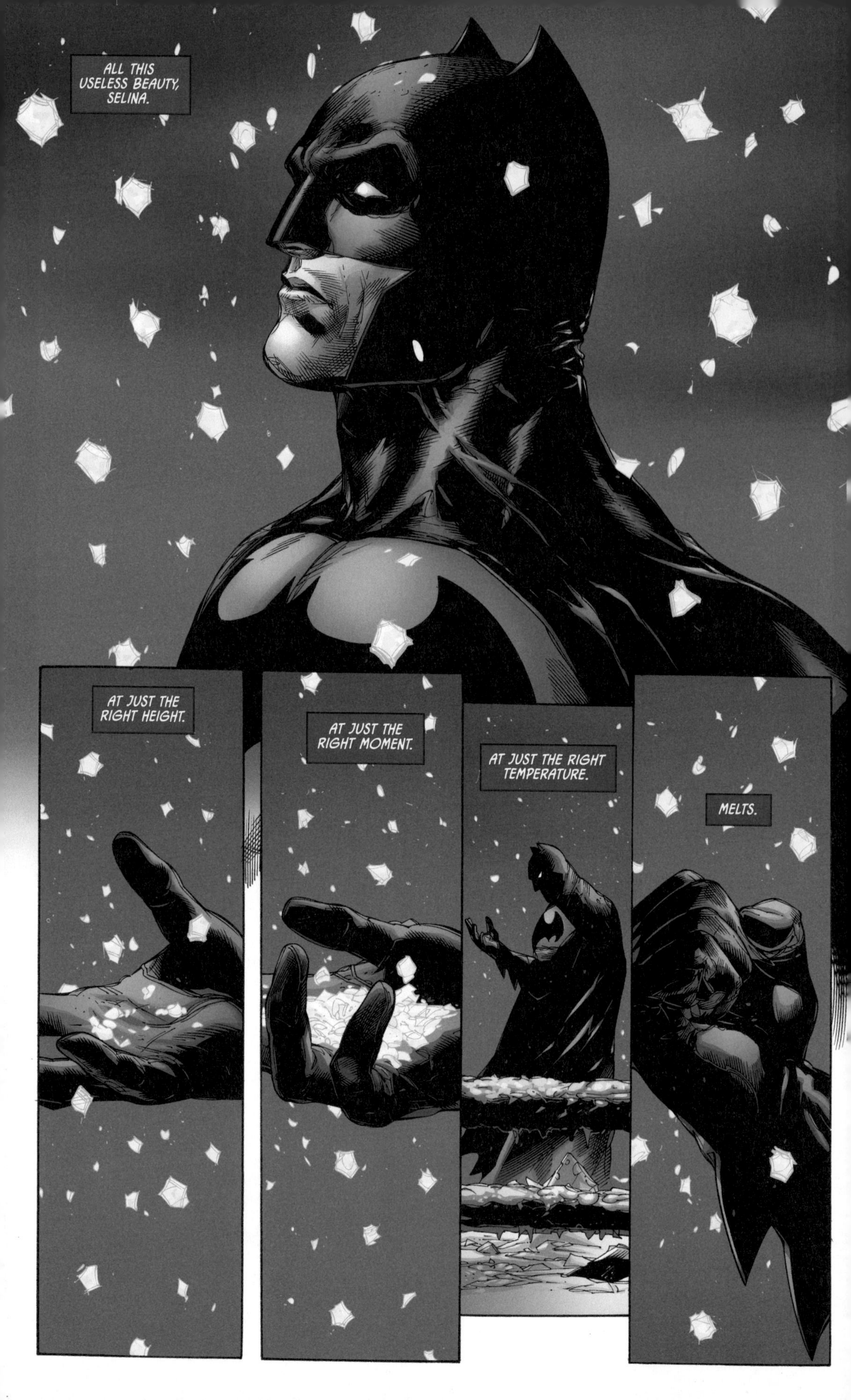
ALL THIS USELESS BEAUTY, SELINA.
AT JUST THE RIGHT HEIGHT.
AT JUST THE RIGHT MOMENT.
AT JUST THE RIGHT TEMPERATURE.
MELTS.

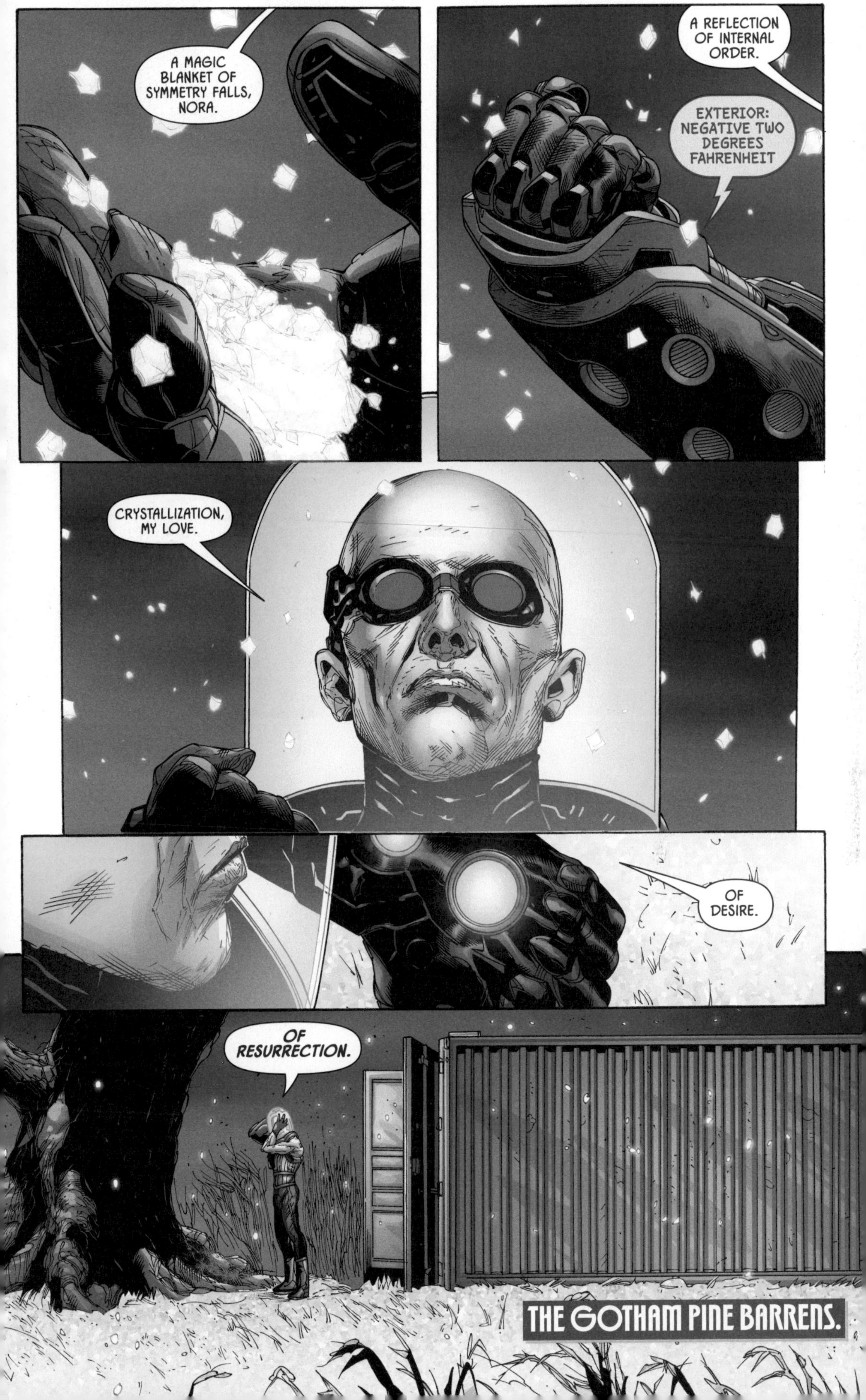
A MAGIC BLANKET OF SYMMETRY FALLS, NORA.
A REFLECTION OF INTERNAL ORDER.
EXTERIOR: NEGATIVE TWO DEGREES FAHRENHEIT
CRYSTALLIZATION, MY LOVE.
OF DESIRE.
OF RESURRECTION.
THE GOTHAM PINE BARRENS.

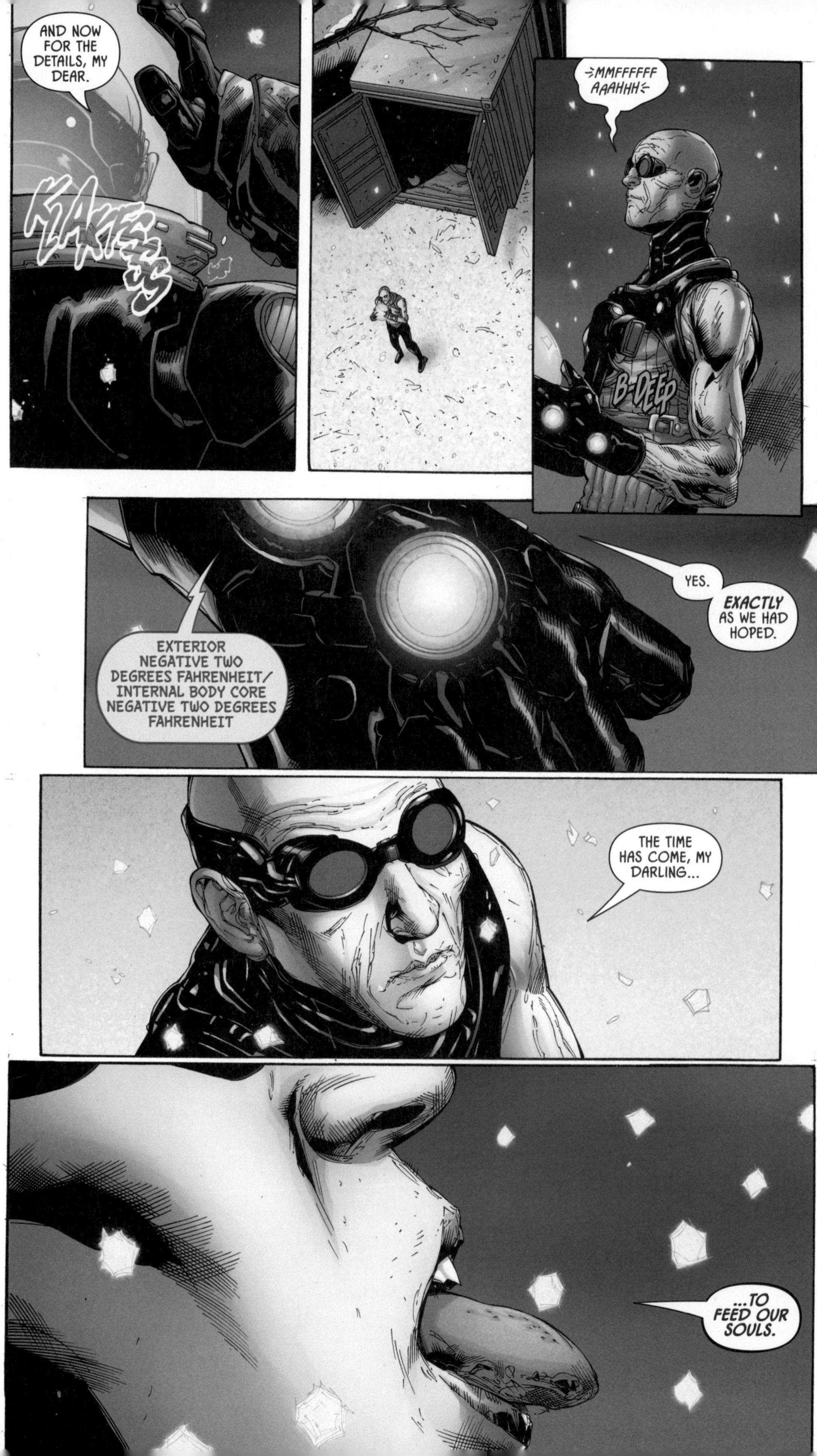
AND NOW FOR THE DETAILS, MY DEAR.
KLAKFSSS
=MMFFFFFF AAAHHH=
B-DEEP
YES. EXACTLY AS WE HAD HOPED.
EXTERIOR NEGATIVE TWO DEGREES FAHRENHEIT/ INTERNAL BODY CORE NEGATIVE TWO DEGREES FAHRENHEIT
THE TIME HAS COME, MY DARLING...
...TO FEED OUR SOULS.

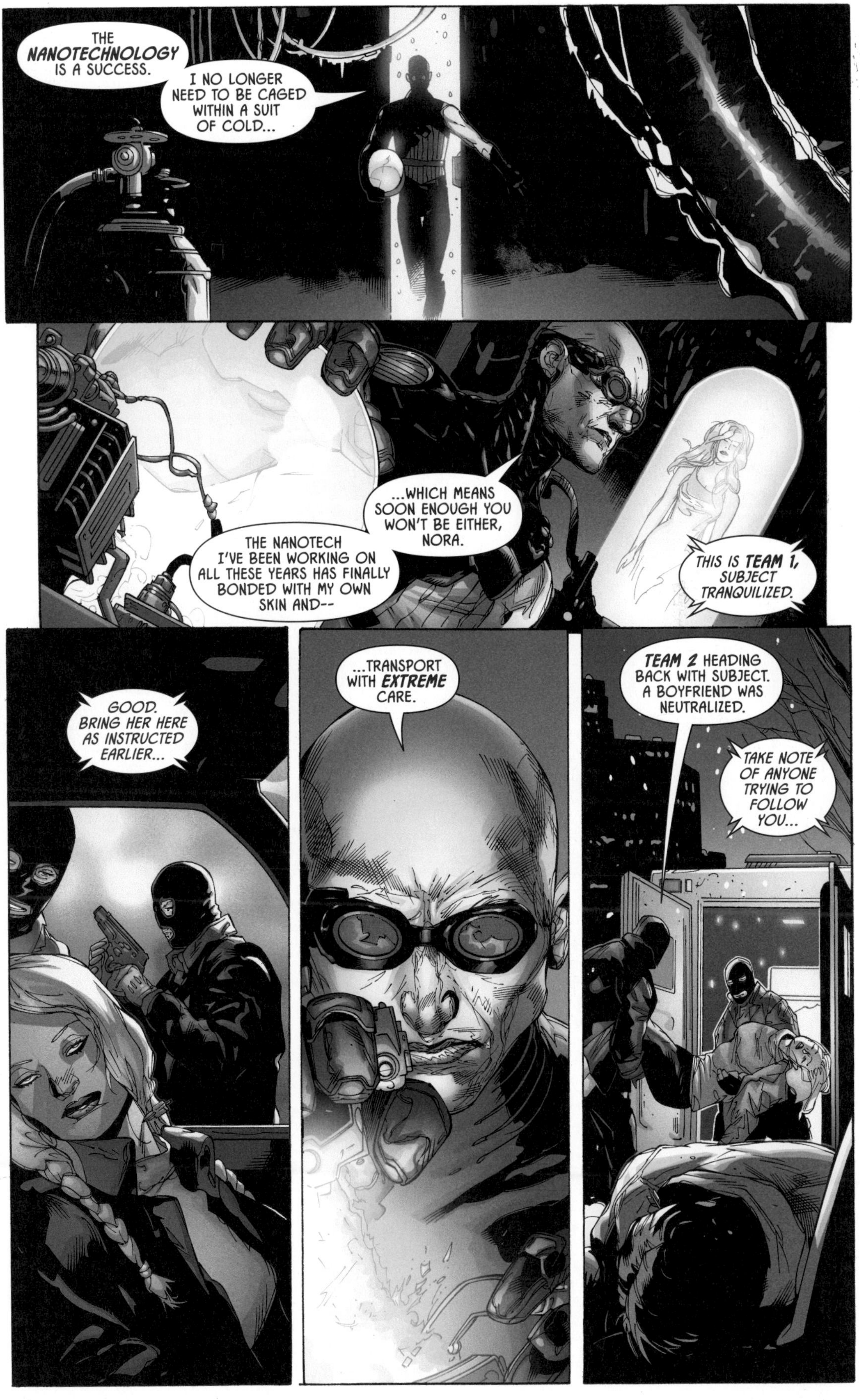
THE NANOTECHNOLOGY IS A SUCCESS.
I NO LONGER NEED TO BE CAGED WITHIN A SUIT OF COLD...
THE NANOTECH I'VE BEEN WORKING ON ALL THESE YEARS HAS FINALLY BONDED WITH MY OWN SKIN AND--
...WHICH MEANS SOON ENOUGH YOU WON'T BE EITHER, NORA.
THIS IS TEAM 1, SUBJECT TRANQUILIZED.
GOOD. BRING HER HERE AS INSTRUCTED EARLIER...
...TRANSPORT WITH EXTREME CARE.
TEAM 2 HEADING BACK WITH SUBJECT. A BOYFRIEND WAS NEUTRALIZED.
TAKE NOTE OF ANYONE TRYING TO FOLLOW YOU...

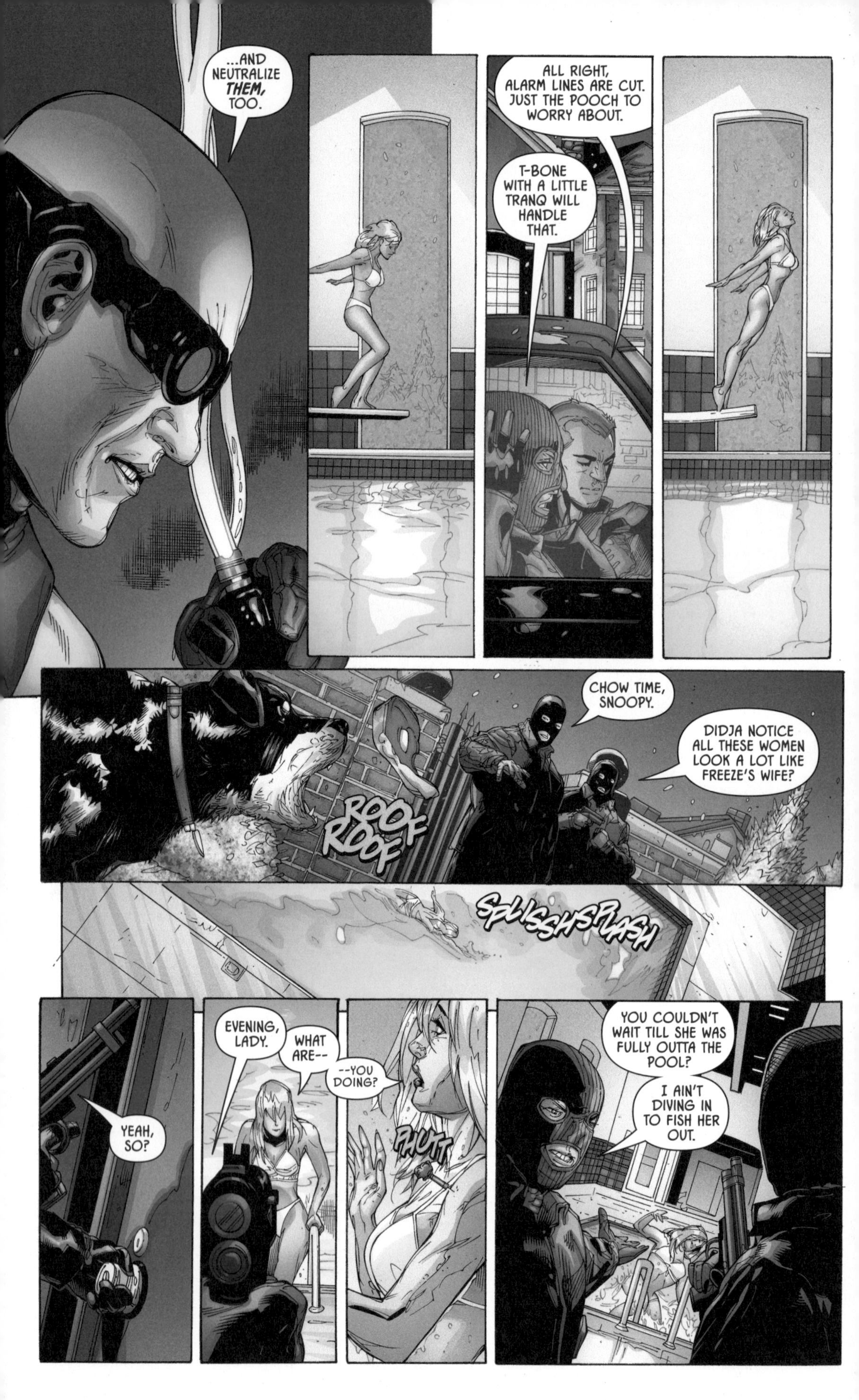
...AND NEUTRALIZE THEM, TOO.
ALL RIGHT, ALARM LINES ARE CUT. JUST THE POOCH TO WORRY ABOUT.
T-BONE WITH A LITTLE TRANQ WILL HANDLE THAT.
ROOF ROOF
CHOW TIME, SNOOPY.
DIDJA NOTICE ALL THESE WOMEN LOOK A LOT LIKE FREEZE'S WIFE?
SPLISSHSPLASH
YEAH, SO?
EVENING, LADY.
WHAT ARE--
--YOU DOING?
PHUTT
YOU COULDN'T WAIT TILL SHE WAS FULLY OUTTA THE POOL?
I AIN'T DIVING IN TO FISH HER OUT.

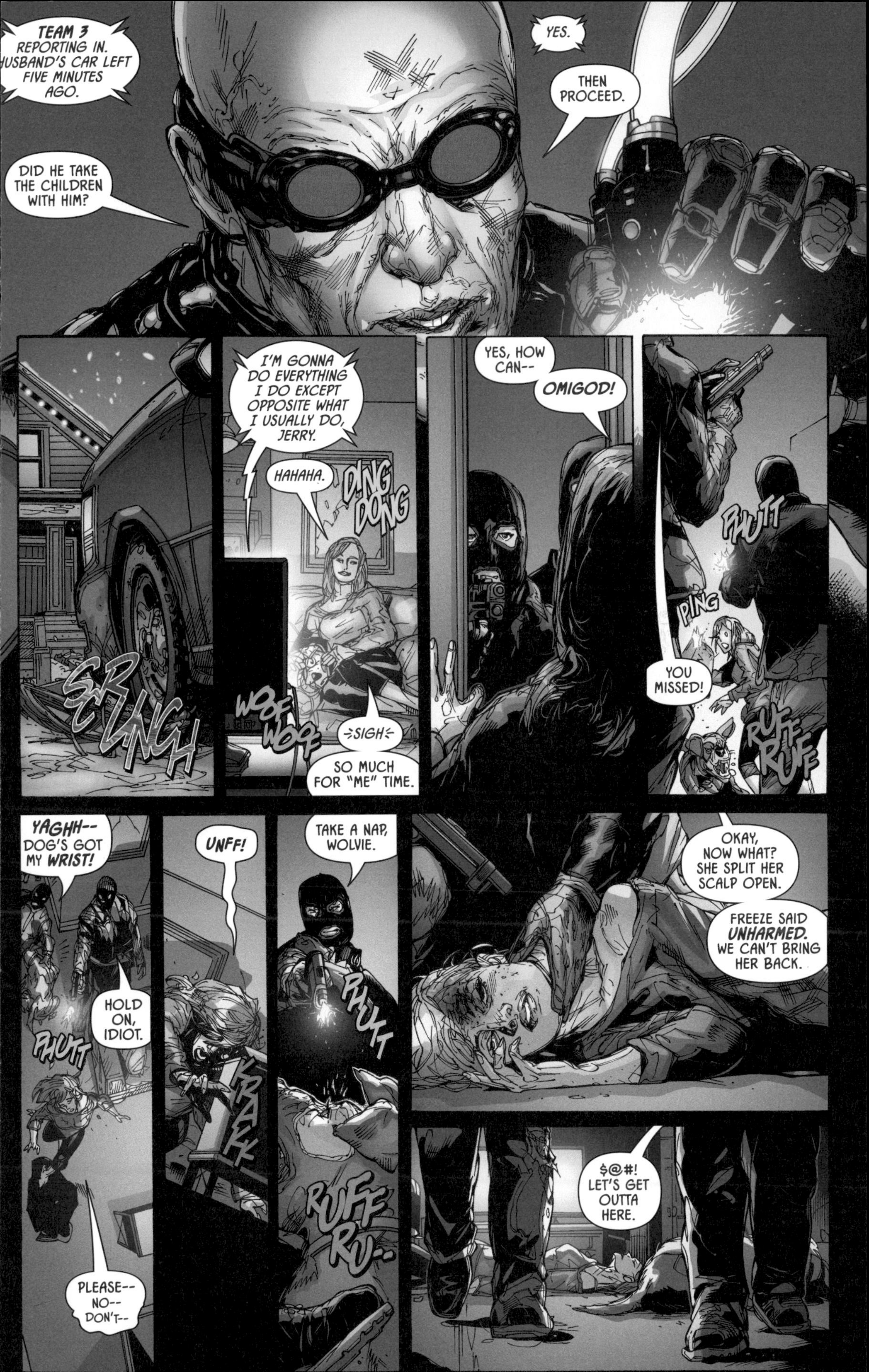
TEAM 3 REPORTING IN. HUSBAND'S CAR LEFT FIVE MINUTES AGO.
YES.
THEN PROCEED.
DID HE TAKE THE CHILDREN WITH HIM?
SCRUNCH
I'M GONNA DO EVERYTHING I DO EXCEPT OPPOSITE WHAT I USUALLY DO, JERRY.
HAHAHA.
DING DONG
WOOF WOOF
SIGH
SO MUCH FOR "ME" TIME.
YES, HOW CAN--
OMIGOD!
PHUTT
PING
YOU MISSED!
RUFF RUFF
YAGHH-- DOG'S GOT MY WRIST!
HOLD ON, IDIOT.
PHUTT
PLEASE-- NO-- DON'T--
UNFF!
KRAKK
TAKE A NAP, WOLVIE.
PHUTT
RUFF RU..
OKAY, NOW WHAT? SHE SPLIT HER SCALP OPEN.
FREEZE SAID UNHARMED. WE CAN'T BRING HER BACK.
$@#! LET'S GET OUTTA HERE.

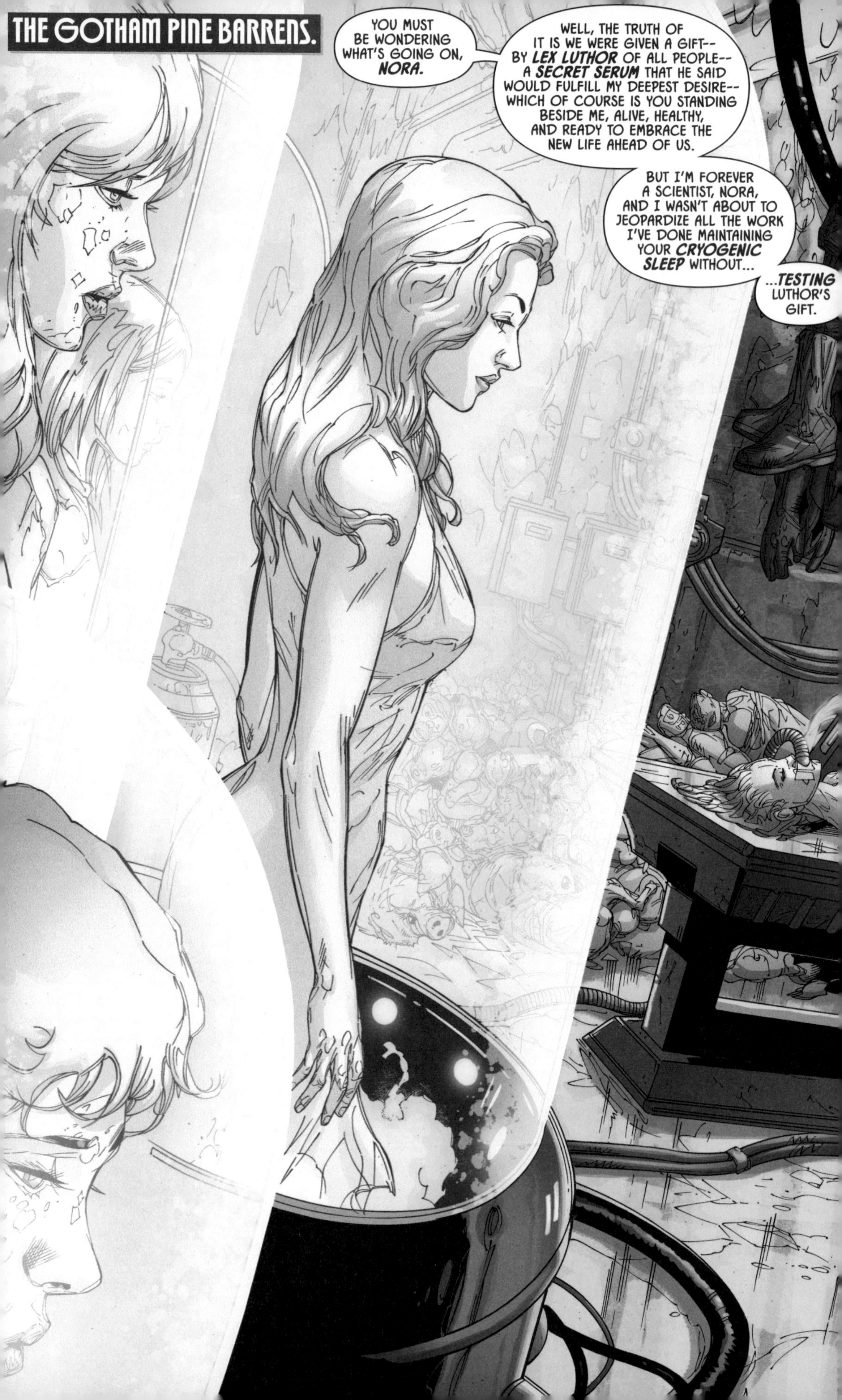
THE GOTHAM PINE BARRENS.
YOU MUST BE WONDERING WHAT'S GOING ON, NORA.
WELL, THE TRUTH OF IT IS WE WERE GIVEN A GIFT-- BY LEX LUTHOR OF ALL PEOPLE-- A SECRET SERUM THAT HE SAID WOULD FULFILL MY DEEPEST DESIRE-- WHICH OF COURSE IS YOU STANDING BESIDE ME, ALIVE, HEALTHY, AND READY TO EMBRACE THE NEW LIFE AHEAD OF US.
BUT I'M FOREVER A SCIENTIST, NORA, AND I WASN'T ABOUT TO JEOPARDIZE ALL THE WORK I'VE DONE MAINTAINING YOUR CRYOGENIC SLEEP WITHOUT...
...TESTING LUTHOR'S GIFT.

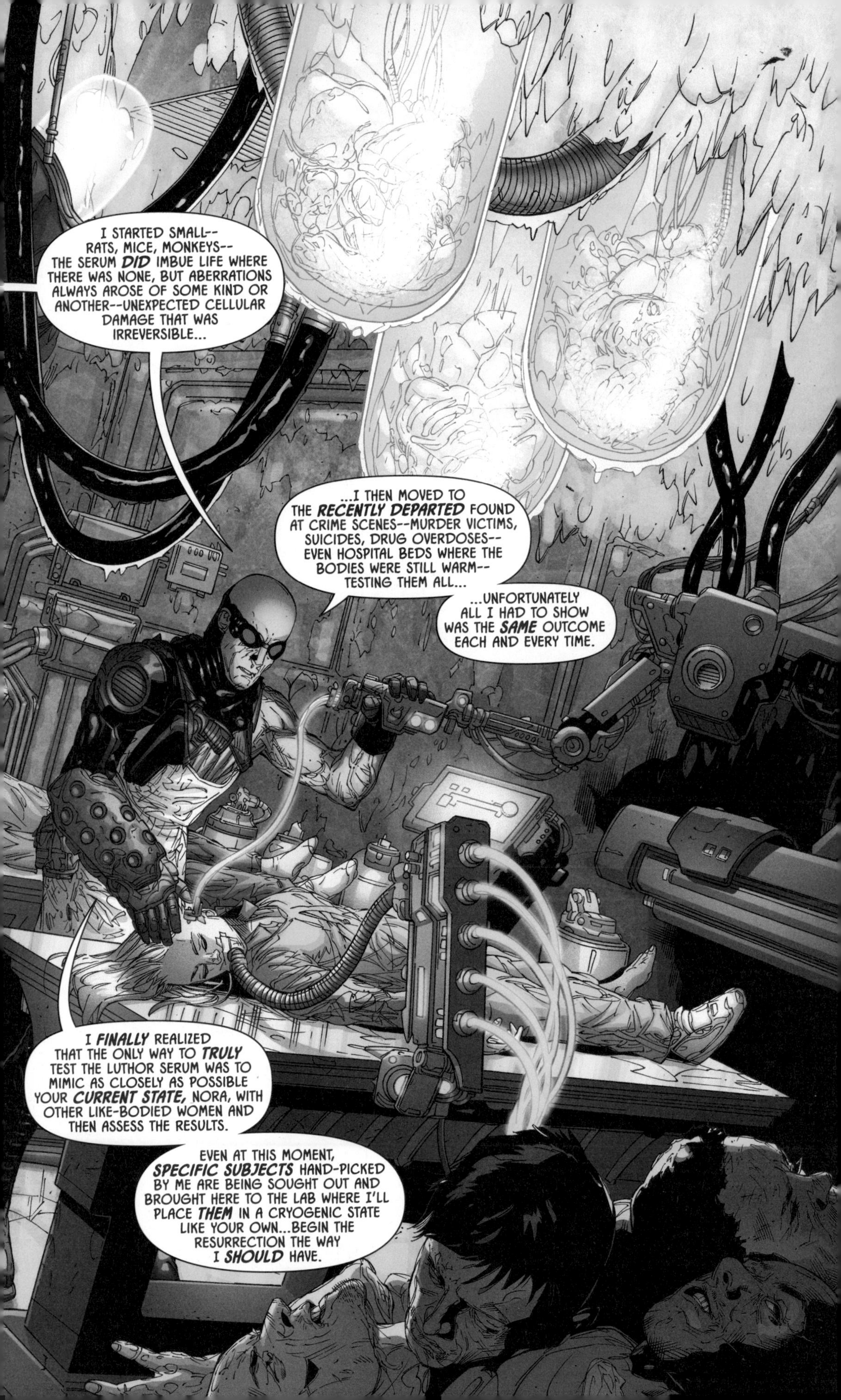

I STARTED SMALL--RATS, MICE, MONKEYS--THE SERUM *DID* IMBUE LIFE WHERE THERE WAS NONE, BUT ABERRATIONS ALWAYS AROSE OF SOME KIND OR ANOTHER--UNEXPECTED CELLULAR DAMAGE THAT WAS IRREVERSIBLE...
...I THEN MOVED TO THE *RECENTLY DEPARTED* FOUND AT CRIME SCENES--MURDER VICTIMS, SUICIDES, DRUG OVERDOSES--EVEN HOSPITAL BEDS WHERE THE BODIES WERE STILL WARM--TESTING THEM ALL...
...UNFORTUNATELY ALL I HAD TO SHOW WAS THE *SAME* OUTCOME EACH AND EVERY TIME.
I *FINALLY* REALIZED THAT THE ONLY WAY TO *TRULY* TEST THE LUTHOR SERUM WAS TO MIMIC AS CLOSELY AS POSSIBLE YOUR *CURRENT STATE,* NORA, WITH OTHER LIKE-BODIED WOMEN AND THEN ASSESS THE RESULTS.
EVEN AT THIS MOMENT, *SPECIFIC SUBJECTS* HAND-PICKED BY ME ARE BEING SOUGHT OUT AND BROUGHT HERE TO THE LAB WHERE I'LL PLACE *THEM* IN A CRYOGENIC STATE LIKE YOUR OWN...BEGIN THE RESURRECTION THE WAY I *SHOULD* HAVE.

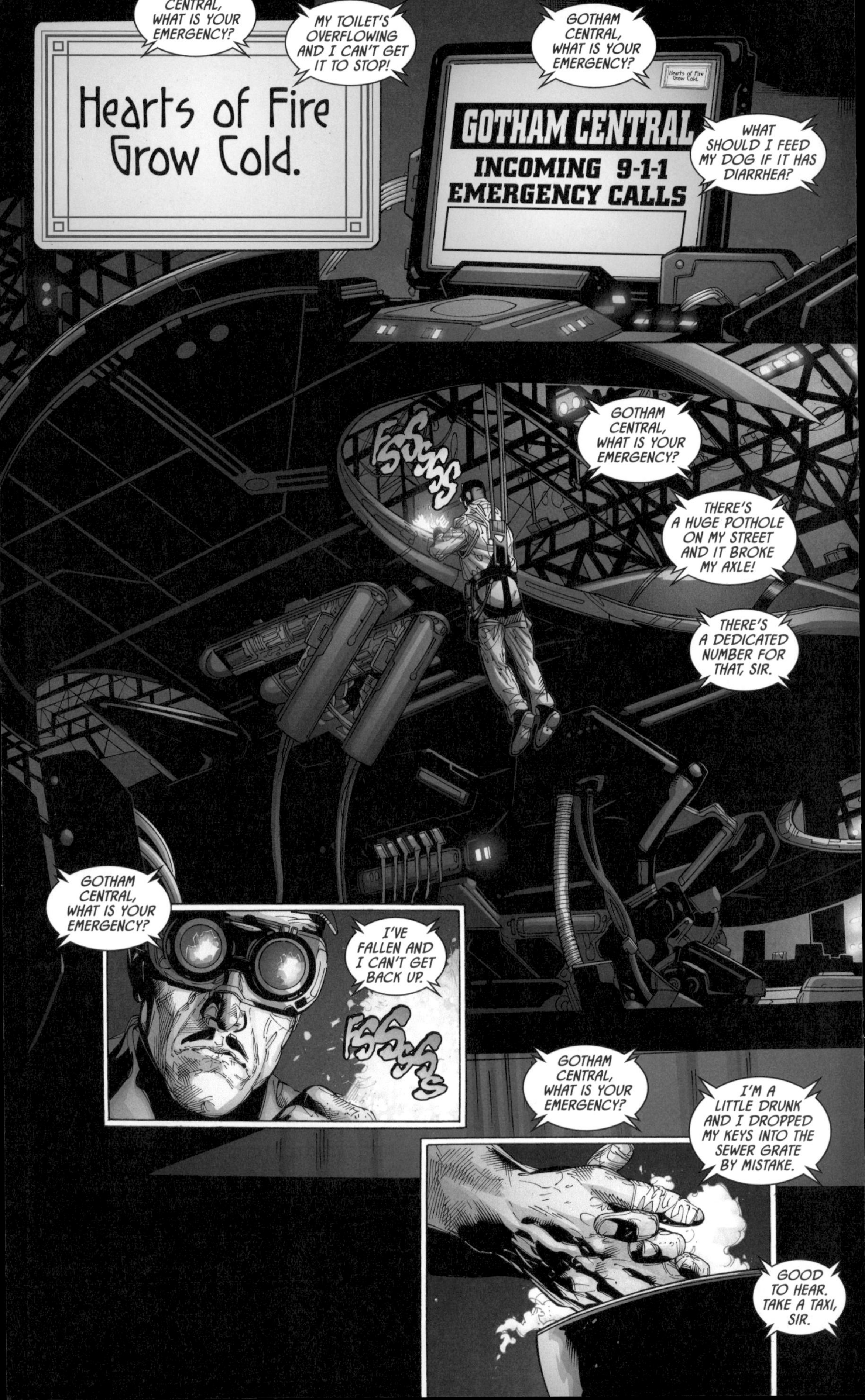
Hearts of Fire Grow Cold.
CENTRAL, WHAT IS YOUR EMERGENCY?
MY TOILET'S OVERFLOWING AND I CAN'T GET IT TO STOP!
GOTHAM CENTRAL, WHAT IS YOUR EMERGENCY?
Hearts of Fire Grow Cold.
GOTHAM CENTRAL
INCOMING 9-1-1 EMERGENCY CALLS
WHAT SHOULD I FEED MY DOG IF IT HAS DIARRHEA?
FSSSSS
GOTHAM CENTRAL, WHAT IS YOUR EMERGENCY?
THERE'S A HUGE POTHOLE ON MY STREET AND IT BROKE MY AXLE!
THERE'S A DEDICATED NUMBER FOR THAT, SIR.
GOTHAM CENTRAL, WHAT IS YOUR EMERGENCY?
I'VE FALLEN AND I CAN'T GET BACK UP.
FSSSSS
GOTHAM CENTRAL, WHAT IS YOUR EMERGENCY?
I'M A LITTLE DRUNK AND I DROPPED MY KEYS INTO THE SEWER GRATE BY MISTAKE.
GOOD TO HEAR. TAKE A TAXI, SIR.

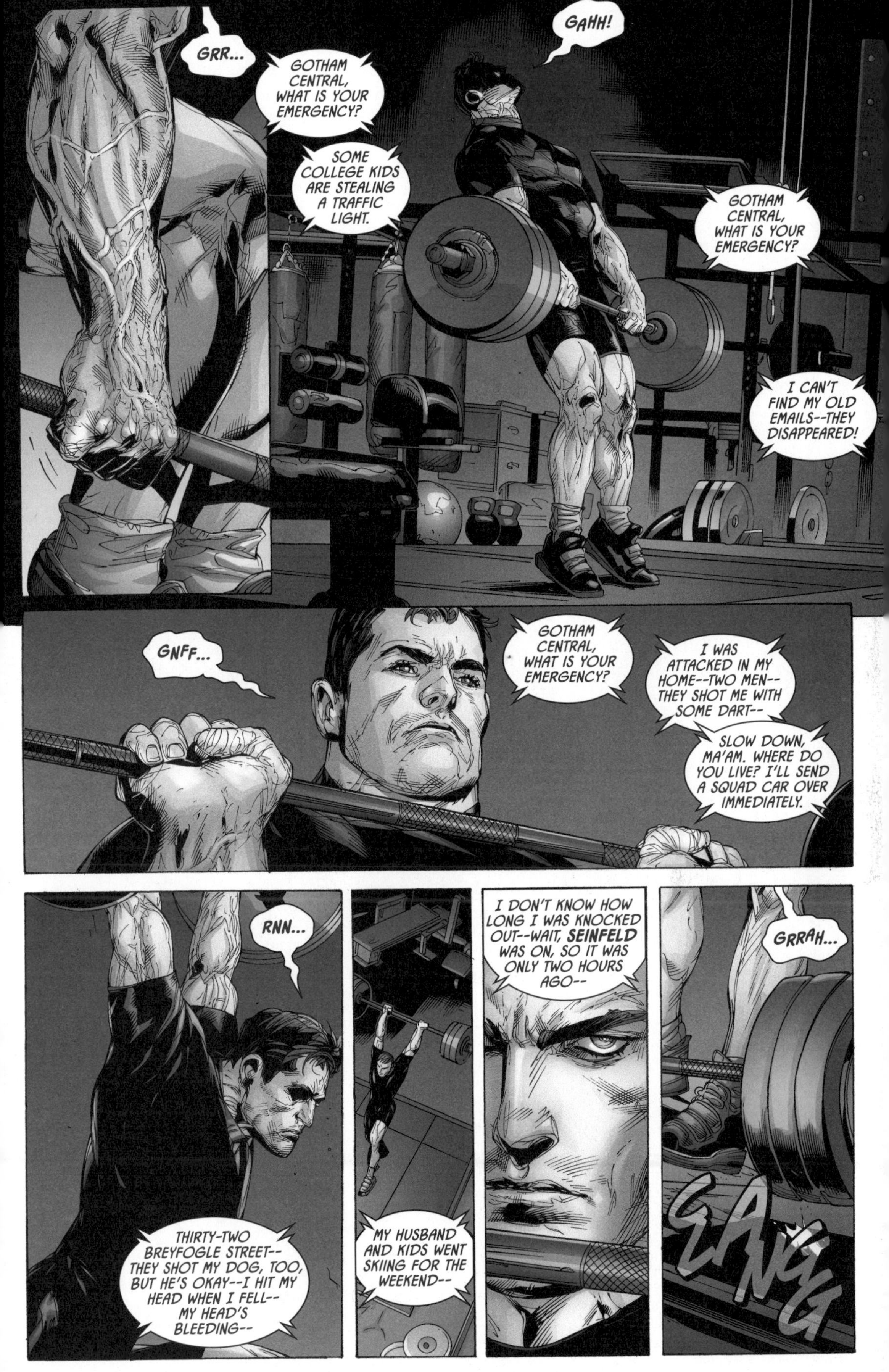
GRR...
GOTHAM CENTRAL, WHAT IS YOUR EMERGENCY?
SOME COLLEGE KIDS ARE STEALING A TRAFFIC LIGHT.
GAHH!
GOTHAM CENTRAL, WHAT IS YOUR EMERGENCY?
I CAN'T FIND MY OLD EMAILS--THEY DISAPPEARED!
GNFF...
GOTHAM CENTRAL, WHAT IS YOUR EMERGENCY?
I WAS ATTACKED IN MY HOME--TWO MEN--THEY SHOT ME WITH SOME DART--
SLOW DOWN, MA'AM. WHERE DO YOU LIVE? I'LL SEND A SQUAD CAR OVER IMMEDIATELY.
RNN...
THIRTY-TWO BREYFOGLE STREET--THEY SHOT MY DOG, TOO, BUT HE'S OKAY--I HIT MY HEAD WHEN I FELL--MY HEAD'S BLEEDING--
MY HUSBAND AND KIDS WENT SKIING FOR THE WEEKEND--
I DON'T KNOW HOW LONG I WAS KNOCKED OUT--WAIT, SEINFELD WAS ON, SO IT WAS ONLY TWO HOURS AGO--
GRRAH...
CLANG

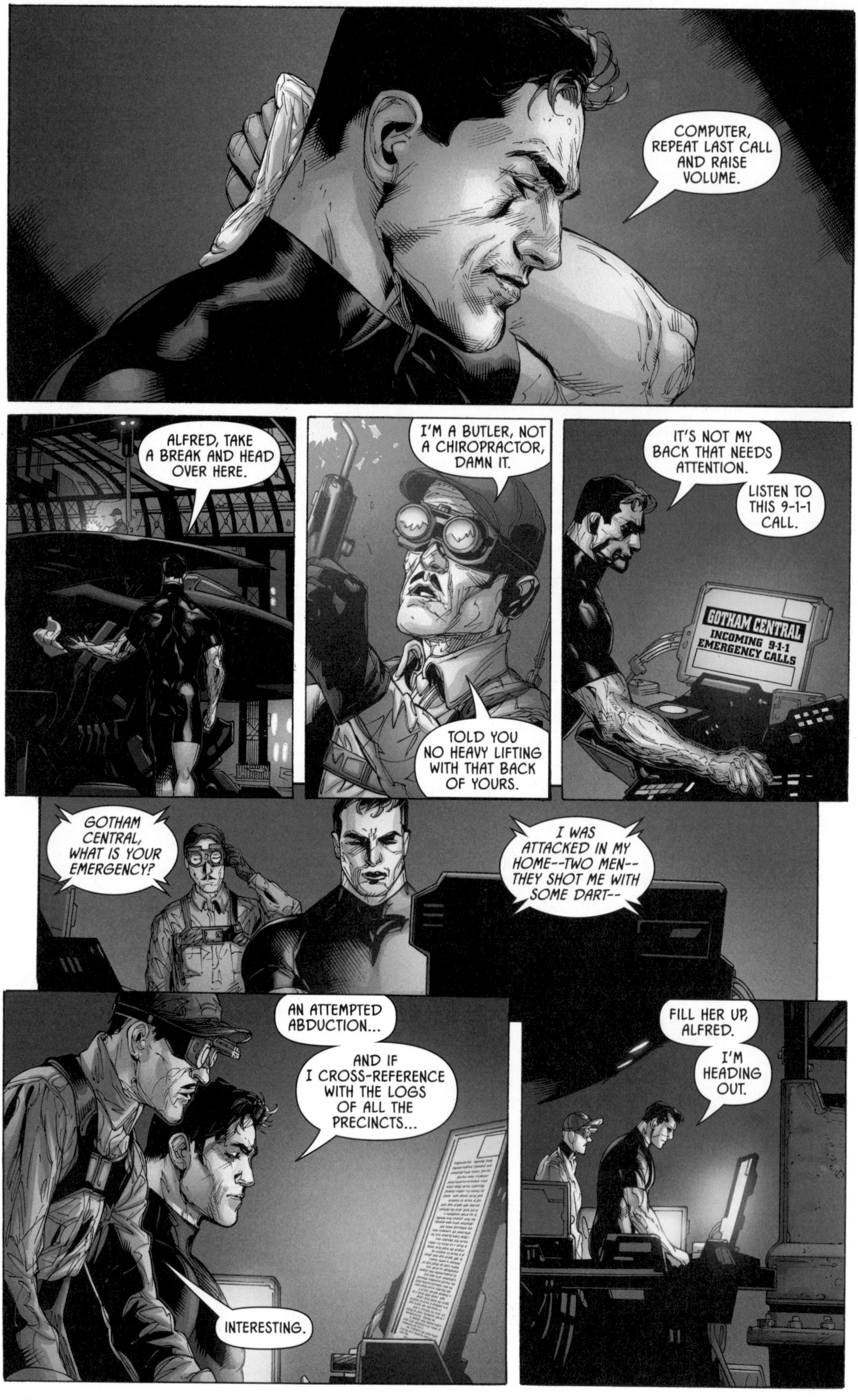
COMPUTER, REPEAT LAST CALL AND RAISE VOLUME.
ALFRED, TAKE A BREAK AND HEAD OVER HERE.
I'M A BUTLER, NOT A CHIROPRACTOR, DAMN IT.
TOLD YOU NO HEAVY LIFTING WITH THAT BACK OF YOURS.
IT'S NOT MY BACK THAT NEEDS ATTENTION.
LISTEN TO THIS 9-1-1 CALL.
GOTHAM CENTRAL
INCOMING 9-1-1 EMERGENCY CALLS
GOTHAM CENTRAL, WHAT IS YOUR EMERGENCY?
I WAS ATTACKED IN MY HOME--TWO MEN--THEY SHOT ME WITH SOME DART--
AN ATTEMPTED ABDUCTION...
AND IF I CROSS-REFERENCE WITH THE LOGS OF ALL THE PRECINCTS...
INTERESTING.
FILL HER UP, ALFRED.
I'M HEADING OUT.

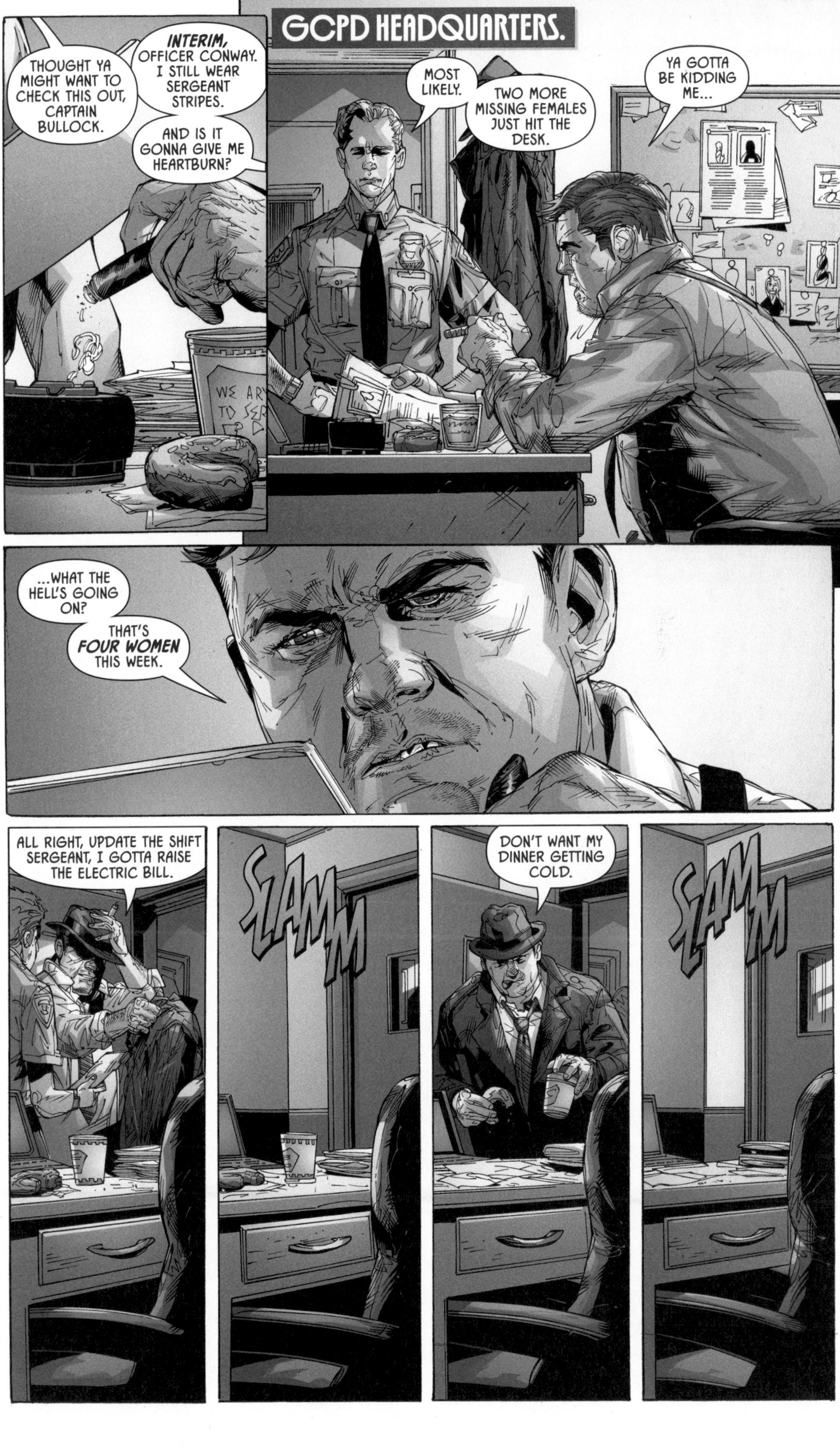
GCPD HEADQUARTERS.
THOUGHT YA MIGHT WANT TO CHECK THIS OUT, CAPTAIN BULLOCK.
INTERIM, OFFICER CONWAY. I STILL WEAR SERGEANT STRIPES.
AND IS IT GONNA GIVE ME HEARTBURN?
MOST LIKELY.
TWO MORE MISSING FEMALES JUST HIT THE DESK.
YA GOTTA BE KIDDING ME...
...WHAT THE HELL'S GOING ON?
THAT'S *FOUR WOMEN* THIS WEEK.
ALL RIGHT, UPDATE THE SHIFT SERGEANT, I GOTTA RAISE THE ELECTRIC BILL.
SLAMM
DON'T WANT MY DINNER GETTING COLD.
SLAMM

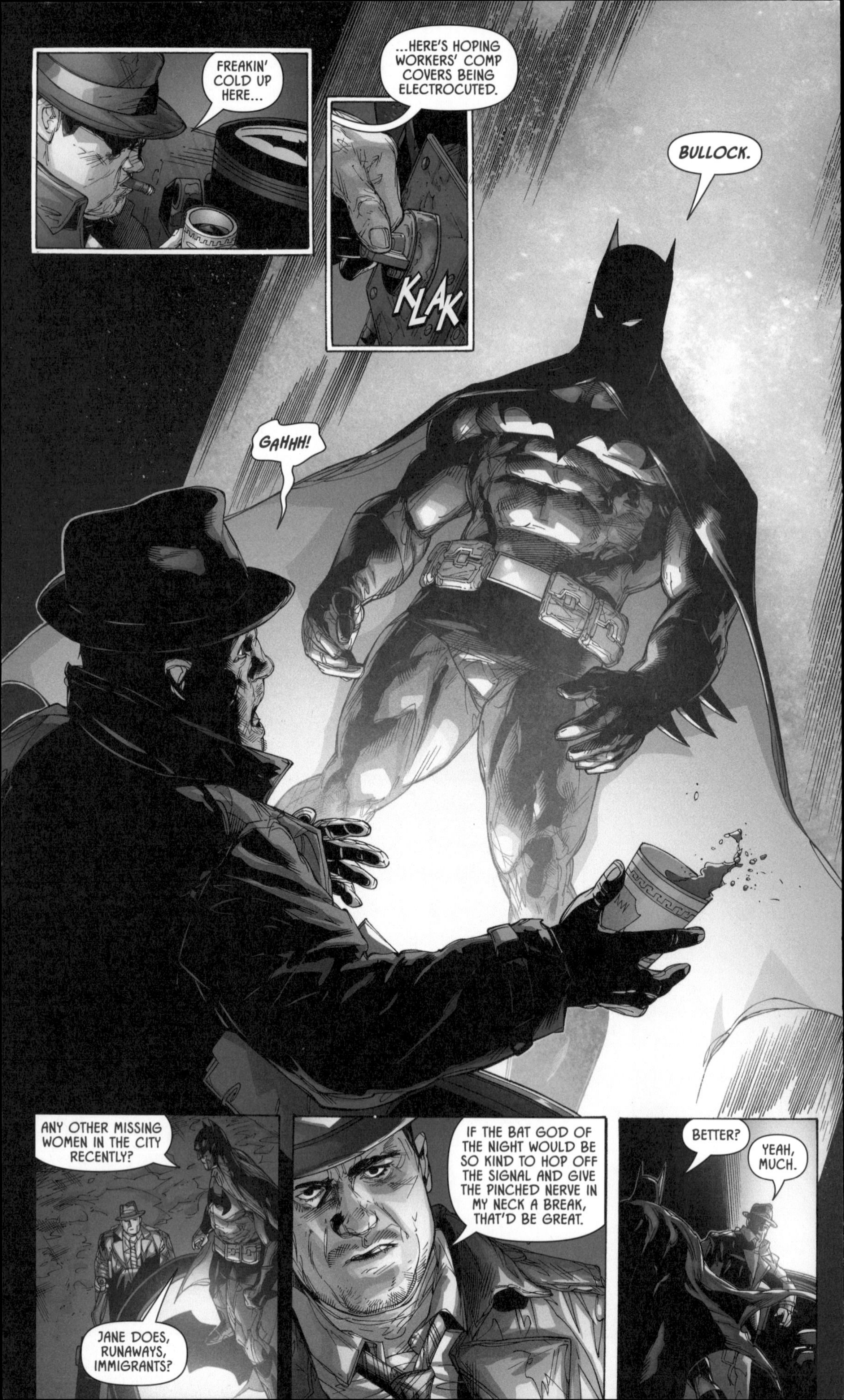
FREAKIN' COLD UP HERE...
...HERE'S HOPING WORKERS' COMP COVERS BEING ELECTROCUTED.
KLAK
BULLOCK.
GAHHH!
ANY OTHER MISSING WOMEN IN THE CITY RECENTLY?
JANE DOES, RUNAWAYS, IMMIGRANTS?
IF THE BAT GOD OF THE NIGHT WOULD BE SO KIND TO HOP OFF THE SIGNAL AND GIVE THE PINCHED NERVE IN MY NECK A BREAK, THAT'D BE GREAT.
BETTER?
YEAH, MUCH.

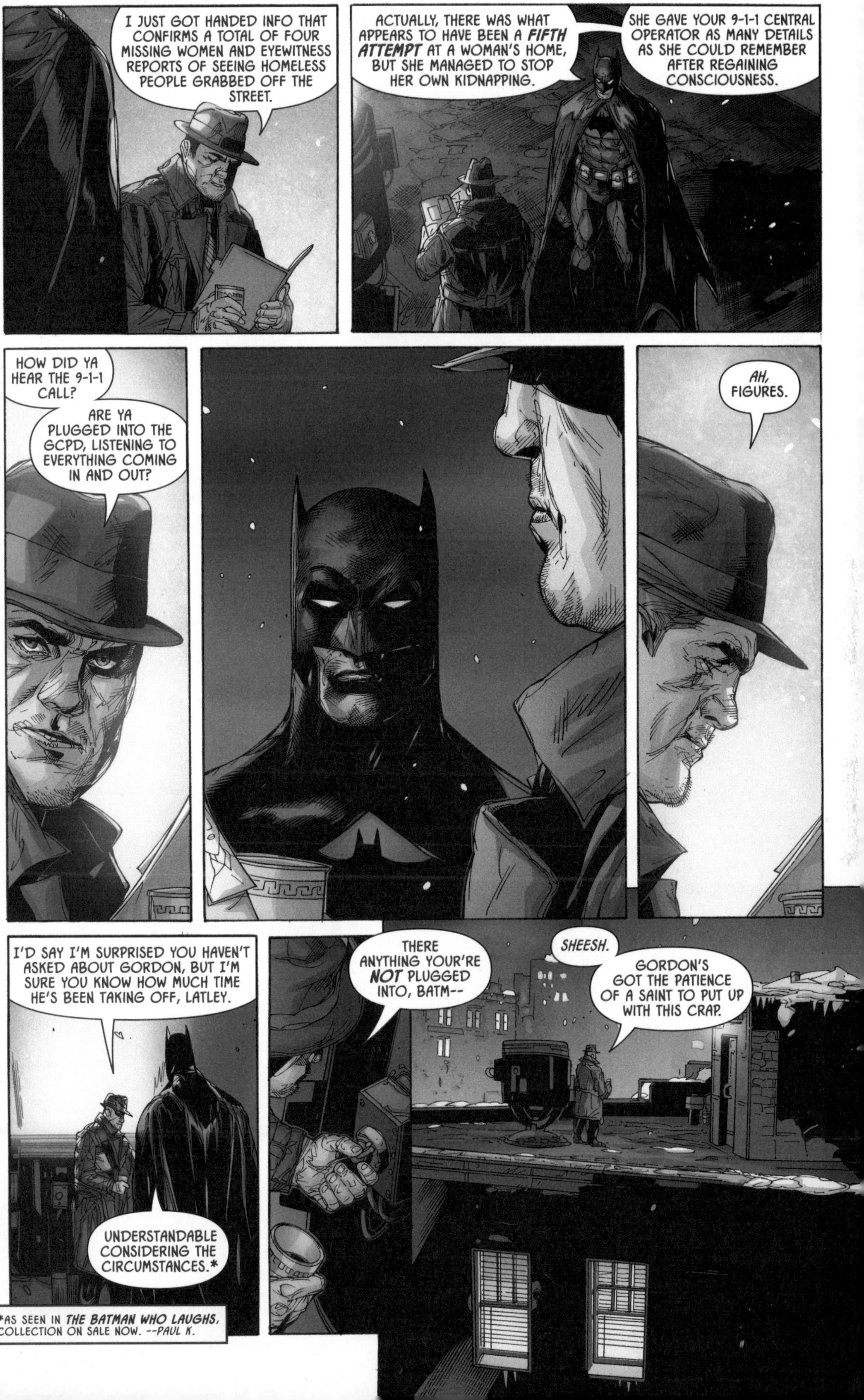
I JUST GOT HANDED INFO THAT CONFIRMS A TOTAL OF FOUR MISSING WOMEN AND EYEWITNESS REPORTS OF SEEING HOMELESS PEOPLE GRABBED OFF THE STREET.
ACTUALLY, THERE WAS WHAT APPEARS TO HAVE BEEN A FIFTH ATTEMPT AT A WOMAN'S HOME, BUT SHE MANAGED TO STOP HER OWN KIDNAPPING.
SHE GAVE YOUR 9-1-1 CENTRAL OPERATOR AS MANY DETAILS AS SHE COULD REMEMBER AFTER REGAINING CONSCIOUSNESS.
HOW DID YA HEAR THE 9-1-1 CALL?
ARE YA PLUGGED INTO THE GCPD, LISTENING TO EVERYTHING COMING IN AND OUT?
AH, FIGURES.
I'D SAY I'M SURPRISED YOU HAVEN'T ASKED ABOUT GORDON, BUT I'M SURE YOU KNOW HOW MUCH TIME HE'S BEEN TAKING OFF, LATLEY.
UNDERSTANDABLE CONSIDERING THE CIRCUMSTANCES.*
THERE ANYTHING YOUR'RE NOT PLUGGED INTO, BATM--
SHEESH.
GORDON'S GOT THE PATIENCE OF A SAINT TO PUT UP WITH THIS CRAP.
*AS SEEN IN THE BATMAN WHO LAUGHS, COLLECTION ON SALE NOW. --PAUL K.

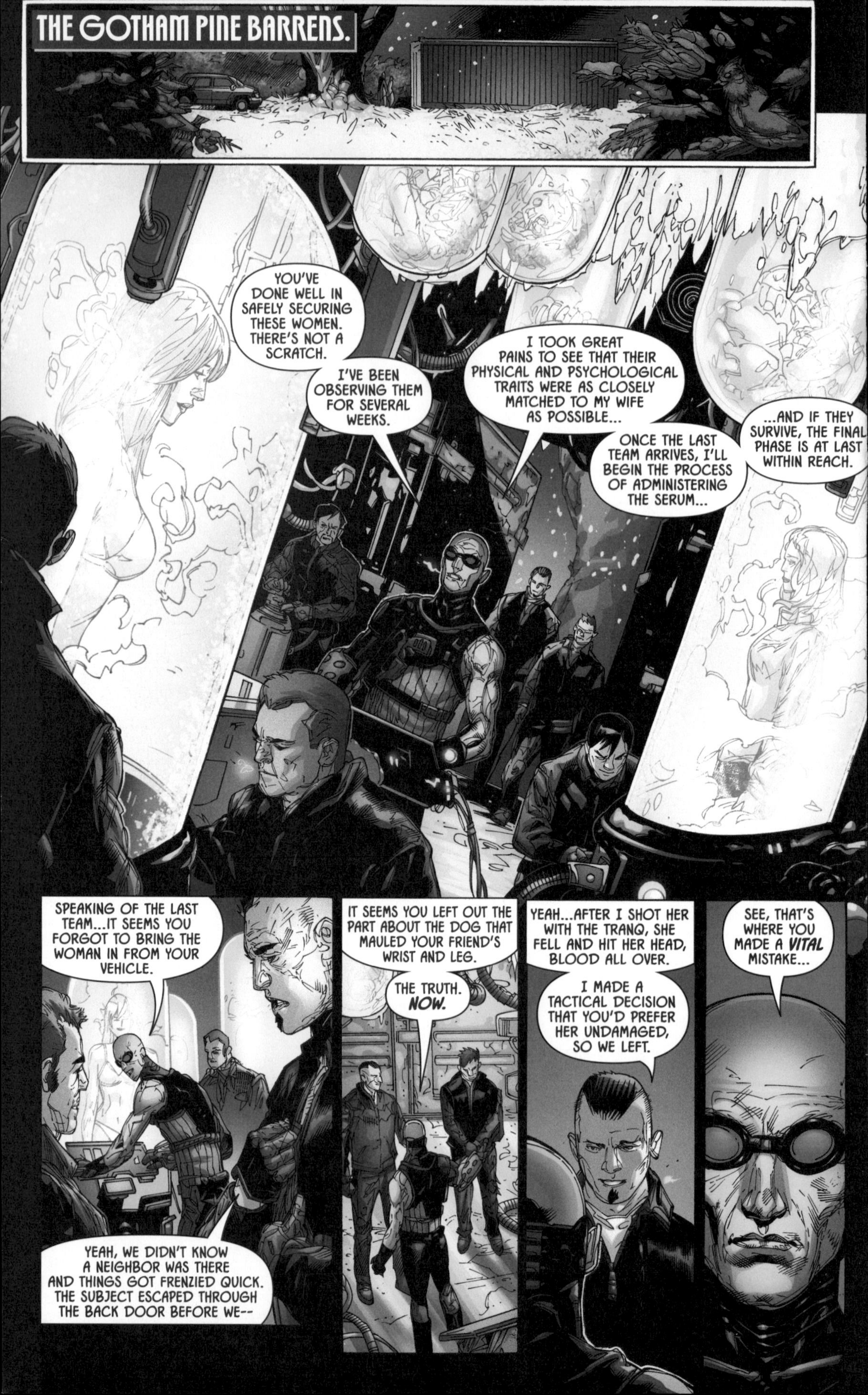
THE GOTHAM PINE BARRENS.
YOU'VE DONE WELL IN SAFELY SECURING THESE WOMEN. THERE'S NOT A SCRATCH.
I'VE BEEN OBSERVING THEM FOR SEVERAL WEEKS.
I TOOK GREAT PAINS TO SEE THAT THEIR PHYSICAL AND PSYCHOLOGICAL TRAITS WERE AS CLOSELY MATCHED TO MY WIFE AS POSSIBLE...
ONCE THE LAST TEAM ARRIVES, I'LL BEGIN THE PROCESS OF ADMINISTERING THE SERUM...
...AND IF THEY SURVIVE, THE FINAL PHASE IS AT LAST WITHIN REACH.
SPEAKING OF THE LAST TEAM...IT SEEMS YOU FORGOT TO BRING THE WOMAN IN FROM YOUR VEHICLE.
YEAH, WE DIDN'T KNOW A NEIGHBOR WAS THERE AND THINGS GOT FRENZIED QUICK. THE SUBJECT ESCAPED THROUGH THE BACK DOOR BEFORE WE--
IT SEEMS YOU LEFT OUT THE PART ABOUT THE DOG THAT MAULED YOUR FRIEND'S WRIST AND LEG.
THE TRUTH. *NOW.*
YEAH...AFTER I SHOT HER WITH THE TRANQ, SHE FELL AND HIT HER HEAD, BLOOD ALL OVER.
I MADE A TACTICAL DECISION THAT YOU'D PREFER HER UNDAMAGED, SO WE LEFT.
SEE, THAT'S WHERE YOU MADE A *VITAL* MISTAKE...

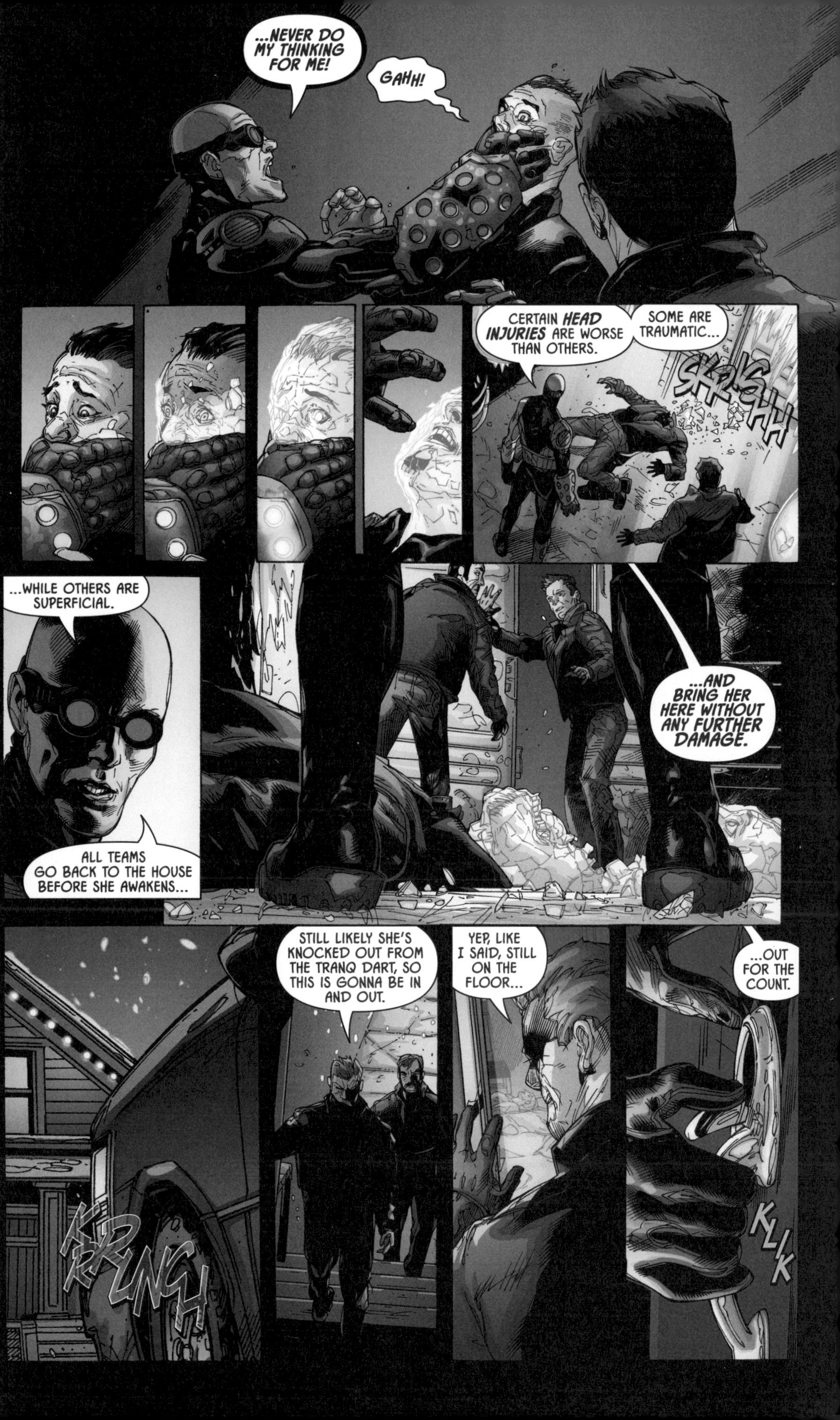
...NEVER DO MY THINKING FOR ME!
GAHH!
CERTAIN HEAD INJURIES ARE WORSE THAN OTHERS.
SOME ARE TRAUMATIC...
SKRSSHH
...WHILE OTHERS ARE SUPERFICIAL.
ALL TEAMS GO BACK TO THE HOUSE BEFORE SHE AWAKENS...
...AND BRING HER HERE WITHOUT ANY FURTHER DAMAGE.
KRRUNCH
STILL LIKELY SHE'S KNOCKED OUT FROM THE TRANQ DART, SO THIS IS GONNA BE IN AND OUT.
YEP, LIKE I SAID, STILL ON THE FLOOR...
...OUT FOR THE COUNT.
KLIK

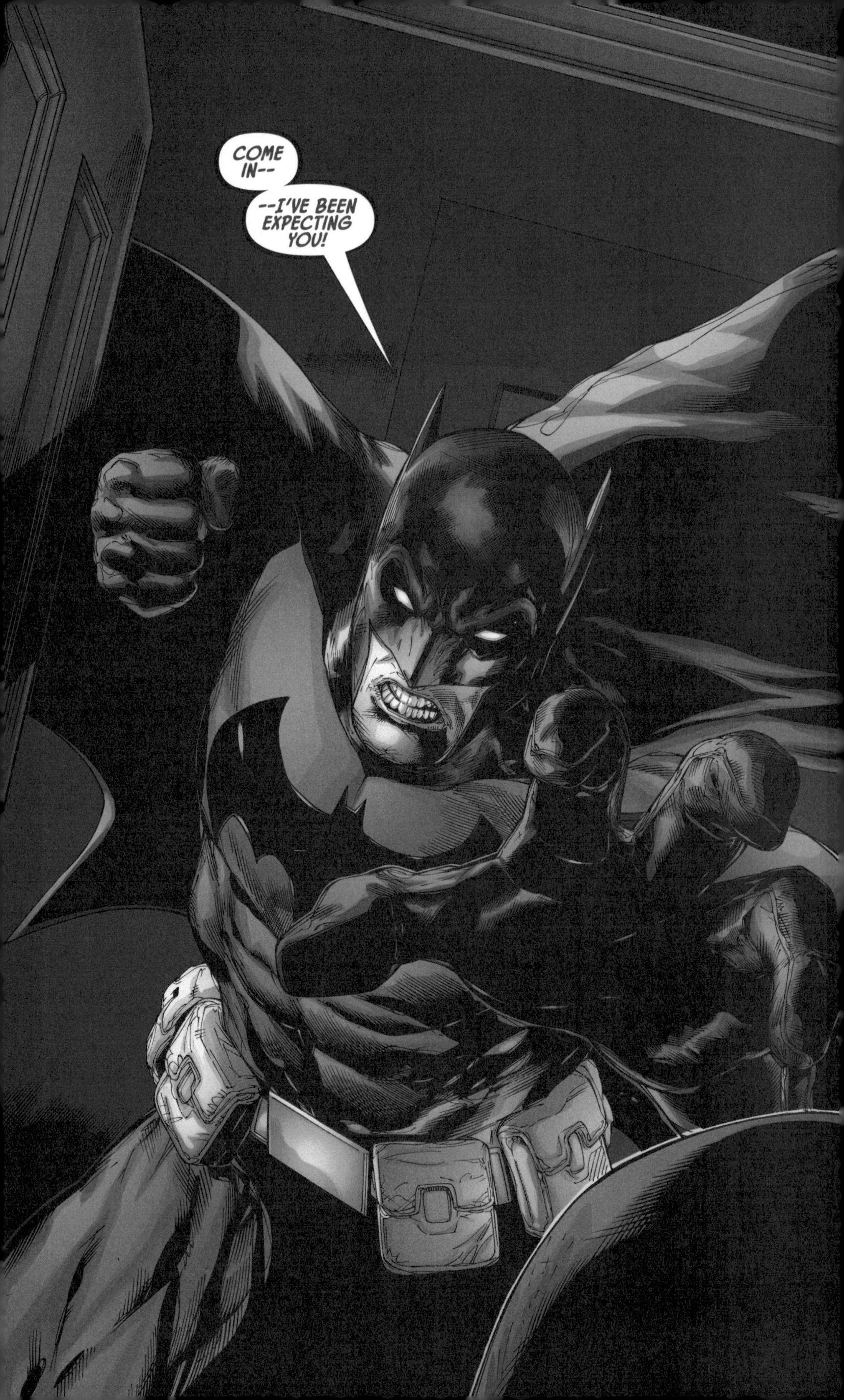
COME IN--
--I'VE BEEN EXPECTING YOU!

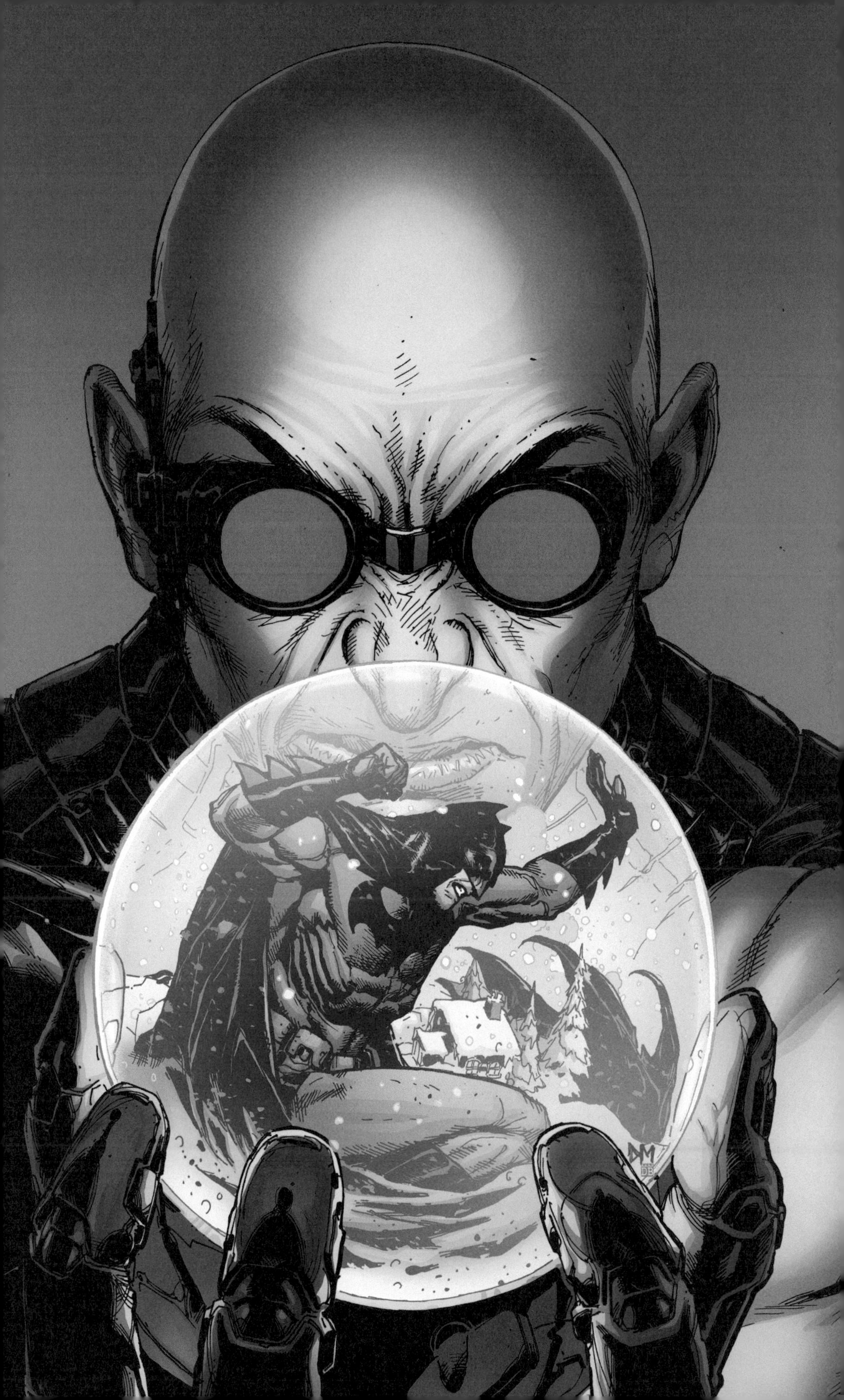

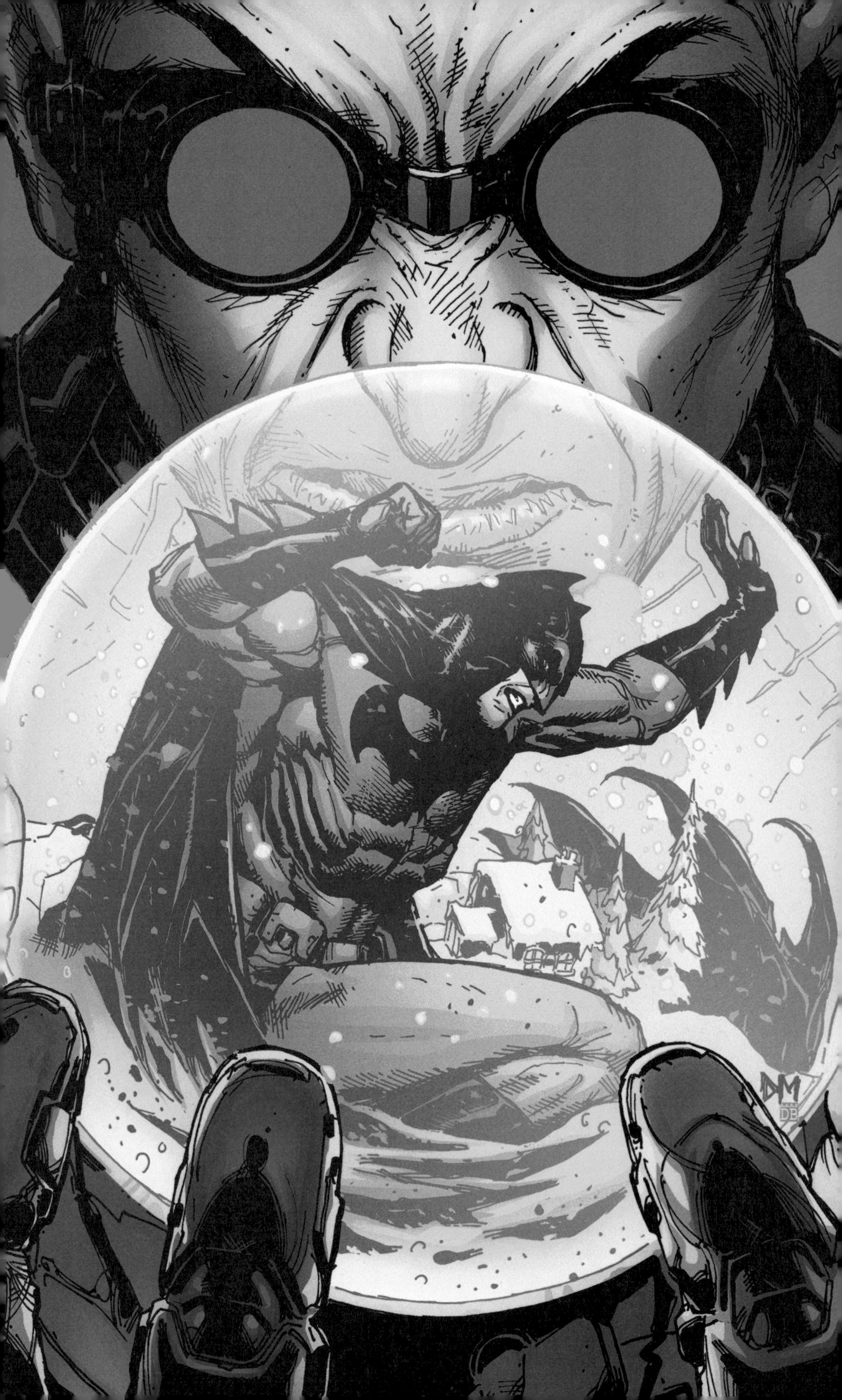

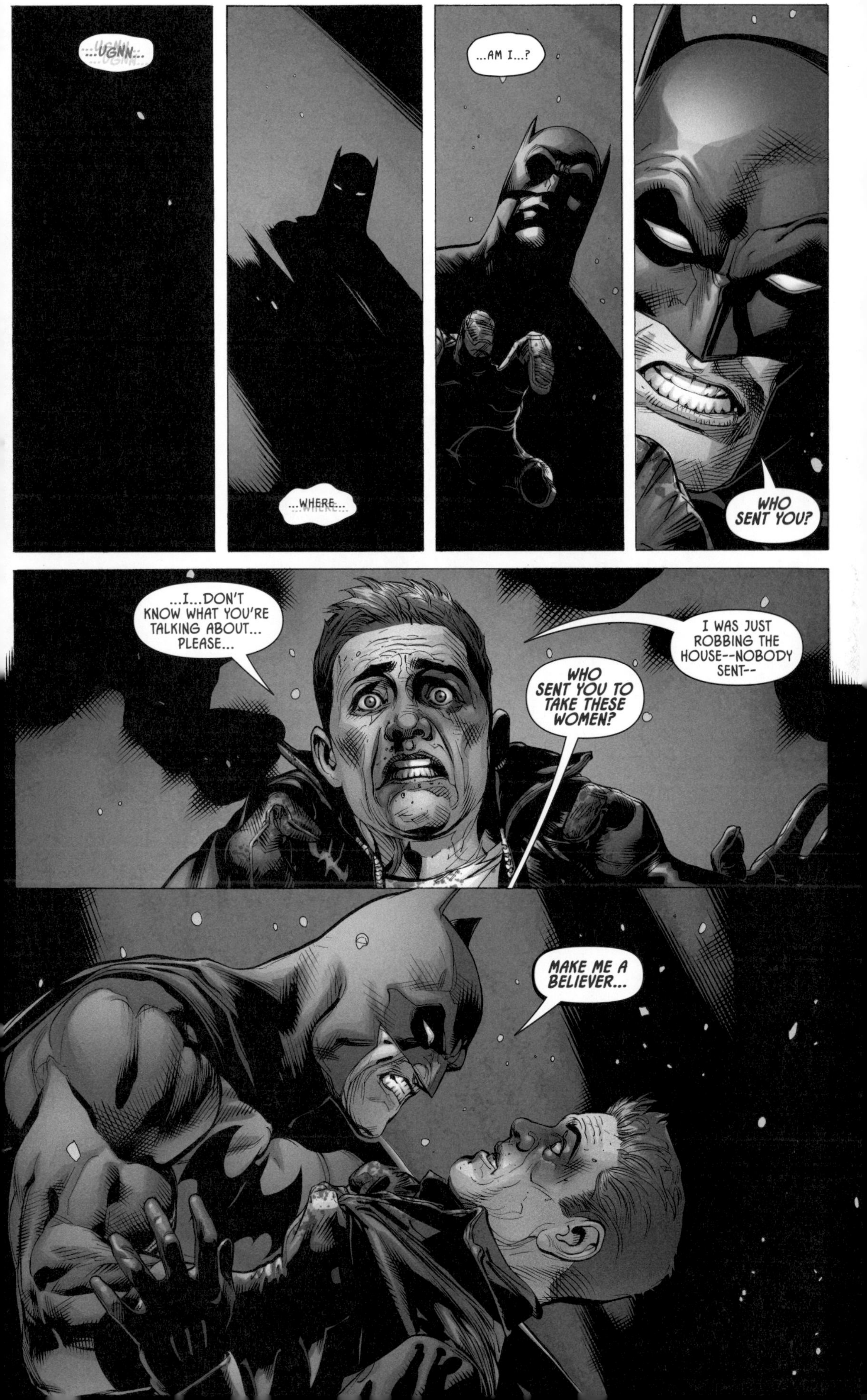
...UGNN...
...WHERE...
...AM I...?
WHO SENT YOU?
...I...DON'T KNOW WHAT YOU'RE TALKING ABOUT... PLEASE...
WHO SENT YOU TO TAKE THESE WOMEN?
I WAS JUST ROBBING THE HOUSE--NOBODY SENT--
MAKE ME A BELIEVER...

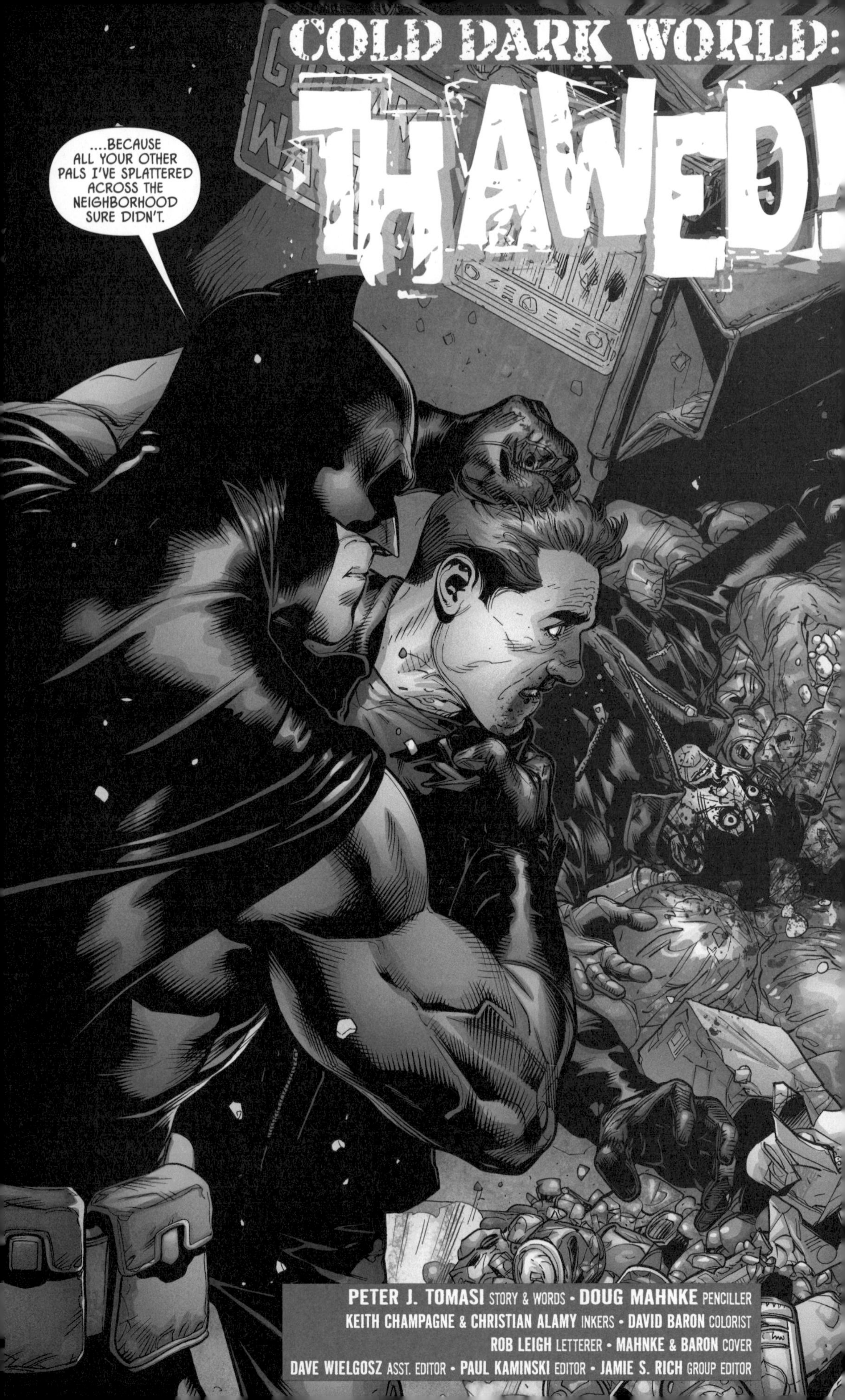
COLD DARK WORLD:
THAWED!
....BECAUSE ALL YOUR OTHER PALS I'VE SPLATTERED ACROSS THE NEIGHBORHOOD SURE DIDN'T.
PETER J. TOMASI STORY & WORDS • DOUG MAHNKE PENCILLER
KEITH CHAMPAGNE & CHRISTIAN ALAMY INKERS • DAVID BARON COLORIST
ROB LEIGH LETTERER • MAHNKE & BARON COVER
DAVE WIELGOSZ ASST. EDITOR • PAUL KAMINSKI EDITOR • JAMIE S. RICH GROUP EDITOR

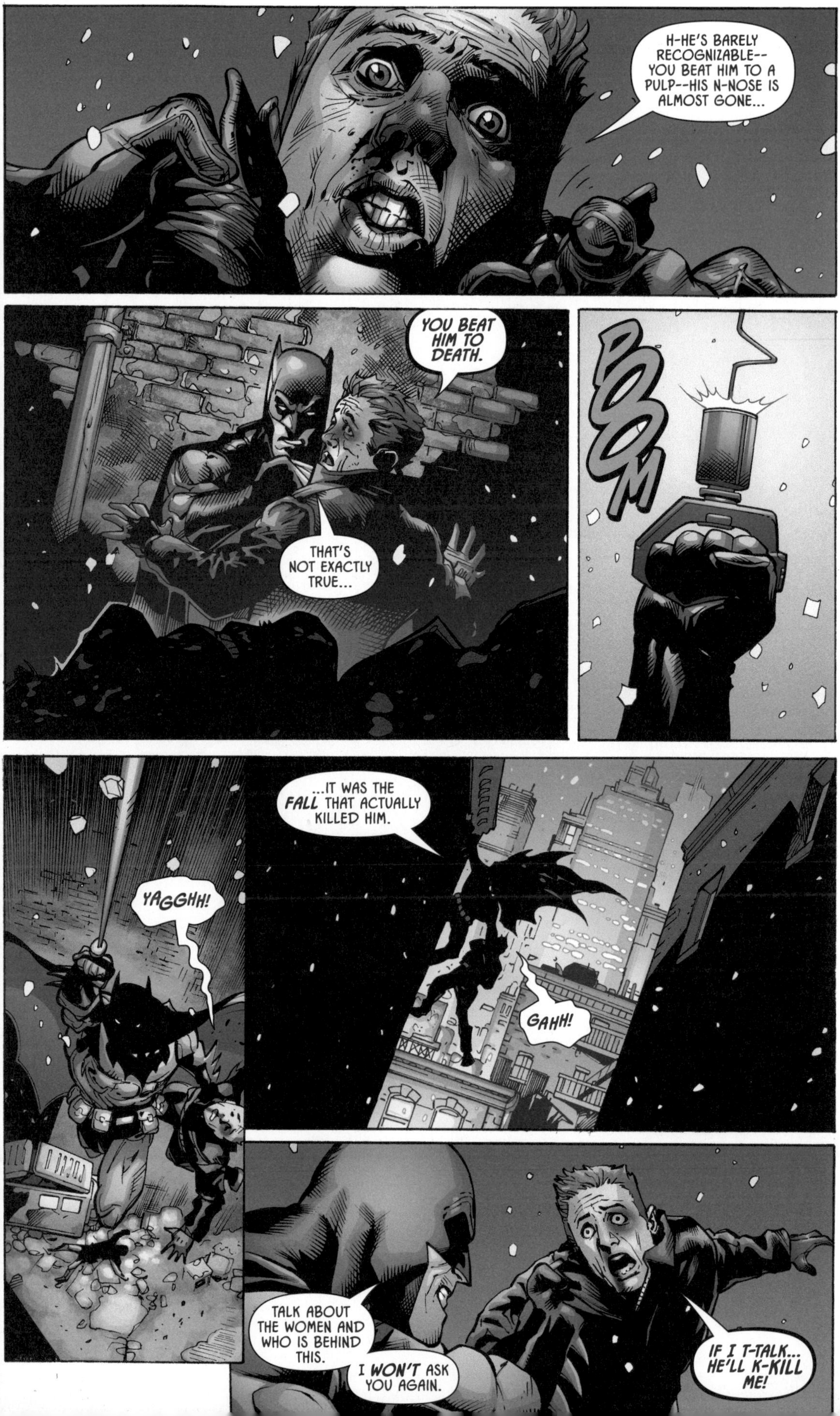
H-HE'S BARELY RECOGNIZABLE-- YOU BEAT HIM TO A PULP--HIS N-NOSE IS ALMOST GONE...
YOU BEAT HIM TO DEATH.
THAT'S NOT EXACTLY TRUE...
BOOM
YAGGHH!
...IT WAS THE FALL THAT ACTUALLY KILLED HIM.
GAHH!
TALK ABOUT THE WOMEN AND WHO IS BEHIND THIS.
I WON'T ASK YOU AGAIN.
IF I T-TALK... HE'LL K-KILL ME!

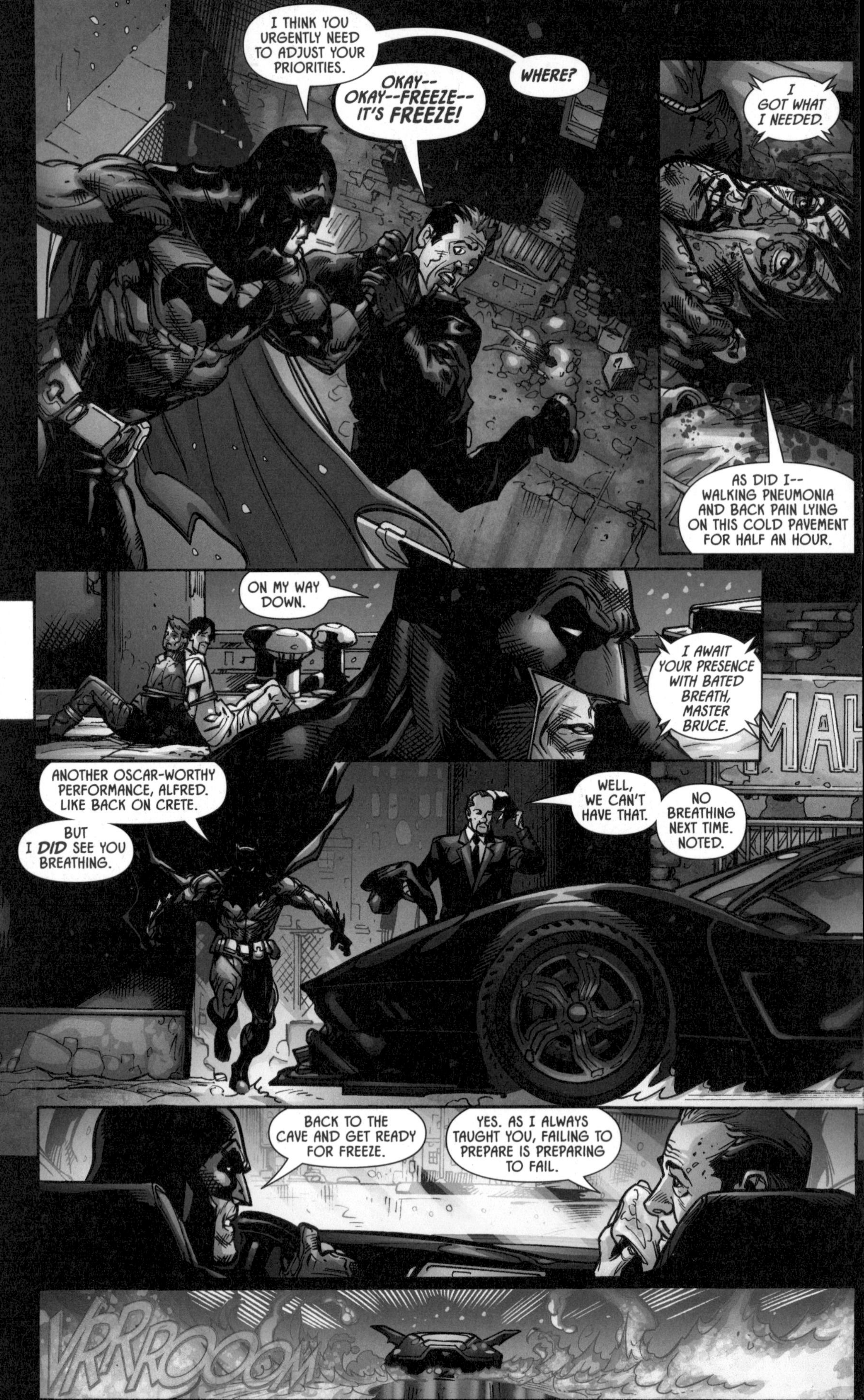
I THINK YOU URGENTLY NEED TO ADJUST YOUR PRIORITIES.
OKAY-- OKAY--FREEZE-- IT'S FREEZE!
WHERE?
I GOT WHAT I NEEDED.
AS DID I-- WALKING PNEUMONIA AND BACK PAIN LYING ON THIS COLD PAVEMENT FOR HALF AN HOUR.
ON MY WAY DOWN.
I AWAIT YOUR PRESENCE WITH BATED BREATH, MASTER BRUCE.
ANOTHER OSCAR-WORTHY PERFORMANCE, ALFRED. LIKE BACK ON CRETE.
BUT I DID SEE YOU BREATHING.
WELL, WE CAN'T HAVE THAT.
NO BREATHING NEXT TIME. NOTED.
BACK TO THE CAVE AND GET READY FOR FREEZE.
YES. AS I ALWAYS TAUGHT YOU, FAILING TO PREPARE IS PREPARING TO FAIL.
VRRROOOM

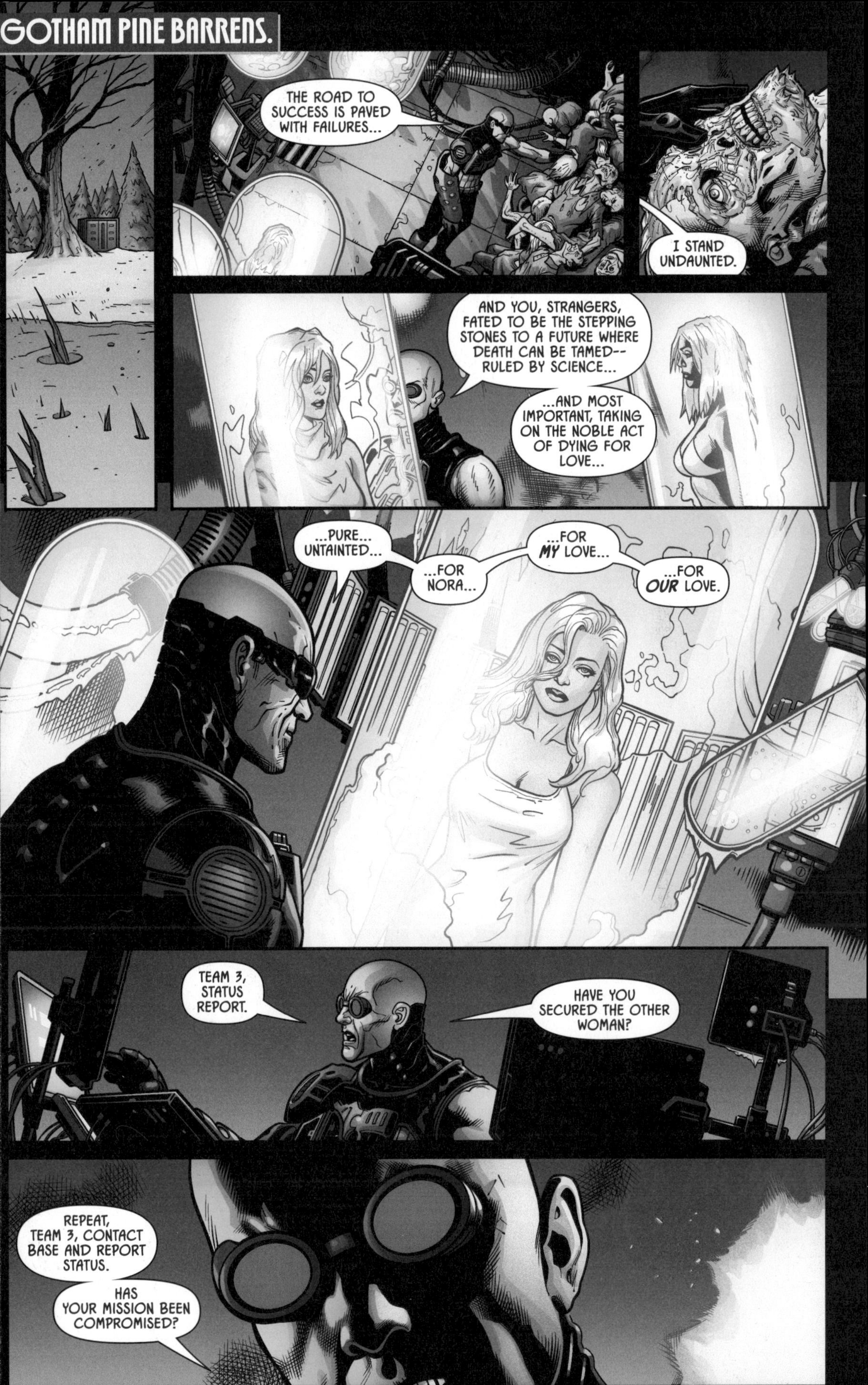
GOTHAM PINE BARRENS.
THE ROAD TO SUCCESS IS PAVED WITH FAILURES...
I STAND UNDAUNTED.
AND YOU, STRANGERS, FATED TO BE THE STEPPING STONES TO A FUTURE WHERE DEATH CAN BE TAMED-- RULED BY SCIENCE...
...AND MOST IMPORTANT, TAKING ON THE NOBLE ACT OF DYING FOR LOVE...
...PURE... UNTAINTED...
...FOR NORA...
...FOR *MY* LOVE...
...FOR *OUR* LOVE.
TEAM 3, STATUS REPORT.
HAVE YOU SECURED THE OTHER WOMAN?
REPEAT, TEAM 3, CONTACT BASE AND REPORT STATUS.
HAS YOUR MISSION BEEN COMPROMISED?

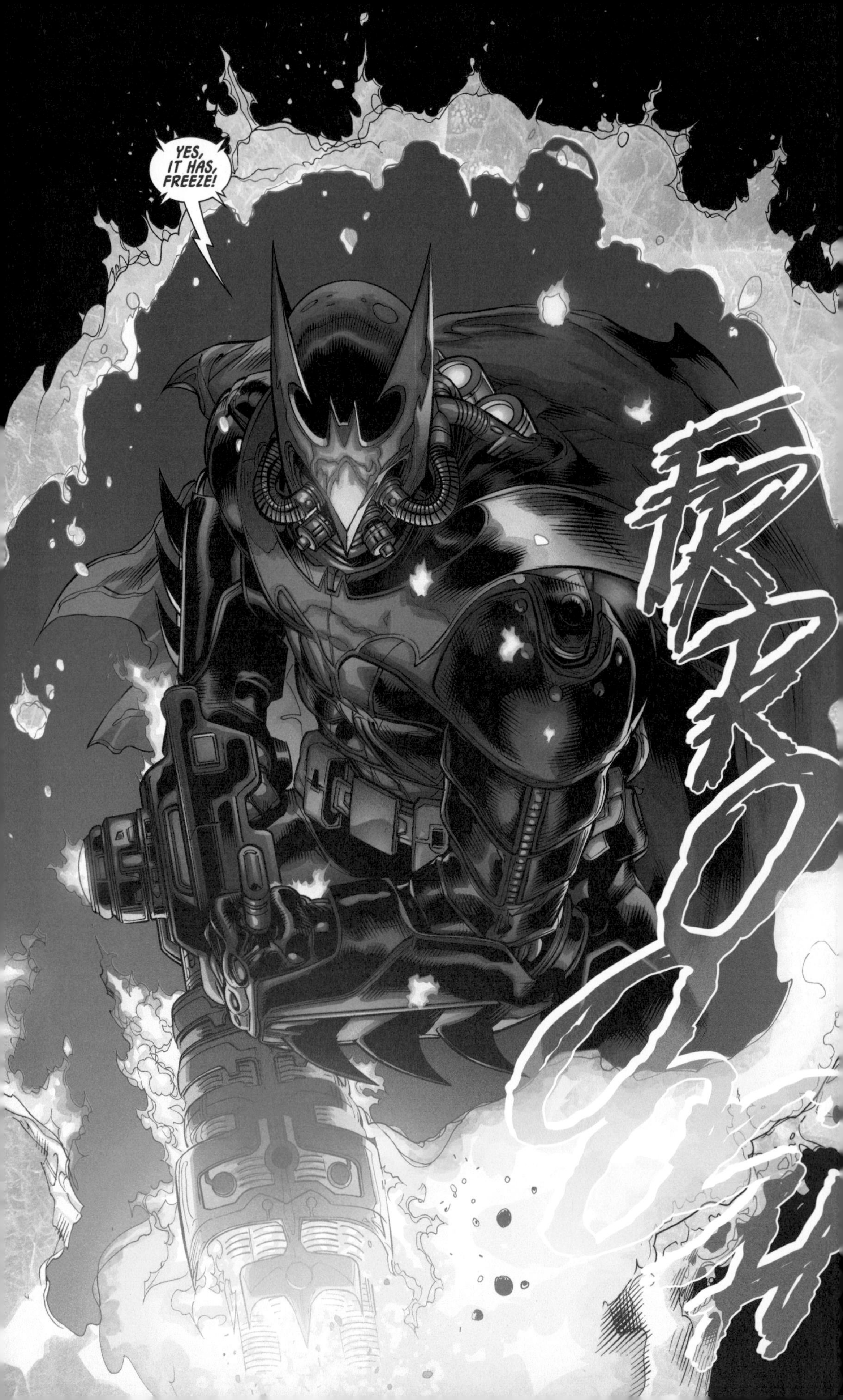
YES, IT HAS, FREEZE!

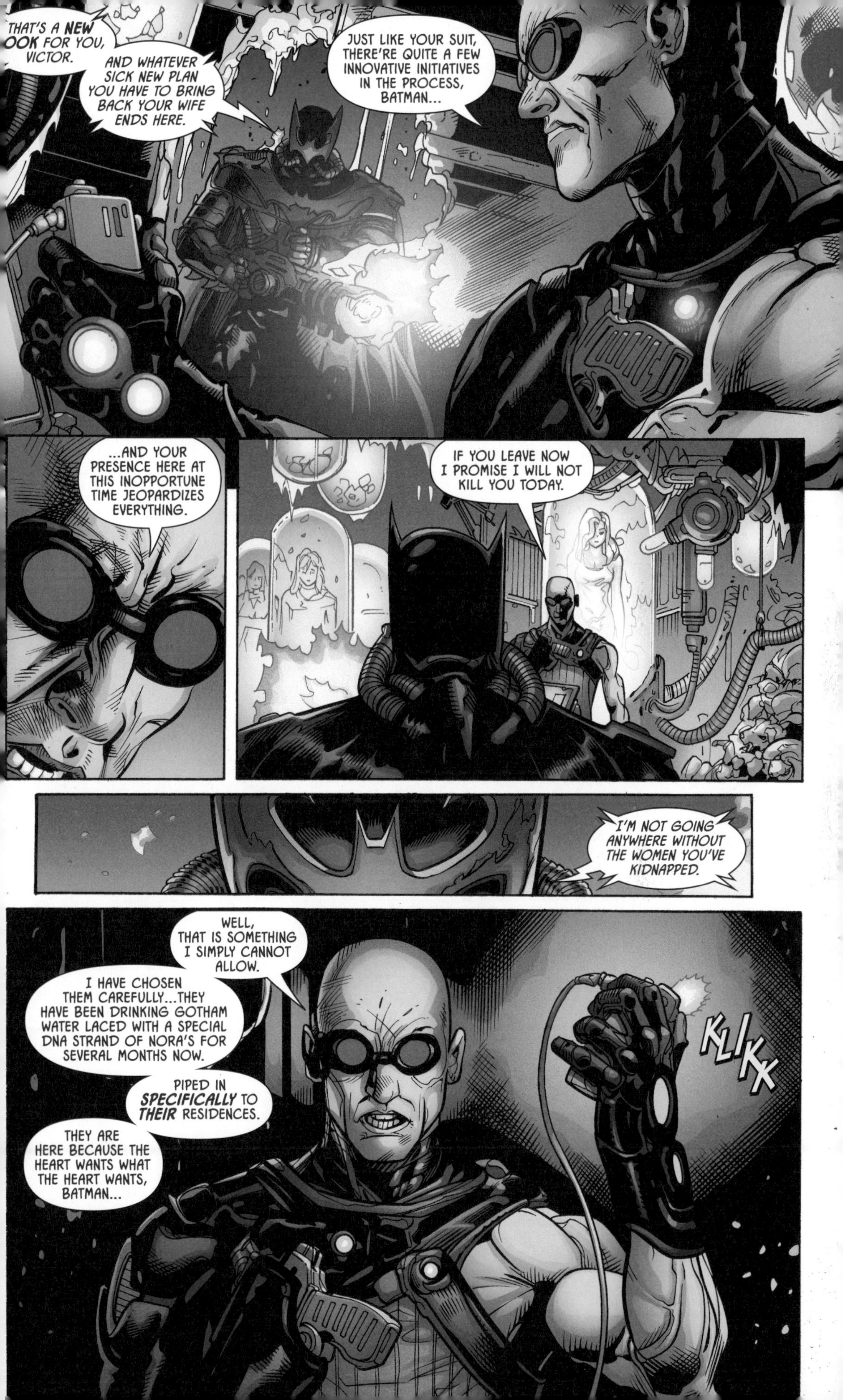

THAT'S A NEW OOK FOR YOU, VICTOR.
AND WHATEVER SICK NEW PLAN YOU HAVE TO BRING BACK YOUR WIFE ENDS HERE.
JUST LIKE YOUR SUIT, THERE'RE QUITE A FEW INNOVATIVE INITIATIVES IN THE PROCESS, BATMAN...
...AND YOUR PRESENCE HERE AT THIS INOPPORTUNE TIME JEOPARDIZES EVERYTHING.
IF YOU LEAVE NOW I PROMISE I WILL NOT KILL YOU TODAY.
I'M NOT GOING ANYWHERE WITHOUT THE WOMEN YOU'VE KIDNAPPED.
WELL, THAT IS SOMETHING I SIMPLY CANNOT ALLOW.
I HAVE CHOSEN THEM CAREFULLY...THEY HAVE BEEN DRINKING GOTHAM WATER LACED WITH A SPECIAL DNA STRAND OF NORA'S FOR SEVERAL MONTHS NOW.
PIPED IN SPECIFICALLY TO THEIR RESIDENCES.
THEY ARE HERE BECAUSE THE HEART WANTS WHAT THE HEART WANTS, BATMAN...
KLIKK

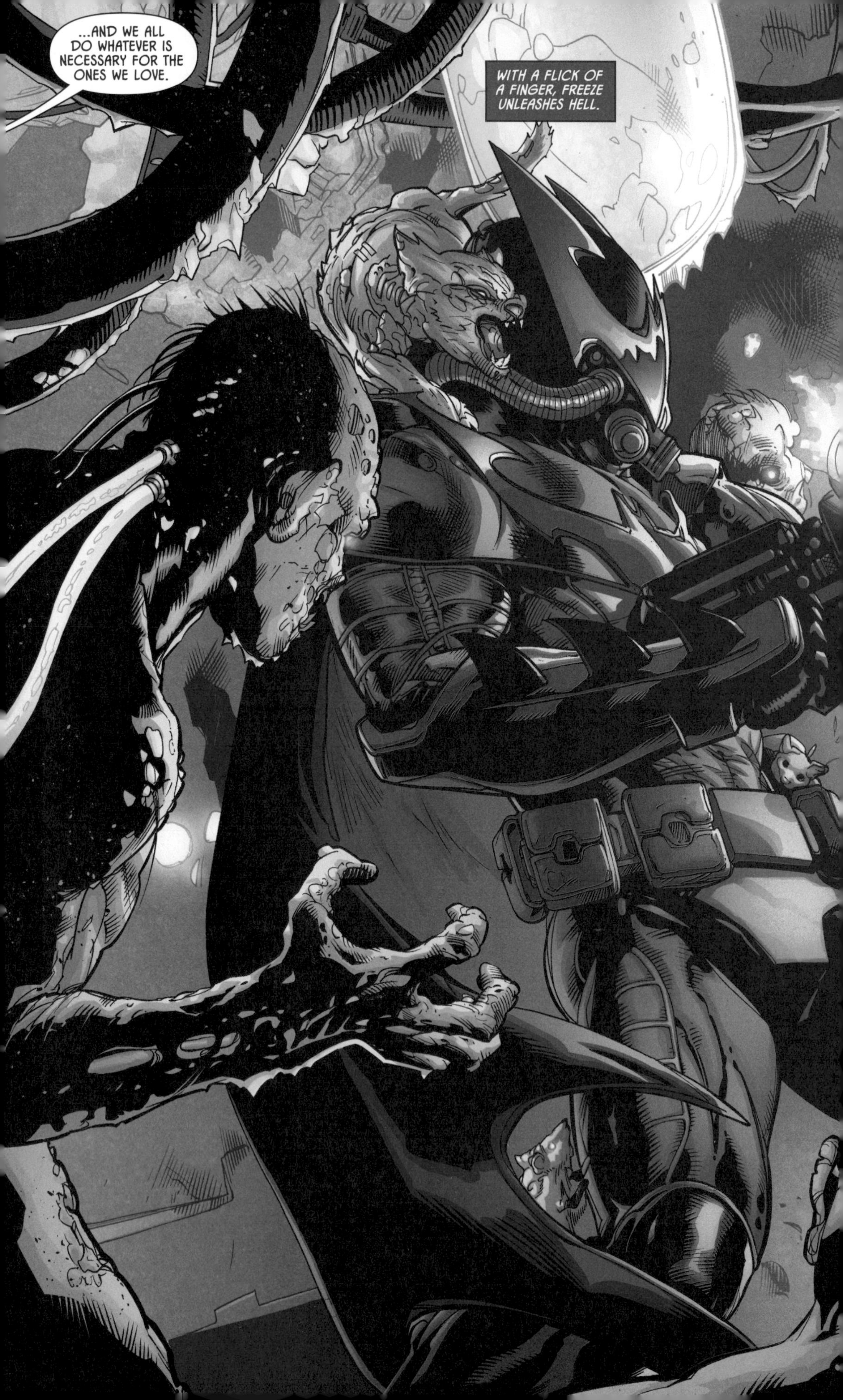
...AND WE ALL DO WHATEVER IS NECESSARY FOR THE ONES WE LOVE.
WITH A FLICK OF A FINGER, FREEZE UNLEASHES HELL.

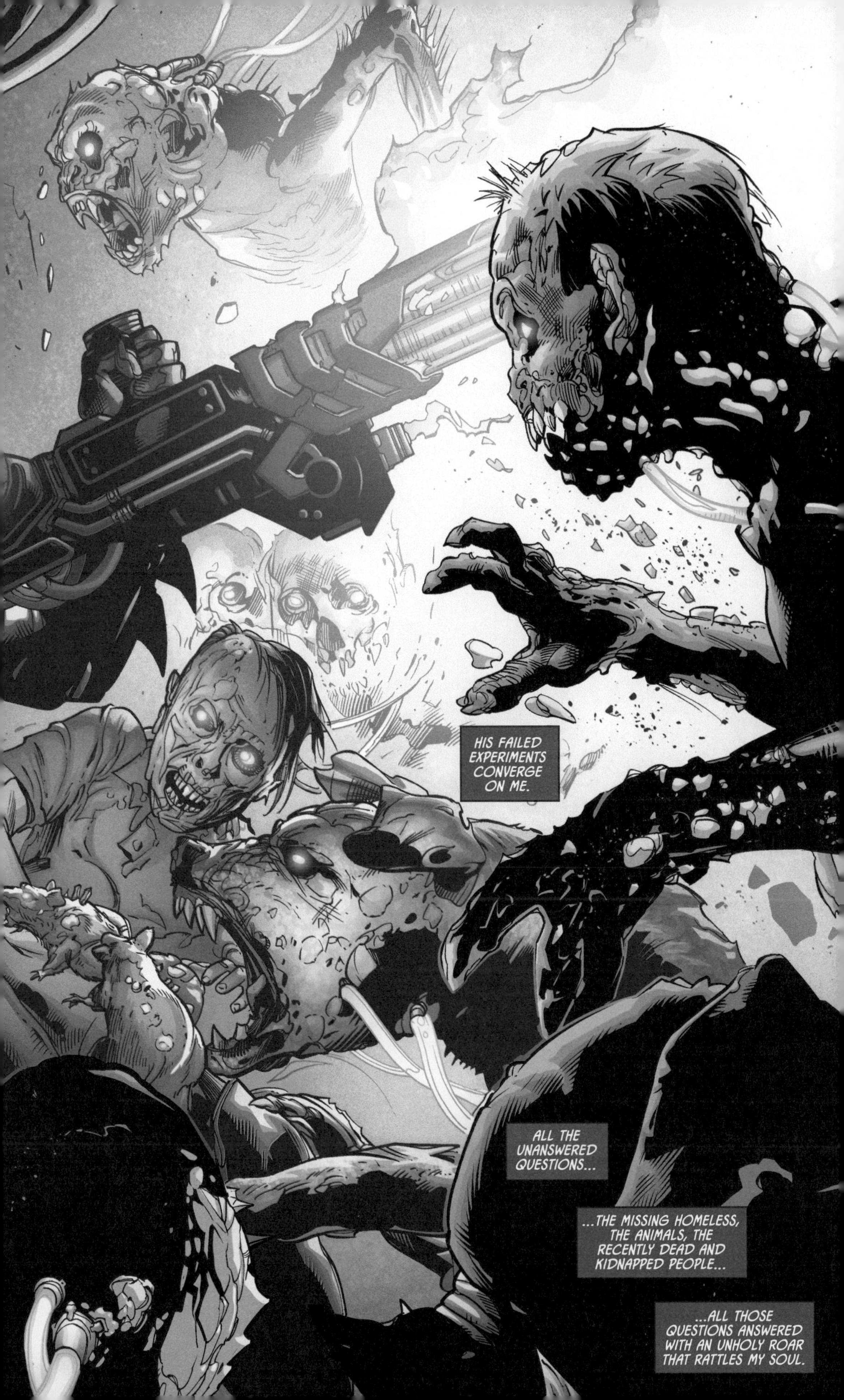
HIS FAILED EXPERIMENTS CONVERGE ON ME.
ALL THE UNANSWERED QUESTIONS...
...THE MISSING HOMELESS, THE ANIMALS, THE RECENTLY DEAD AND KIDNAPPED PEOPLE...
...ALL THOSE QUESTIONS ANSWERED WITH AN UNHOLY ROAR THAT RATTLES MY SOUL.

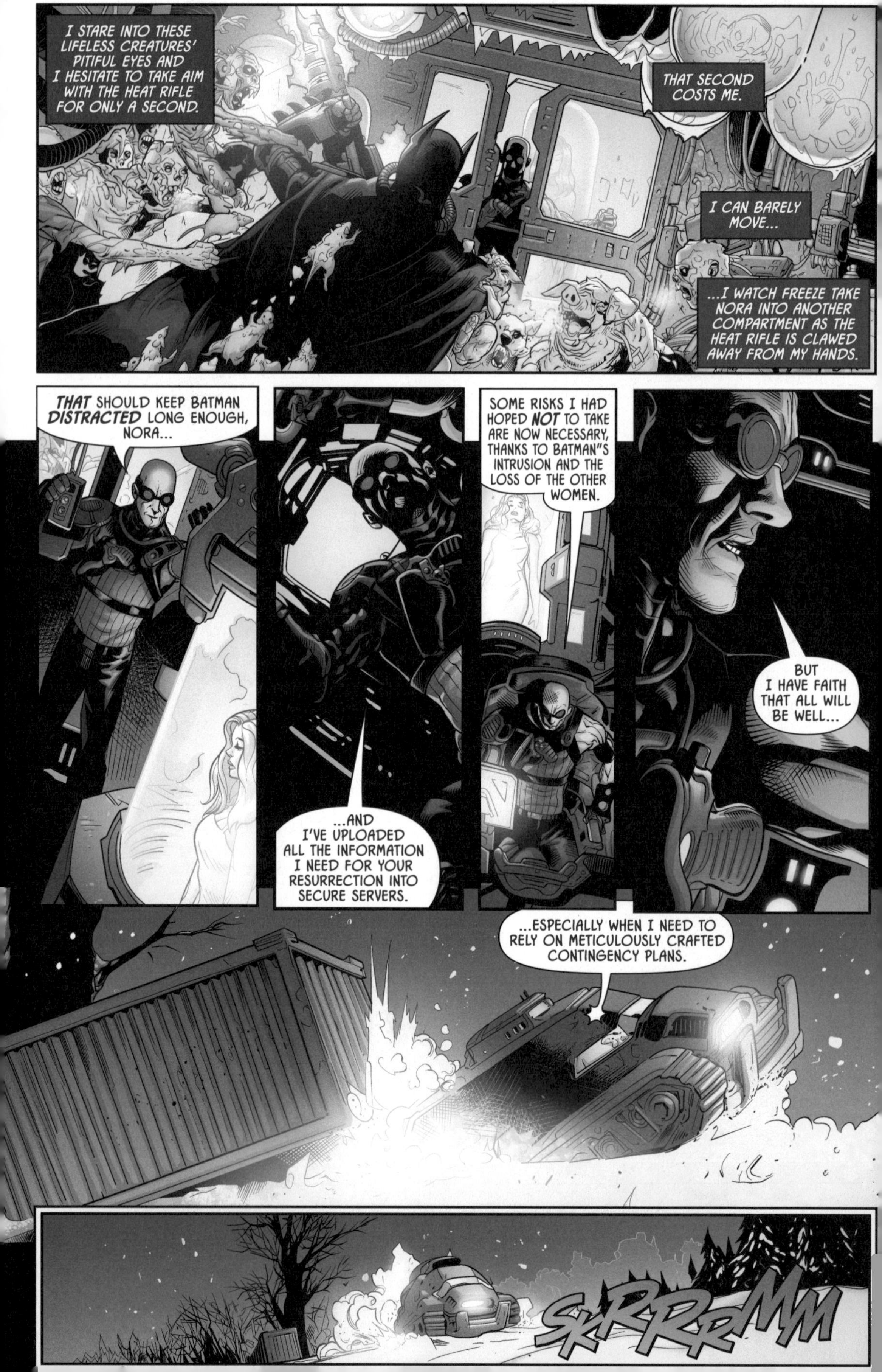
I STARE INTO THESE LIFELESS CREATURES' PITIFUL EYES AND I HESITATE TO TAKE AIM WITH THE HEAT RIFLE FOR ONLY A SECOND.
THAT SECOND COSTS ME.
I CAN BARELY MOVE...
...I WATCH FREEZE TAKE NORA INTO ANOTHER COMPARTMENT AS THE HEAT RIFLE IS CLAWED AWAY FROM MY HANDS.
THAT SHOULD KEEP BATMAN DISTRACTED LONG ENOUGH, NORA...
...AND I'VE UPLOADED ALL THE INFORMATION I NEED FOR YOUR RESURRECTION INTO SECURE SERVERS.
SOME RISKS I HAD HOPED NOT TO TAKE ARE NOW NECESSARY, THANKS TO BATMAN"S INTRUSION AND THE LOSS OF THE OTHER WOMEN.
BUT I HAVE FAITH THAT ALL WILL BE WELL...
...ESPECIALLY WHEN I NEED TO RELY ON METICULOUSLY CRAFTED CONTINGENCY PLANS.
SKRRRMM

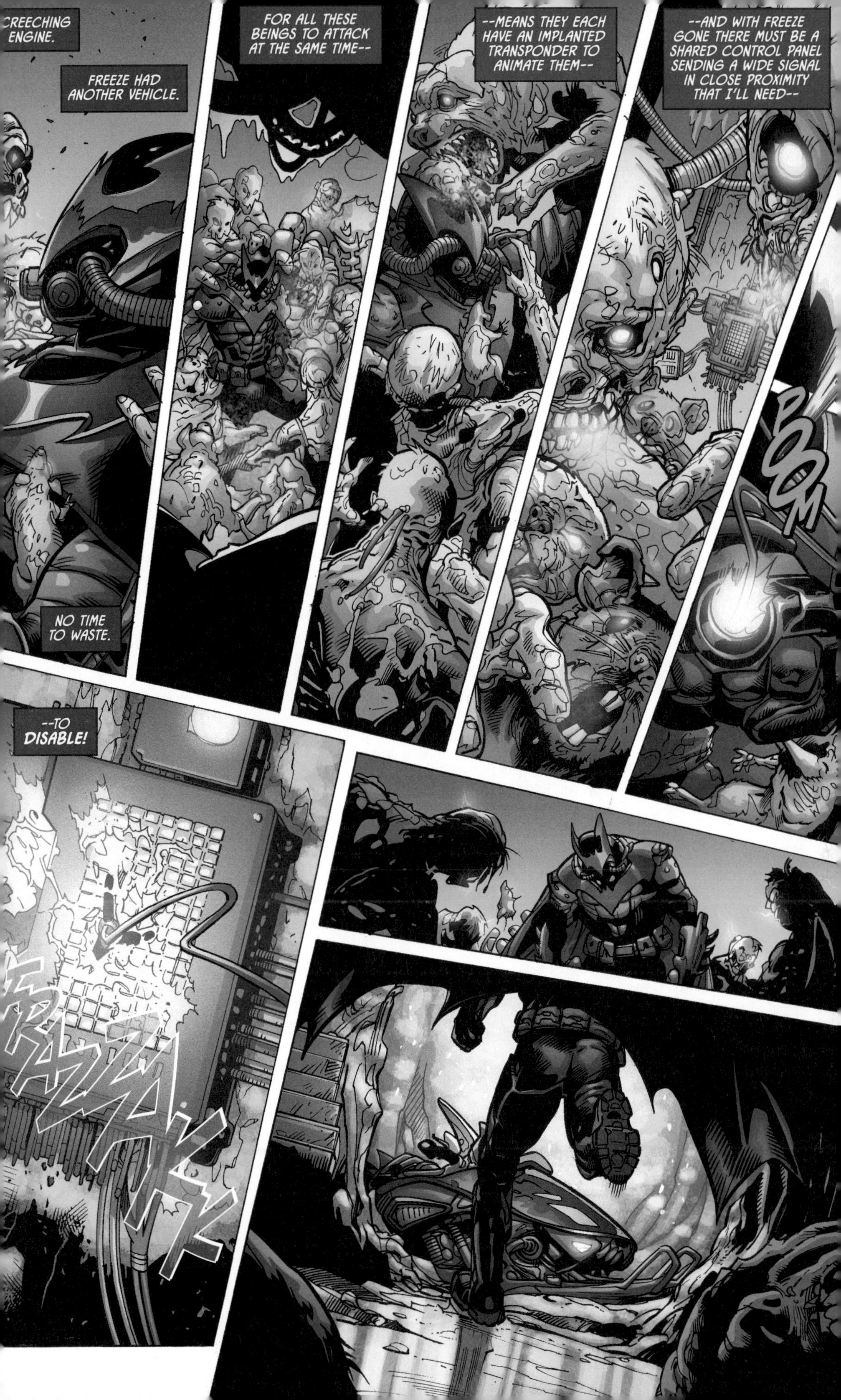
CREECHING ENGINE.
FREEZE HAD ANOTHER VEHICLE.
NO TIME TO WASTE.
FOR ALL THESE BEINGS TO ATTACK AT THE SAME TIME--
--MEANS THEY EACH HAVE AN IMPLANTED TRANSPONDER TO ANIMATE THEM--
--AND WITH FREEZE GONE THERE MUST BE A SHARED CONTROL PANEL SENDING A WIDE SIGNAL IN CLOSE PROXIMITY THAT I'LL NEED--
POOM
--TO DISABLE!

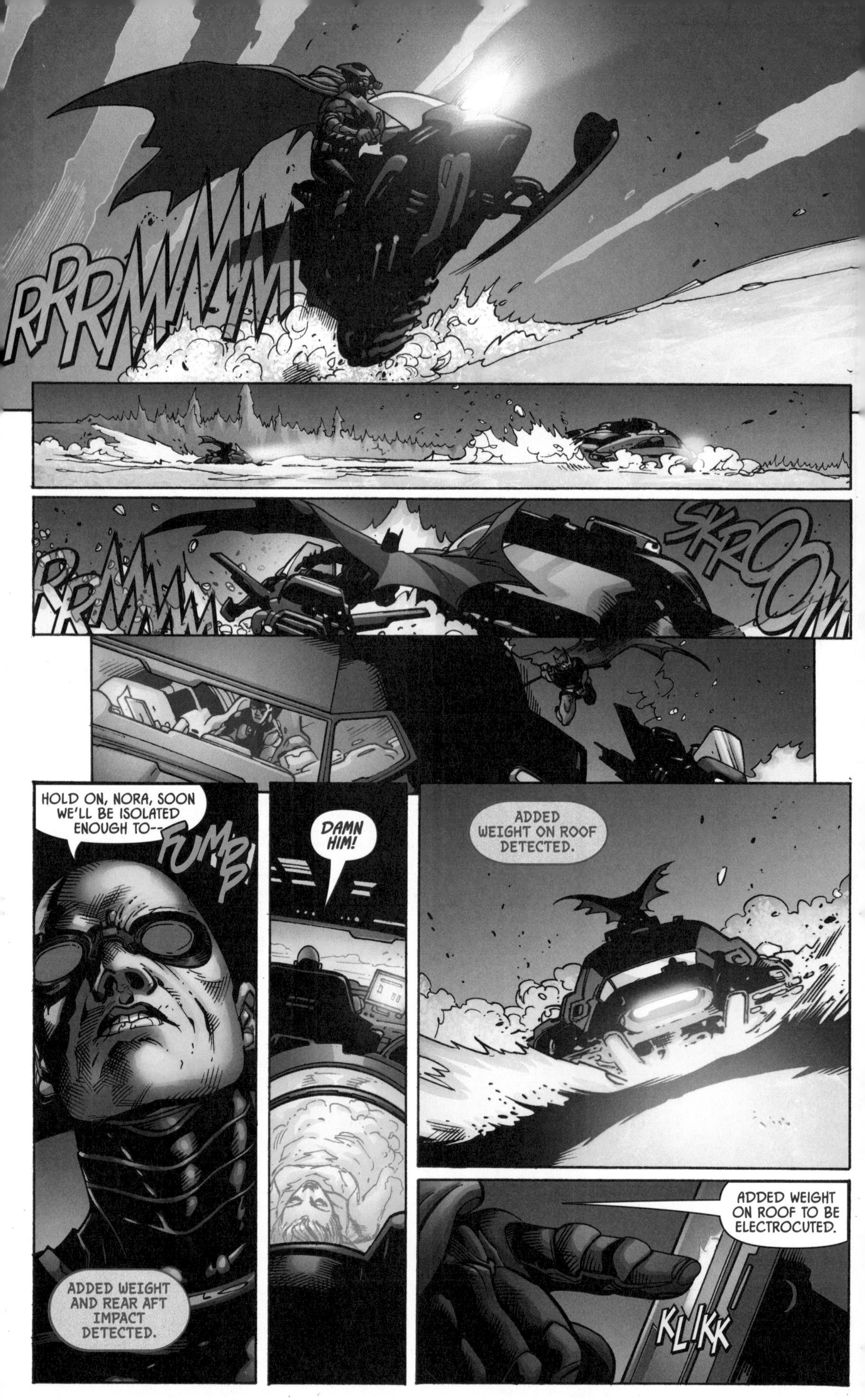

RRRMMMM
SKROOOM
RRRMMMM
HOLD ON, NORA, SOON WE'LL BE ISOLATED ENOUGH TO--
FUMP
ADDED WEIGHT AND REAR AFT IMPACT DETECTED.
DAMN HIM!
ADDED WEIGHT ON ROOF DETECTED.
ADDED WEIGHT ON ROOF TO BE ELECTROCUTED.
KLIKK

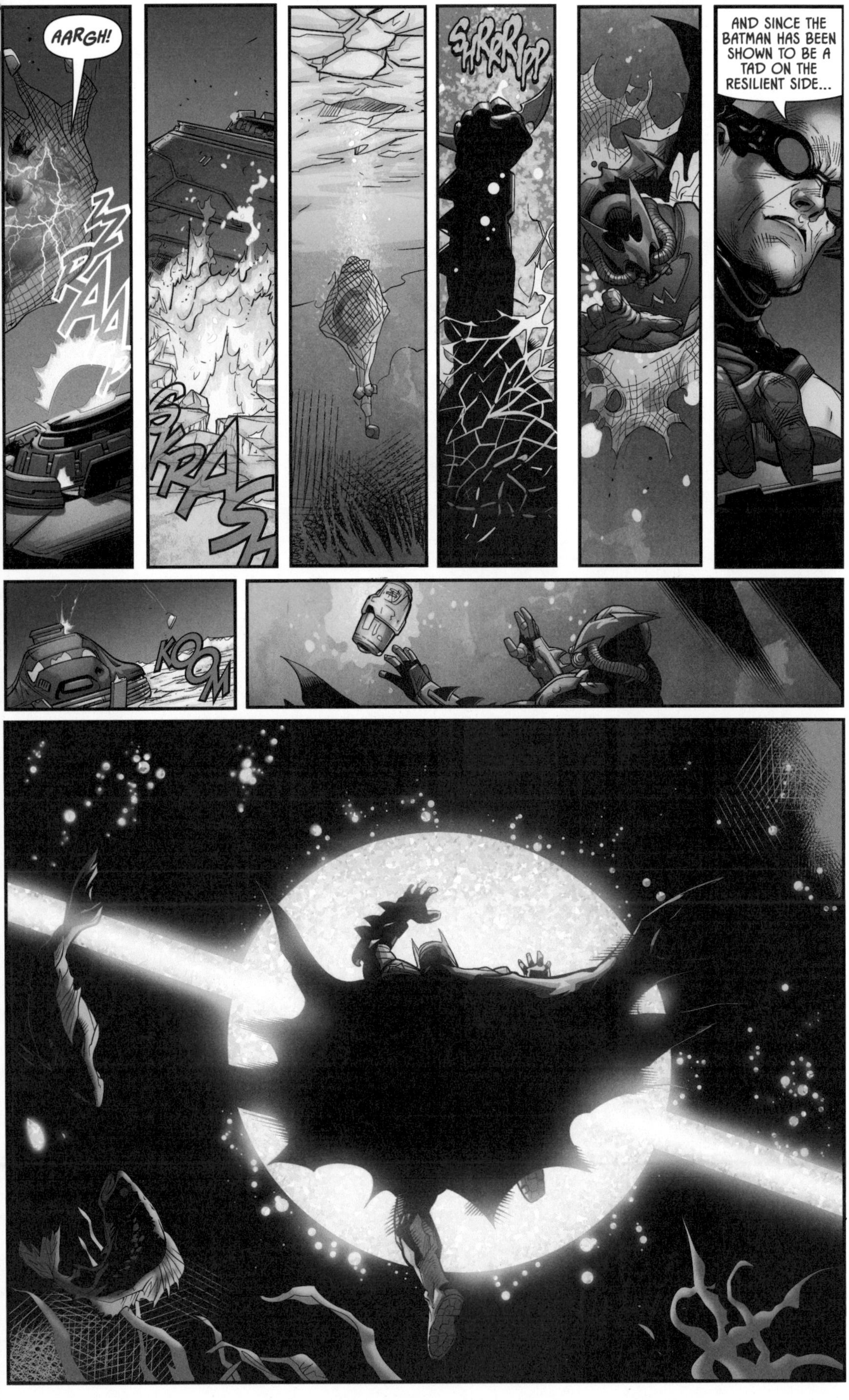
AARGH!
ZZRAAAAP
SKRASH
SHRRRIPP
AND SINCE THE BATMAN HAS BEEN SHOWN TO BE A TAD ON THE RESILIENT SIDE...
KOOM

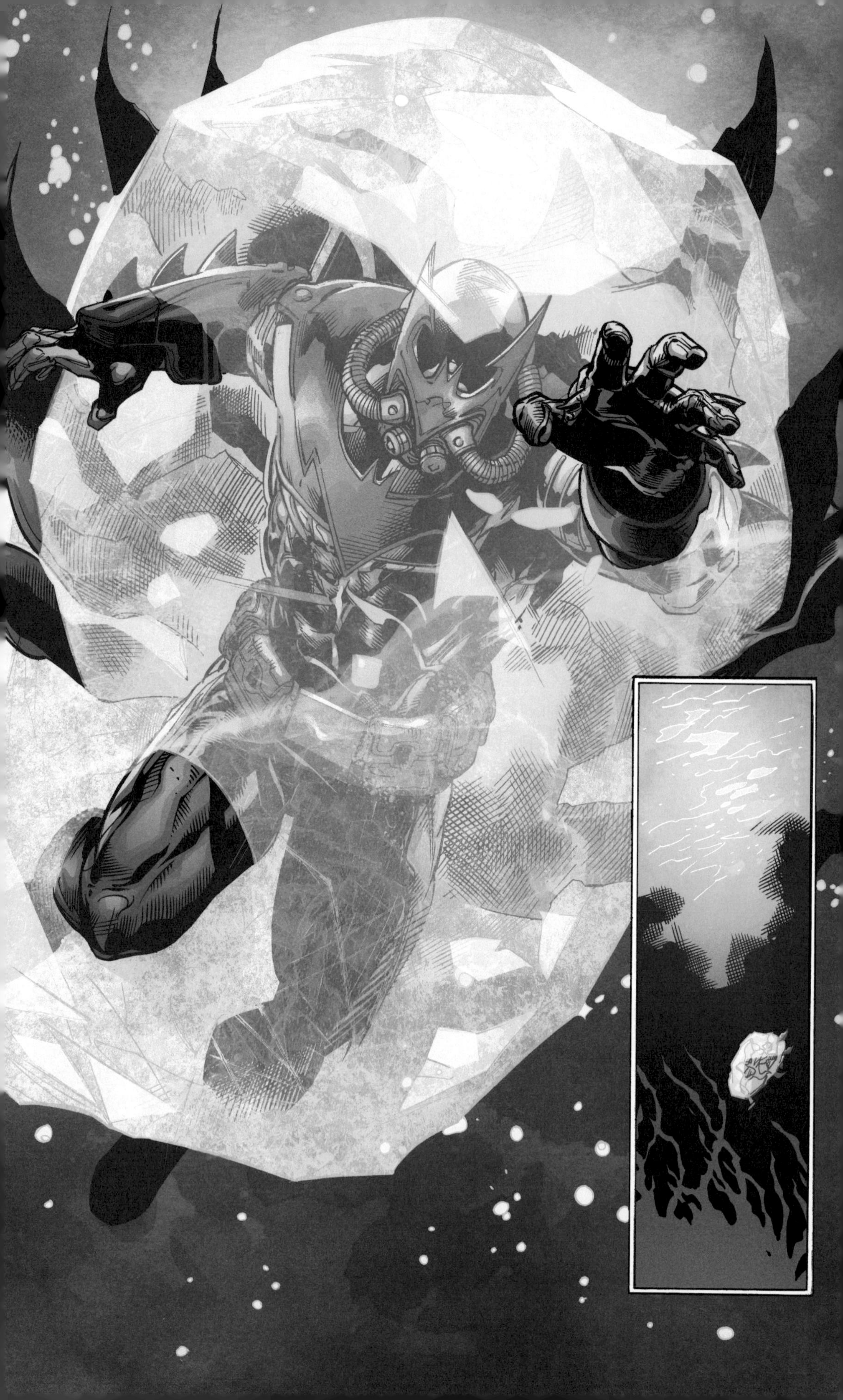

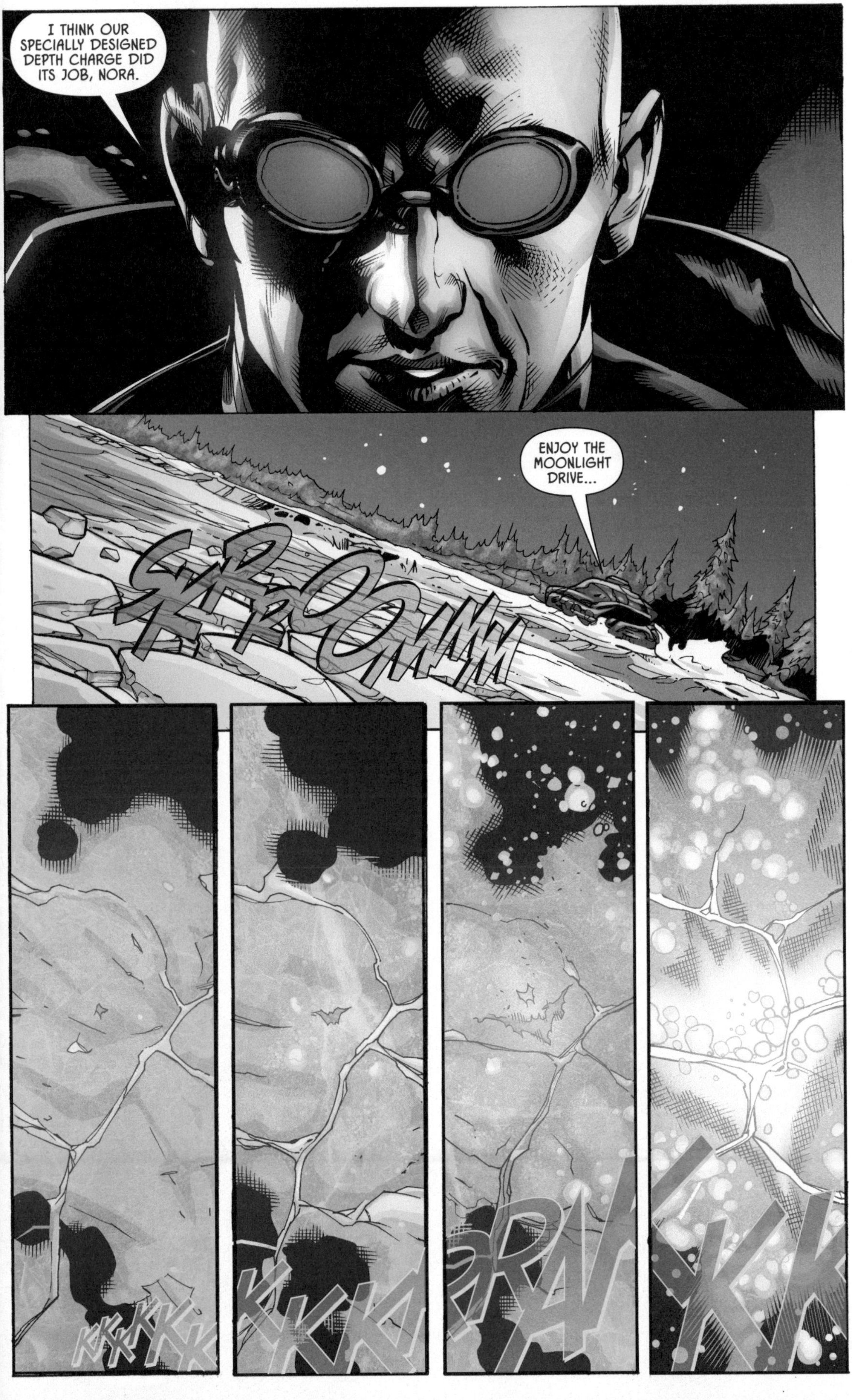
I THINK OUR SPECIALLY DESIGNED DEPTH CHARGE DID ITS JOB, NORA.
ENJOY THE MOONLIGHT DRIVE...

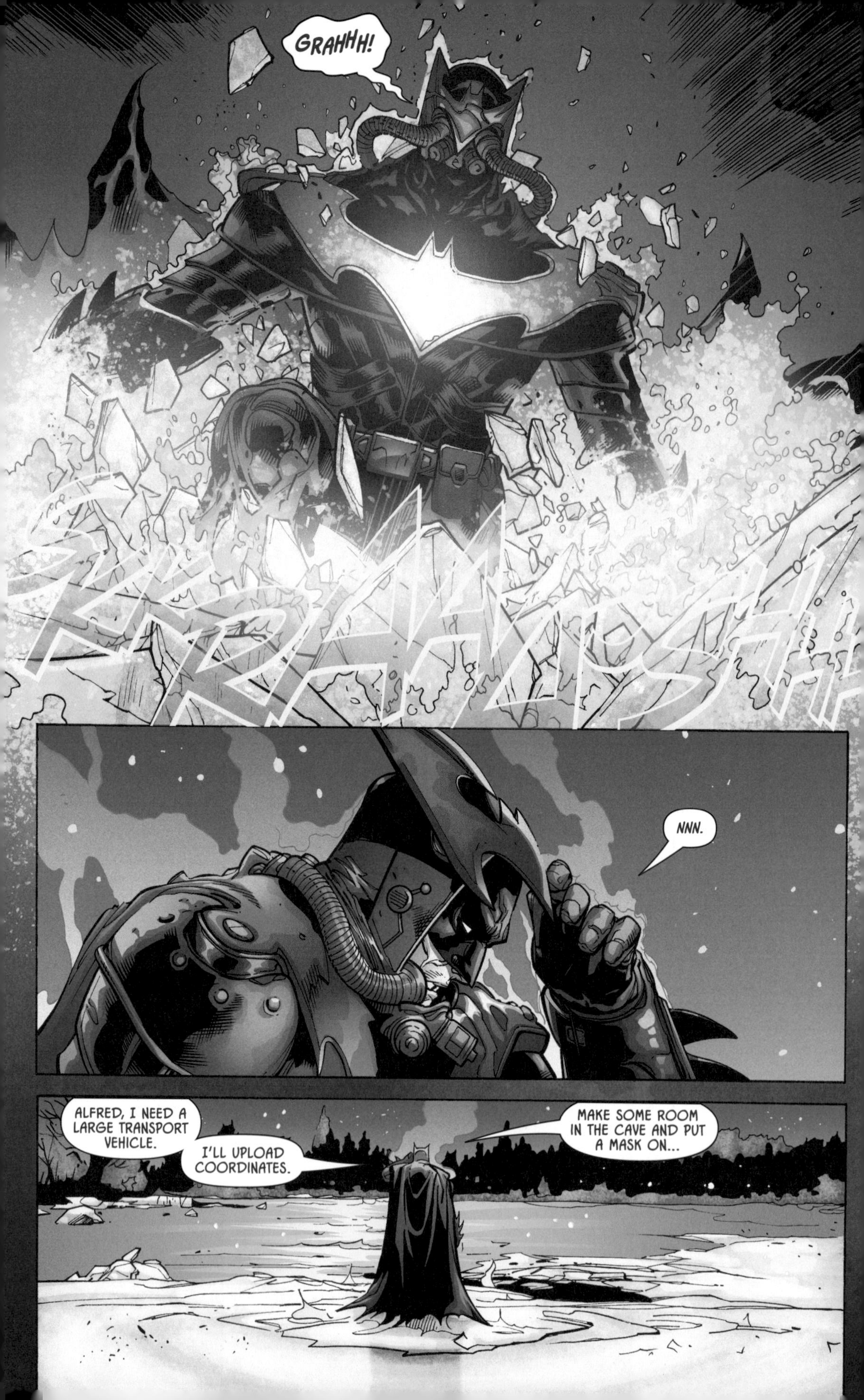
GRAHHH!
NNN.
ALFRED, I NEED A LARGE TRANSPORT VEHICLE.
I'LL UPLOAD COORDINATES.
MAKE SOME ROOM IN THE CAVE AND PUT A MASK ON...

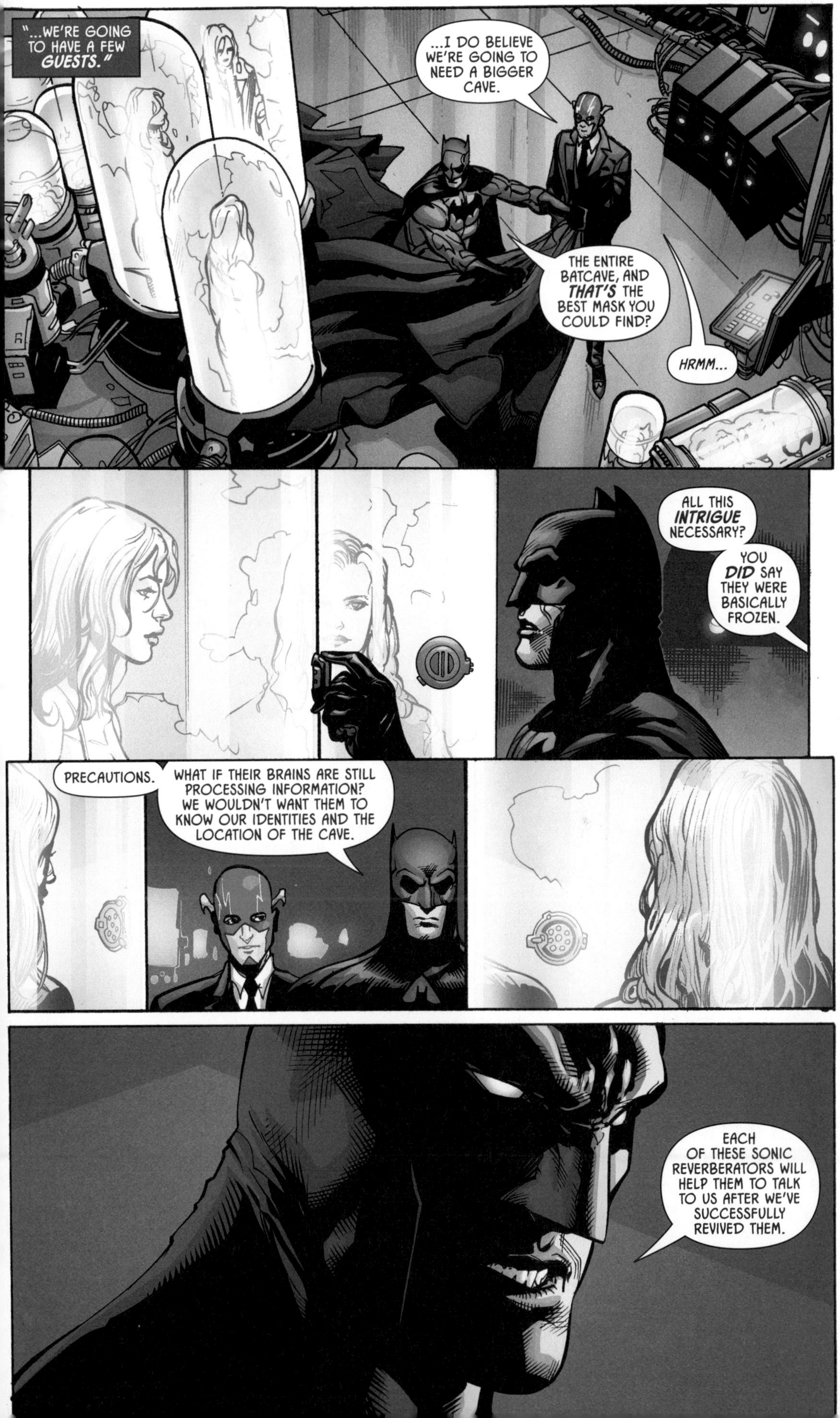
"...WE'RE GOING TO HAVE A FEW *GUESTS.*"
...I DO BELIEVE WE'RE GOING TO NEED A BIGGER CAVE.
THE ENTIRE BATCAVE, AND ***THAT'S*** THE BEST MASK YOU COULD FIND?
HRMM...
ALL THIS ***INTRIGUE*** NECESSARY?
YOU ***DID*** SAY THEY WERE BASICALLY FROZEN.
PRECAUTIONS.
WHAT IF THEIR BRAINS ARE STILL PROCESSING INFORMATION? WE WOULDN'T WANT THEM TO KNOW OUR IDENTITIES AND THE LOCATION OF THE CAVE.
EACH OF THESE SONIC REVERBERATORS WILL HELP THEM TO TALK TO US AFTER WE'VE SUCCESSFULLY REVIVED THEM.

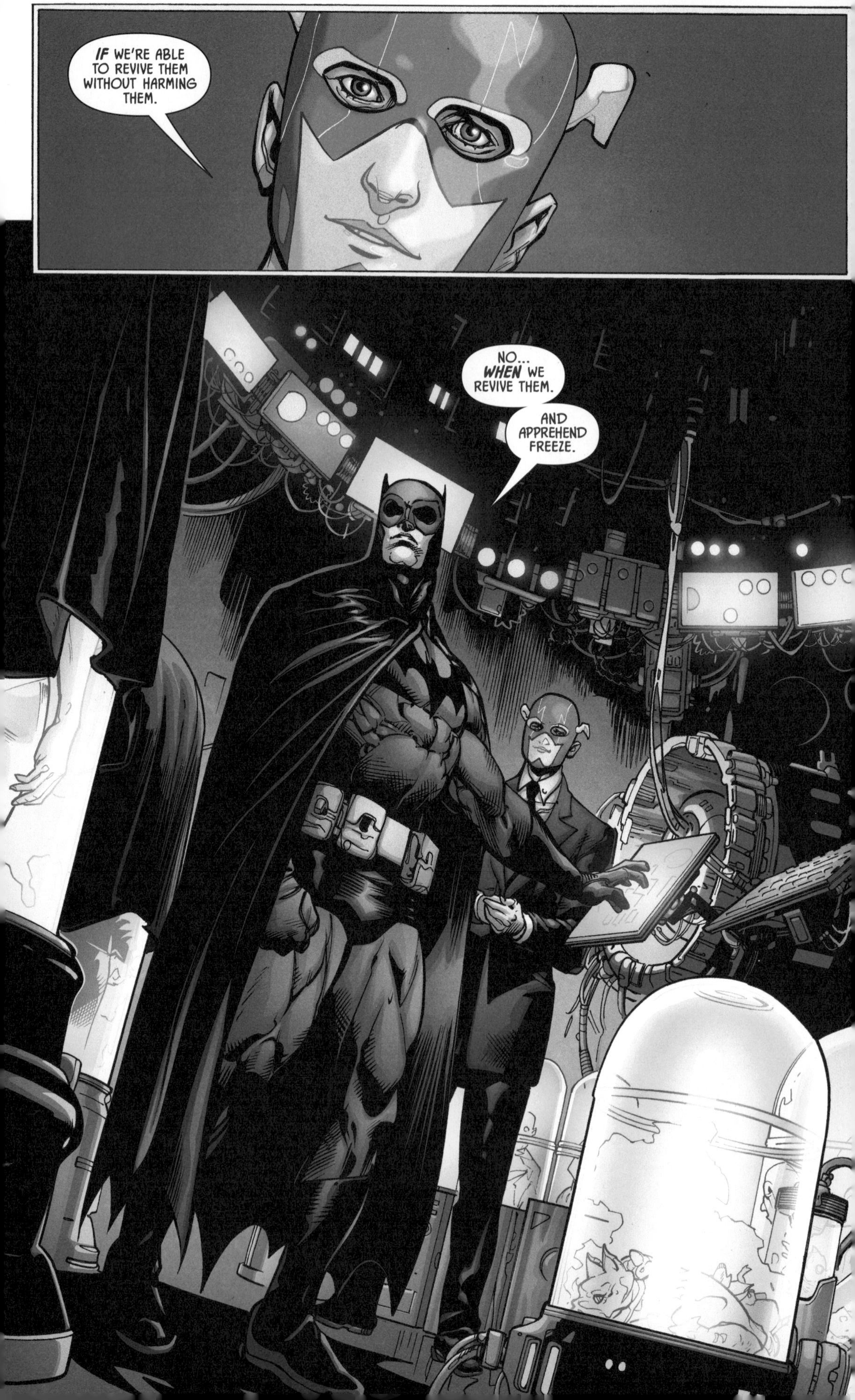
IF WE'RE ABLE TO REVIVE THEM WITHOUT HARMING THEM.
NO... WHEN WE REVIVE THEM.
AND APPREHEND FREEZE.

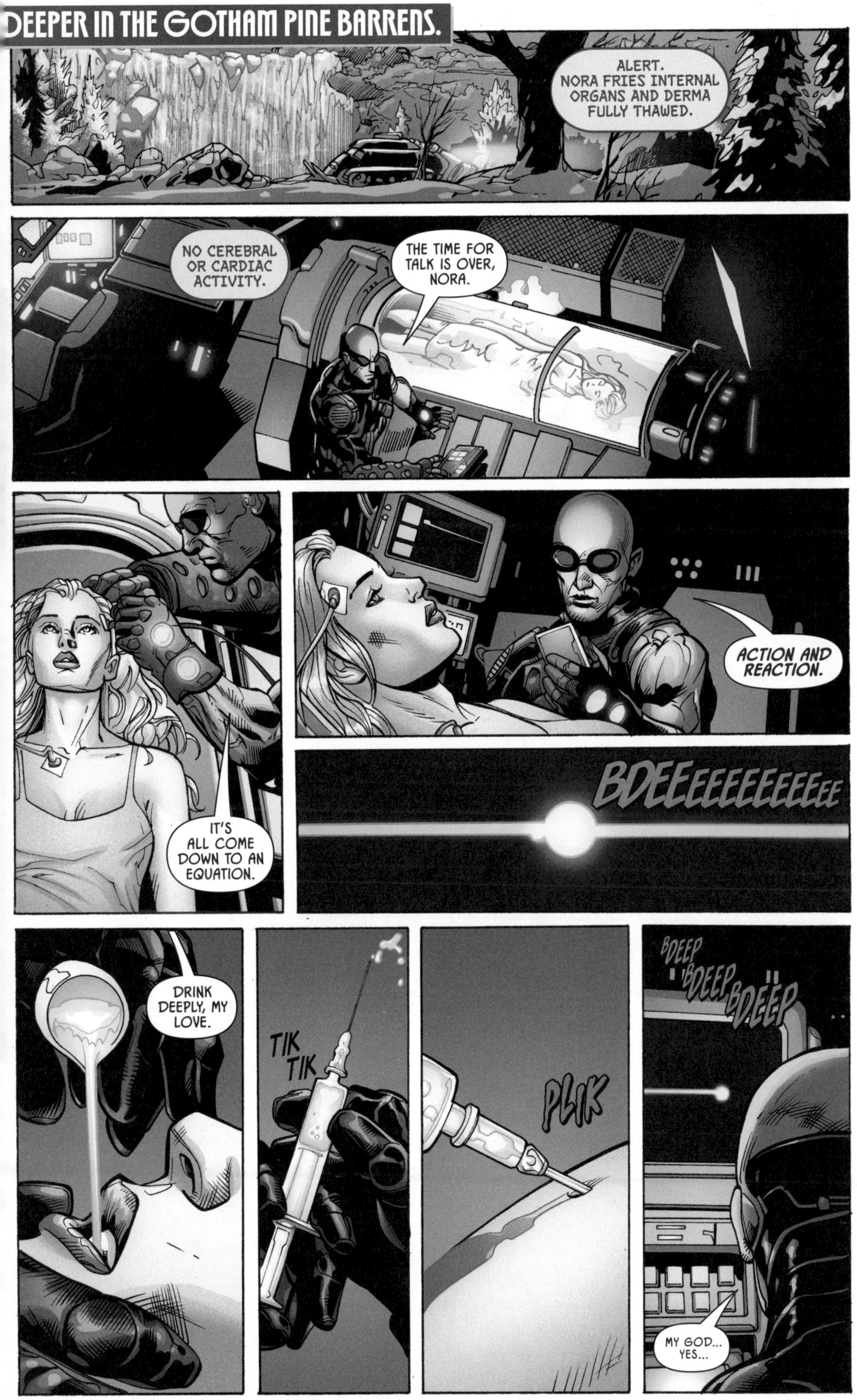

DEEPER IN THE GOTHAM PINE BARRENS.
ALERT. NORA FRIES INTERNAL ORGANS AND DERMA FULLY THAWED.
NO CEREBRAL OR CARDIAC ACTIVITY.
THE TIME FOR TALK IS OVER, NORA.
IT'S ALL COME DOWN TO AN EQUATION.
ACTION AND REACTION.
BDEEEEEEEEEEEEE
DRINK DEEPLY, MY LOVE.
TIK TIK
PLIK
BDEEP BDEEP BDEEP
MY GOD... YES...

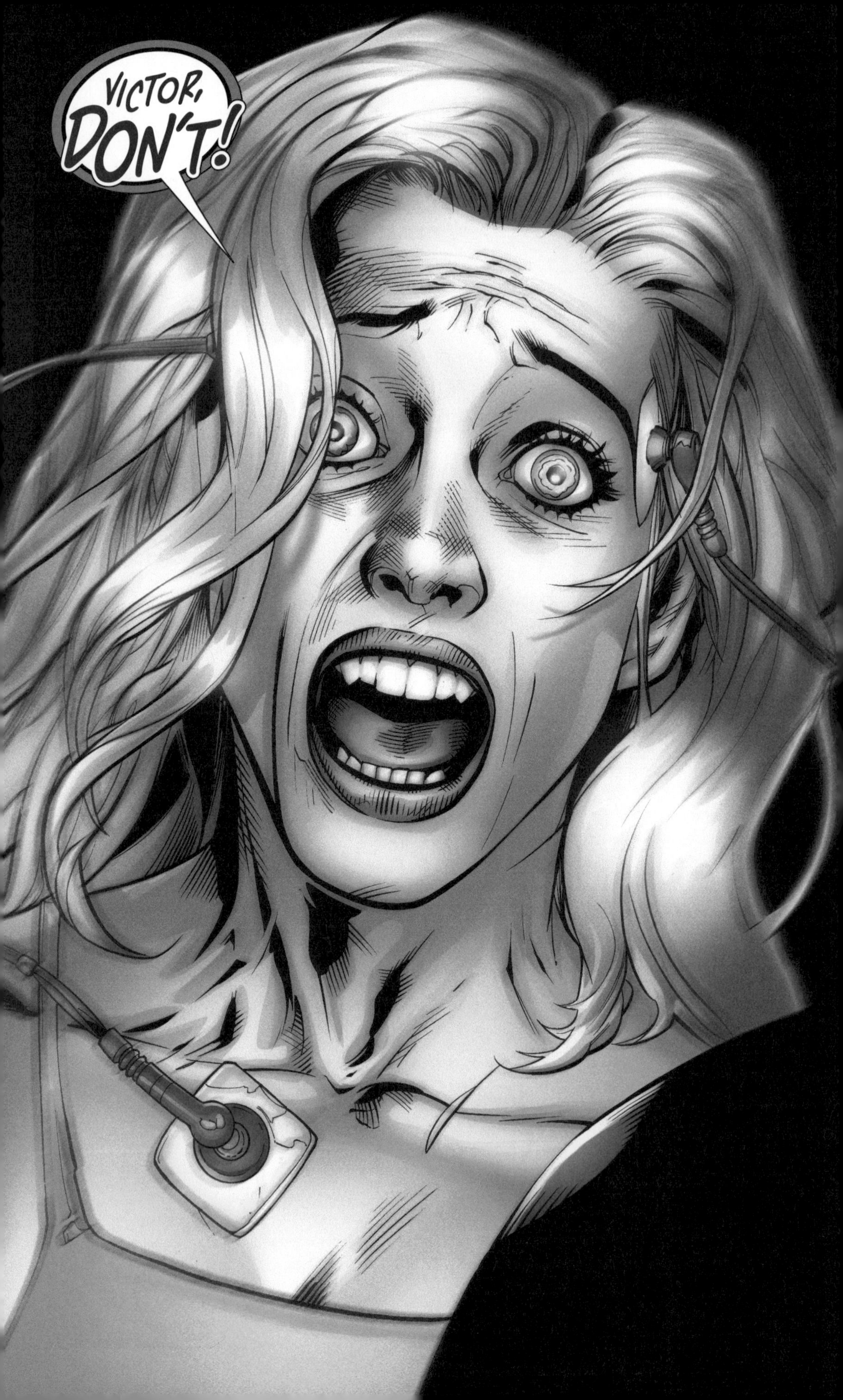
VICTOR, DON'T!

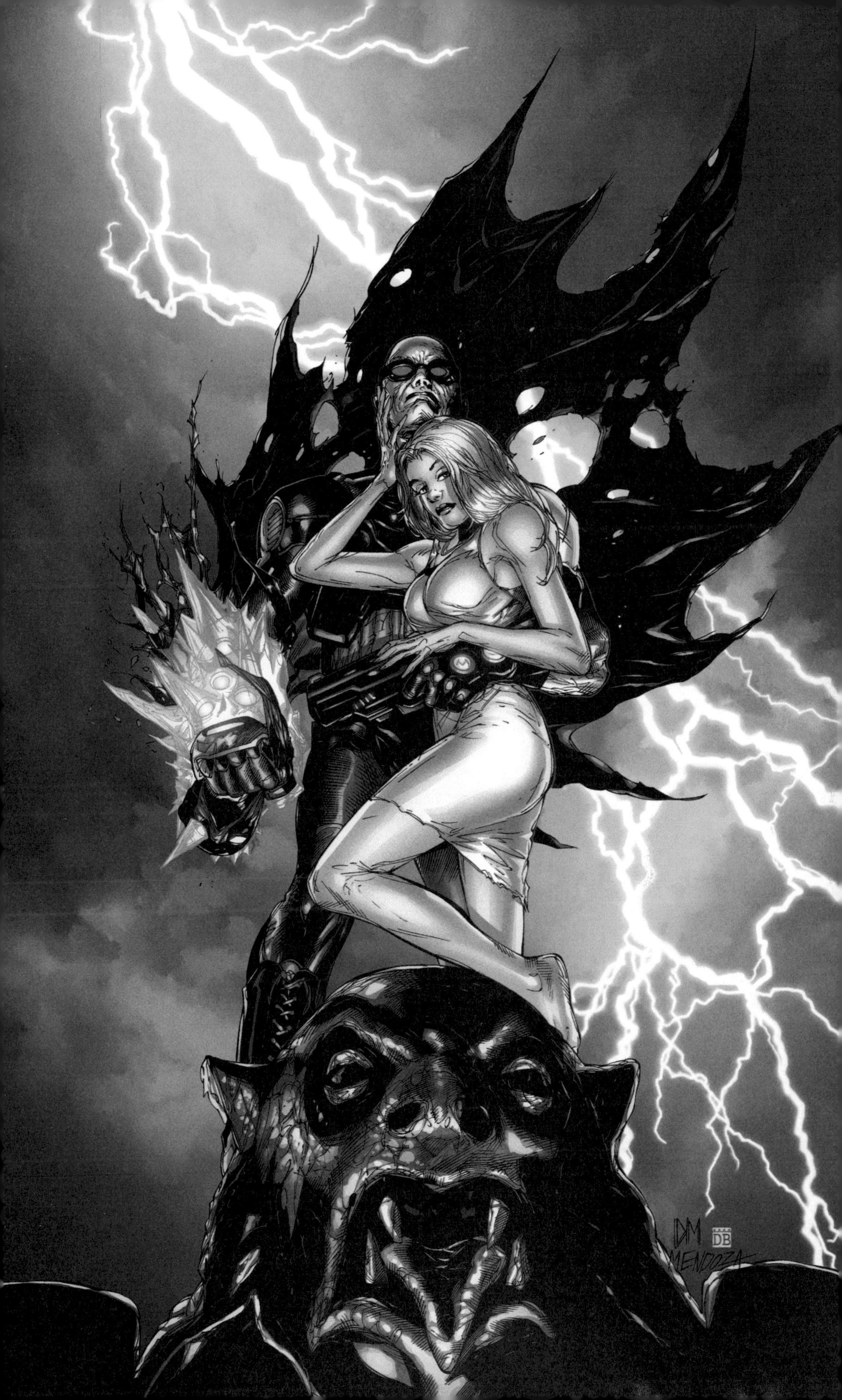
MENDOZA

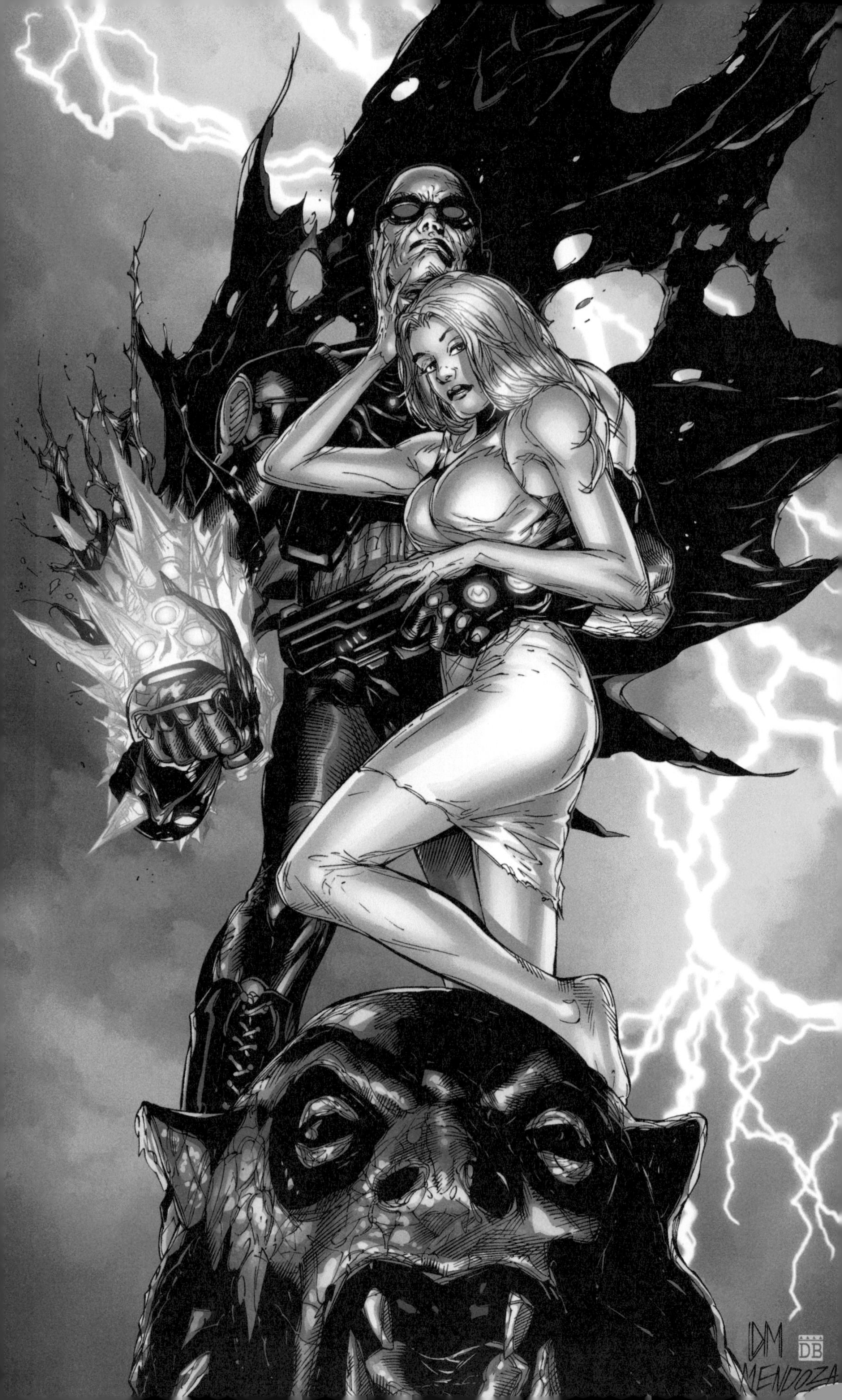
MENDOZA
DB

...BUT I *BEGGED* YOU NOT TO DO IT, VICTOR...

...I *PLEADED* WITH YOU THAT I WANTED TO *FIGHT* THE CANCER ON MY OWN TERMS...

...I *DIDN'T* WANT TO BE FROZEN.

ABSOLUTE ZERO IN T MINUS FIFTEEN SECONDS...

I HAD NO CHOICE, NORA.

I HAD A CHANCE TO SAVE YOU AND I TOOK IT.

A *CHANCE?*

YOU WEREN'T SURE IT WOULD WORK?

ABSOLUTE ZERO IN T MINUS FOURTEEN SECONDS...

NO, I WASN'T.

I'M NOT GOING TO LIE TO YOU.

IT WAS A GAMBLE.

ABSOLUTE ZERO IN T MINUS THIRTEEN SECONDS...

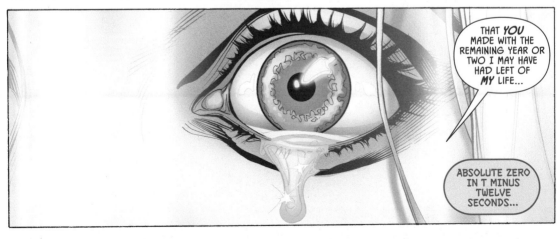

THAT *YOU* MADE WITH THE REMAINING YEAR OR TWO I MAY HAVE HAD LEFT OF *MY* LIFE...

ABSOLUTE ZERO IN T MINUS TWELVE SECONDS...

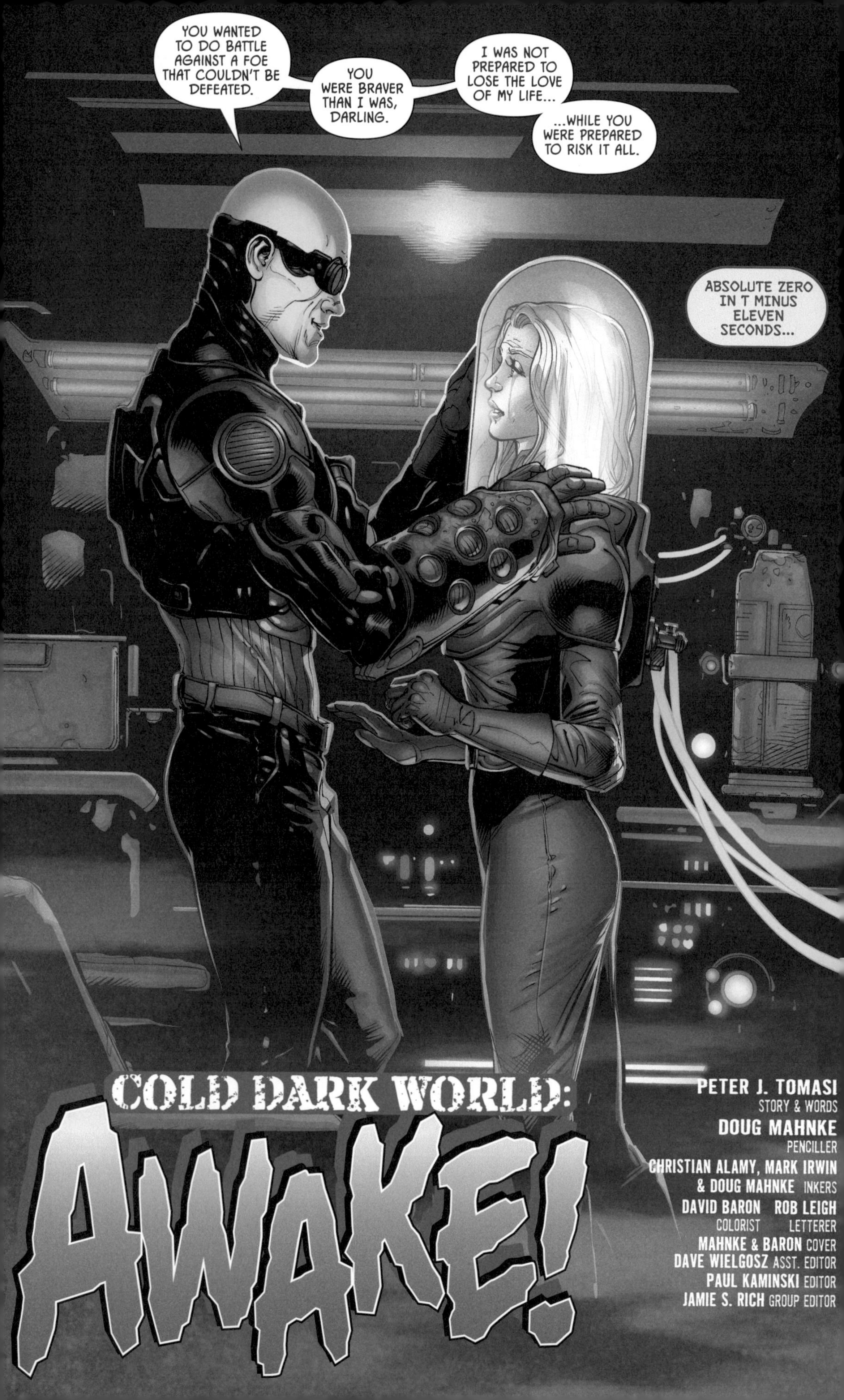
YOU WANTED TO DO BATTLE AGAINST A FOE THAT COULDN'T BE DEFEATED.
YOU WERE BRAVER THAN I WAS, DARLING.
I WAS NOT PREPARED TO LOSE THE LOVE OF MY LIFE...
...WHILE YOU WERE PREPARED TO RISK IT ALL.
ABSOLUTE ZERO IN T MINUS ELEVEN SECONDS...
COLD DARK WORLD:
AWAKE!
PETER J. TOMASI STORY & WORDS
DOUG MAHNKE PENCILLER
CHRISTIAN ALAMY, MARK IRWIN & DOUG MAHNKE INKERS
DAVID BARON COLORIST
ROB LEIGH LETTERER
MAHNKE & BARON COVER
DAVE WIELGOSZ ASST. EDITOR
PAUL KAMINSKI EDITOR
JAMIE S. RICH GROUP EDITOR

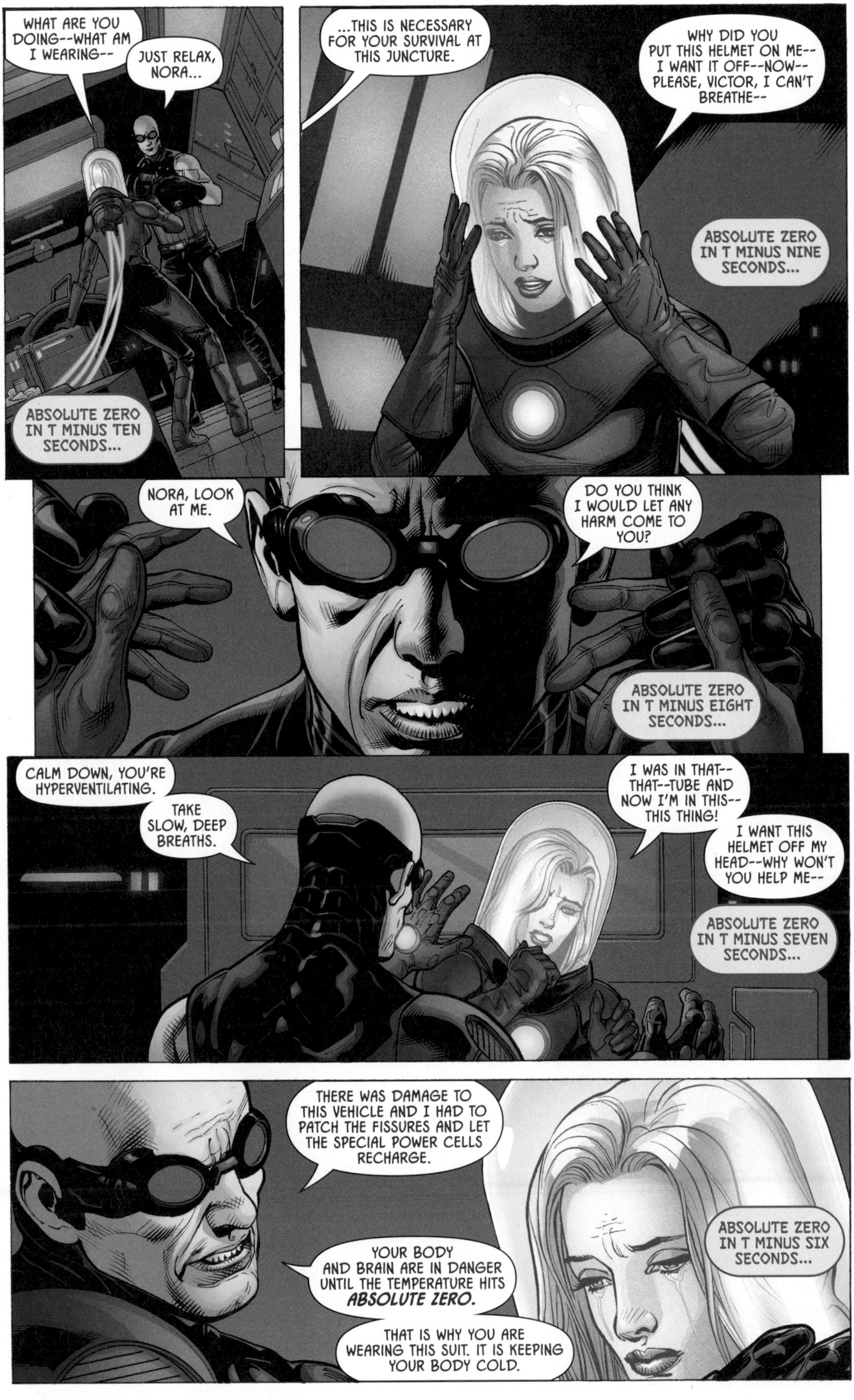

WHAT ARE YOU DOING--WHAT AM I WEARING--
JUST RELAX, NORA...
ABSOLUTE ZERO IN T MINUS TEN SECONDS...
...THIS IS NECESSARY FOR YOUR SURVIVAL AT THIS JUNCTURE.
WHY DID YOU PUT THIS HELMET ON ME-- I WANT IT OFF--NOW-- PLEASE, VICTOR, I CAN'T BREATHE--
ABSOLUTE ZERO IN T MINUS NINE SECONDS...
NORA, LOOK AT ME.
DO YOU THINK I WOULD LET ANY HARM COME TO YOU?
ABSOLUTE ZERO IN T MINUS EIGHT SECONDS...
CALM DOWN, YOU'RE HYPERVENTILATING.
TAKE SLOW, DEEP BREATHS.
I WAS IN THAT-- THAT--TUBE AND NOW I'M IN THIS-- THIS THING!
I WANT THIS HELMET OFF MY HEAD--WHY WON'T YOU HELP ME--
ABSOLUTE ZERO IN T MINUS SEVEN SECONDS...
THERE WAS DAMAGE TO THIS VEHICLE AND I HAD TO PATCH THE FISSURES AND LET THE SPECIAL POWER CELLS RECHARGE.
YOUR BODY AND BRAIN ARE IN DANGER UNTIL THE TEMPERATURE HITS *ABSOLUTE ZERO.*
THAT IS WHY YOU ARE WEARING THIS SUIT. IT IS KEEPING YOUR BODY COLD.
ABSOLUTE ZERO IN T MINUS SIX SECONDS...

I DON'T CARE, VICTOR. I NEED TO BREATHE--I NEED TO FEEL THE AIR ON MY SKIN--I'M TAKING THIS OFF EVEN IF IT MEANS BREAKING IT!

ABSOLUTE ZERO IN T MINUS FIVE SECONDS...

IT'S ONLY A MATTER OF MOMENTS BEFORE *ABSOLUTE ZERO* IS ACHIEVED.

NORA--

ABSOLUTE ZERO IN T MINUS FOUR SECONDS...

I'M NOT WAITING TO LIVE MY LIFE ANY LONGER!

KLIK KLAK

ABSOLUTE ZERO IN T MINUS THREE SECONDS...

I BEG YOU, NORA-- DON'T REMOVE YOUR HELMET UNTIL--

ABSOLUTE ZERO IN T MINUS TWO SECONDS... ONE SECOND...

FSSSS

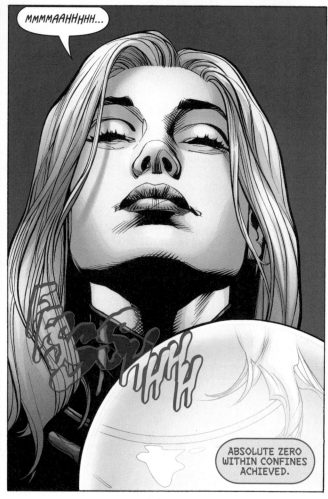

MMMMAAHHHHH...

FSSSS HHHH

ABSOLUTE ZERO WITHIN CONFINES ACHIEVED.

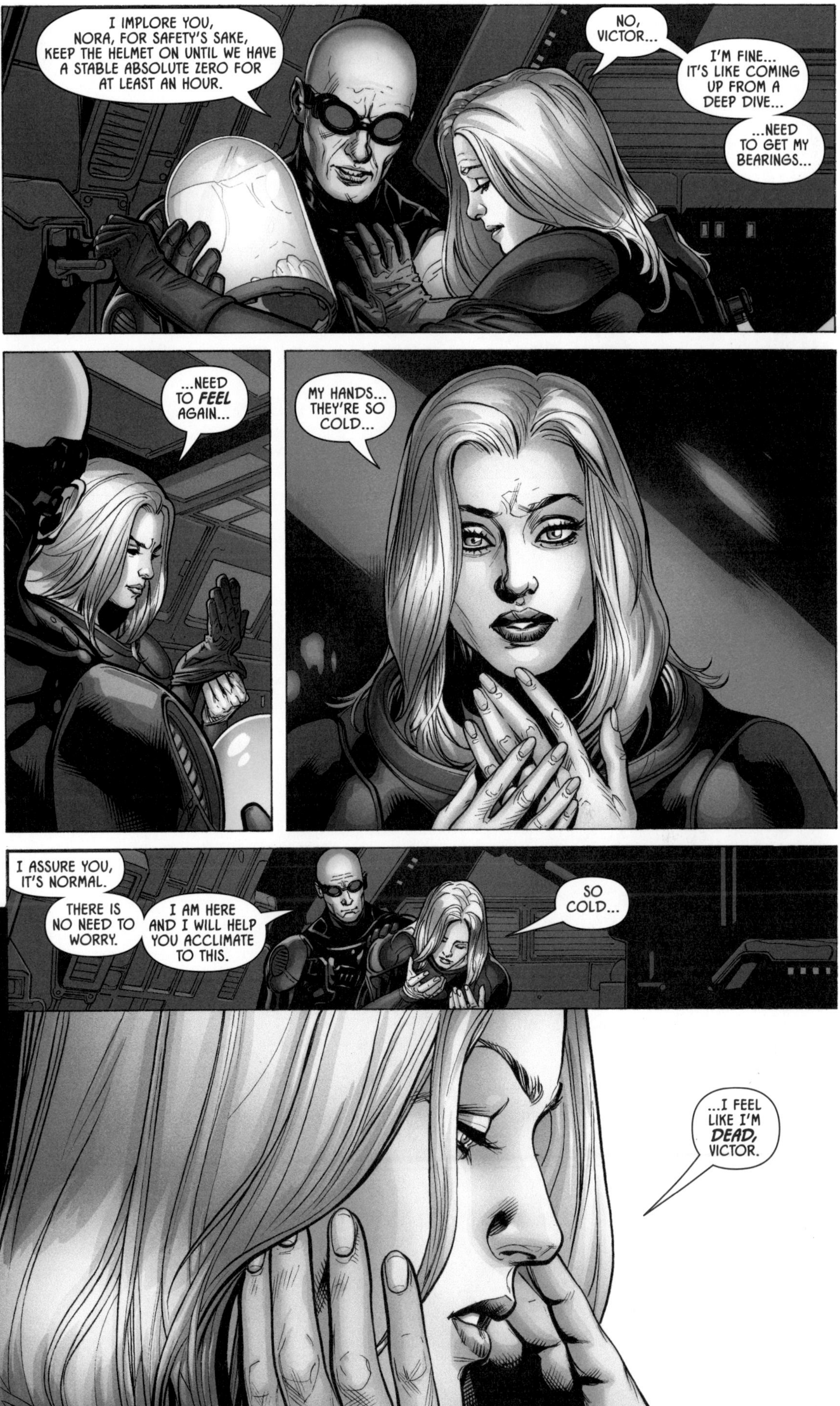
I IMPLORE YOU, NORA, FOR SAFETY'S SAKE, KEEP THE HELMET ON UNTIL WE HAVE A STABLE ABSOLUTE ZERO FOR AT LEAST AN HOUR.
NO, VICTOR...
I'M FINE... IT'S LIKE COMING UP FROM A DEEP DIVE...
...NEED TO GET MY BEARINGS...
...NEED TO *FEEL* AGAIN...
MY HANDS... THEY'RE SO COLD...
I ASSURE YOU, IT'S NORMAL.
THERE IS NO NEED TO WORRY.
I AM HERE AND I WILL HELP YOU ACCLIMATE TO THIS.
SO COLD...
...I FEEL LIKE I'M *DEAD,* VICTOR.

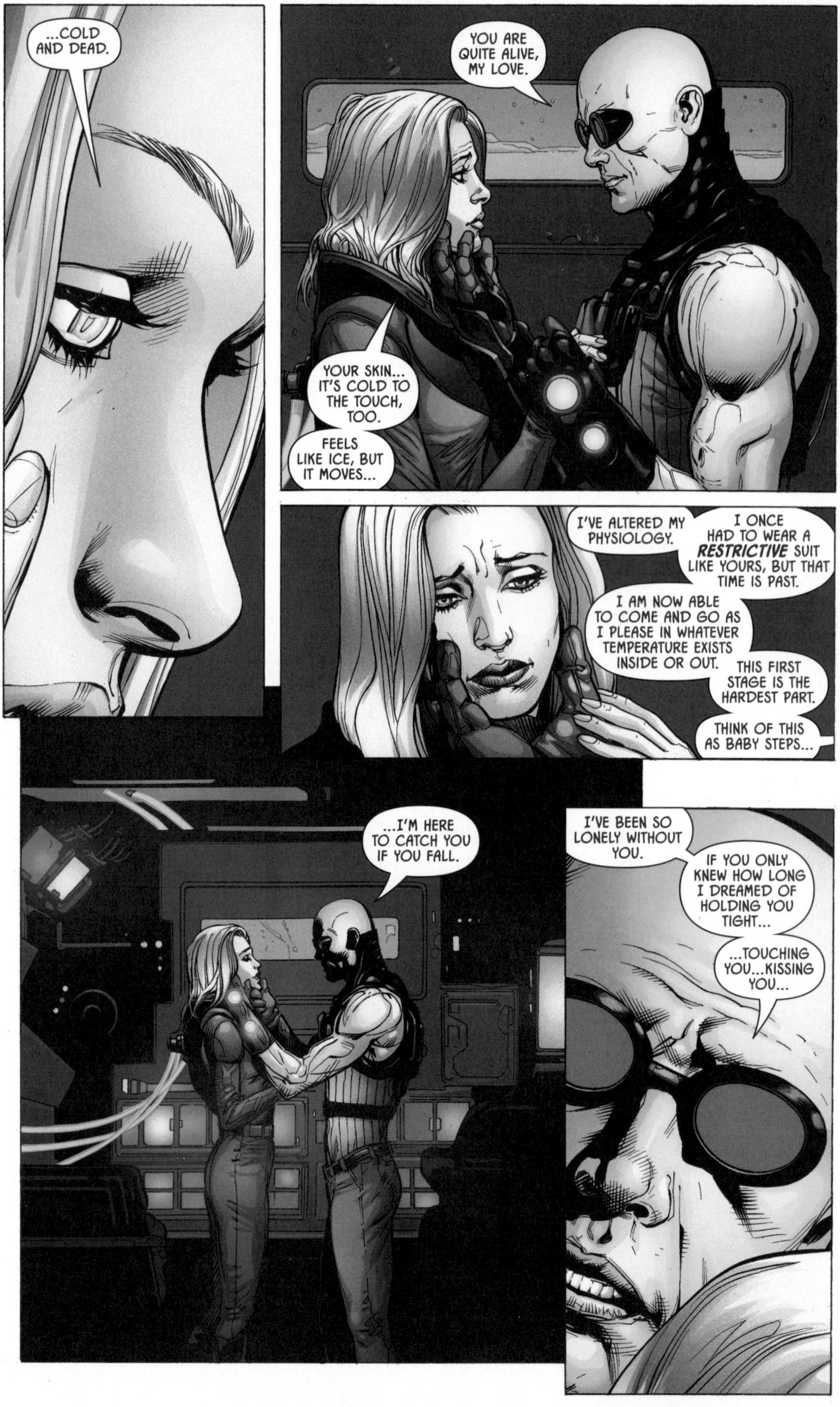
...COLD AND DEAD.
YOU ARE QUITE ALIVE, MY LOVE.
YOUR SKIN... IT'S COLD TO THE TOUCH, TOO.
FEELS LIKE ICE, BUT IT MOVES...
I'VE ALTERED MY PHYSIOLOGY.
I ONCE HAD TO WEAR A RESTRICTIVE SUIT LIKE YOURS, BUT THAT TIME IS PAST.
I AM NOW ABLE TO COME AND GO AS I PLEASE IN WHATEVER TEMPERATURE EXISTS INSIDE OR OUT.
THIS FIRST STAGE IS THE HARDEST PART.
THINK OF THIS AS BABY STEPS...
...I'M HERE TO CATCH YOU IF YOU FALL.
I'VE BEEN SO LONELY WITHOUT YOU.
IF YOU ONLY KNEW HOW LONG I DREAMED OF HOLDING YOU TIGHT...
...TOUCHING YOU...KISSING YOU...

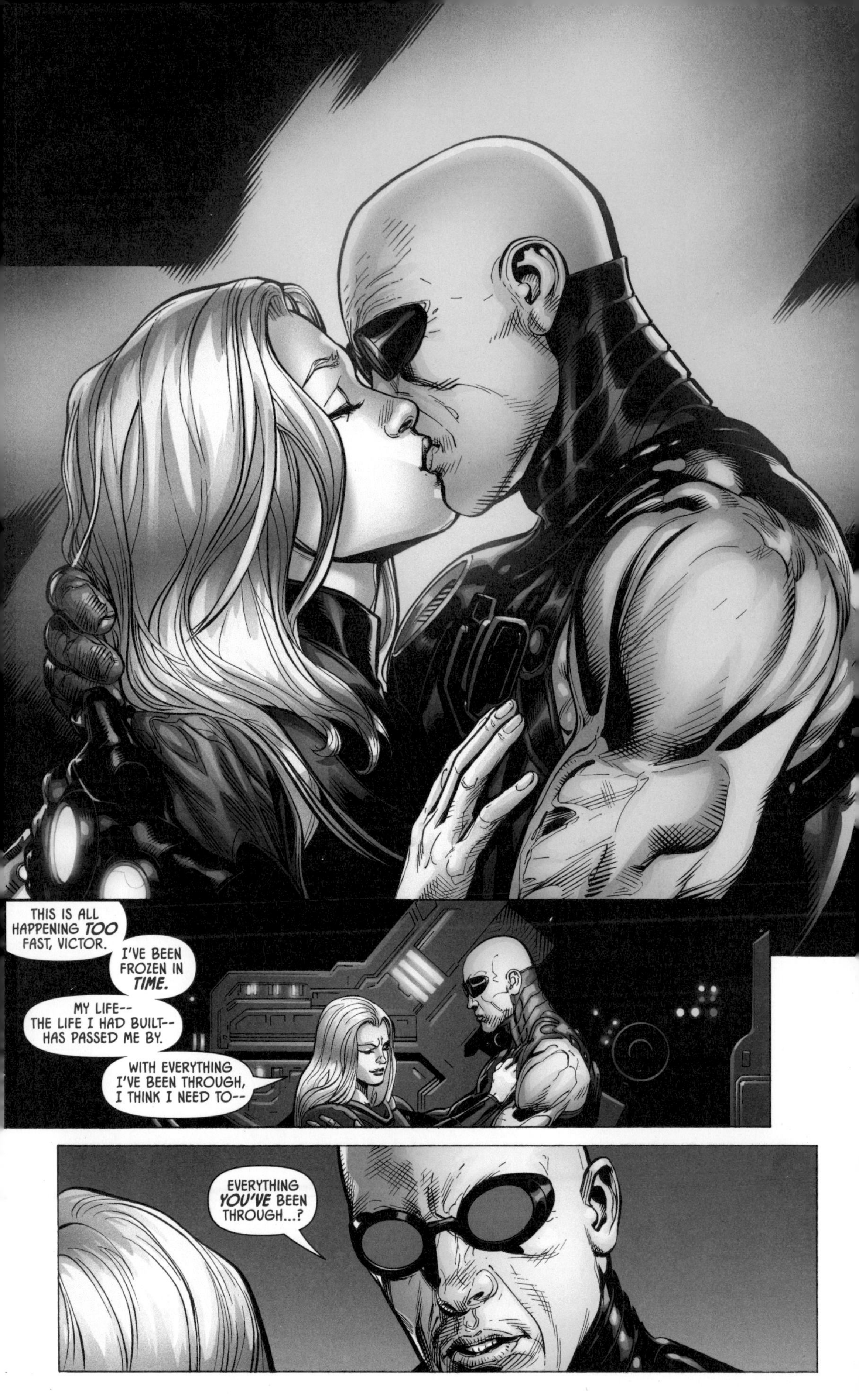
THIS IS ALL HAPPENING *TOO* FAST, VICTOR.
I'VE BEEN FROZEN IN *TIME.*
MY LIFE-- THE LIFE I HAD BUILT-- HAS PASSED ME BY.
WITH EVERYTHING I'VE BEEN THROUGH, I THINK I NEED TO--
EVERYTHING *YOU'VE* BEEN THROUGH...?

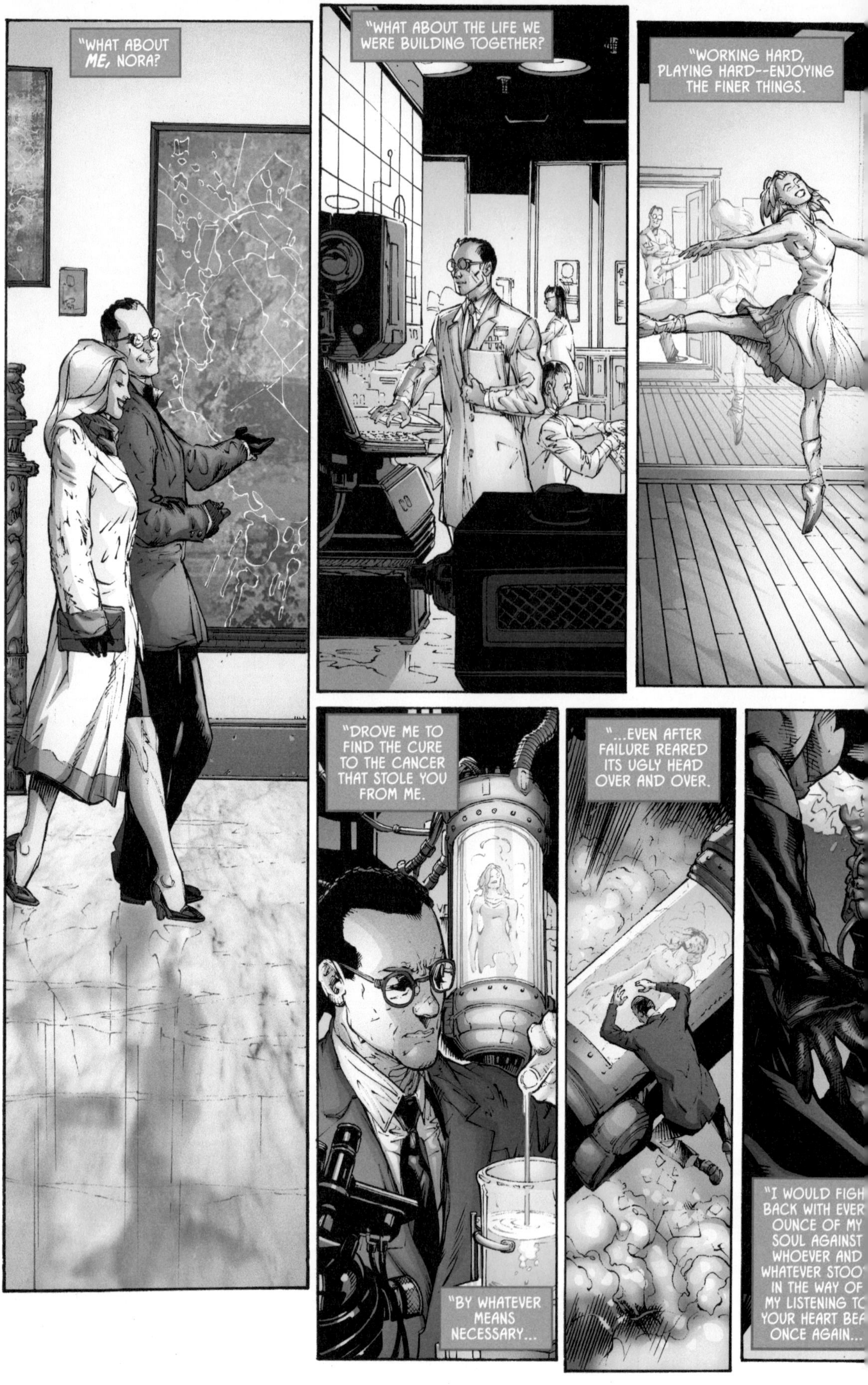
"WHAT ABOUT *ME,* NORA?
"WHAT ABOUT THE LIFE WE WERE BUILDING TOGETHER?
"WORKING HARD, PLAYING HARD--ENJOYING THE FINER THINGS.
"DROVE ME TO FIND THE CURE TO THE CANCER THAT STOLE YOU FROM ME.
"BY WHATEVER MEANS NECESSARY...
"...EVEN AFTER FAILURE REARED ITS UGLY HEAD OVER AND OVER.
"I WOULD FIGH BACK WITH EVER OUNCE OF MY SOUL AGAINST WHOEVER AND WHATEVER STOO IN THE WAY OF MY LISTENING TO YOUR HEART BEA ONCE AGAIN...

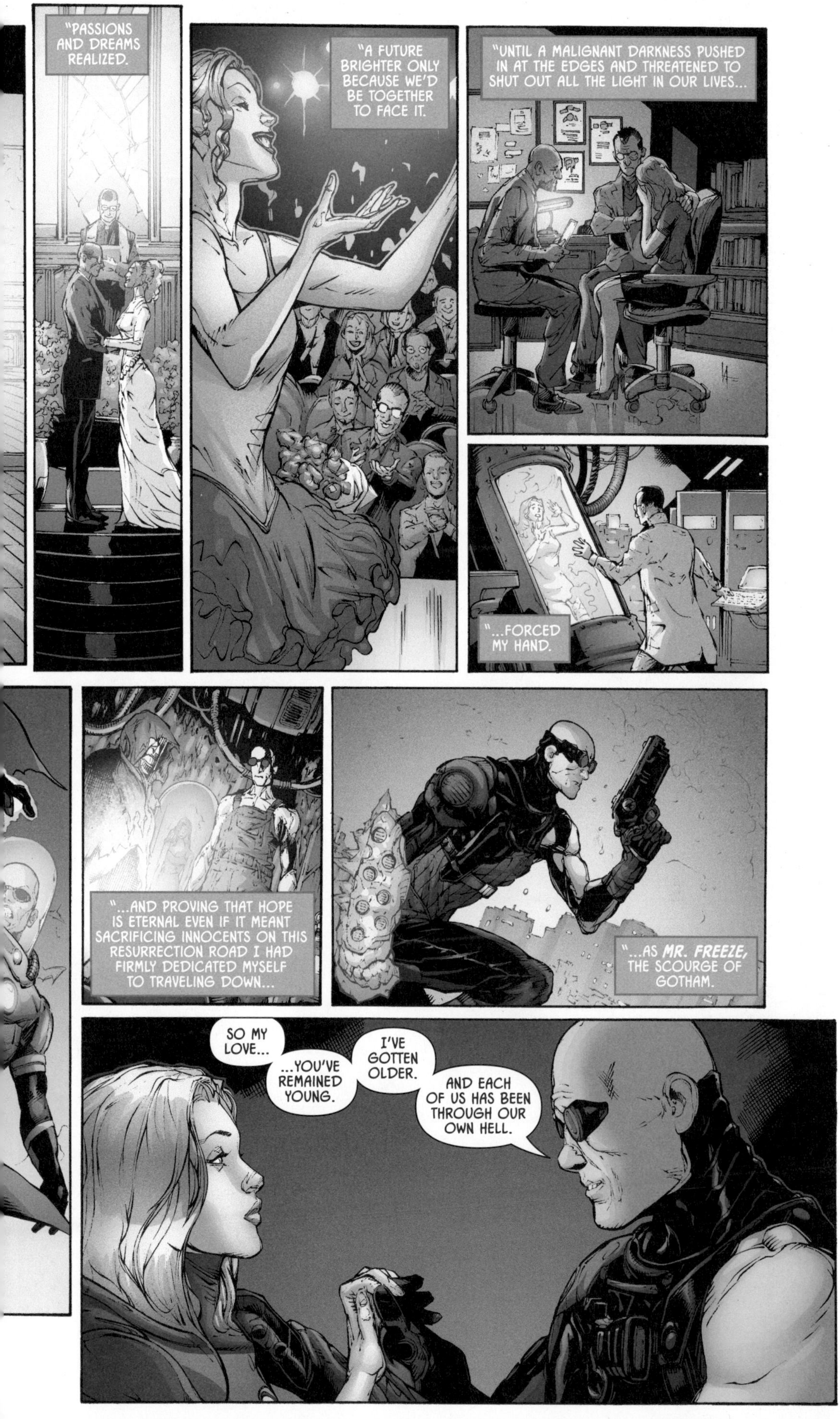
"PASSIONS AND DREAMS REALIZED.
"A FUTURE BRIGHTER ONLY BECAUSE WE'D BE TOGETHER TO FACE IT.
"UNTIL A MALIGNANT DARKNESS PUSHED IN AT THE EDGES AND THREATENED TO SHUT OUT ALL THE LIGHT IN OUR LIVES...
"...FORCED MY HAND.
"...AND PROVING THAT HOPE IS ETERNAL EVEN IF IT MEANT SACRIFICING INNOCENTS ON THIS RESURRECTION ROAD I HAD FIRMLY DEDICATED MYSELF TO TRAVELING DOWN...
"...AS MR. FREEZE, THE SCOURGE OF GOTHAM.
SO MY LOVE...
...YOU'VE REMAINED YOUNG.
I'VE GOTTEN OLDER.
AND EACH OF US HAS BEEN THROUGH OUR OWN HELL.

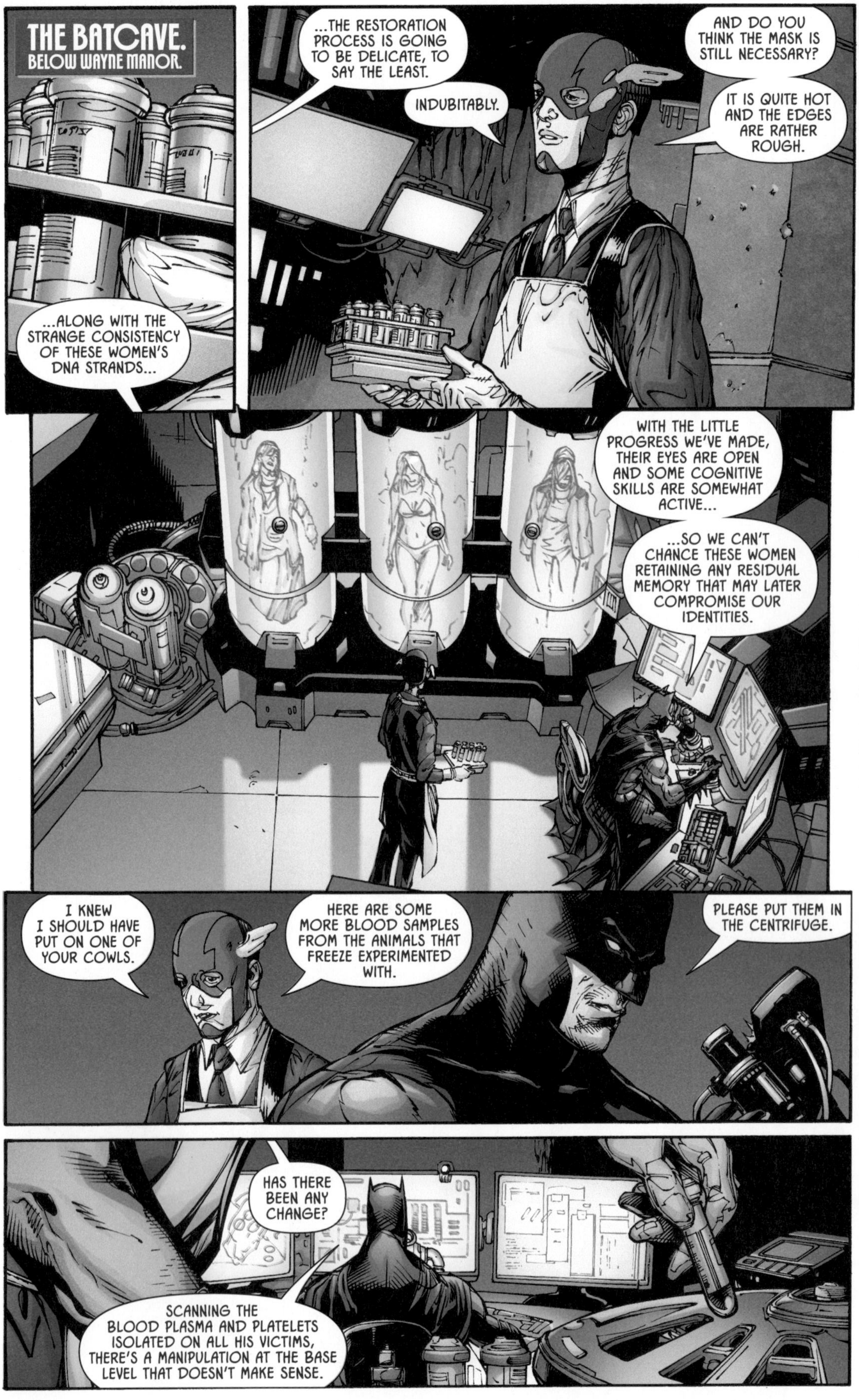
THE BATCAVE. BELOW WAYNE MANOR.
...THE RESTORATION PROCESS IS GOING TO BE DELICATE, TO SAY THE LEAST.
INDUBITABLY.
AND DO YOU THINK THE MASK IS STILL NECESSARY?
IT IS QUITE HOT AND THE EDGES ARE RATHER ROUGH.
...ALONG WITH THE STRANGE CONSISTENCY OF THESE WOMEN'S DNA STRANDS...
WITH THE LITTLE PROGRESS WE'VE MADE, THEIR EYES ARE OPEN AND SOME COGNITIVE SKILLS ARE SOMEWHAT ACTIVE...
...SO WE CAN'T CHANCE THESE WOMEN RETAINING ANY RESIDUAL MEMORY THAT MAY LATER COMPROMISE OUR IDENTITIES.
I KNEW I SHOULD HAVE PUT ON ONE OF YOUR COWLS.
HERE ARE SOME MORE BLOOD SAMPLES FROM THE ANIMALS THAT FREEZE EXPERIMENTED WITH.
PLEASE PUT THEM IN THE CENTRIFUGE.
HAS THERE BEEN ANY CHANGE?
SCANNING THE BLOOD PLASMA AND PLATELETS ISOLATED ON ALL HIS VICTIMS, THERE'S A MANIPULATION AT THE BASE LEVEL THAT DOESN'T MAKE SENSE.

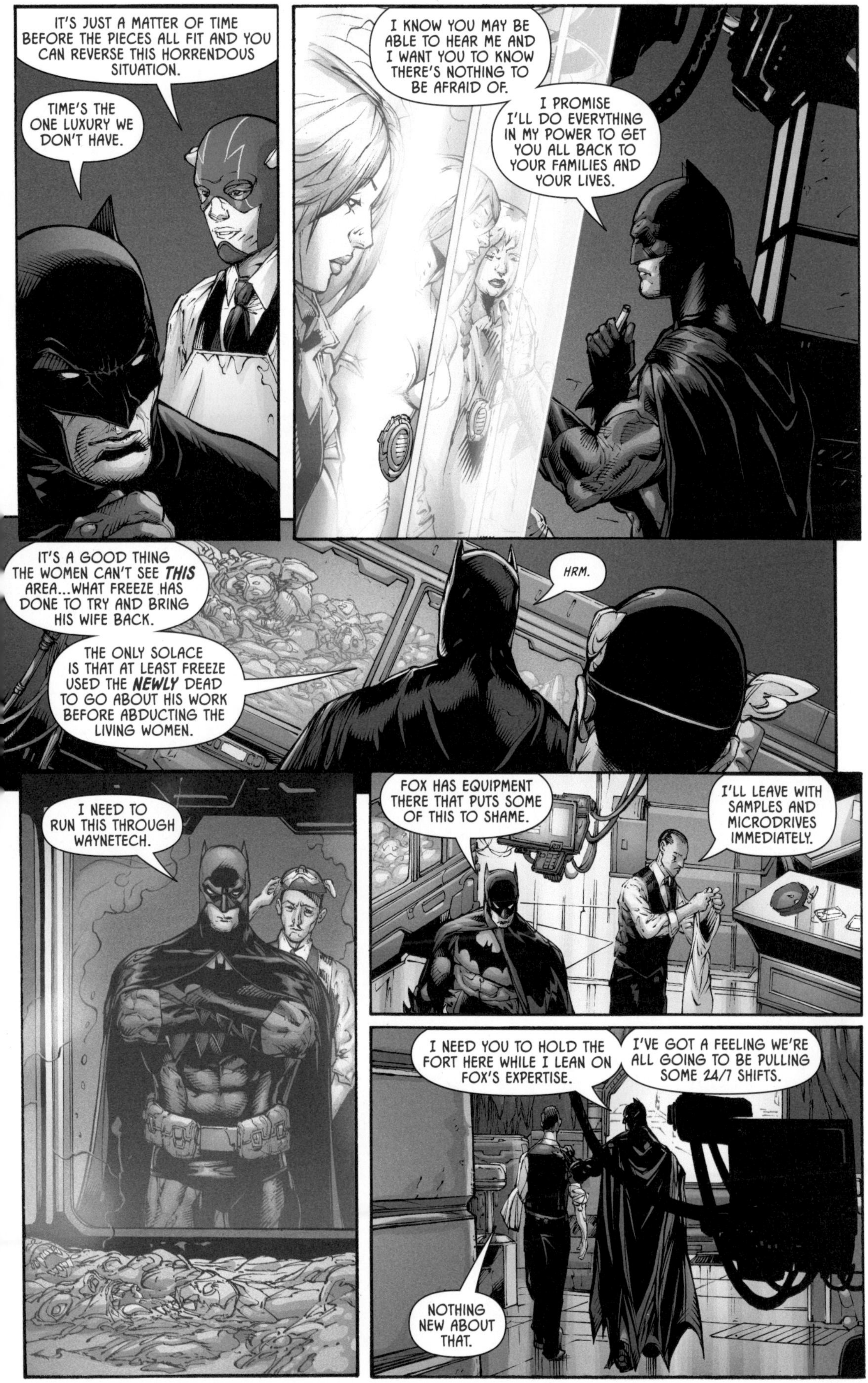
IT'S JUST A MATTER OF TIME BEFORE THE PIECES ALL FIT AND YOU CAN REVERSE THIS HORRENDOUS SITUATION.
TIME'S THE ONE LUXURY WE DON'T HAVE.
I KNOW YOU MAY BE ABLE TO HEAR ME AND I WANT YOU TO KNOW THERE'S NOTHING TO BE AFRAID OF.
I PROMISE I'LL DO EVERYTHING IN MY POWER TO GET YOU ALL BACK TO YOUR FAMILIES AND YOUR LIVES.
IT'S A GOOD THING THE WOMEN CAN'T SEE THIS AREA...WHAT FREEZE HAS DONE TO TRY AND BRING HIS WIFE BACK.
THE ONLY SOLACE IS THAT AT LEAST FREEZE USED THE NEWLY DEAD TO GO ABOUT HIS WORK BEFORE ABDUCTING THE LIVING WOMEN.
HRM.
I NEED TO RUN THIS THROUGH WAYNETECH.
FOX HAS EQUIPMENT THERE THAT PUTS SOME OF THIS TO SHAME.
I'LL LEAVE WITH SAMPLES AND MICRODRIVES IMMEDIATELY.
I NEED YOU TO HOLD THE FORT HERE WHILE I LEAN ON FOX'S EXPERTISE.
I'VE GOT A FEELING WE'RE ALL GOING TO BE PULLING SOME 24/7 SHIFTS.
NOTHING NEW ABOUT THAT.

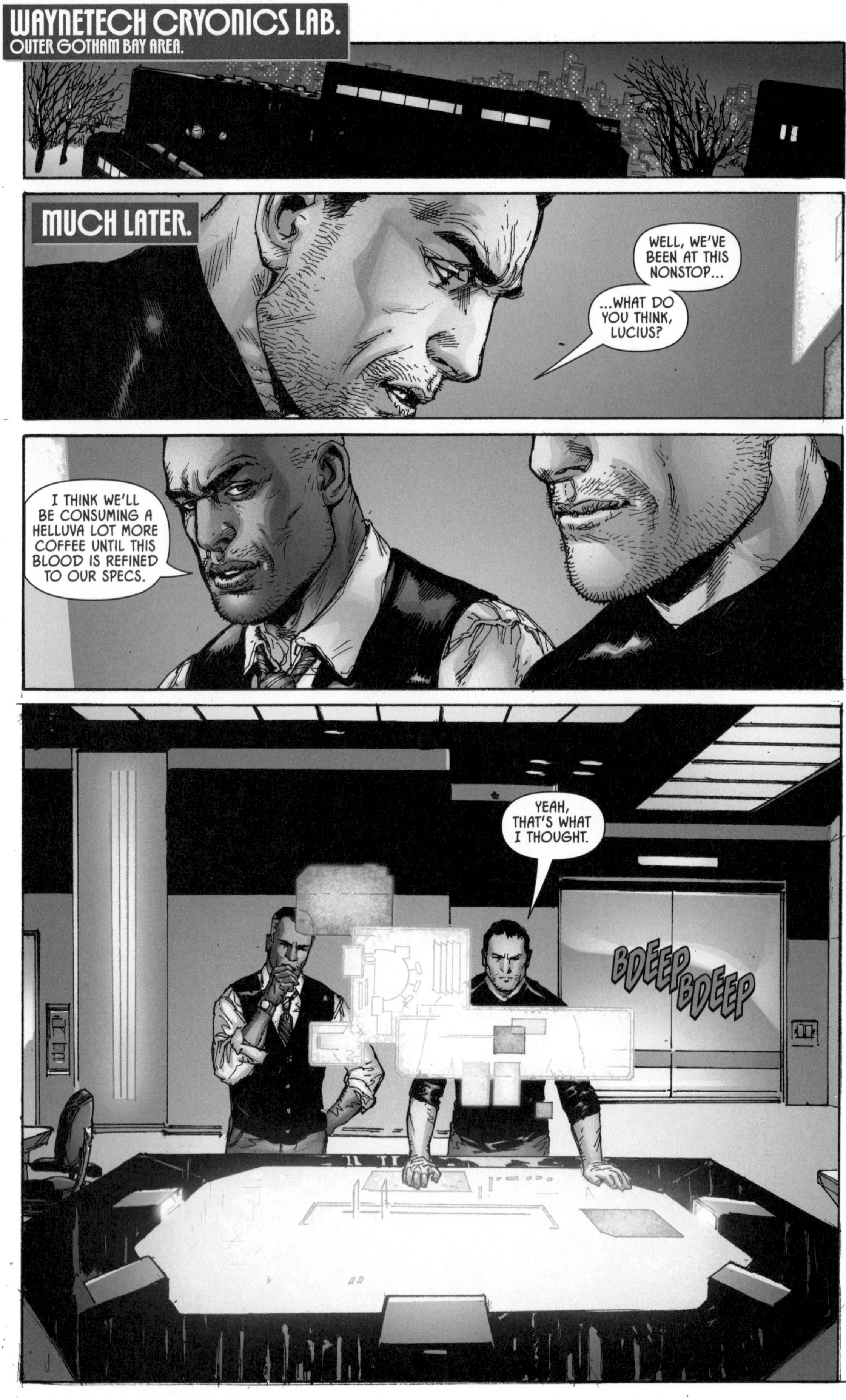
WAYNETECH CRYONICS LAB.
OUTER GOTHAM BAY AREA.
MUCH LATER.
WELL, WE'VE BEEN AT THIS NONSTOP...
...WHAT DO YOU THINK, LUCIUS?
I THINK WE'LL BE CONSUMING A HELLUVA LOT MORE COFFEE UNTIL THIS BLOOD IS REFINED TO OUR SPECS.
YEAH, THAT'S WHAT I THOUGHT.
BDEEP BDEEP

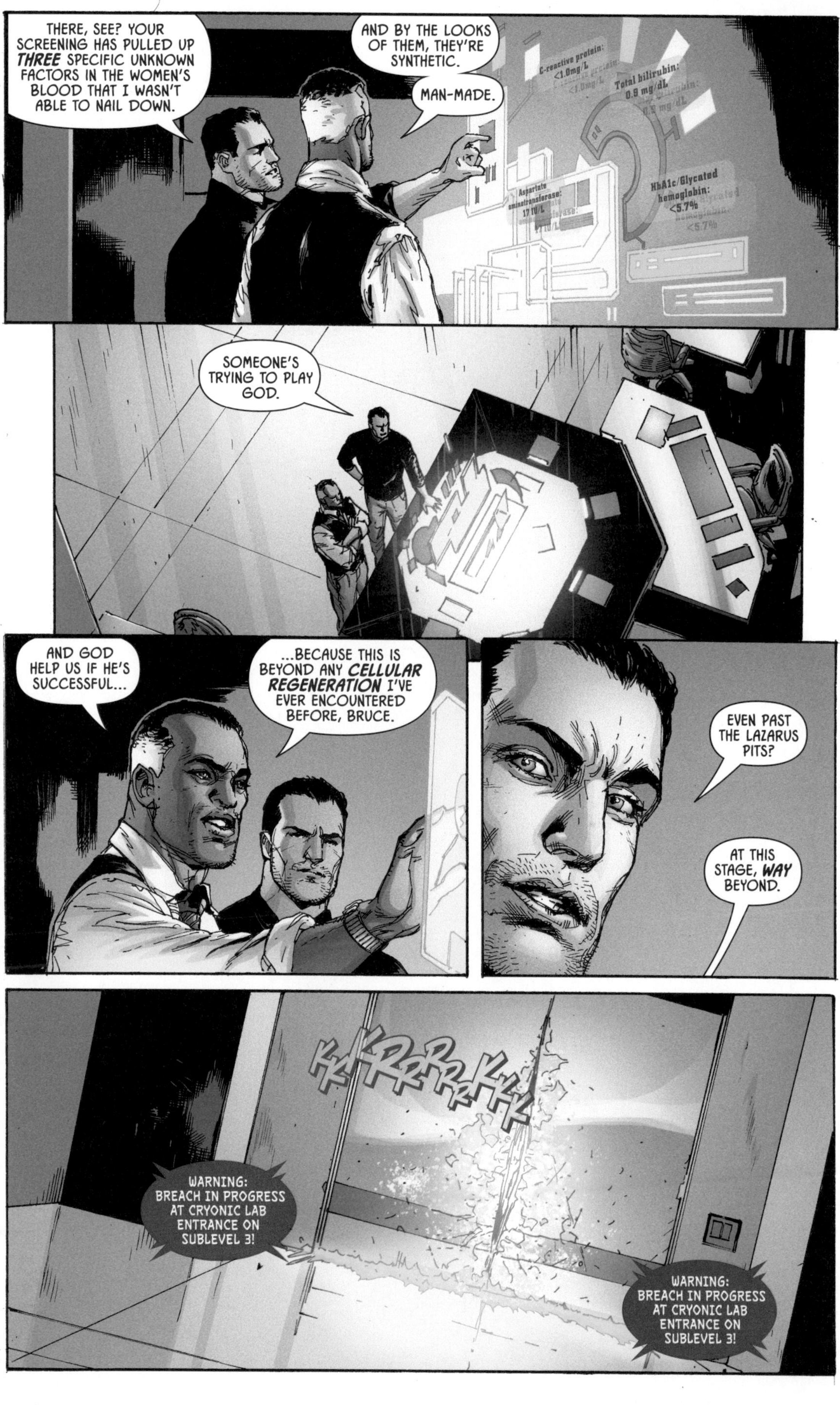
THERE, SEE? YOUR SCREENING HAS PULLED UP ***THREE*** SPECIFIC UNKNOWN FACTORS IN THE WOMEN'S BLOOD THAT I WASN'T ABLE TO NAIL DOWN.
AND BY THE LOOKS OF THEM, THEY'RE SYNTHETIC.
MAN-MADE.
C-reactive protein: <1.0mg/L
Total bilirubin: 0.9 mg/dL
Aspartate aminotransferase: 17 IU/L
HbA1c/Glycated hemoglobin: <5.7%
SOMEONE'S TRYING TO PLAY GOD.
AND GOD HELP US IF HE'S SUCCESSFUL...
...BECAUSE THIS IS BEYOND ANY ***CELLULAR REGENERATION*** I'VE EVER ENCOUNTERED BEFORE, BRUCE.
EVEN PAST THE LAZARUS PITS?
AT THIS STAGE, ***WAY*** BEYOND.
KKKRRRRRKKK
WARNING: BREACH IN PROGRESS AT CRYONIC LAB ENTRANCE ON SUBLEVEL 3!
WARNING: BREACH IN PROGRESS AT CRYONIC LAB ENTRANCE ON SUBLEVEL 3!

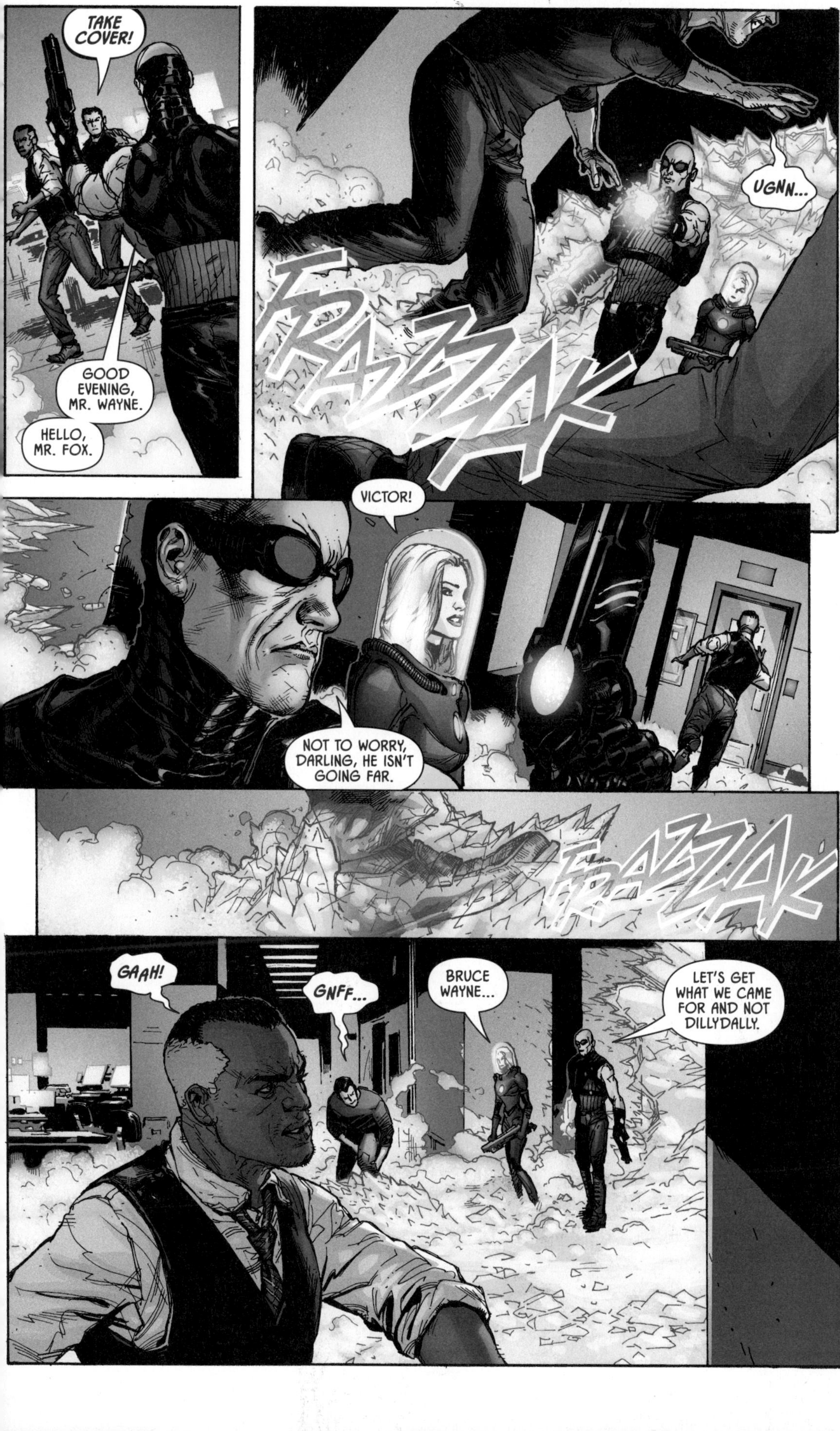
TAKE COVER!
GOOD EVENING, MR. WAYNE.
HELLO, MR. FOX.
UGNN...
FRAZZAK
VICTOR!
NOT TO WORRY, DARLING, HE ISN'T GOING FAR.
FRAZZAK
GAAH!
GNFF...
BRUCE WAYNE...
LET'S GET WHAT WE CAME FOR AND NOT DILLYDALLY.

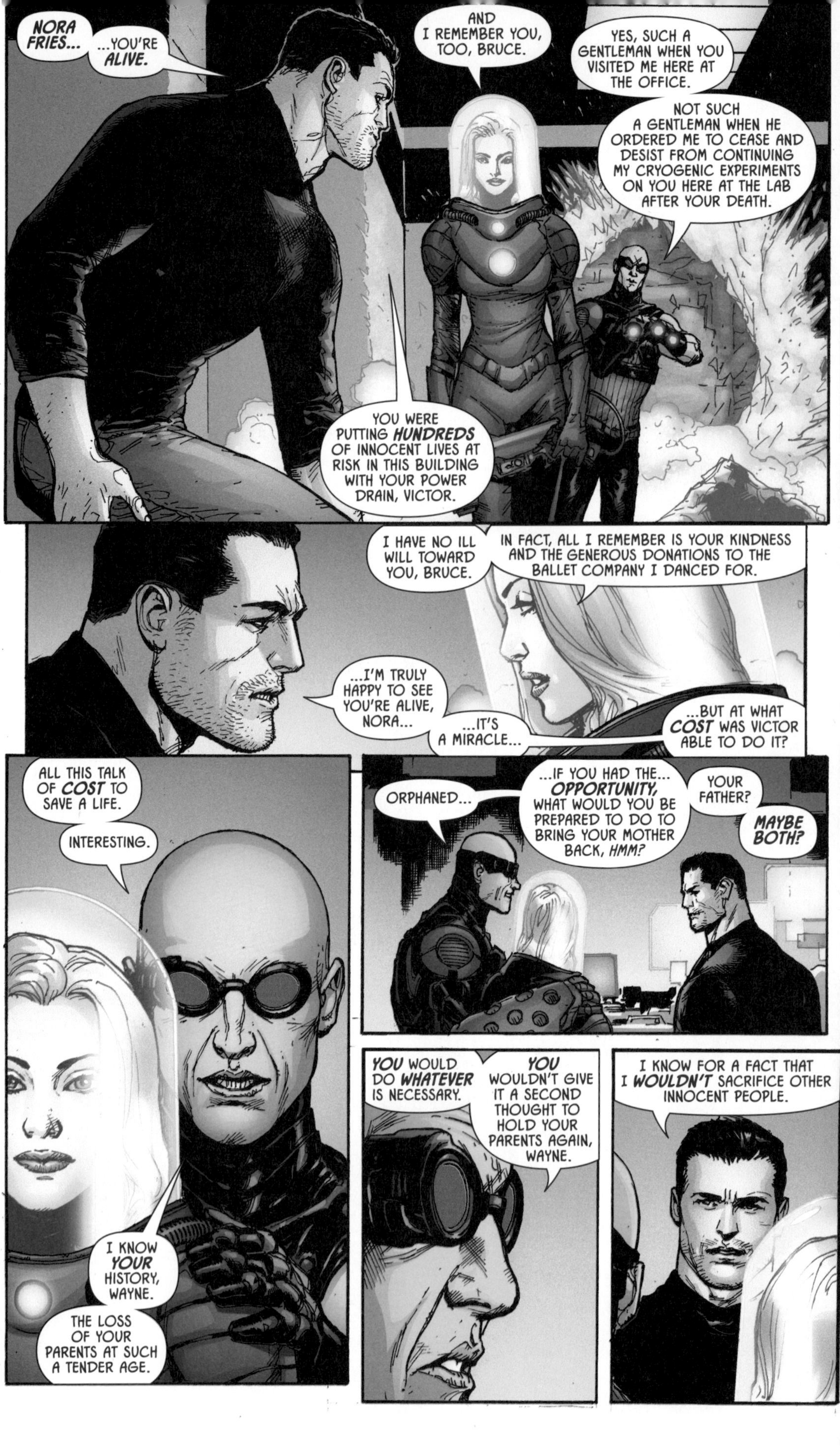
NORA FRIES...
...YOU'RE ALIVE.
AND I REMEMBER YOU, TOO, BRUCE.
YES, SUCH A GENTLEMAN WHEN YOU VISITED ME HERE AT THE OFFICE.
NOT SUCH A GENTLEMAN WHEN HE ORDERED ME TO CEASE AND DESIST FROM CONTINUING MY CRYOGENIC EXPERIMENTS ON YOU HERE AT THE LAB AFTER YOUR DEATH.
YOU WERE PUTTING HUNDREDS OF INNOCENT LIVES AT RISK IN THIS BUILDING WITH YOUR POWER DRAIN, VICTOR.
I HAVE NO ILL WILL TOWARD YOU, BRUCE.
IN FACT, ALL I REMEMBER IS YOUR KINDNESS AND THE GENEROUS DONATIONS TO THE BALLET COMPANY I DANCED FOR.
...I'M TRULY HAPPY TO SEE YOU'RE ALIVE, NORA...
...IT'S A MIRACLE...
...BUT AT WHAT COST WAS VICTOR ABLE TO DO IT?
ALL THIS TALK OF COST TO SAVE A LIFE.
INTERESTING.
I KNOW YOUR HISTORY, WAYNE.
THE LOSS OF YOUR PARENTS AT SUCH A TENDER AGE.
ORPHANED...
...IF YOU HAD THE... OPPORTUNITY, WHAT WOULD YOU BE PREPARED TO DO TO BRING YOUR MOTHER BACK, HMM?
YOUR FATHER?
MAYBE BOTH?
YOU WOULD DO WHATEVER IS NECESSARY.
YOU WOULDN'T GIVE IT A SECOND THOUGHT TO HOLD YOUR PARENTS AGAIN, WAYNE.
I KNOW FOR A FACT THAT I WOULDN'T SACRIFICE OTHER INNOCENT PEOPLE.

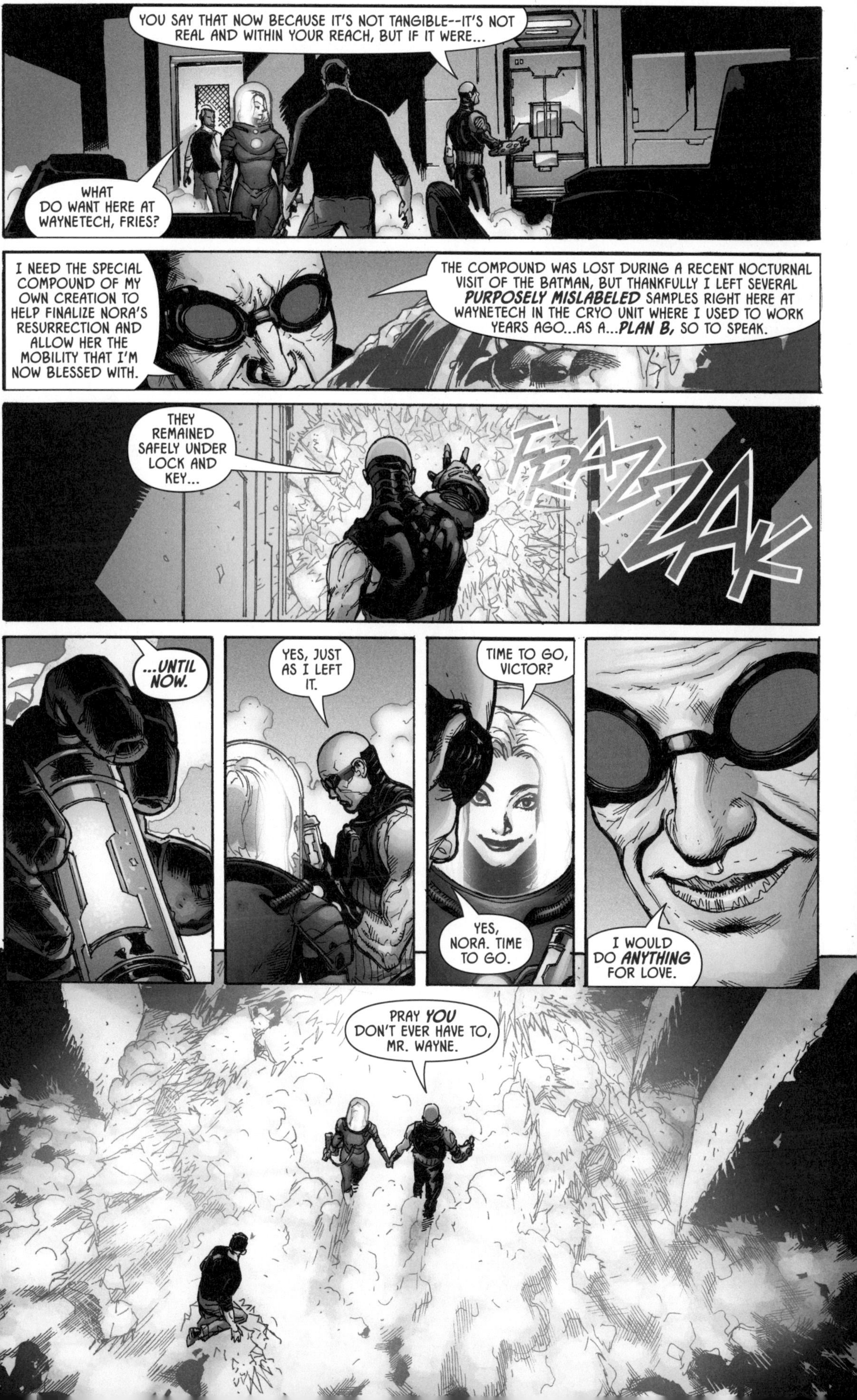

YOU SAY THAT NOW BECAUSE IT'S NOT TANGIBLE--IT'S NOT REAL AND WITHIN YOUR REACH, BUT IF IT WERE...
WHAT DO WANT HERE AT WAYNETECH, FRIES?
I NEED THE SPECIAL COMPOUND OF MY OWN CREATION TO HELP FINALIZE NORA'S RESURRECTION AND ALLOW HER THE MOBILITY THAT I'M NOW BLESSED WITH.
THE COMPOUND WAS LOST DURING A RECENT NOCTURNAL VISIT OF THE BATMAN, BUT THANKFULLY I LEFT SEVERAL PURPOSELY MISLABELED SAMPLES RIGHT HERE AT WAYNETECH IN THE CRYO UNIT WHERE I USED TO WORK YEARS AGO...AS A...PLAN B, SO TO SPEAK.
THEY REMAINED SAFELY UNDER LOCK AND KEY...
FRAZZAK
...UNTIL NOW.
YES, JUST AS I LEFT IT.
TIME TO GO, VICTOR?
YES, NORA. TIME TO GO.
I WOULD DO ANYTHING FOR LOVE.
PRAY YOU DON'T EVER HAVE TO, MR. WAYNE.

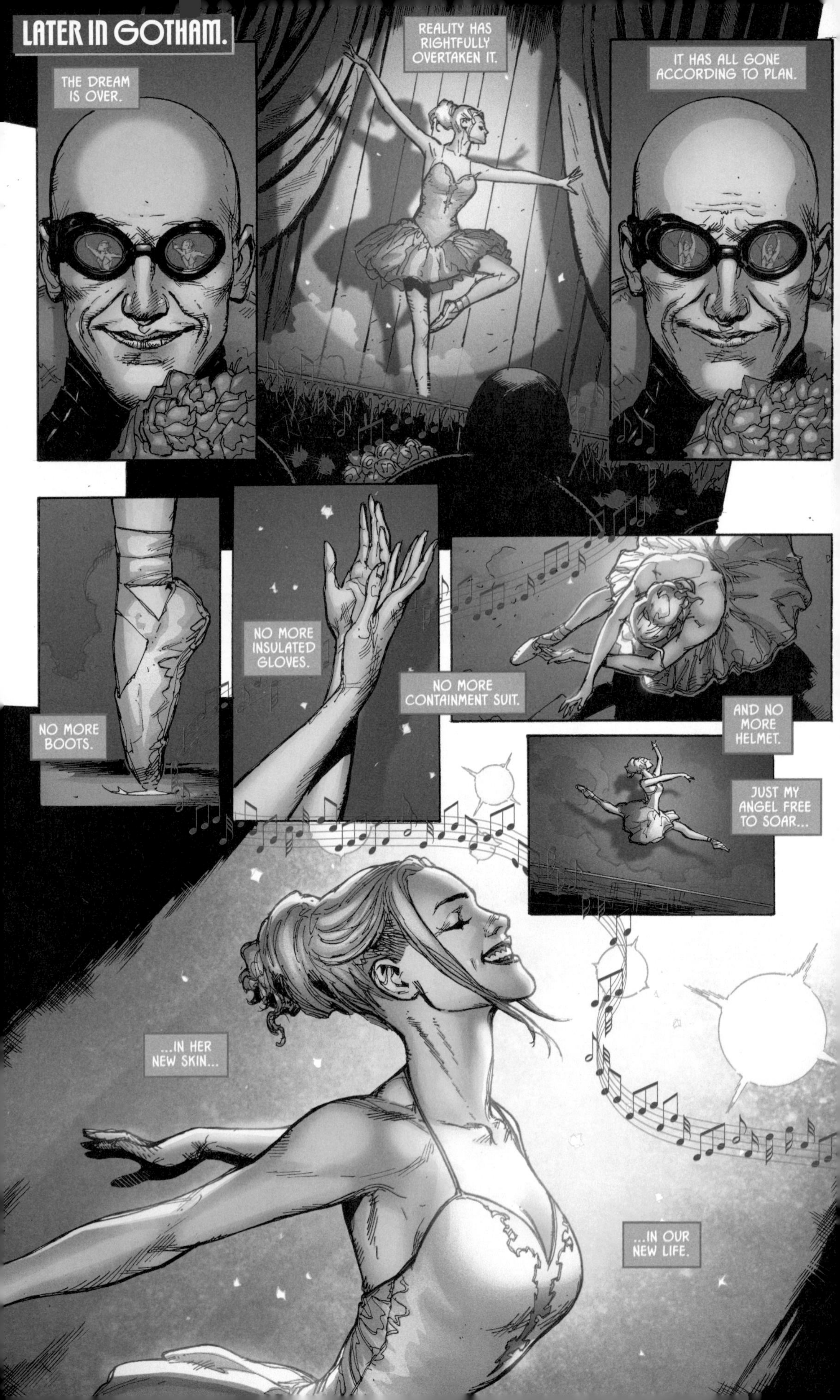
LATER IN GOTHAM.
THE DREAM IS OVER.
REALITY HAS RIGHTFULLY OVERTAKEN IT.
IT HAS ALL GONE ACCORDING TO PLAN.
NO MORE BOOTS.
NO MORE INSULATED GLOVES.
NO MORE CONTAINMENT SUIT.
AND NO MORE HELMET.
JUST MY ANGEL FREE TO SOAR...
...IN HER NEW SKIN...
...IN OUR NEW LIFE.

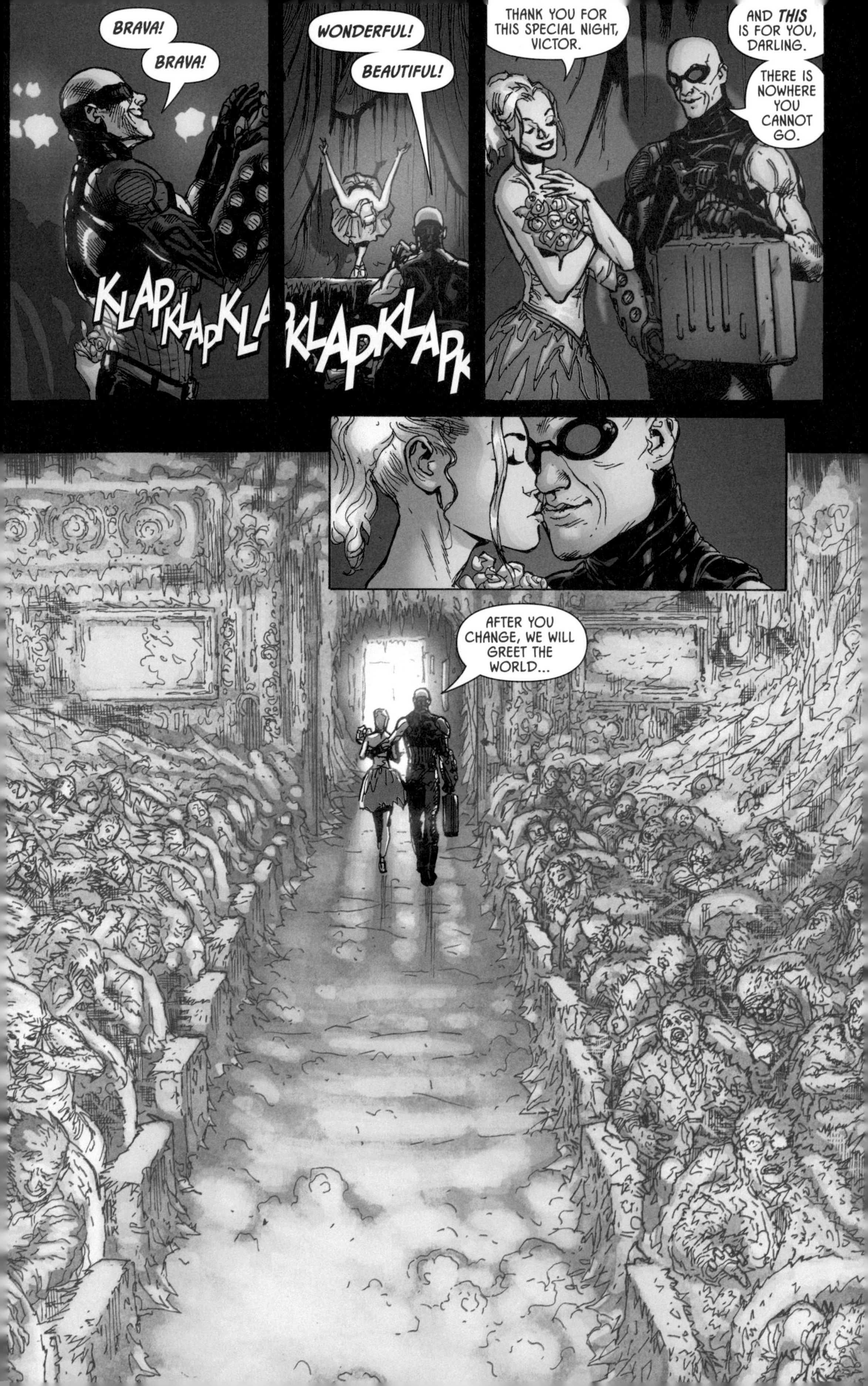
BRAVA!
BRAVA!
KLAPKLAPKLA
WONDERFUL!
BEAUTIFUL!
KLAPKLAPK
THANK YOU FOR THIS SPECIAL NIGHT, VICTOR.
AND THIS IS FOR YOU, DARLING.
THERE IS NOWHERE YOU CANNOT GO.
AFTER YOU CHANGE, WE WILL GREET THE WORLD...

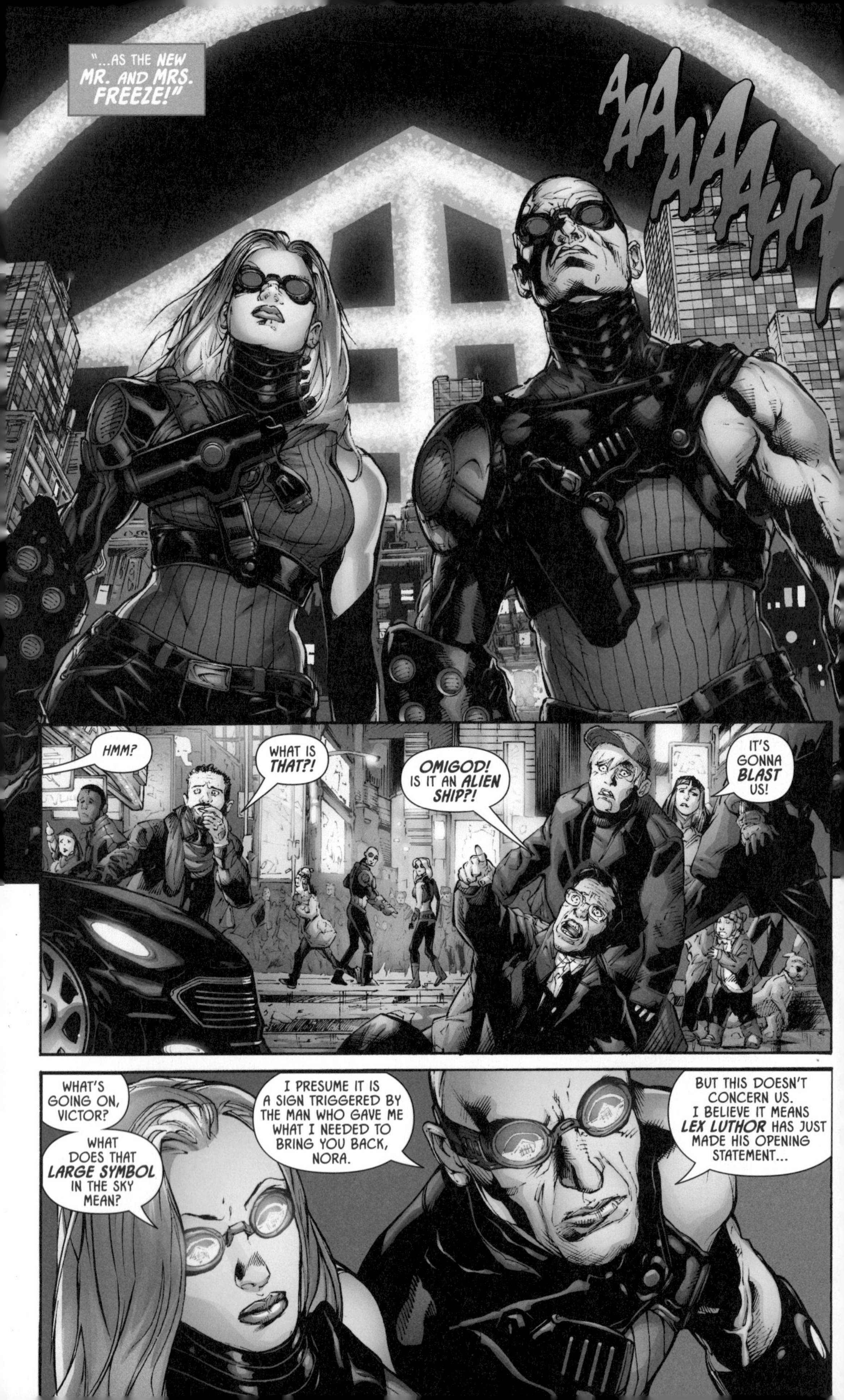
"...AS THE NEW MR. AND MRS. FREEZE!"
AAAAAAAHH
HMM?
WHAT IS THAT?!
OMIGOD! IS IT AN ALIEN SHIP?!
IT'S GONNA BLAST US!
WHAT'S GOING ON, VICTOR?
WHAT DOES THAT LARGE SYMBOL IN THE SKY MEAN?
I PRESUME IT IS A SIGN TRIGGERED BY THE MAN WHO GAVE ME WHAT I NEEDED TO BRING YOU BACK, NORA.
BUT THIS DOESN'T CONCERN US. I BELIEVE IT MEANS LEX LUTHOR HAS JUST MADE HIS OPENING STATEMENT...

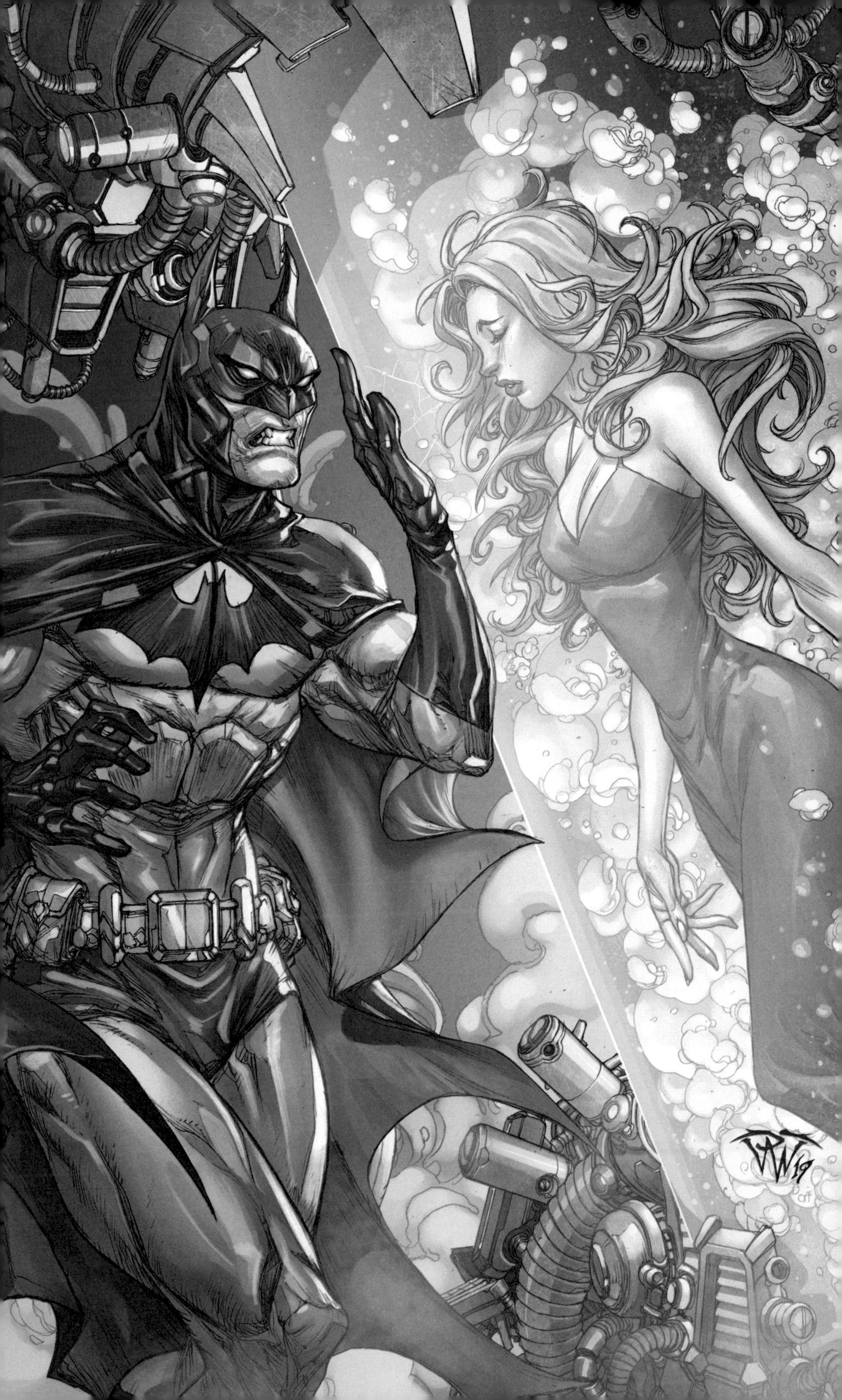

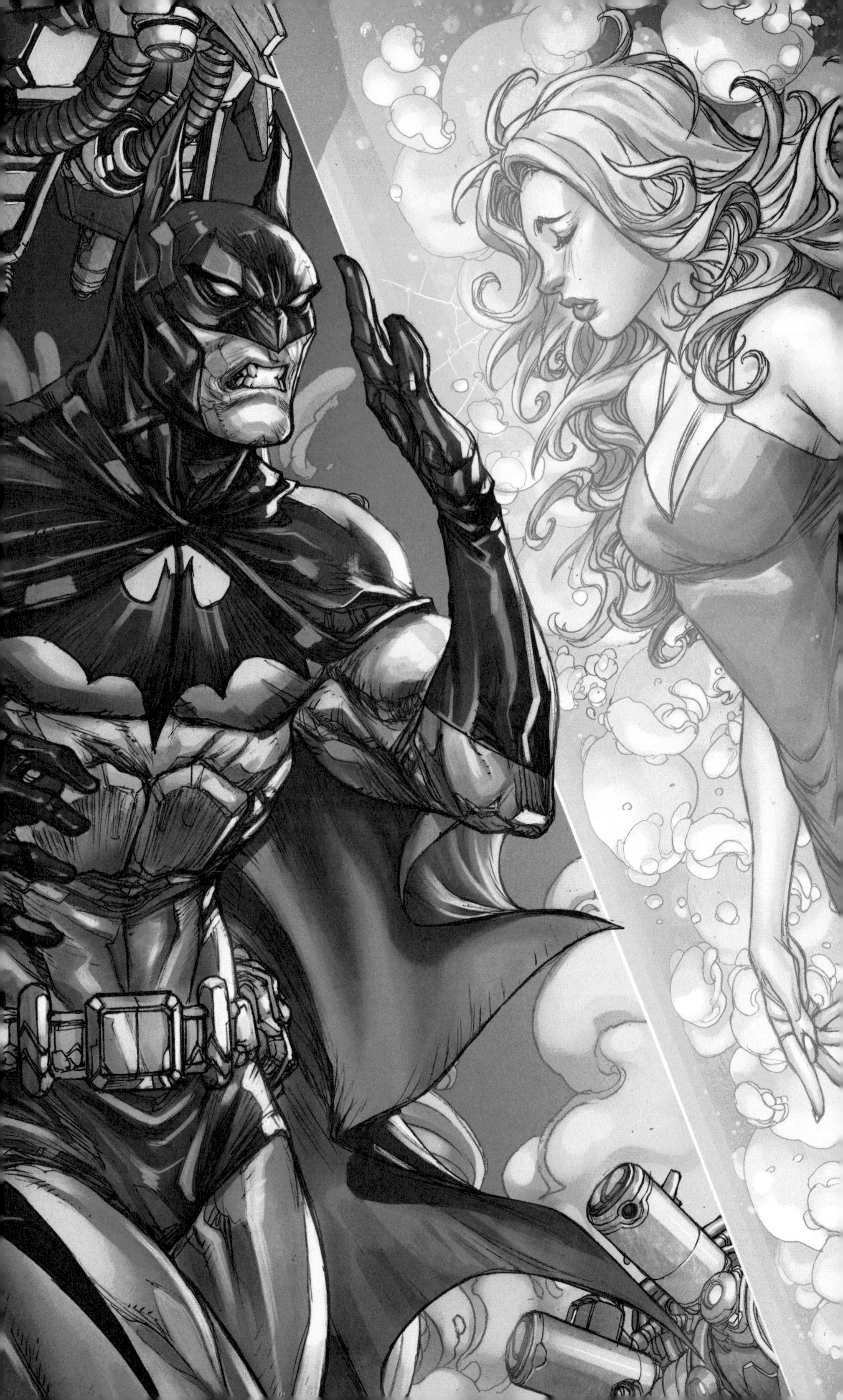

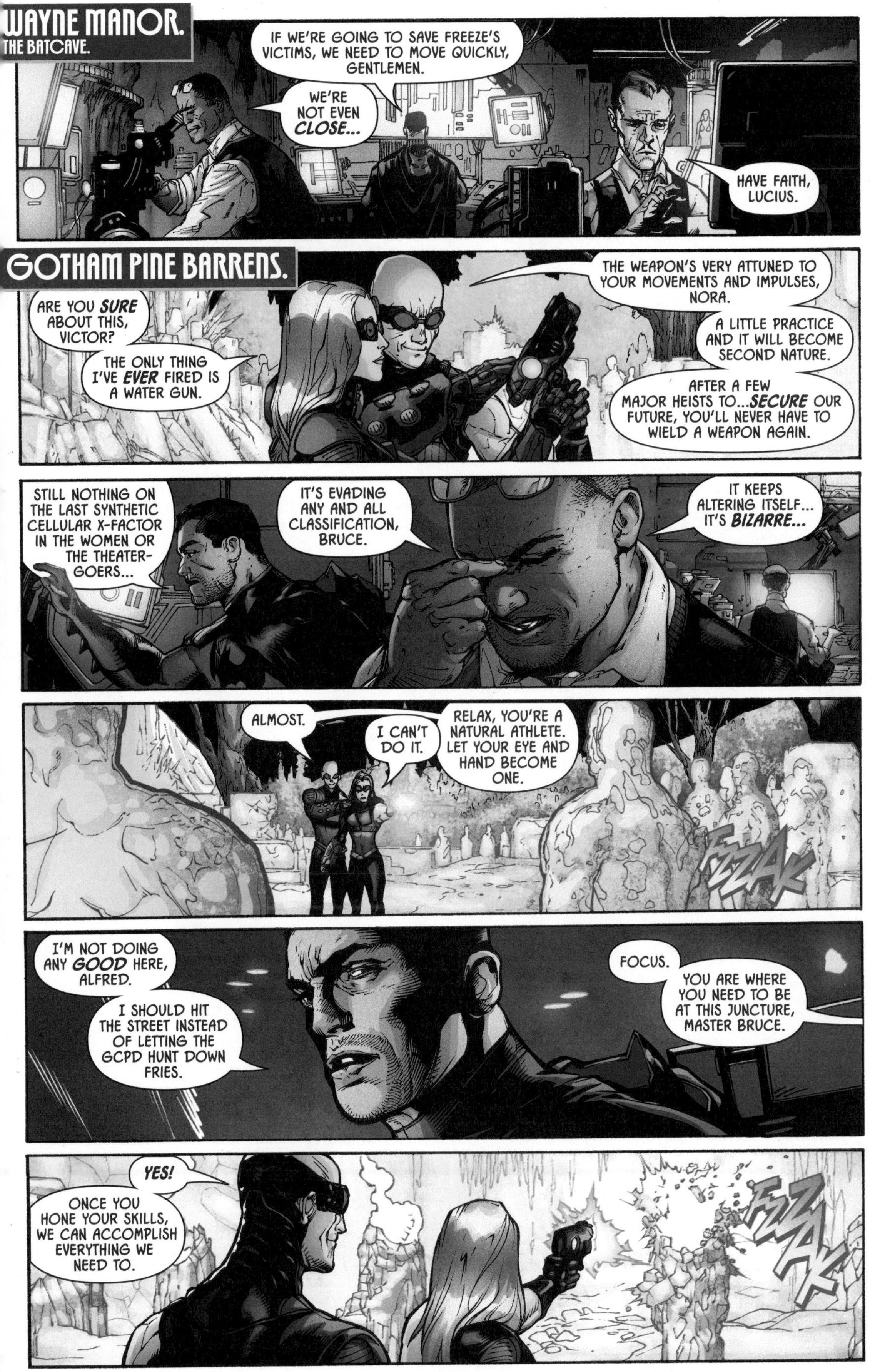
WAYNE MANOR.
THE BATCAVE.
IF WE'RE GOING TO SAVE FREEZE'S VICTIMS, WE NEED TO MOVE QUICKLY, GENTLEMEN.
WE'RE NOT EVEN CLOSE...
HAVE FAITH, LUCIUS.
GOTHAM PINE BARRENS.
ARE YOU SURE ABOUT THIS, VICTOR?
THE ONLY THING I'VE EVER FIRED IS A WATER GUN.
THE WEAPON'S VERY ATTUNED TO YOUR MOVEMENTS AND IMPULSES, NORA.
A LITTLE PRACTICE AND IT WILL BECOME SECOND NATURE.
AFTER A FEW MAJOR HEISTS TO...SECURE OUR FUTURE, YOU'LL NEVER HAVE TO WIELD A WEAPON AGAIN.
STILL NOTHING ON THE LAST SYNTHETIC CELLULAR X-FACTOR IN THE WOMEN OR THE THEATER-GOERS...
IT'S EVADING ANY AND ALL CLASSIFICATION, BRUCE.
IT KEEPS ALTERING ITSELF... IT'S BIZARRE...
ALMOST.
I CAN'T DO IT.
RELAX, YOU'RE A NATURAL ATHLETE. LET YOUR EYE AND HAND BECOME ONE.
FZZAK
I'M NOT DOING ANY GOOD HERE, ALFRED.
I SHOULD HIT THE STREET INSTEAD OF LETTING THE GCPD HUNT DOWN FRIES.
FOCUS.
YOU ARE WHERE YOU NEED TO BE AT THIS JUNCTURE, MASTER BRUCE.
YES!
ONCE YOU HONE YOUR SKILLS, WE CAN ACCOMPLISH EVERYTHING WE NEED TO.
FZZAK

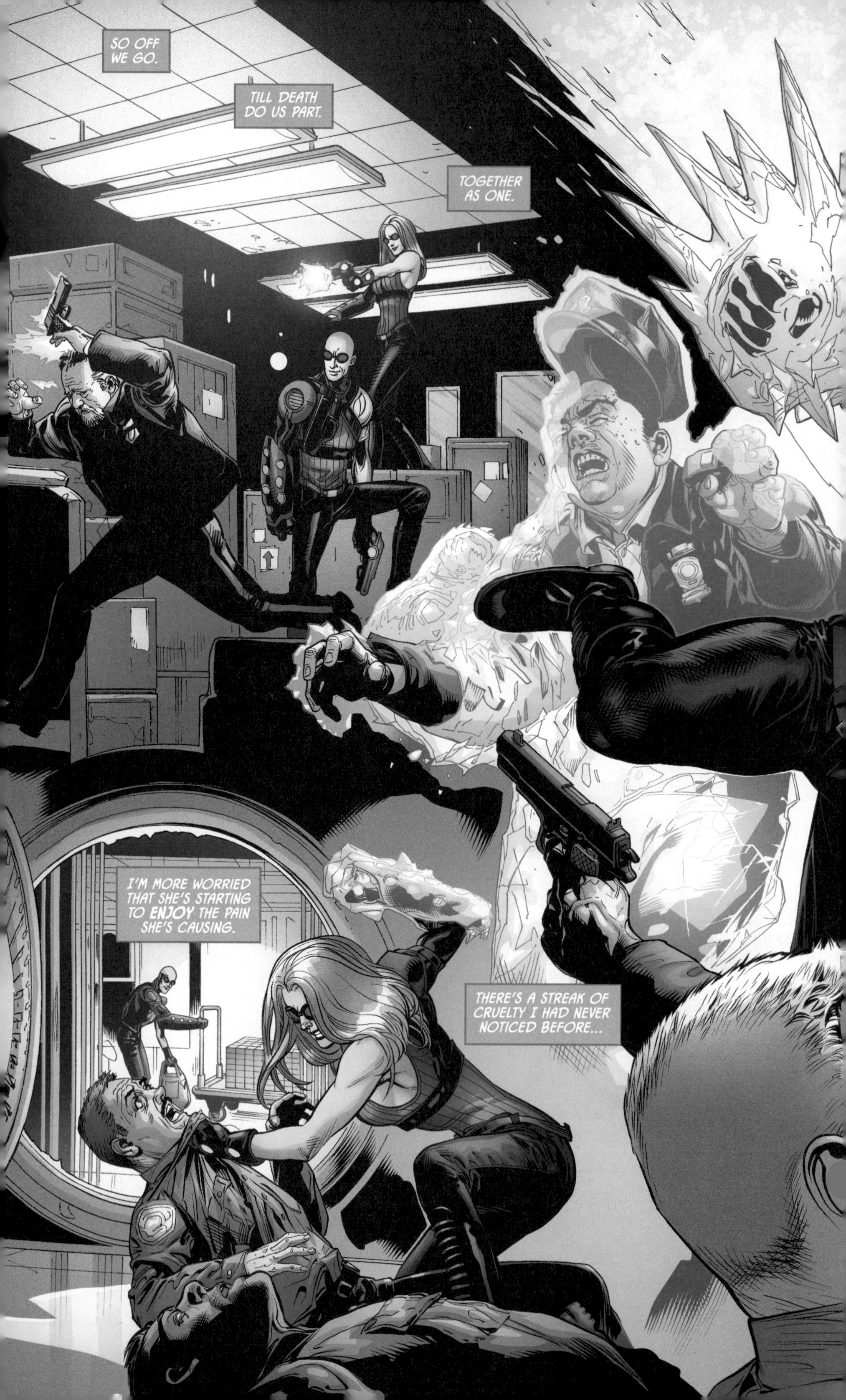
SO OFF WE GO.
TILL DEATH DO US PART.
TOGETHER AS ONE.
I'M MORE WORRIED THAT SHE'S STARTING TO **ENJOY** THE PAIN SHE'S CAUSING.
THERE'S A STREAK OF CRUELTY I HAD NEVER NOTICED BEFORE...

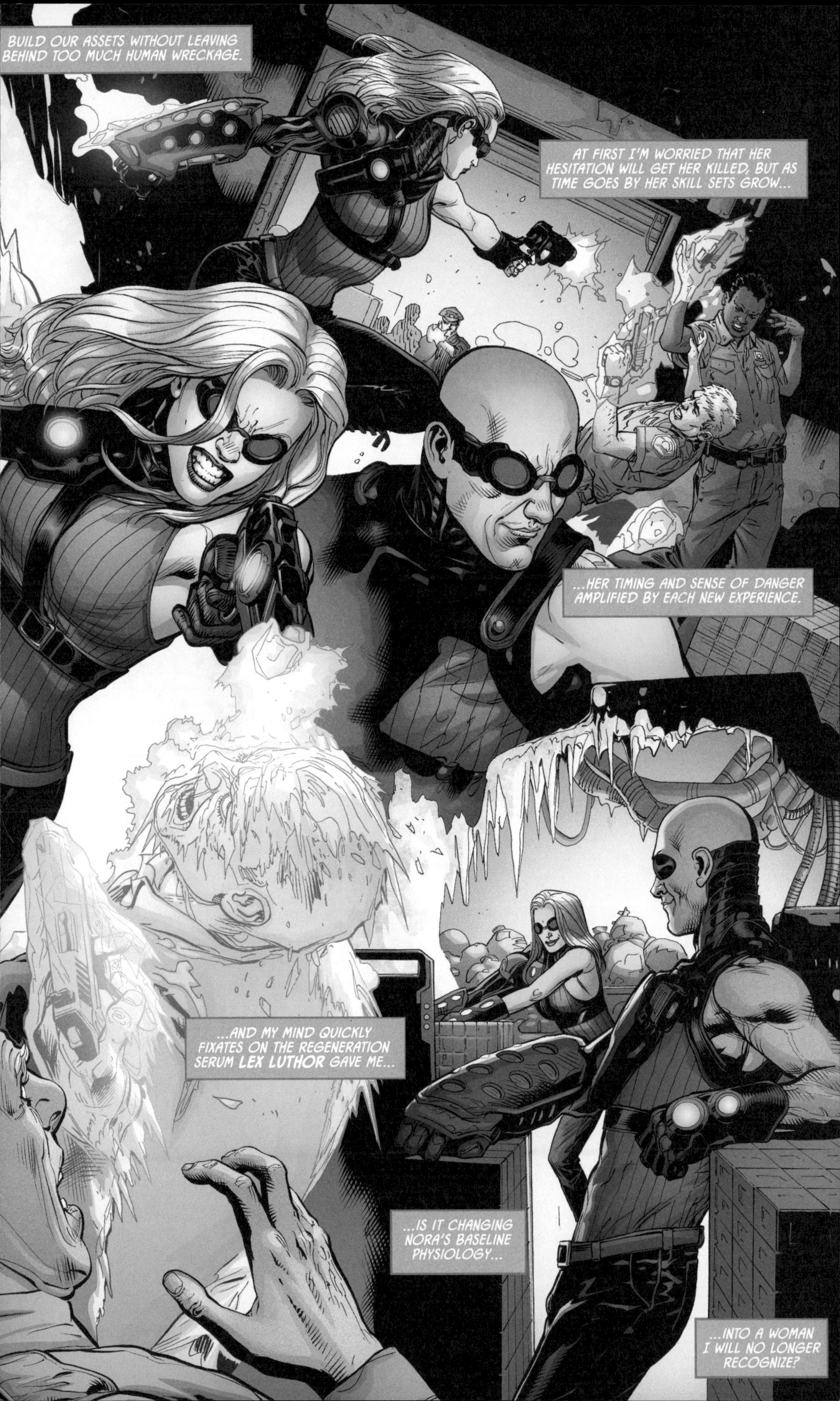

BUILD OUR ASSETS WITHOUT LEAVING BEHIND TOO MUCH HUMAN WRECKAGE.
AT FIRST I'M WORRIED THAT HER HESITATION WILL GET HER KILLED, BUT AS TIME GOES BY HER SKILL SETS GROW...
...HER TIMING AND SENSE OF DANGER AMPLIFIED BY EACH NEW EXPERIENCE.
...AND MY MIND QUICKLY FIXATES ON THE REGENERATION SERUM LEX LUTHOR GAVE ME...
...IS IT CHANGING NORA'S BASELINE PHYSIOLOGY...
...INTO A WOMAN I WILL NO LONGER RECOGNIZE?

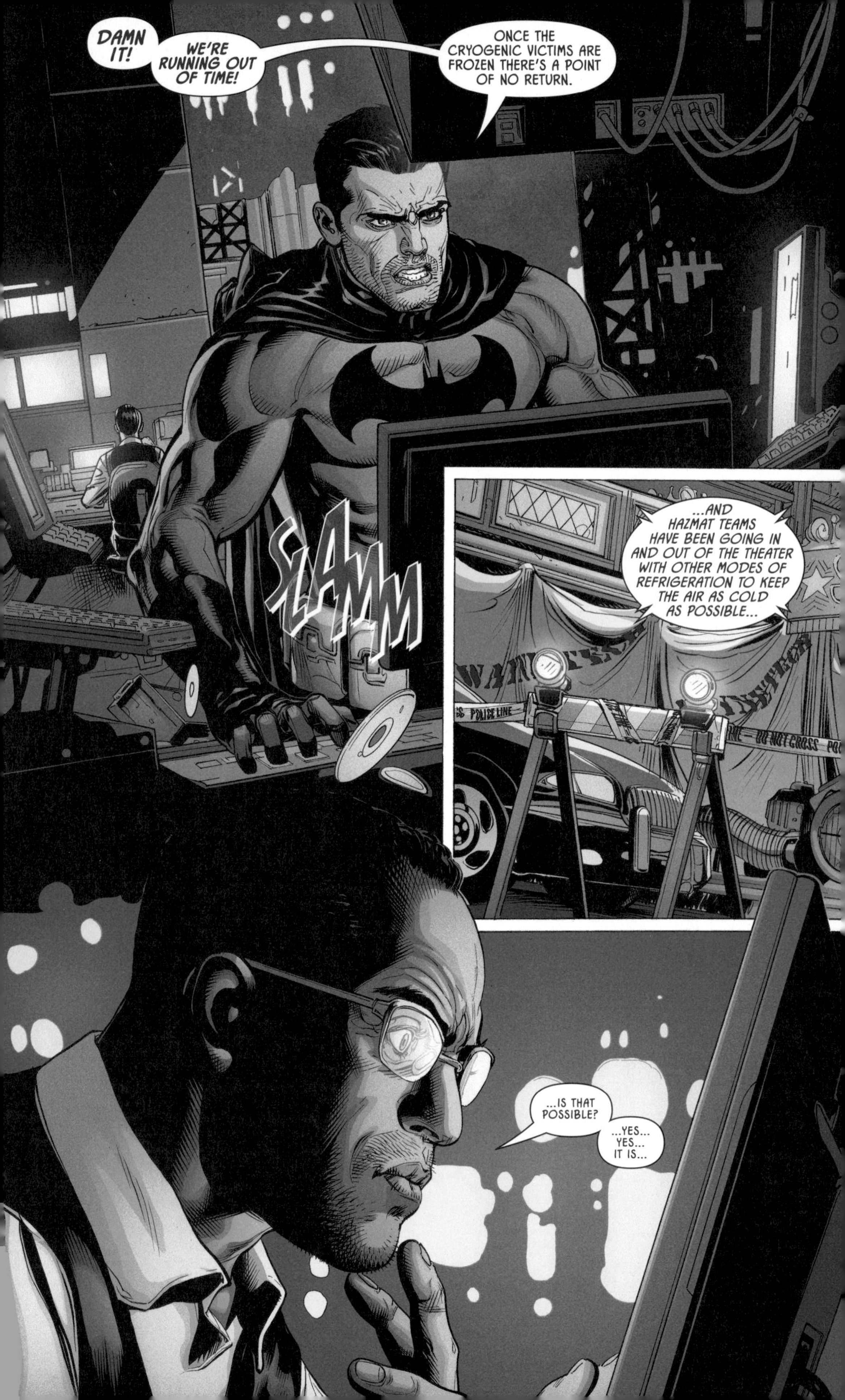
DAMN IT!
WE'RE RUNNING OUT OF TIME!
ONCE THE CRYOGENIC VICTIMS ARE FROZEN THERE'S A POINT OF NO RETURN.
SLAMM
...AND HAZMAT TEAMS HAVE BEEN GOING IN AND OUT OF THE THEATER WITH OTHER MODES OF REFRIGERATION TO KEEP THE AIR AS COLD AS POSSIBLE...
POLICE LINE
...IS THAT POSSIBLE?
...YES... YES... IT IS...

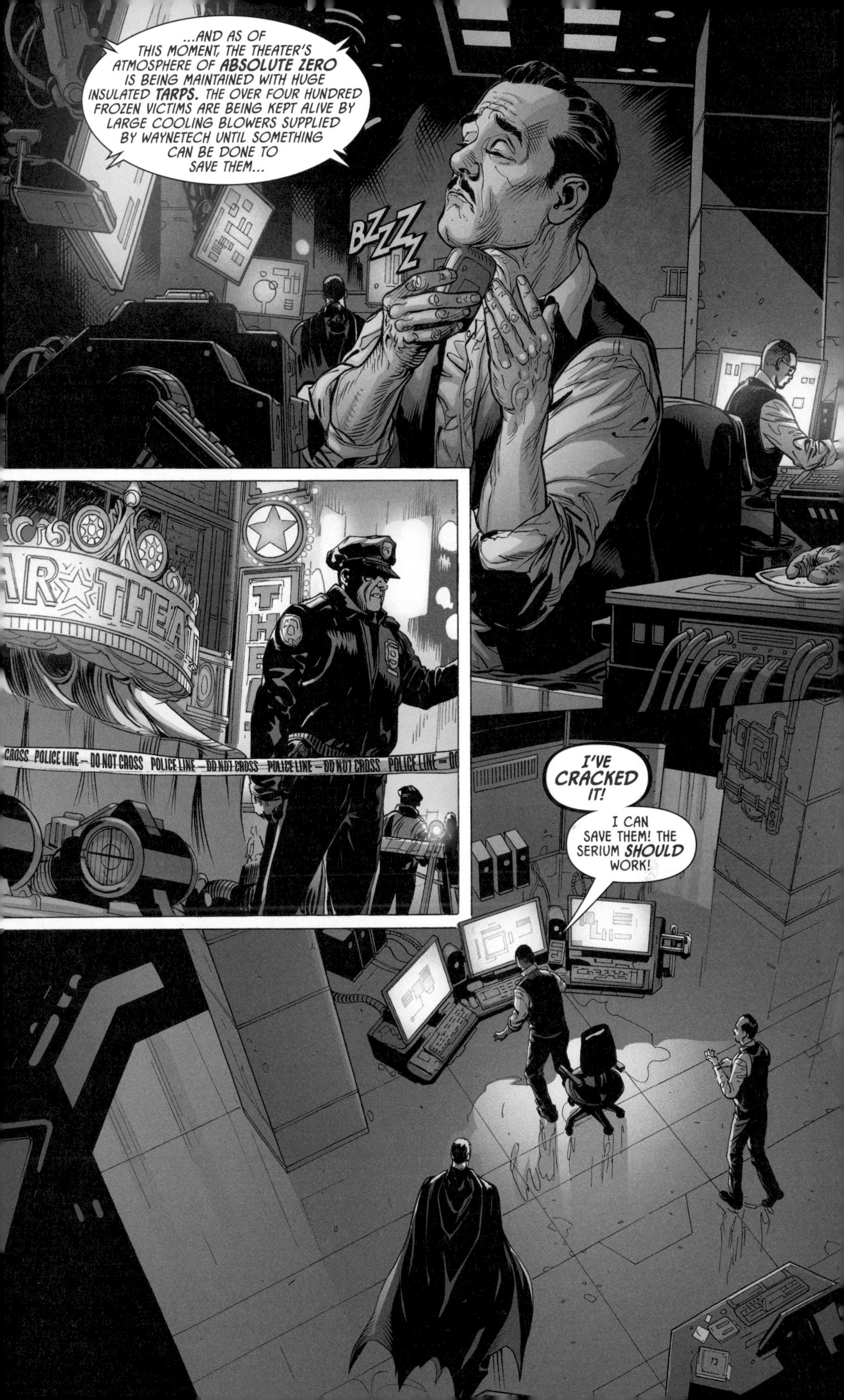
...AND AS OF THIS MOMENT, THE THEATER'S ATMOSPHERE OF ABSOLUTE ZERO IS BEING MAINTAINED WITH HUGE INSULATED TARPS. THE OVER FOUR HUNDRED FROZEN VICTIMS ARE BEING KEPT ALIVE BY LARGE COOLING BLOWERS SUPPLIED BY WAYNETECH UNTIL SOMETHING CAN BE DONE TO SAVE THEM...
BZZZZ
THEAT
CROSS POLICE LINE – DO NOT CROSS POLICE LINE – DO NOT CROSS POLICE LINE – DO NOT CROSS POLICE LINE – D
I'VE CRACKED IT!
I CAN SAVE THEM! THE SERIUM SHOULD WORK!

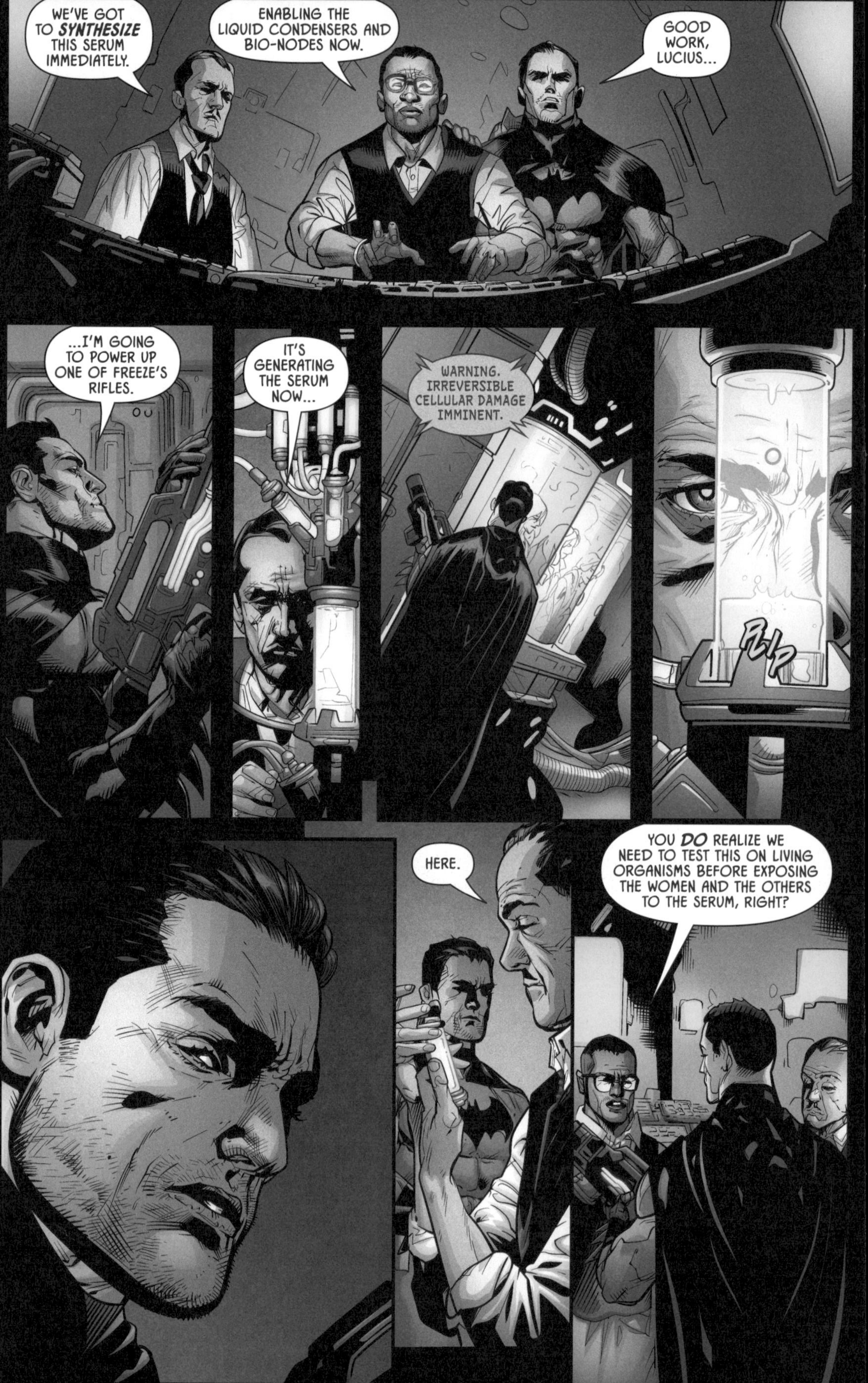
WE'VE GOT TO SYNTHESIZE THIS SERUM IMMEDIATELY.
ENABLING THE LIQUID CONDENSERS AND BIO-NODES NOW.
GOOD WORK, LUCIUS...
...I'M GOING TO POWER UP ONE OF FREEZE'S RIFLES.
IT'S GENERATING THE SERUM NOW...
WARNING. IRREVERSIBLE CELLULAR DAMAGE IMMINENT.
PLIP
HERE.
YOU DO REALIZE WE NEED TO TEST THIS ON LIVING ORGANISMS BEFORE EXPOSING THE WOMEN AND THE OTHERS TO THE SERUM, RIGHT?

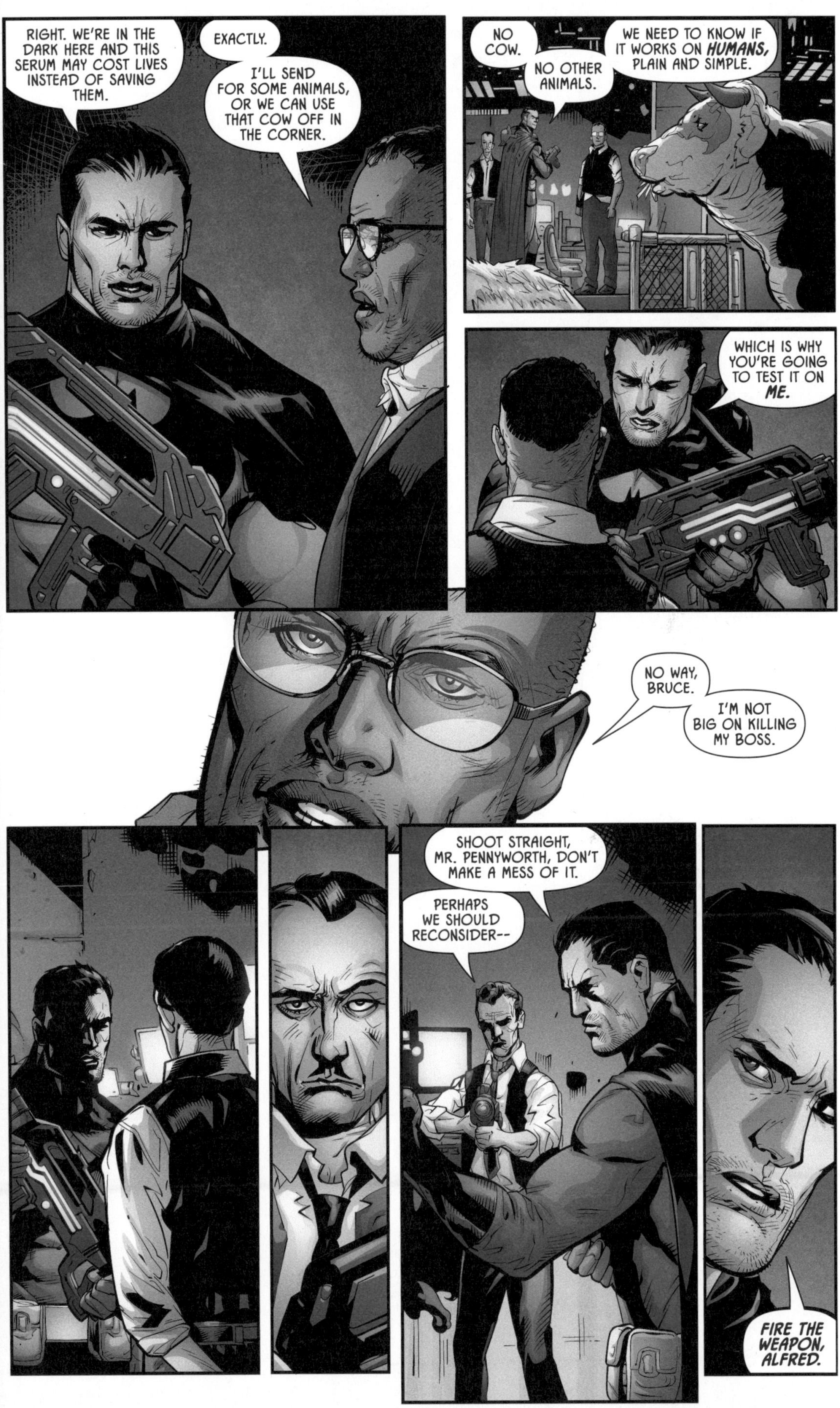
RIGHT. WE'RE IN THE DARK HERE AND THIS SERUM MAY COST LIVES INSTEAD OF SAVING THEM.
EXACTLY.
I'LL SEND FOR SOME ANIMALS, OR WE CAN USE THAT COW OFF IN THE CORNER.
NO COW.
NO OTHER ANIMALS.
WE NEED TO KNOW IF IT WORKS ON *HUMANS*, PLAIN AND SIMPLE.
WHICH IS WHY YOU'RE GOING TO TEST IT ON *ME.*
NO WAY, BRUCE.
I'M NOT BIG ON KILLING MY BOSS.
SHOOT STRAIGHT, MR. PENNYWORTH, DON'T MAKE A MESS OF IT.
PERHAPS WE SHOULD RECONSIDER--
FIRE THE WEAPON, ALFRED.

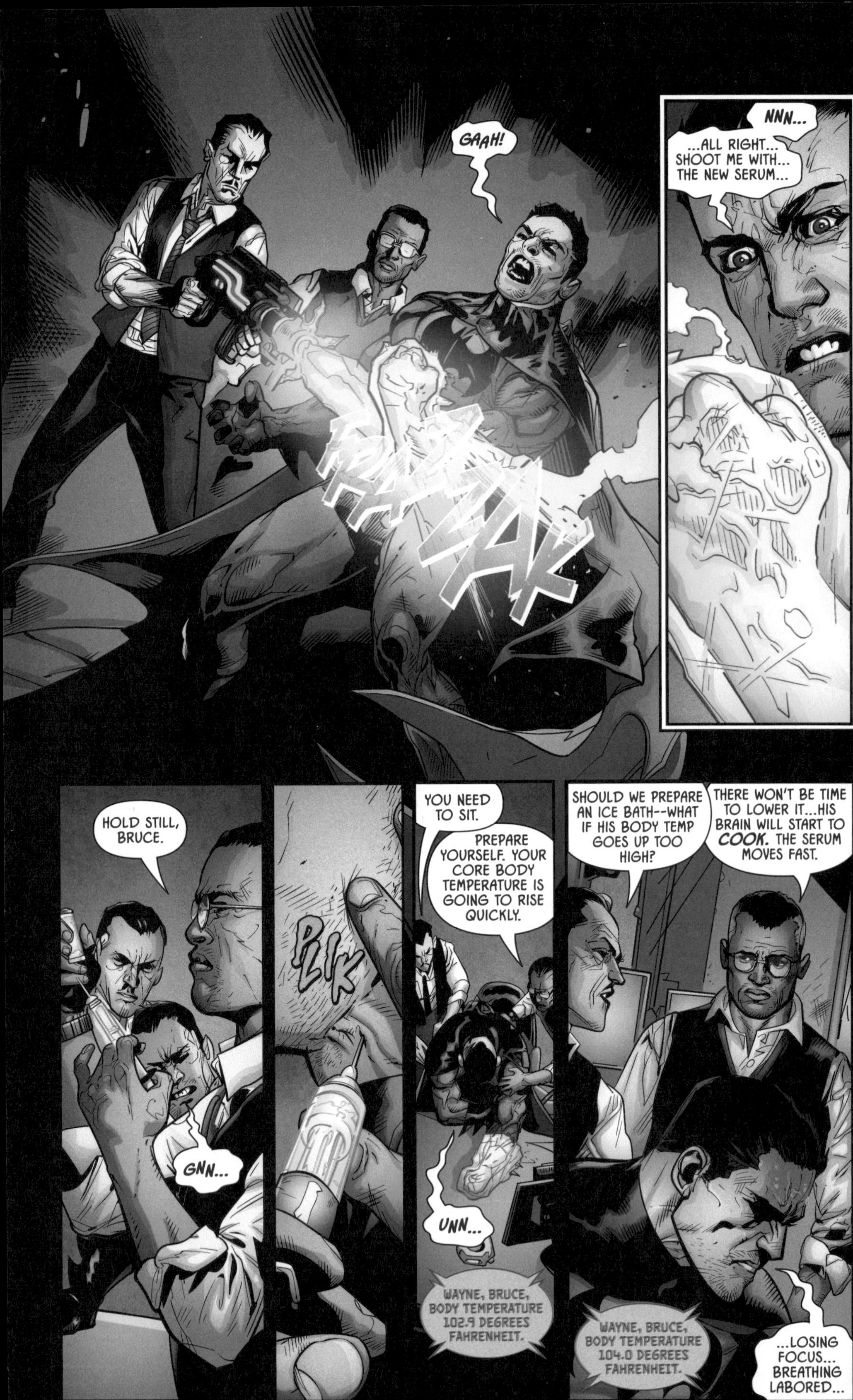
GAAH!
NNN...
...ALL RIGHT... SHOOT ME WITH... THE NEW SERUM...
HOLD STILL, BRUCE.
GNN...
PLIK
YOU NEED TO SIT.
PREPARE YOURSELF. YOUR CORE BODY TEMPERATURE IS GOING TO RISE QUICKLY.
UNN...
WAYNE, BRUCE, BODY TEMPERATURE 102.9 DEGREES FAHRENHEIT.
SHOULD WE PREPARE AN ICE BATH--WHAT IF HIS BODY TEMP GOES UP TOO HIGH?
THERE WON'T BE TIME TO LOWER IT...HIS BRAIN WILL START TO COOK. THE SERUM MOVES FAST.
WAYNE, BRUCE, BODY TEMPERATURE 104.0 DEGREES FAHRENHEIT.
...LOSING FOCUS... BREATHING LABORED...

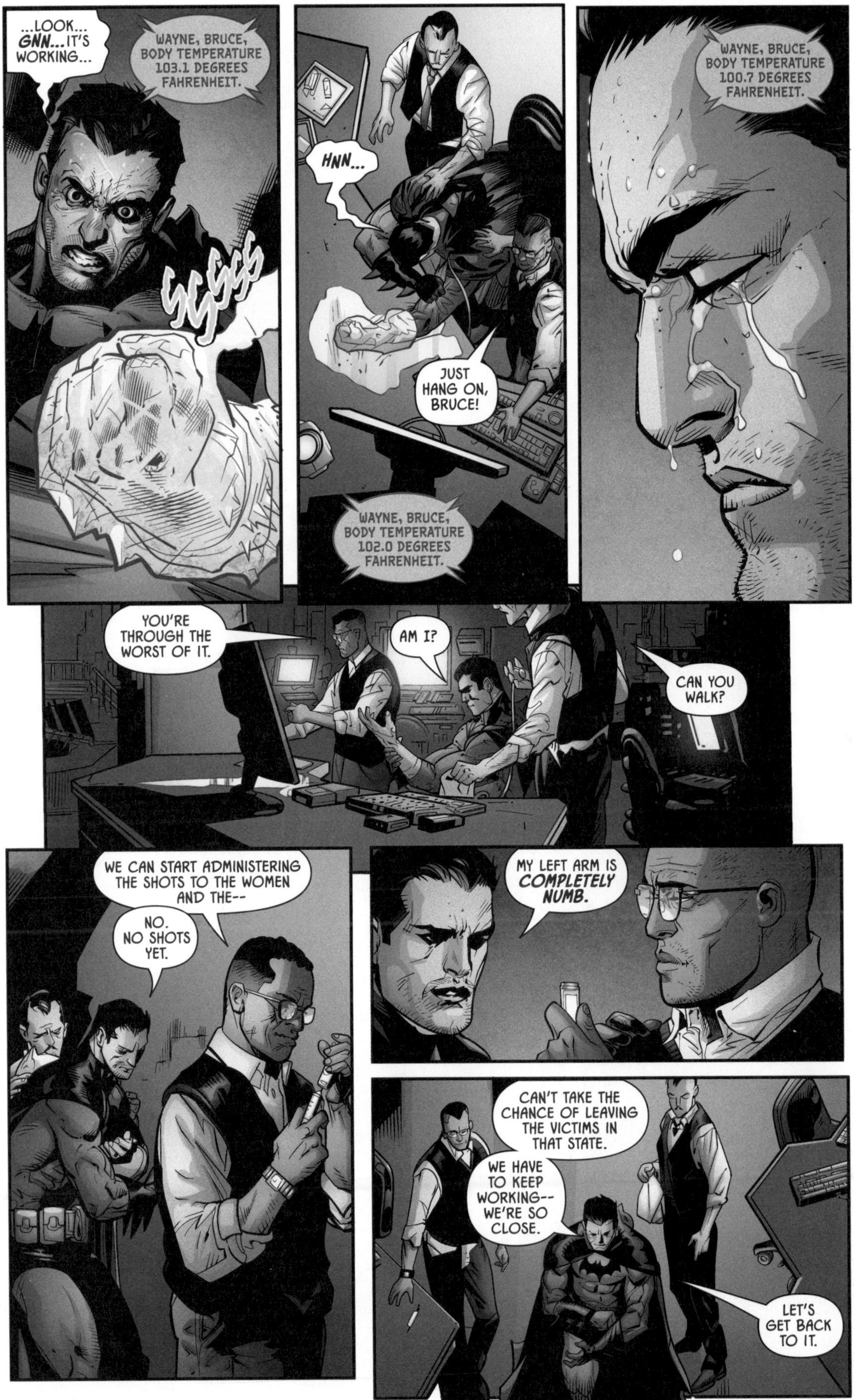
...LOOK... GNN... IT'S WORKING...
WAYNE, BRUCE, BODY TEMPERATURE 103.1 DEGREES FAHRENHEIT.
SSSSS
HNN...
JUST HANG ON, BRUCE!
WAYNE, BRUCE, BODY TEMPERATURE 102.0 DEGREES FAHRENHEIT.
WAYNE, BRUCE, BODY TEMPERATURE 100.7 DEGREES FAHRENHEIT.
YOU'RE THROUGH THE WORST OF IT.
AM I?
CAN YOU WALK?
WE CAN START ADMINISTERING THE SHOTS TO THE WOMEN AND THE--
NO. NO SHOTS YET.
MY LEFT ARM IS COMPLETELY NUMB.
CAN'T TAKE THE CHANCE OF LEAVING THE VICTIMS IN THAT STATE.
WE HAVE TO KEEP WORKING-- WE'RE SO CLOSE.
LET'S GET BACK TO IT.

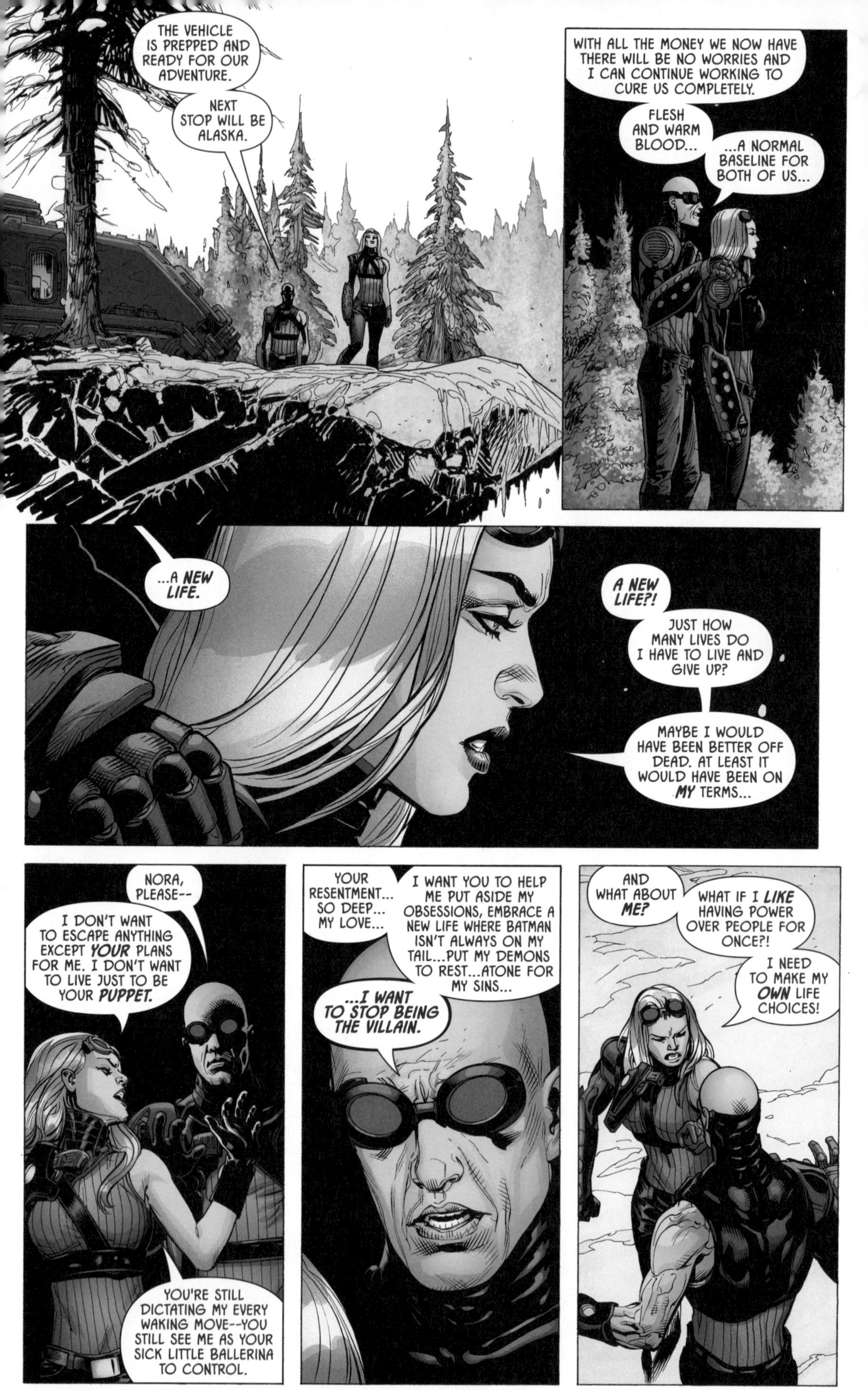
THE VEHICLE IS PREPPED AND READY FOR OUR ADVENTURE.
NEXT STOP WILL BE ALASKA.
WITH ALL THE MONEY WE NOW HAVE THERE WILL BE NO WORRIES AND I CAN CONTINUE WORKING TO CURE US COMPLETELY.
FLESH AND WARM BLOOD...
...A NORMAL BASELINE FOR BOTH OF US...
...A NEW LIFE.
A NEW LIFE?!
JUST HOW MANY LIVES DO I HAVE TO LIVE AND GIVE UP?
MAYBE I WOULD HAVE BEEN BETTER OFF DEAD. AT LEAST IT WOULD HAVE BEEN ON MY TERMS...
NORA, PLEASE--
I DON'T WANT TO ESCAPE ANYTHING EXCEPT YOUR PLANS FOR ME. I DON'T WANT TO LIVE JUST TO BE YOUR PUPPET.
YOU'RE STILL DICTATING MY EVERY WAKING MOVE--YOU STILL SEE ME AS YOUR SICK LITTLE BALLERINA TO CONTROL.
YOUR RESENTMENT... SO DEEP... MY LOVE...
I WANT YOU TO HELP ME PUT ASIDE MY OBSESSIONS, EMBRACE A NEW LIFE WHERE BATMAN ISN'T ALWAYS ON MY TAIL...PUT MY DEMONS TO REST...ATONE FOR MY SINS...
...I WANT TO STOP BEING THE VILLAIN.
AND WHAT ABOUT ME?
WHAT IF I LIKE HAVING POWER OVER PEOPLE FOR ONCE?!
I NEED TO MAKE MY OWN LIFE CHOICES!

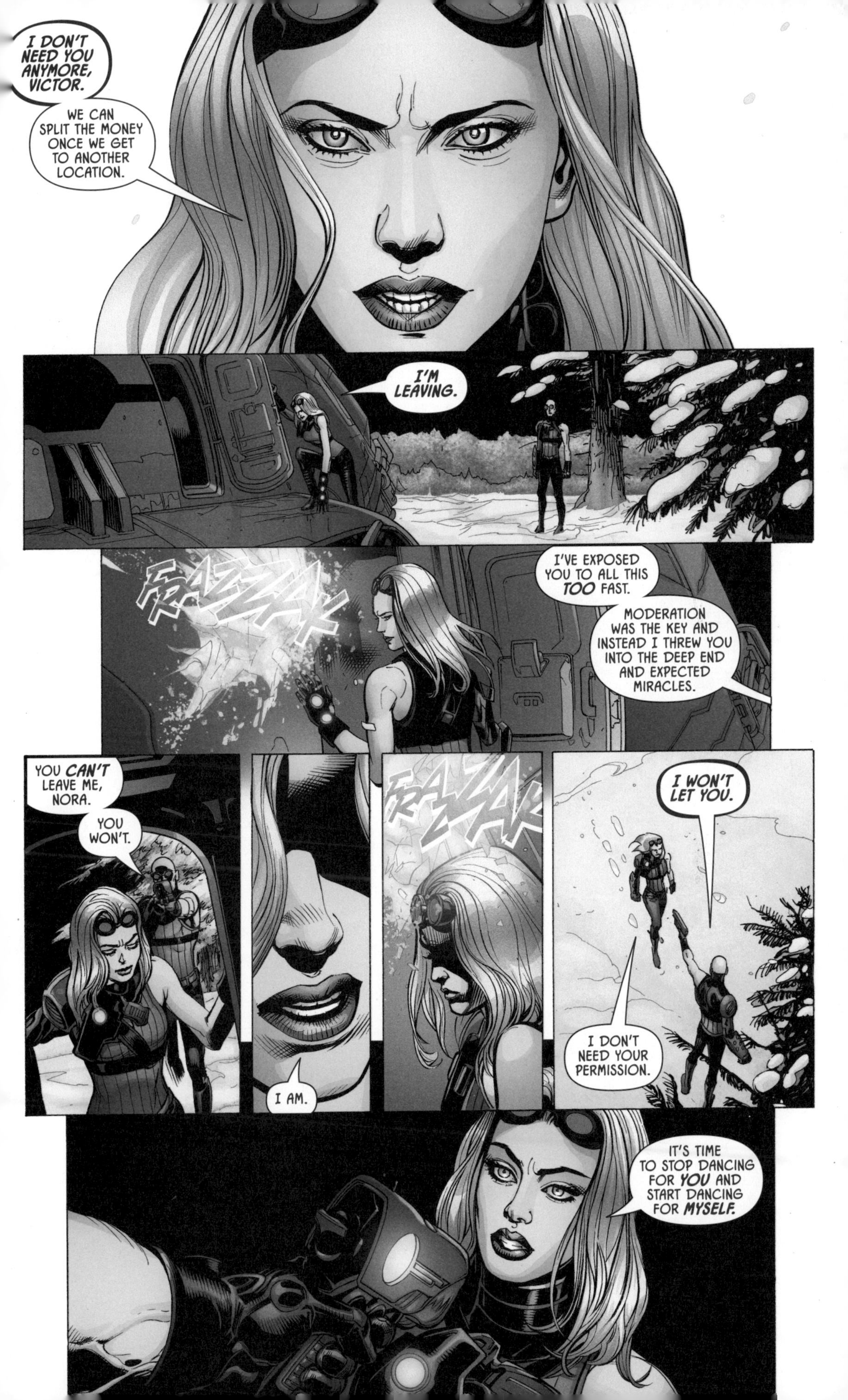
I DON'T NEED YOU ANYMORE, VICTOR.
WE CAN SPLIT THE MONEY ONCE WE GET TO ANOTHER LOCATION.
I'M LEAVING.
FRAZZAK
I'VE EXPOSED YOU TO ALL THIS TOO FAST.
MODERATION WAS THE KEY AND INSTEAD I THREW YOU INTO THE DEEP END AND EXPECTED MIRACLES.
YOU CAN'T LEAVE ME, NORA.
YOU WON'T.
I AM.
FRAZZAK
I WON'T LET YOU.
I DON'T NEED YOUR PERMISSION.
IT'S TIME TO STOP DANCING FOR YOU AND START DANCING FOR MYSELF.

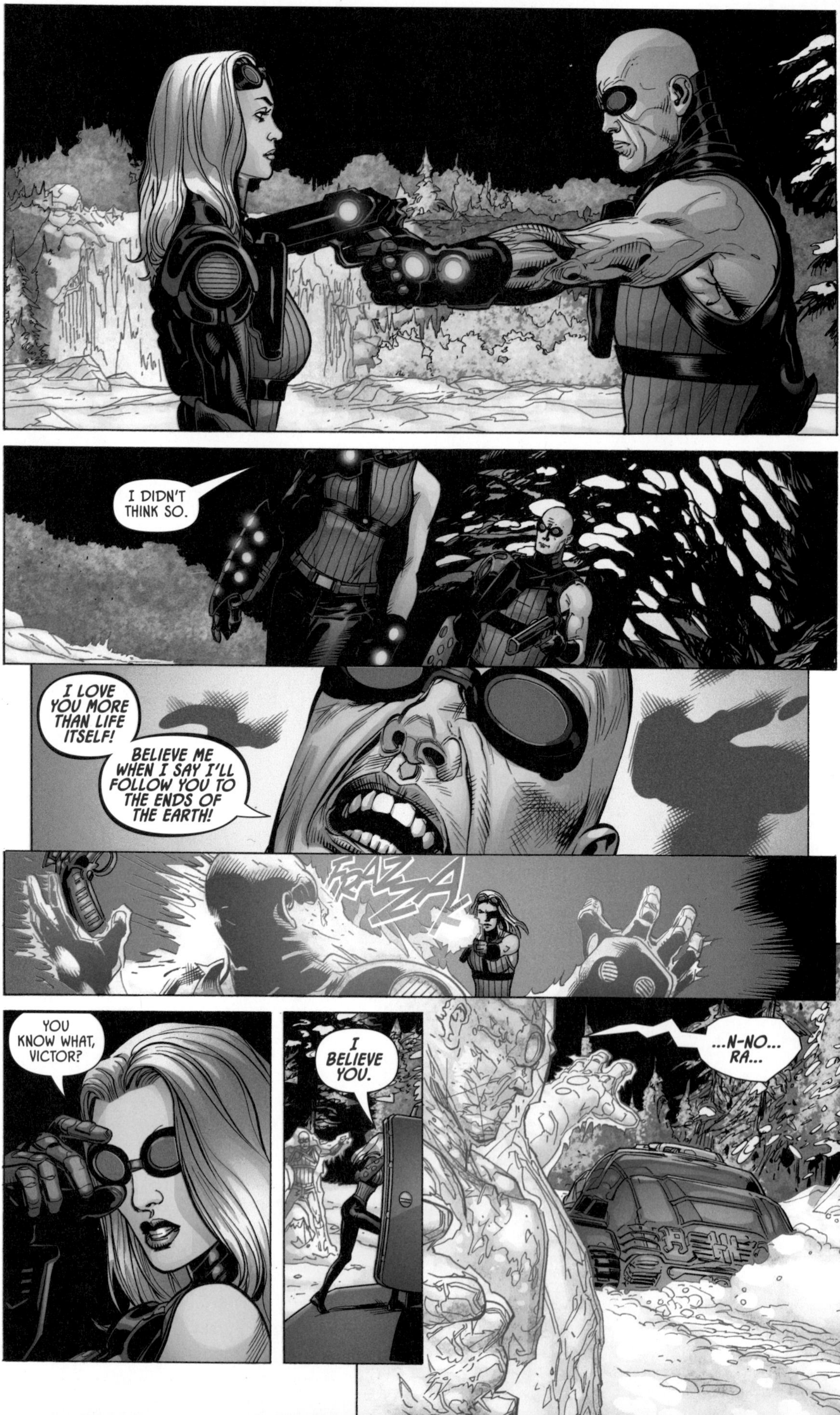
I DIDN'T THINK SO.
I LOVE YOU MORE THAN LIFE ITSELF!
BELIEVE ME WHEN I SAY I'LL FOLLOW YOU TO THE ENDS OF THE EARTH!
FRAZZAK
YOU KNOW WHAT, VICTOR?
I BELIEVE YOU.
...N-NO... RA...

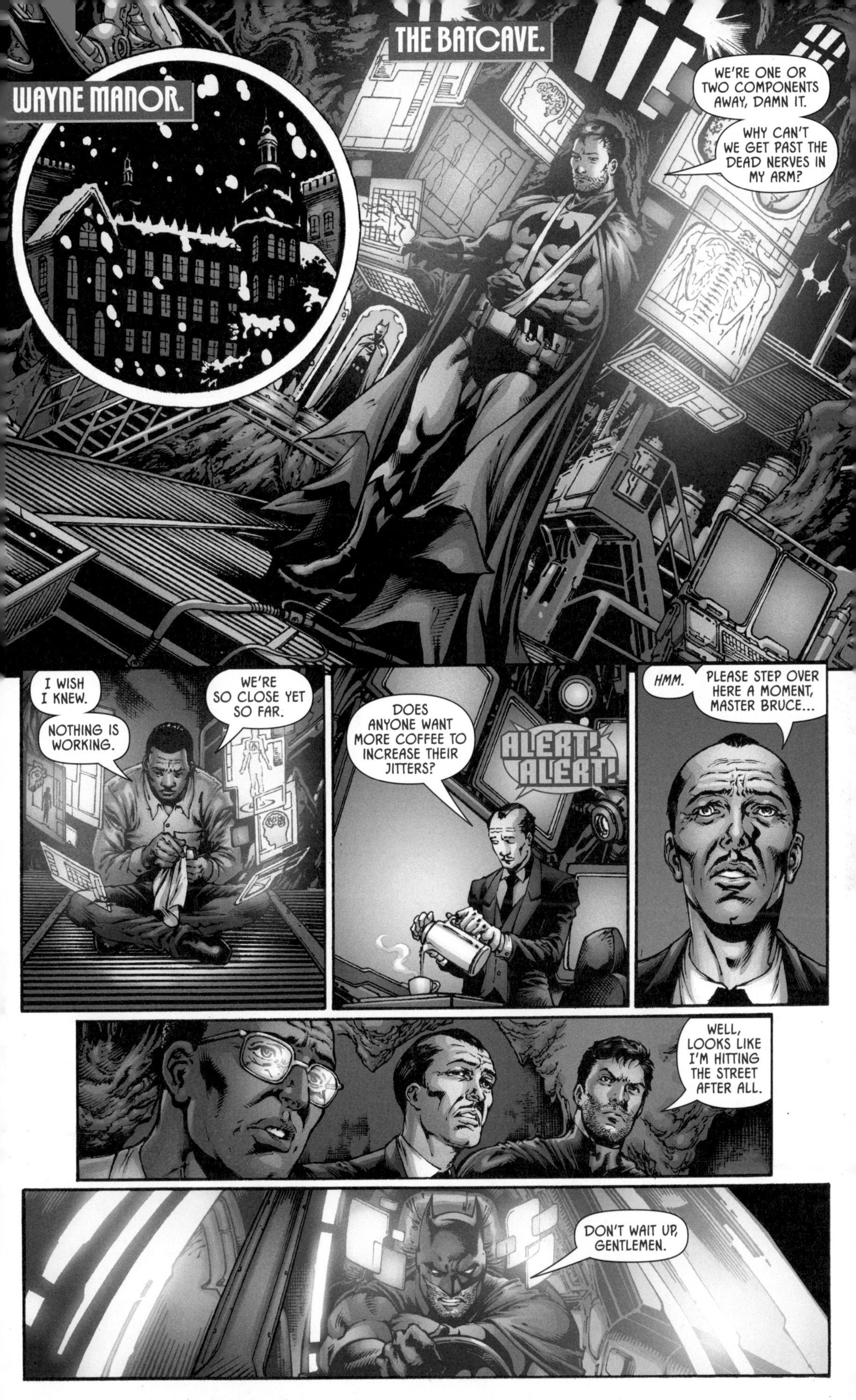
WAYNE MANOR.
THE BATCAVE.
WE'RE ONE OR TWO COMPONENTS AWAY, DAMN IT.
WHY CAN'T WE GET PAST THE DEAD NERVES IN MY ARM?
I WISH I KNEW.
NOTHING IS WORKING.
WE'RE SO CLOSE YET SO FAR.
DOES ANYONE WANT MORE COFFEE TO INCREASE THEIR JITTERS?
ALERT! ALERT!
HMM.
PLEASE STEP OVER HERE A MOMENT, MASTER BRUCE...
WELL, LOOKS LIKE I'M HITTING THE STREET AFTER ALL.
DON'T WAIT UP, GENTLEMEN.

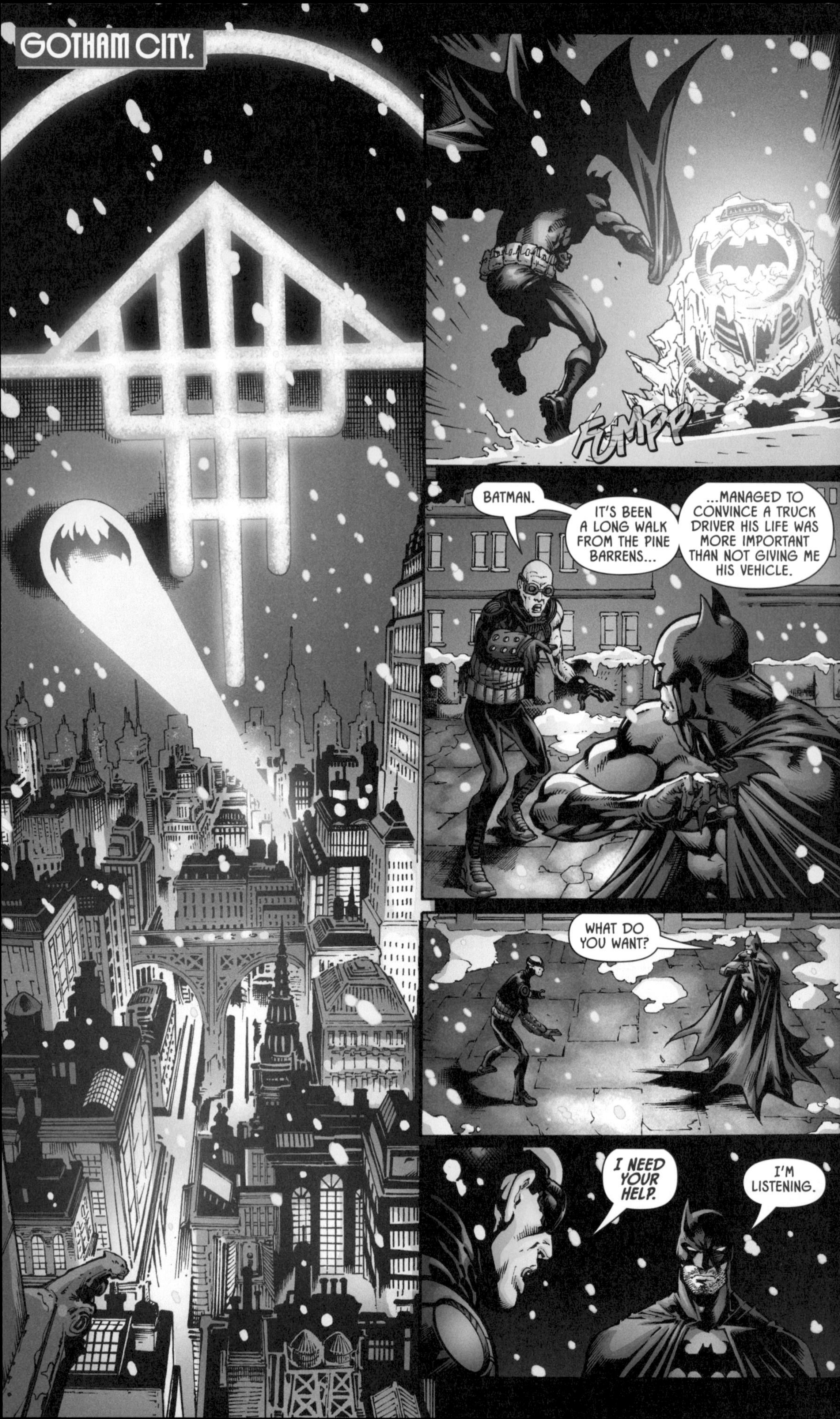
GOTHAM CITY.
FUMPP
BATMAN.
IT'S BEEN A LONG WALK FROM THE PINE BARRENS...
...MANAGED TO CONVINCE A TRUCK DRIVER HIS LIFE WAS MORE IMPORTANT THAN NOT GIVING ME HIS VEHICLE.
WHAT DO YOU WANT?
I NEED YOUR HELP.
I'M LISTENING.

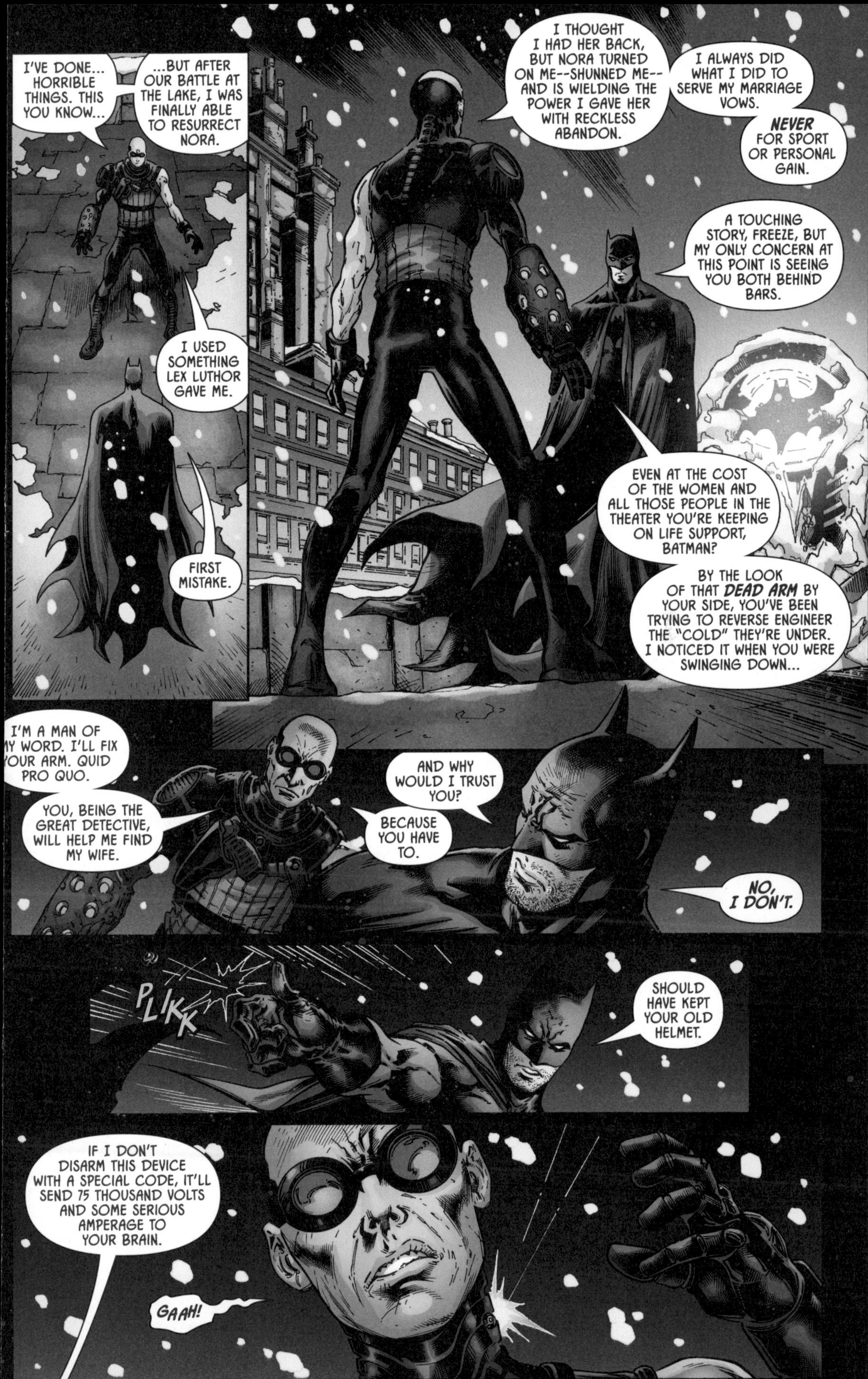
I'VE DONE... HORRIBLE THINGS. THIS YOU KNOW...
...BUT AFTER OUR BATTLE AT THE LAKE, I WAS FINALLY ABLE TO RESURRECT NORA.
I USED SOMETHING LEX LUTHOR GAVE ME.
FIRST MISTAKE.
I THOUGHT I HAD HER BACK, BUT NORA TURNED ON ME--SHUNNED ME--AND IS WIELDING THE POWER I GAVE HER WITH RECKLESS ABANDON.
I ALWAYS DID WHAT I DID TO SERVE MY MARRIAGE VOWS.
NEVER FOR SPORT OR PERSONAL GAIN.
A TOUCHING STORY, FREEZE, BUT MY ONLY CONCERN AT THIS POINT IS SEEING YOU BOTH BEHIND BARS.
EVEN AT THE COST OF THE WOMEN AND ALL THOSE PEOPLE IN THE THEATER YOU'RE KEEPING ON LIFE SUPPORT, BATMAN?
BY THE LOOK OF THAT DEAD ARM BY YOUR SIDE, YOU'VE BEEN TRYING TO REVERSE ENGINEER THE "COLD" THEY'RE UNDER. I NOTICED IT WHEN YOU WERE SWINGING DOWN...
I'M A MAN OF MY WORD. I'LL FIX YOUR ARM. QUID PRO QUO.
YOU, BEING THE GREAT DETECTIVE, WILL HELP ME FIND MY WIFE.
AND WHY WOULD I TRUST YOU?
BECAUSE YOU HAVE TO.
NO, I DON'T.
PLIKK
SHOULD HAVE KEPT YOUR OLD HELMET.
IF I DON'T DISARM THIS DEVICE WITH A SPECIAL CODE, IT'LL SEND 75 THOUSAND VOLTS AND SOME SERIOUS AMPERAGE TO YOUR BRAIN.
GAAH!

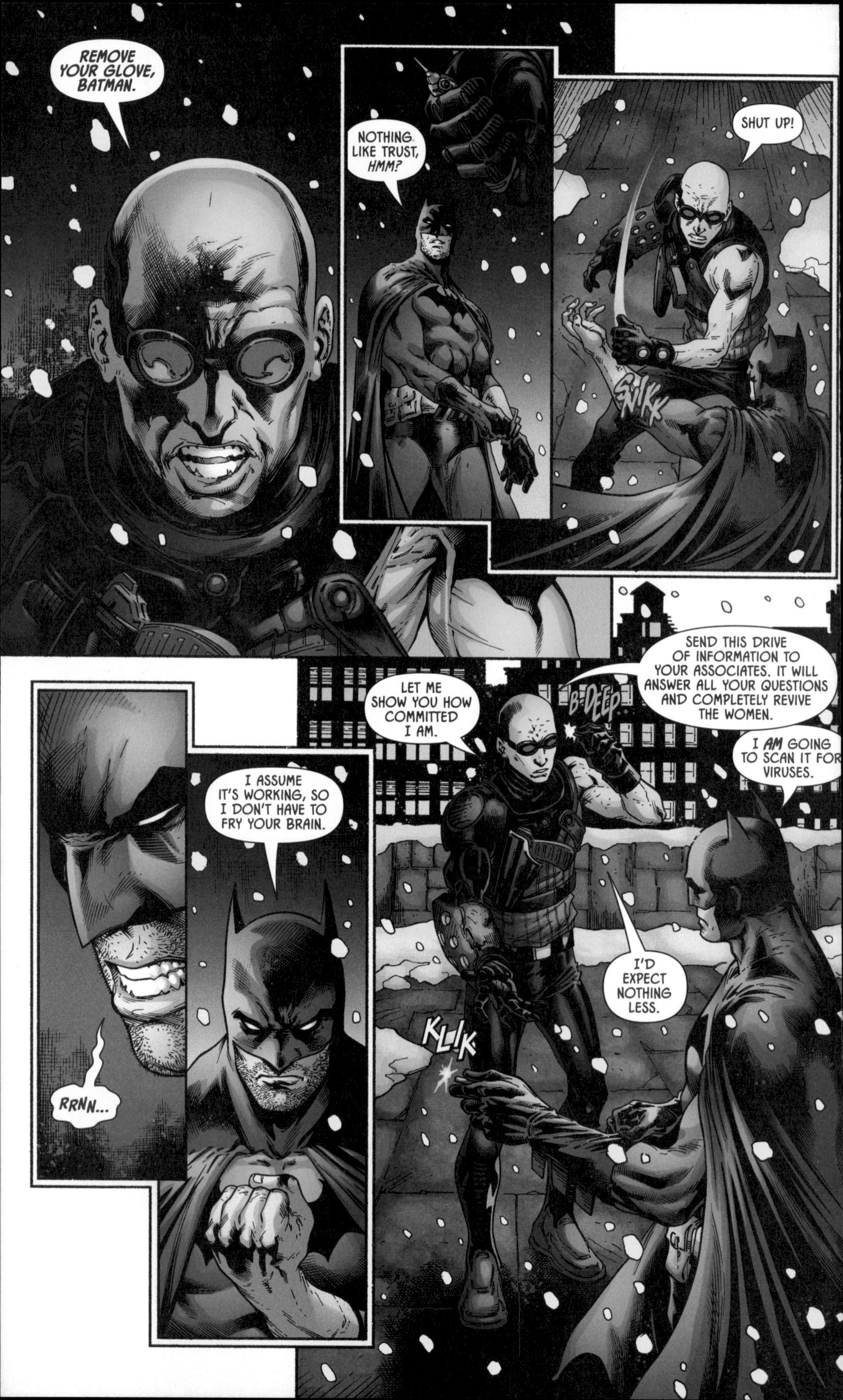
REMOVE YOUR GLOVE, BATMAN.
NOTHING LIKE TRUST, HMM?
SHUT UP!
SNIKK
I ASSUME IT'S WORKING, SO I DON'T HAVE TO FRY YOUR BRAIN.
RRNN...
LET ME SHOW YOU HOW COMMITTED I AM.
B-DEEP
SEND THIS DRIVE OF INFORMATION TO YOUR ASSOCIATES. IT WILL ANSWER ALL YOUR QUESTIONS AND COMPLETELY REVIVE THE WOMEN.
I AM GOING TO SCAN IT FOR VIRUSES.
I'D EXPECT NOTHING LESS.
KLIK

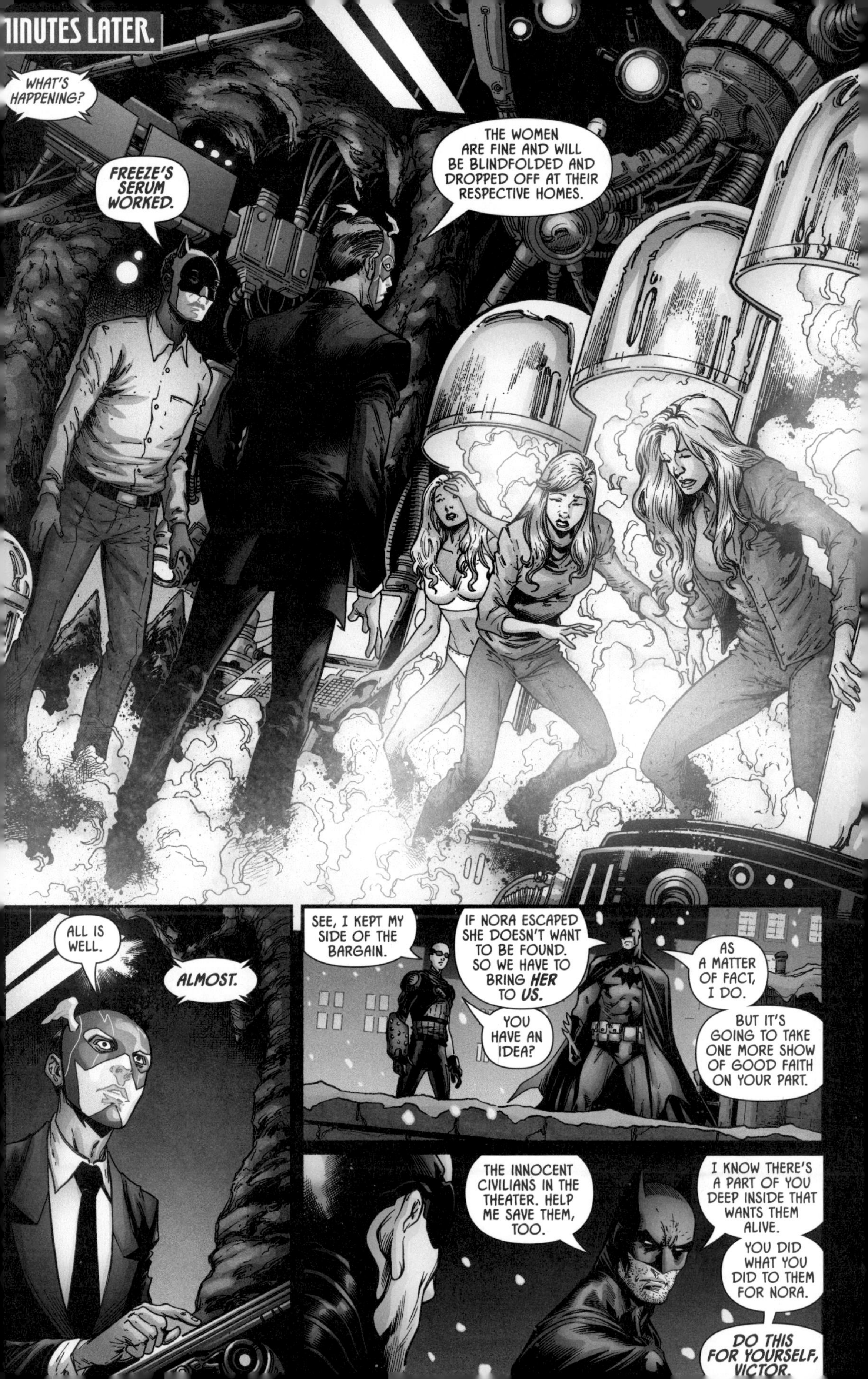

IINUTES LATER.
WHAT'S HAPPENING?
FREEZE'S SERUM WORKED.
THE WOMEN ARE FINE AND WILL BE BLINDFOLDED AND DROPPED OFF AT THEIR RESPECTIVE HOMES.
ALL IS WELL.
ALMOST.
SEE, I KEPT MY SIDE OF THE BARGAIN.
IF NORA ESCAPED SHE DOESN'T WANT TO BE FOUND. SO WE HAVE TO BRING HER TO US.
YOU HAVE AN IDEA?
AS A MATTER OF FACT, I DO.
BUT IT'S GOING TO TAKE ONE MORE SHOW OF GOOD FAITH ON YOUR PART.
THE INNOCENT CIVILIANS IN THE THEATER. HELP ME SAVE THEM, TOO.
I KNOW THERE'S A PART OF YOU DEEP INSIDE THAT WANTS THEM ALIVE.
YOU DID WHAT YOU DID TO THEM FOR NORA.
DO THIS FOR YOURSELF, VICTOR.

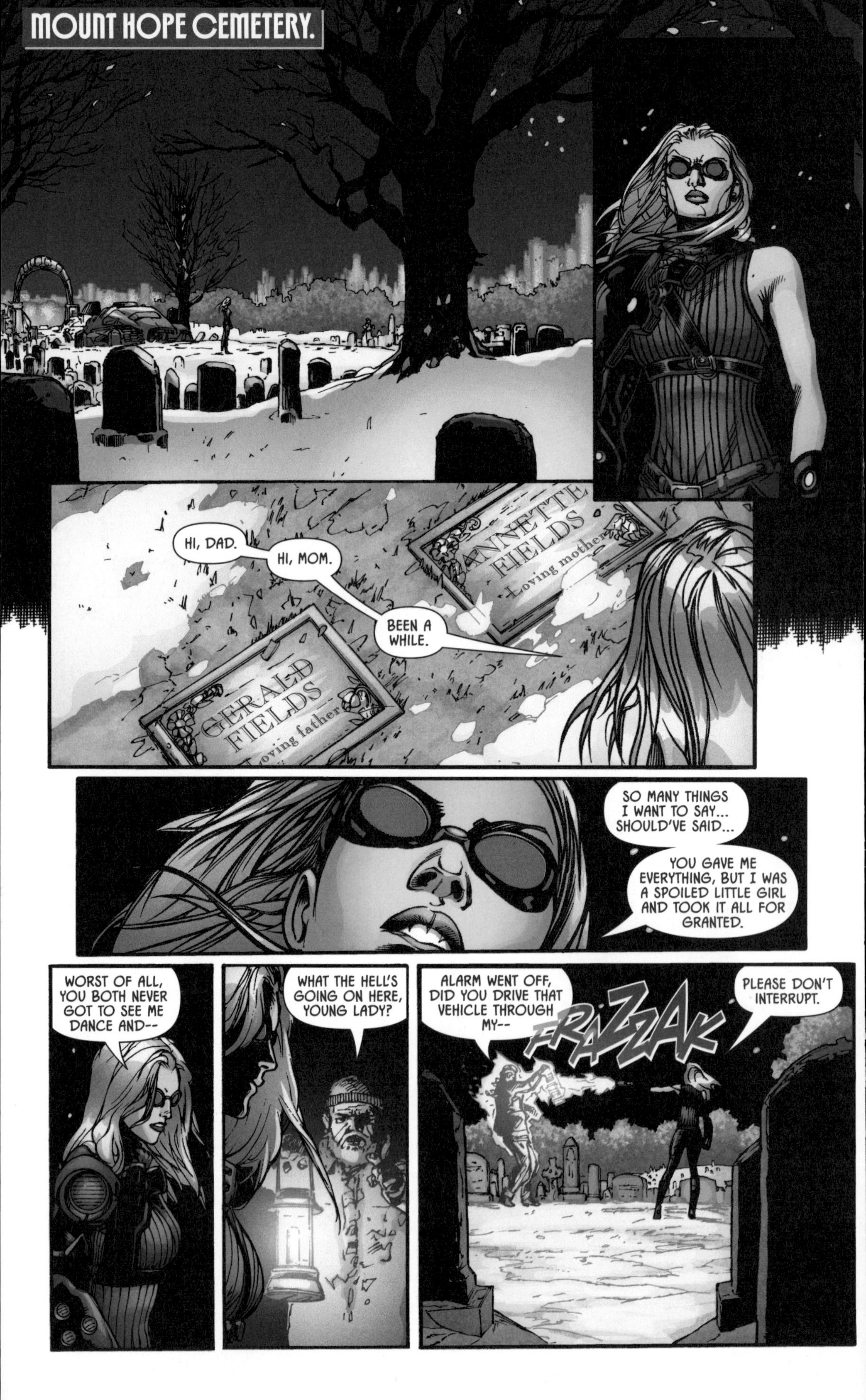
MOUNT HOPE CEMETERY.
HI, DAD.
HI, MOM.
BEEN A WHILE.
ANNETTE FIELDS Loving mother
GERALD FIELDS Loving father
SO MANY THINGS I WANT TO SAY... SHOULD'VE SAID...
YOU GAVE ME EVERYTHING, BUT I WAS A SPOILED LITTLE GIRL AND TOOK IT ALL FOR GRANTED.
WORST OF ALL, YOU BOTH NEVER GOT TO SEE ME DANCE AND--
WHAT THE HELL'S GOING ON HERE, YOUNG LADY?
ALARM WENT OFF, DID YOU DRIVE THAT VEHICLE THROUGH MY--
FRAZZAK
PLEASE DON'T INTERRUPT.

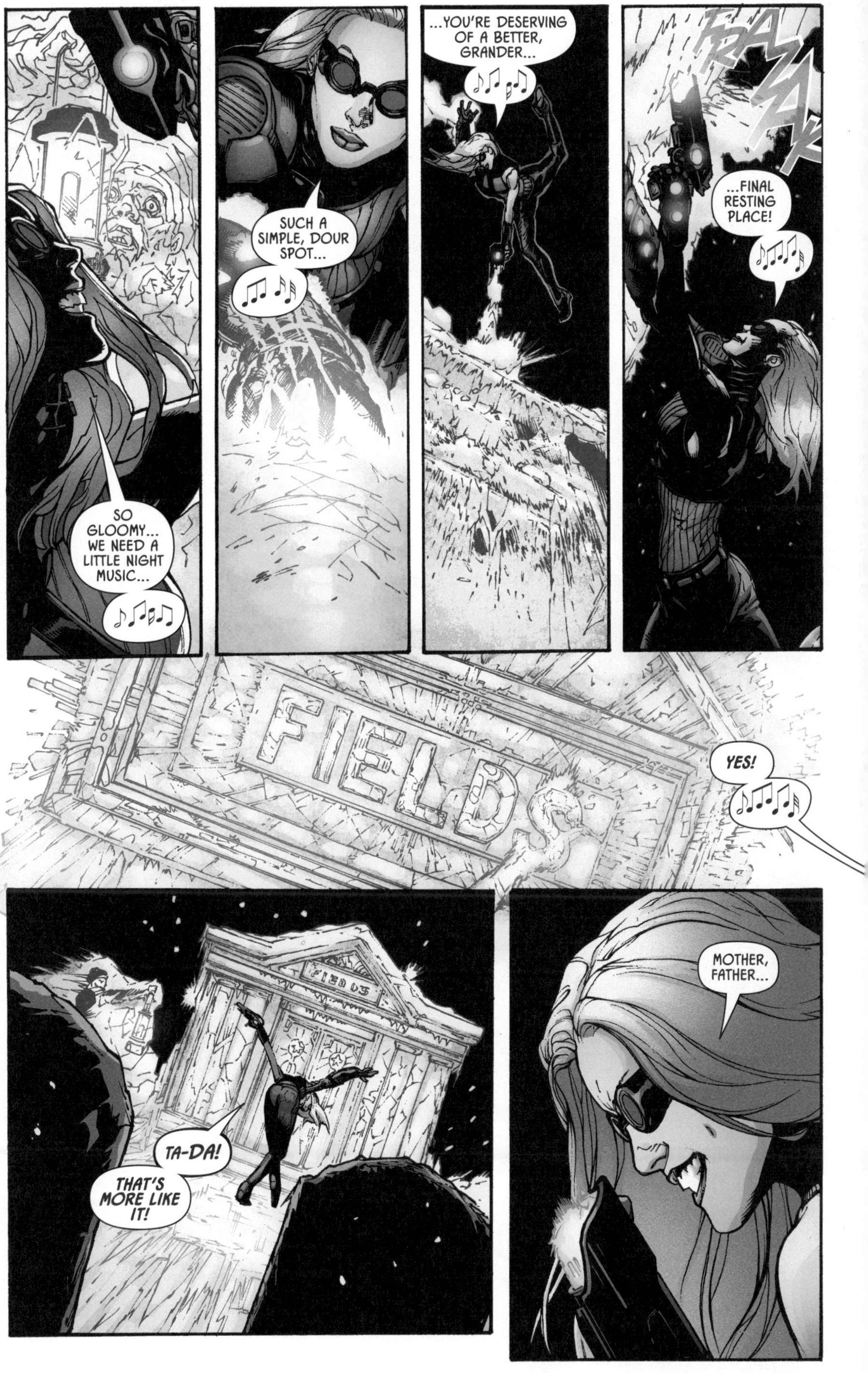

SO GLOOMY... WE NEED A LITTLE NIGHT MUSIC...
SUCH A SIMPLE, DOUR SPOT...
...YOU'RE DESERVING OF A BETTER, GRANDER...
FRA-AK
...FINAL RESTING PLACE!
FIELDS
YES!
FIELDS
TA-DA!
THAT'S MORE LIKE IT!
MOTHER, FATHER...

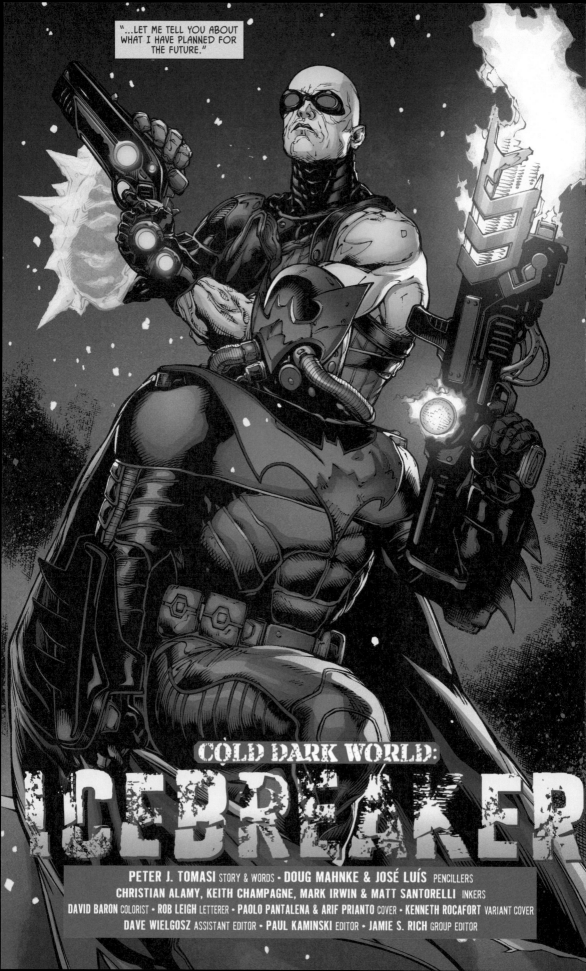

"...LET ME TELL YOU ABOUT WHAT I HAVE PLANNED FOR THE FUTURE."

COLD DARK WORLD:
ICEBREAKER

PETER J. TOMASI STORY & WORDS • **DOUG MAHNKE & JOSÉ LUÍS** PENCILLERS

CHRISTIAN ALAMY, KEITH CHAMPAGNE, MARK IRWIN & MATT SANTORELLI INKERS

DAVID BARON COLORIST • **ROB LEIGH** LETTERER • **PAOLO PANTALENA & ARIF PRIANTO** COVER • **KENNETH ROCAFORT** VARIANT COVER

DAVE WIELGOSZ ASSISTANT EDITOR • **PAUL KAMINSKI** EDITOR • **JAMIE S. RICH** GROUP EDITOR

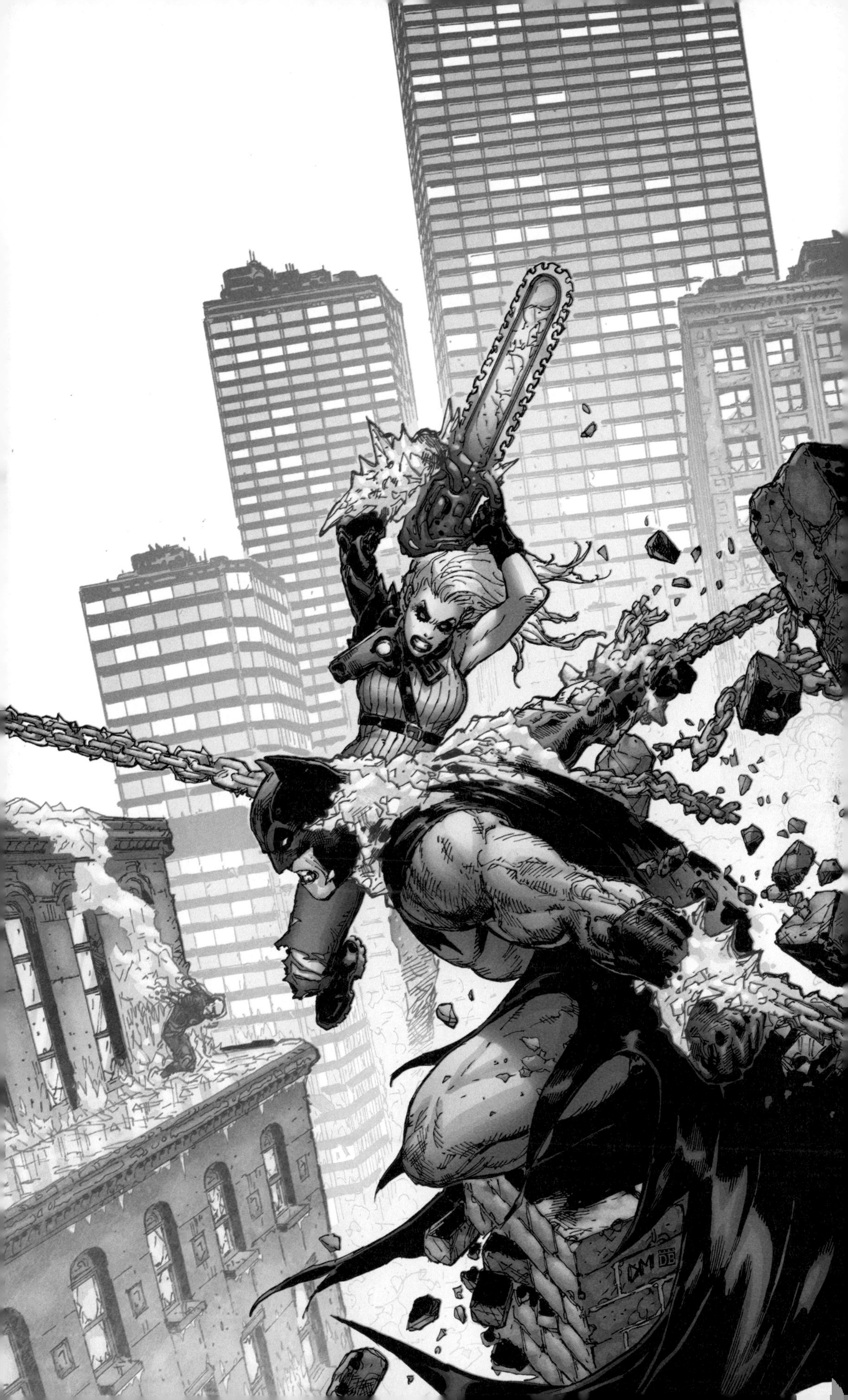

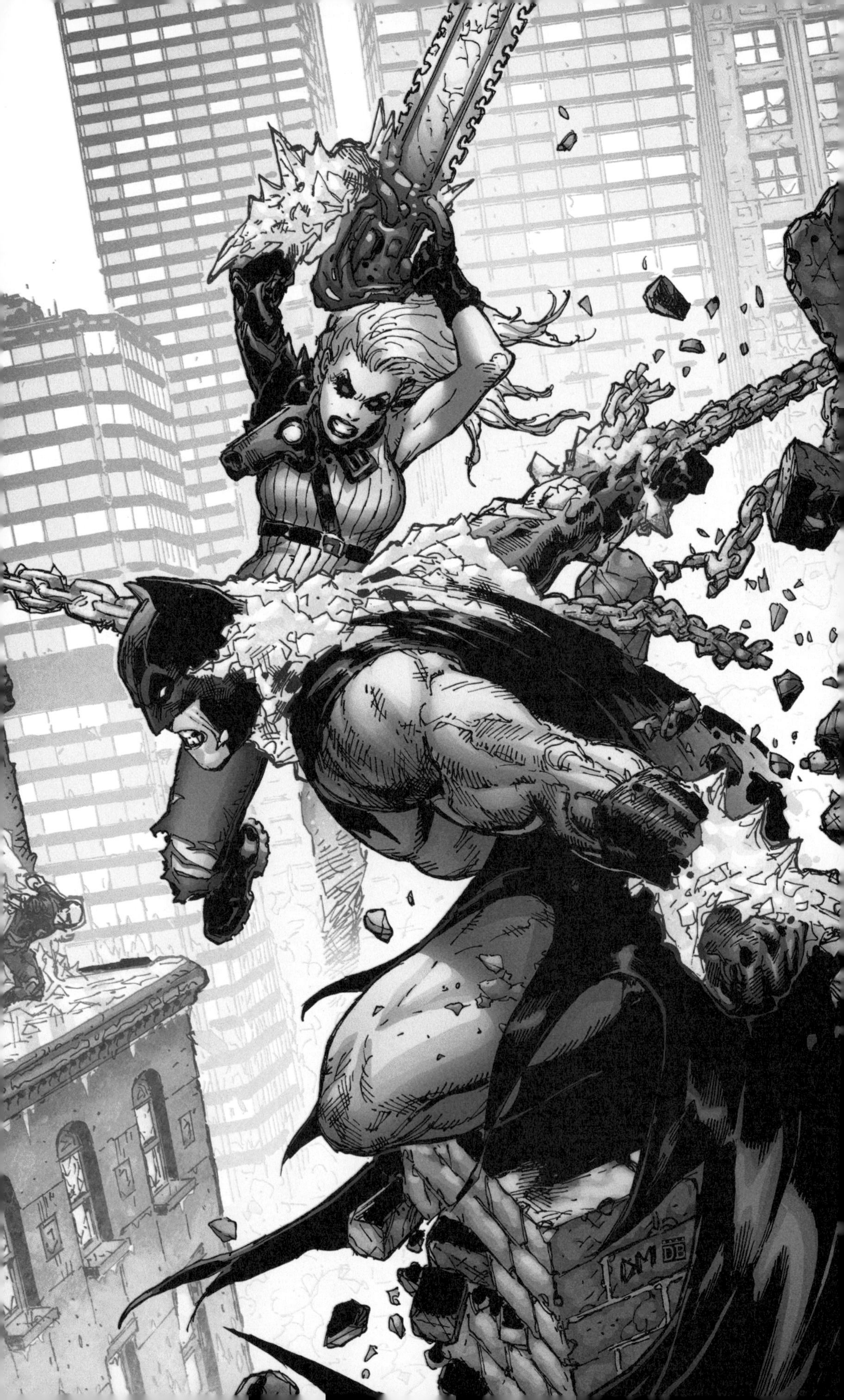

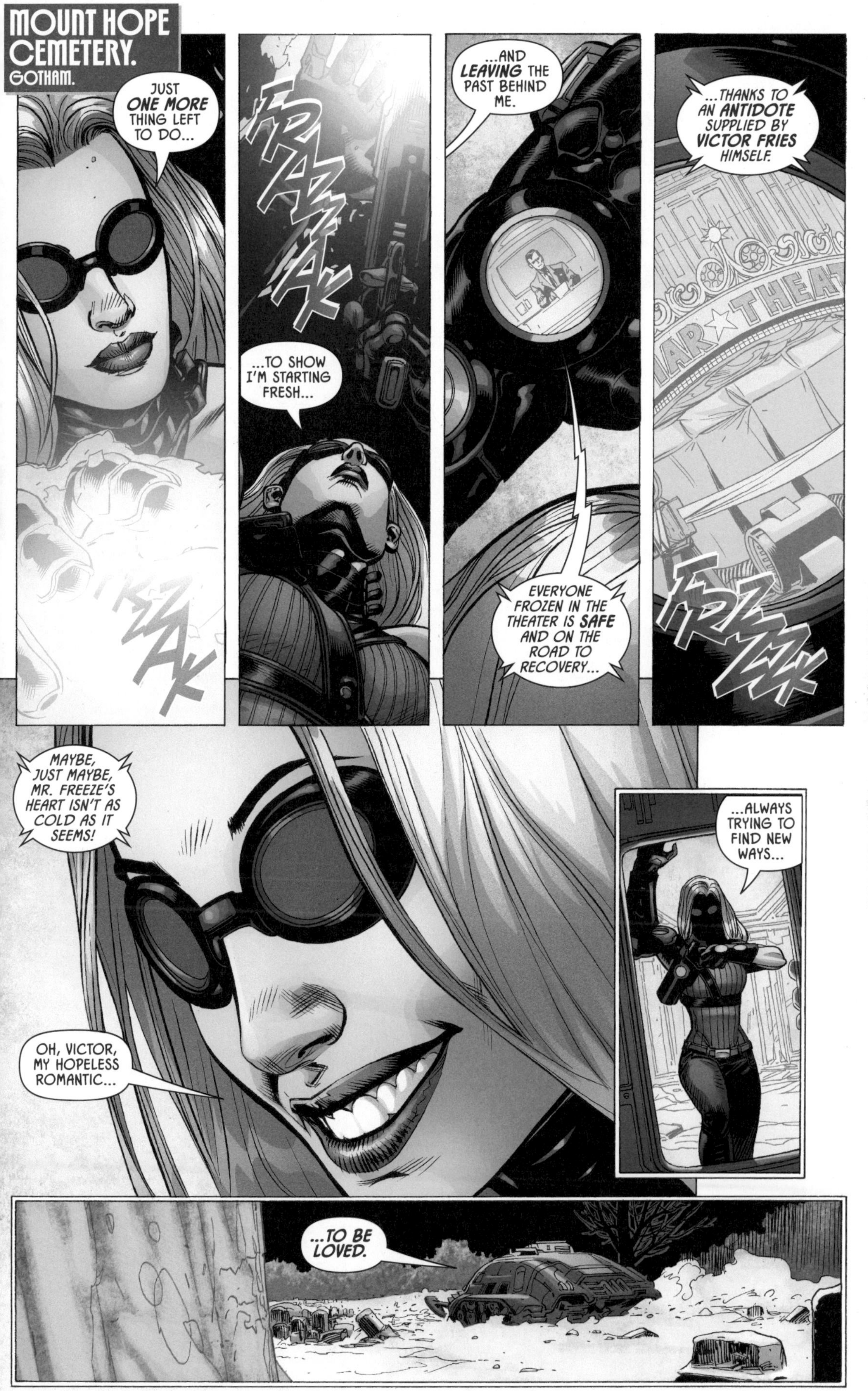
MOUNT HOPE CEMETERY. GOTHAM.
JUST ONE MORE THING LEFT TO DO...
...TO SHOW I'M STARTING FRESH...
...AND LEAVING THE PAST BEHIND ME.
EVERYONE FROZEN IN THE THEATER IS SAFE AND ON THE ROAD TO RECOVERY...
...THANKS TO AN ANTIDOTE SUPPLIED BY VICTOR FRIES HIMSELF.
MAYBE, JUST MAYBE, MR. FREEZE'S HEART ISN'T AS COLD AS IT SEEMS!
OH, VICTOR, MY HOPELESS ROMANTIC...
...ALWAYS TRYING TO FIND NEW WAYS...
...TO BE LOVED.

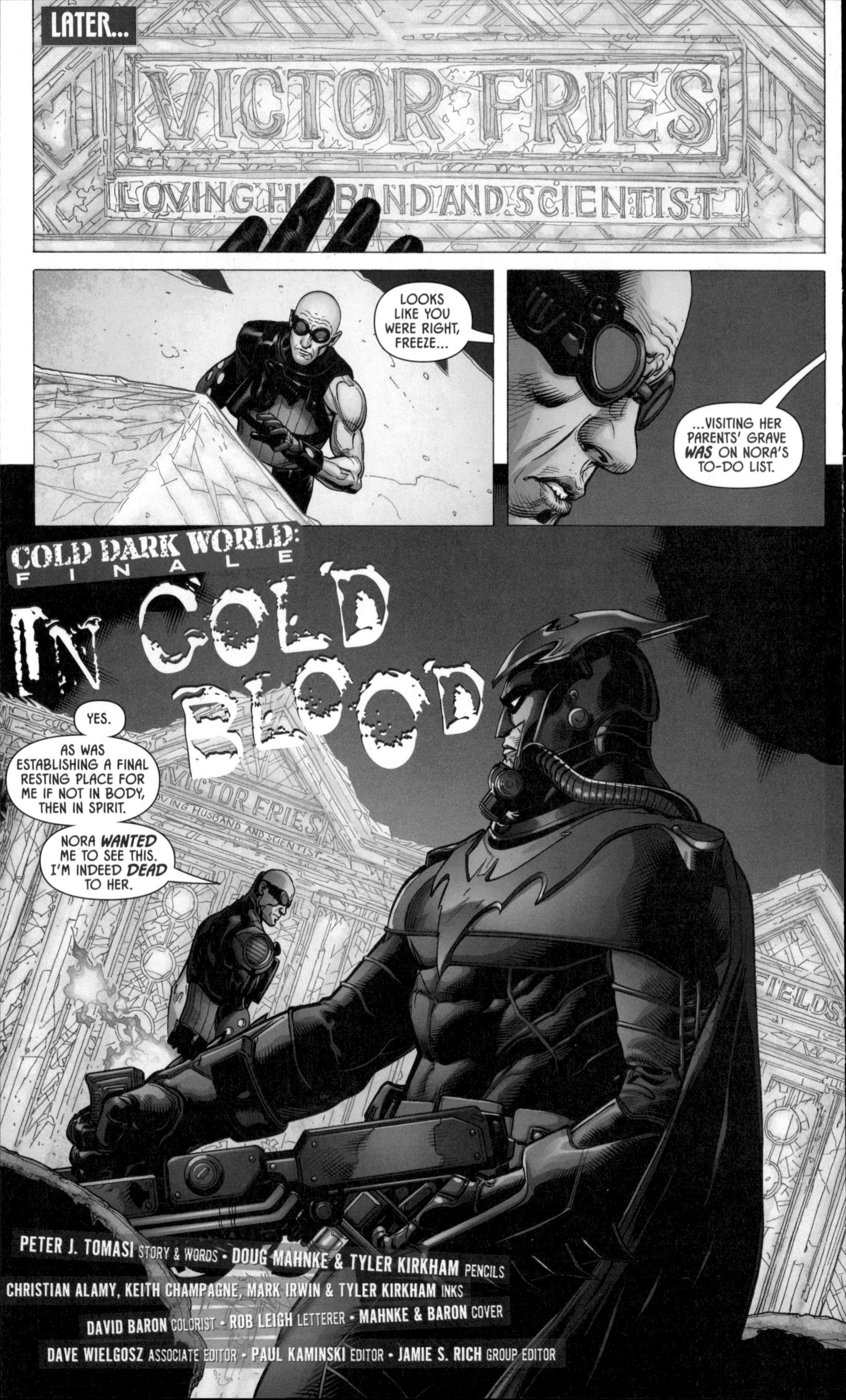
LATER...
VICTOR FRIES
LOVING HUSBAND AND SCIENTIST
LOOKS LIKE YOU WERE RIGHT, FREEZE...
...VISITING HER PARENTS' GRAVE *WAS* ON NORA'S TO-DO LIST.
COLD DARK WORLD: FINALE
IN COLD BLOOD
YES.
AS WAS ESTABLISHING A FINAL RESTING PLACE FOR ME IF NOT IN BODY, THEN IN SPIRIT.
NORA *WANTED* ME TO SEE THIS. I'M INDEED *DEAD* TO HER.
PETER J. TOMASI STORY & WORDS • DOUG MAHNKE & TYLER KIRKHAM PENCILS
CHRISTIAN ALAMY, KEITH CHAMPAGNE, MARK IRWIN & TYLER KIRKHAM INKS
DAVID BARON COLORIST • ROB LEIGH LETTERER • MAHNKE & BARON COVER
DAVE WIELGOSZ ASSOCIATE EDITOR • PAUL KAMINSKI EDITOR • JAMIE S. RICH GROUP EDITOR

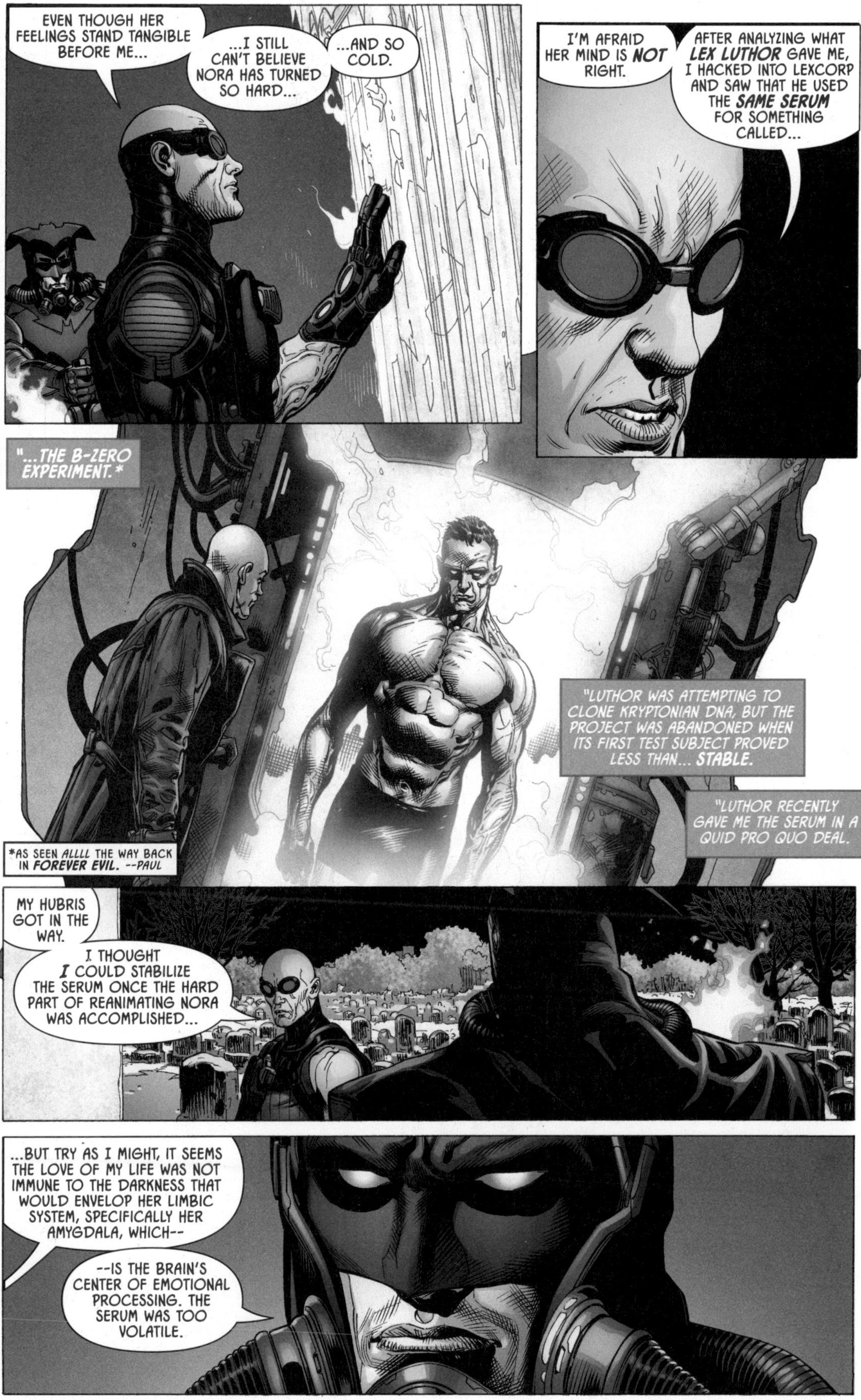
EVEN THOUGH HER FEELINGS STAND TANGIBLE BEFORE ME...
...I STILL CAN'T BELIEVE NORA HAS TURNED SO HARD...
...AND SO COLD.
I'M AFRAID HER MIND IS NOT RIGHT.
AFTER ANALYZING WHAT LEX LUTHOR GAVE ME, I HACKED INTO LEXCORP AND SAW THAT HE USED THE SAME SERUM FOR SOMETHING CALLED...
"...THE B-ZERO EXPERIMENT.*
"LUTHOR WAS ATTEMPTING TO CLONE KRYPTONIAN DNA, BUT THE PROJECT WAS ABANDONED WHEN ITS FIRST TEST SUBJECT PROVED LESS THAN... STABLE.
"LUTHOR RECENTLY GAVE ME THE SERUM IN A QUID PRO QUO DEAL.
*AS SEEN ALLLL THE WAY BACK IN FOREVER EVIL. --PAUL
MY HUBRIS GOT IN THE WAY.
I THOUGHT I COULD STABILIZE THE SERUM ONCE THE HARD PART OF REANIMATING NORA WAS ACCOMPLISHED...
...BUT TRY AS I MIGHT, IT SEEMS THE LOVE OF MY LIFE WAS NOT IMMUNE TO THE DARKNESS THAT WOULD ENVELOP HER LIMBIC SYSTEM, SPECIFICALLY HER AMYGDALA, WHICH--
--IS THE BRAIN'S CENTER OF EMOTIONAL PROCESSING. THE SERUM WAS TOO VOLATILE.

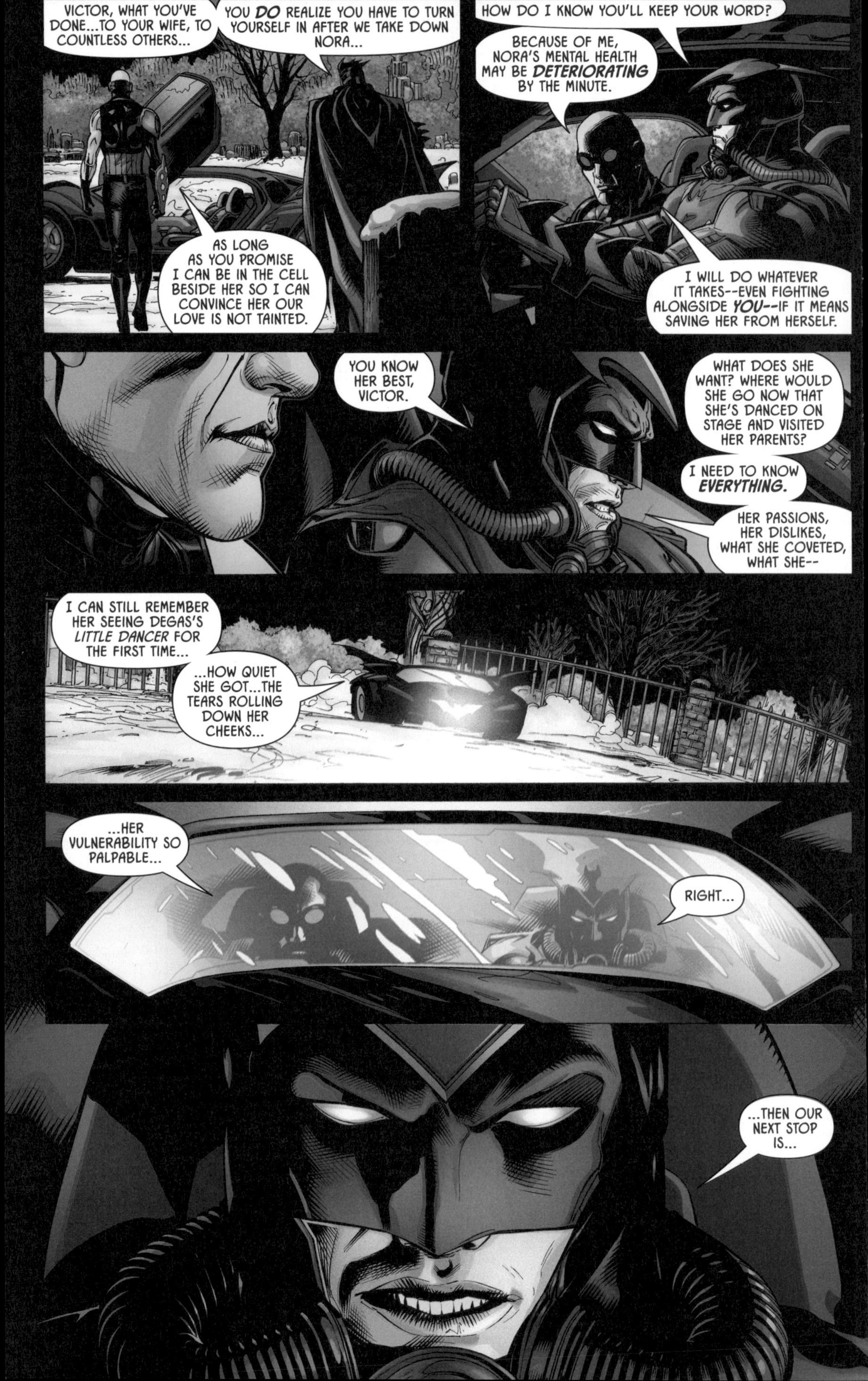
VICTOR, WHAT YOU'VE DONE...TO YOUR WIFE, TO COUNTLESS OTHERS...
YOU *DO* REALIZE YOU HAVE TO TURN YOURSELF IN AFTER WE TAKE DOWN NORA...
AS LONG AS YOU PROMISE I CAN BE IN THE CELL BESIDE HER SO I CAN CONVINCE HER OUR LOVE IS NOT TAINTED.
HOW DO I KNOW YOU'LL KEEP YOUR WORD?
BECAUSE OF ME, NORA'S MENTAL HEALTH MAY BE *DETERIORATING* BY THE MINUTE.
I WILL DO WHATEVER IT TAKES--EVEN FIGHTING ALONGSIDE *YOU*--IF IT MEANS SAVING HER FROM HERSELF.
YOU KNOW HER BEST, VICTOR.
WHAT DOES SHE WANT? WHERE WOULD SHE GO NOW THAT SHE'S DANCED ON STAGE AND VISITED HER PARENTS?
I NEED TO KNOW *EVERYTHING.*
HER PASSIONS, HER DISLIKES, WHAT SHE COVETED, WHAT SHE--
I CAN STILL REMEMBER HER SEEING DEGAS'S *LITTLE DANCER* FOR THE FIRST TIME...
...HOW QUIET SHE GOT...THE TEARS ROLLING DOWN HER CHEEKS...
...HER VULNERABILITY SO PALPABLE...
RIGHT...
...THEN OUR NEXT STOP IS...

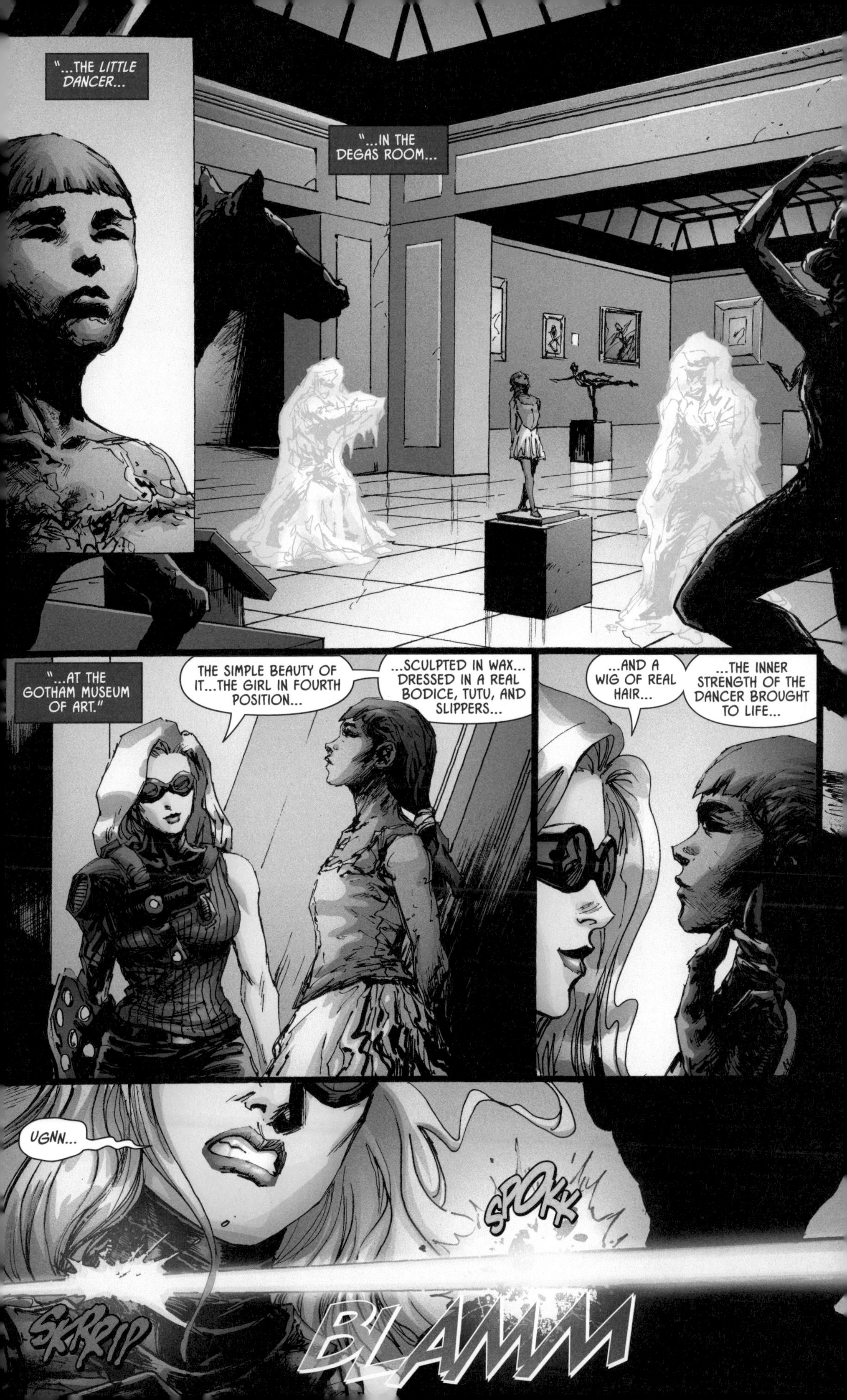
"...THE *LITTLE* DANCER...
"...IN THE DEGAS ROOM...
"...AT THE GOTHAM MUSEUM OF ART."
THE SIMPLE BEAUTY OF IT...THE GIRL IN FOURTH POSITION...
...SCULPTED IN WAX... DRESSED IN A REAL BODICE, TUTU, AND SLIPPERS...
...AND A WIG OF REAL HAIR...
...THE INNER STRENGTH OF THE DANCER BROUGHT TO LIFE...
UGNN...
SPOKK
SKRRIP
BLAMM

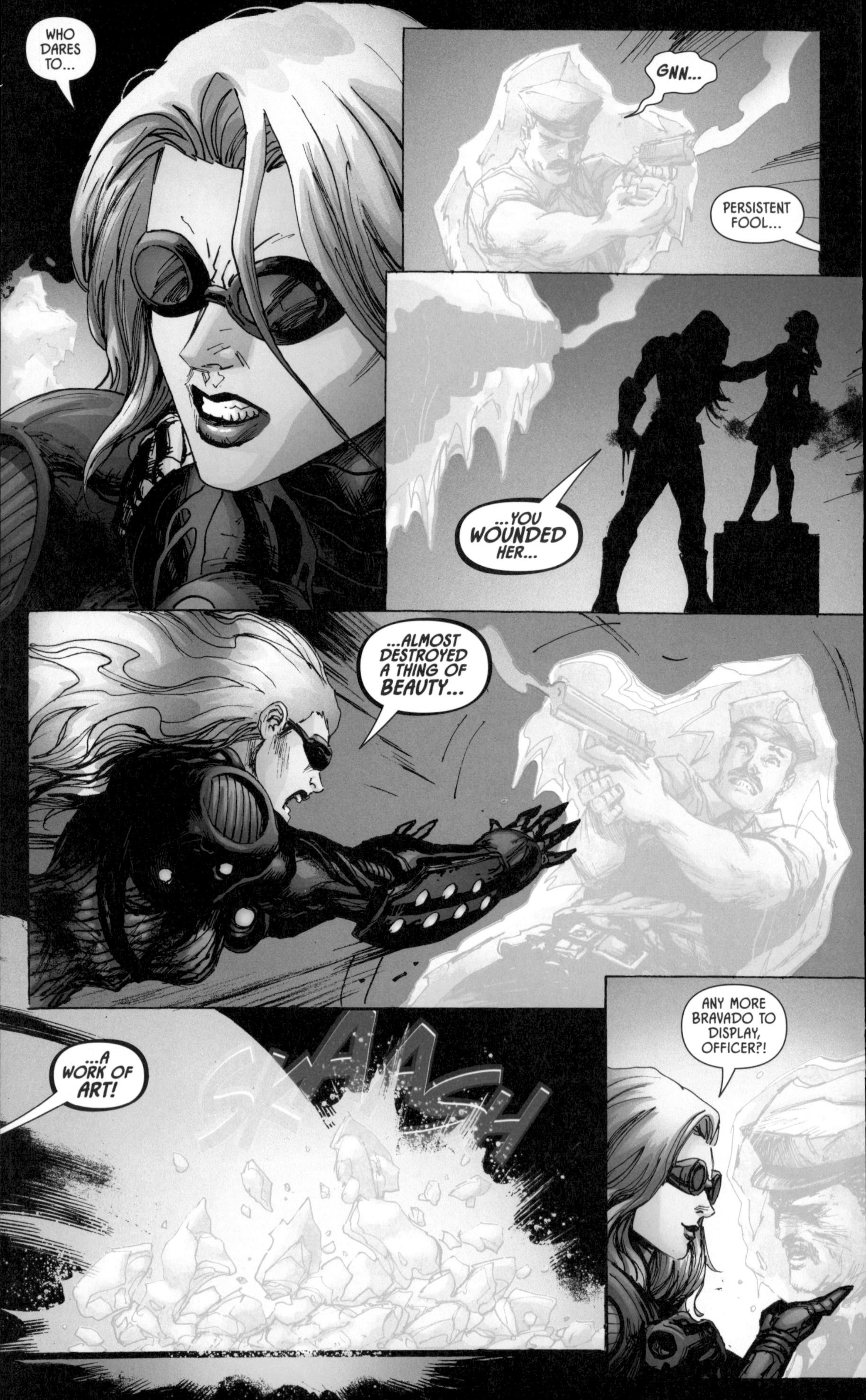
WHO DARES TO...
GNN...
PERSISTENT FOOL...
...YOU WOUNDED HER...
...ALMOST DESTROYED A THING OF BEAUTY...
...A WORK OF ART!
SMASH
ANY MORE BRAVADO TO DISPLAY, OFFICER?!

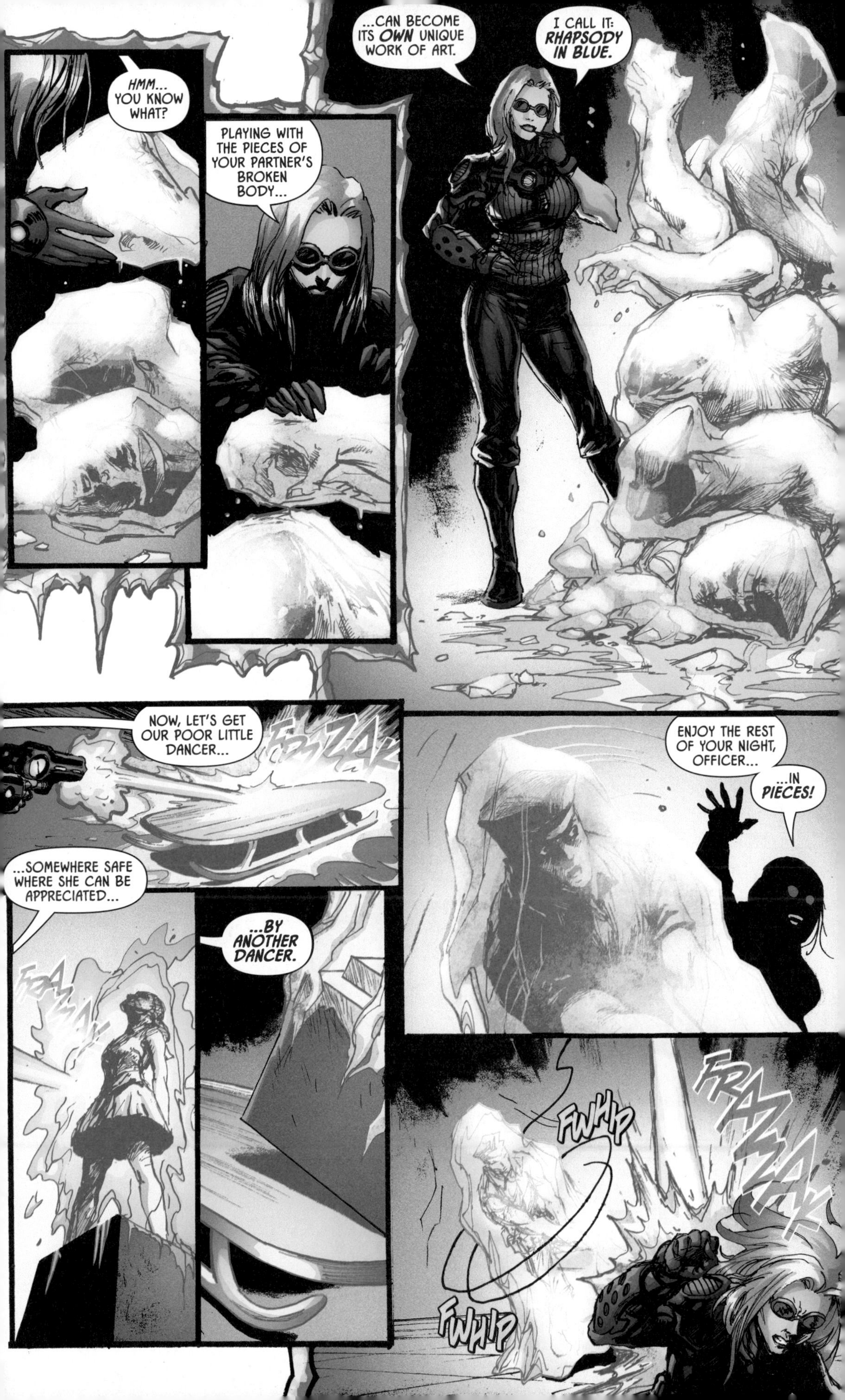
HMM... YOU KNOW WHAT?
PLAYING WITH THE PIECES OF YOUR PARTNER'S BROKEN BODY...
...CAN BECOME ITS OWN UNIQUE WORK OF ART.
I CALL IT: RHAPSODY IN BLUE.
NOW, LET'S GET OUR POOR LITTLE DANCER...
FRAZAK
...SOMEWHERE SAFE WHERE SHE CAN BE APPRECIATED...
...BY ANOTHER DANCER.
ENJOY THE REST OF YOUR NIGHT, OFFICER...
...IN PIECES!
FWHIP
FRAZAK
FWHIP

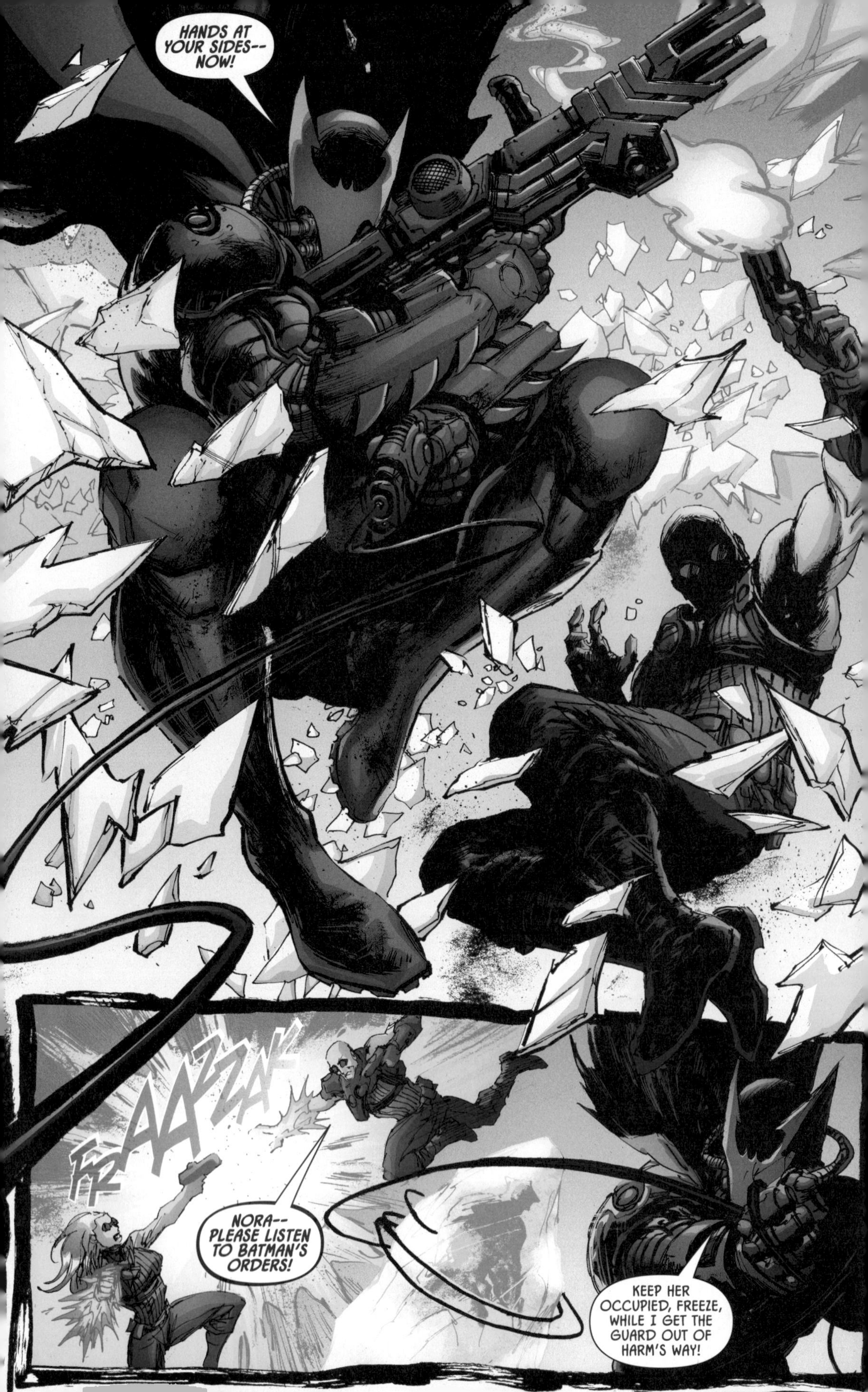
HANDS AT YOUR SIDES-- NOW!
FRAAZZAK
NORA-- PLEASE LISTEN TO BATMAN'S ORDERS!
KEEP HER OCCUPIED, FREEZE, WHILE I GET THE GUARD OUT OF HARM'S WAY!

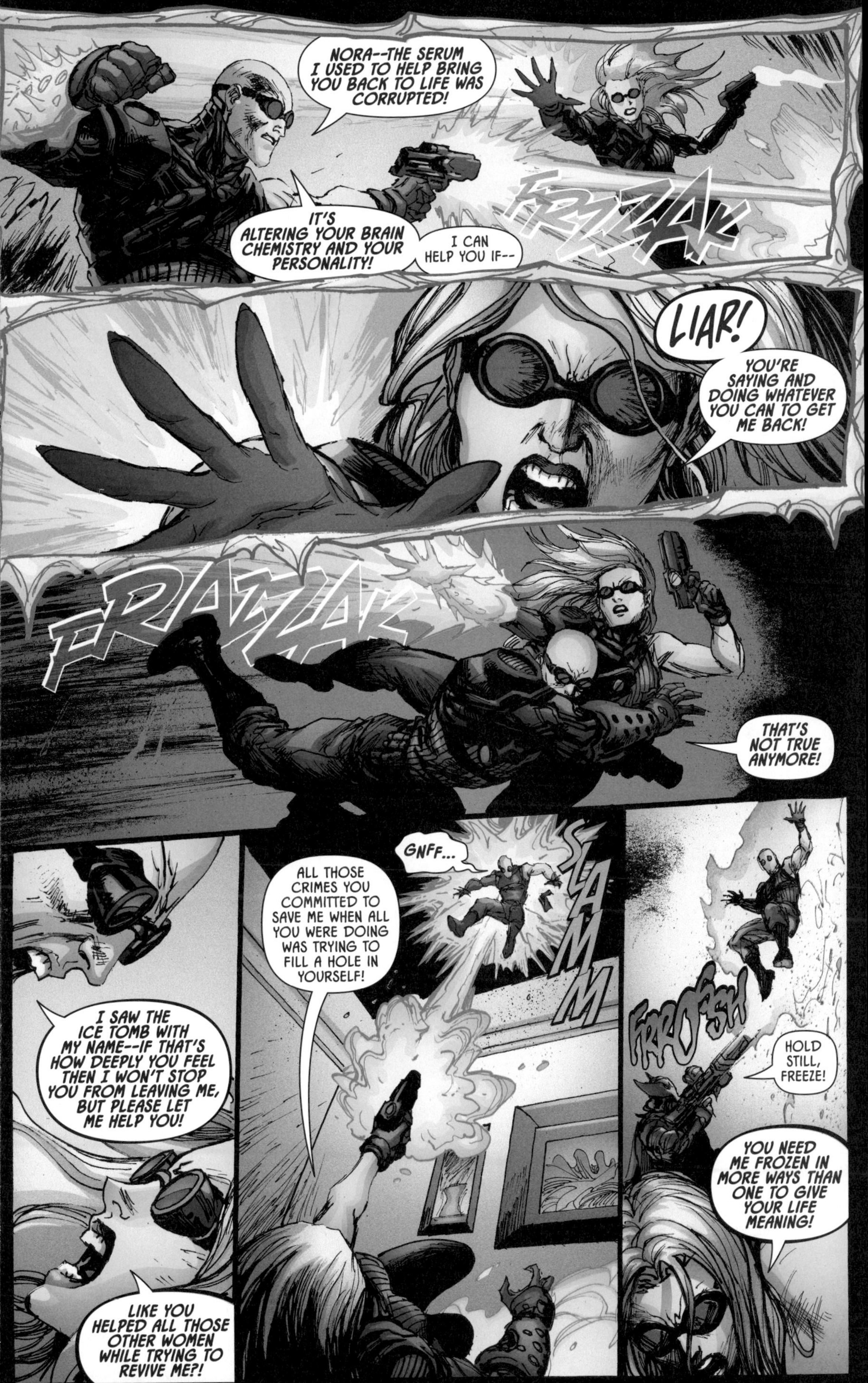
NORA--THE SERUM I USED TO HELP BRING YOU BACK TO LIFE WAS CORRUPTED!
IT'S ALTERING YOUR BRAIN CHEMISTRY AND YOUR PERSONALITY!
I CAN HELP YOU IF--
FRZZAK
LIAR!
YOU'RE SAYING AND DOING WHATEVER YOU CAN TO GET ME BACK!
FRAZZAK
THAT'S NOT TRUE ANYMORE!
I SAW THE ICE TOMB WITH MY NAME--IF THAT'S HOW DEEPLY YOU FEEL THEN I WON'T STOP YOU FROM LEAVING ME, BUT PLEASE LET ME HELP YOU!
LIKE YOU HELPED ALL THOSE OTHER WOMEN WHILE TRYING TO REVIVE ME?!
GNFF...
SLAMM
ALL THOSE CRIMES YOU COMMITTED TO SAVE ME WHEN ALL YOU WERE DOING WAS TRYING TO FILL A HOLE IN YOURSELF!
FRROOSH
HOLD STILL, FREEZE!
YOU NEED ME FROZEN IN MORE WAYS THAN ONE TO GIVE YOUR LIFE MEANING!

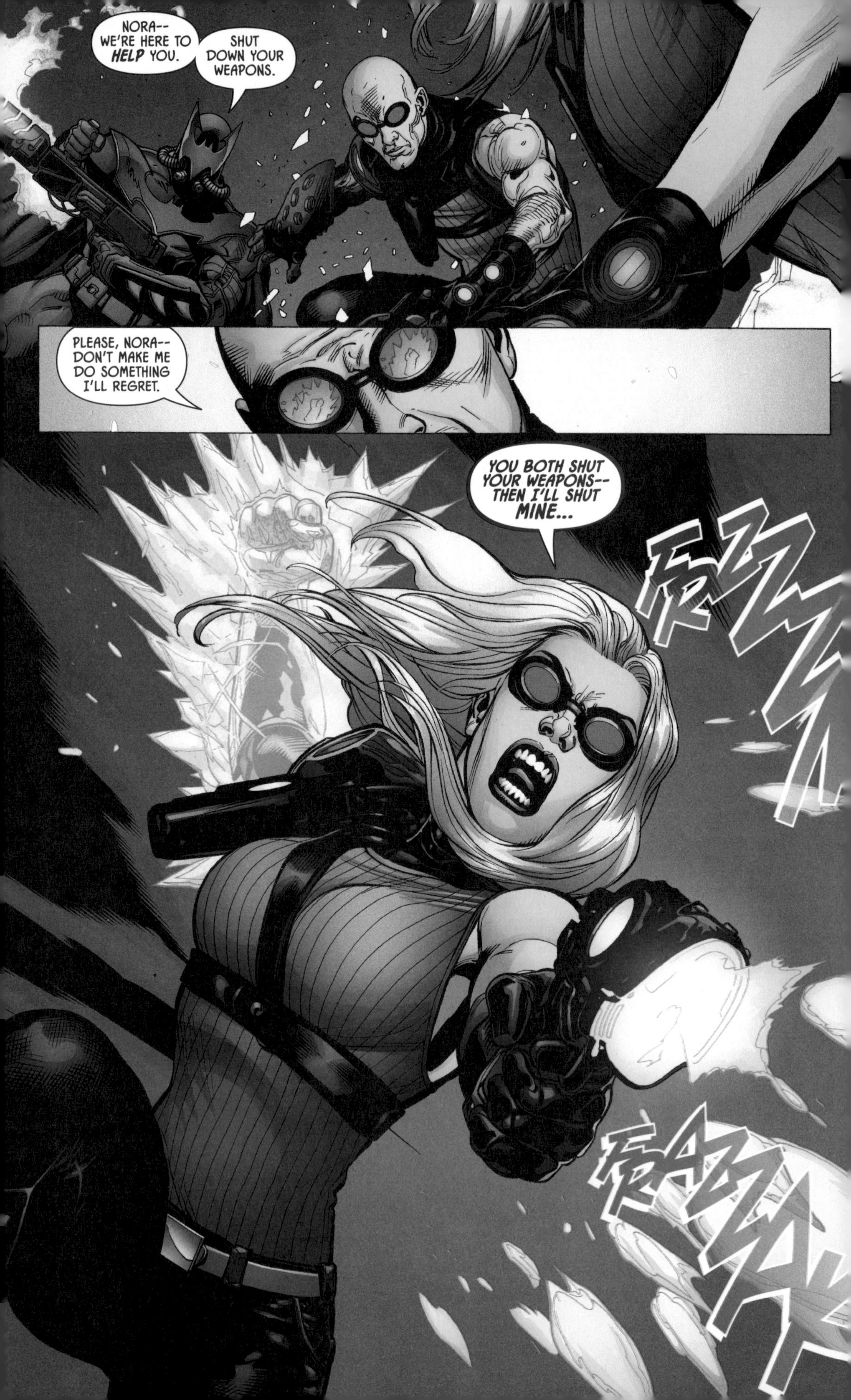
NORA-- WE'RE HERE TO HELP YOU.
SHUT DOWN YOUR WEAPONS.
PLEASE, NORA-- DON'T MAKE ME DO SOMETHING I'LL REGRET.
YOU BOTH SHUT YOUR WEAPONS-- THEN I'LL SHUT MINE...
FRZZZ
FRAZZ

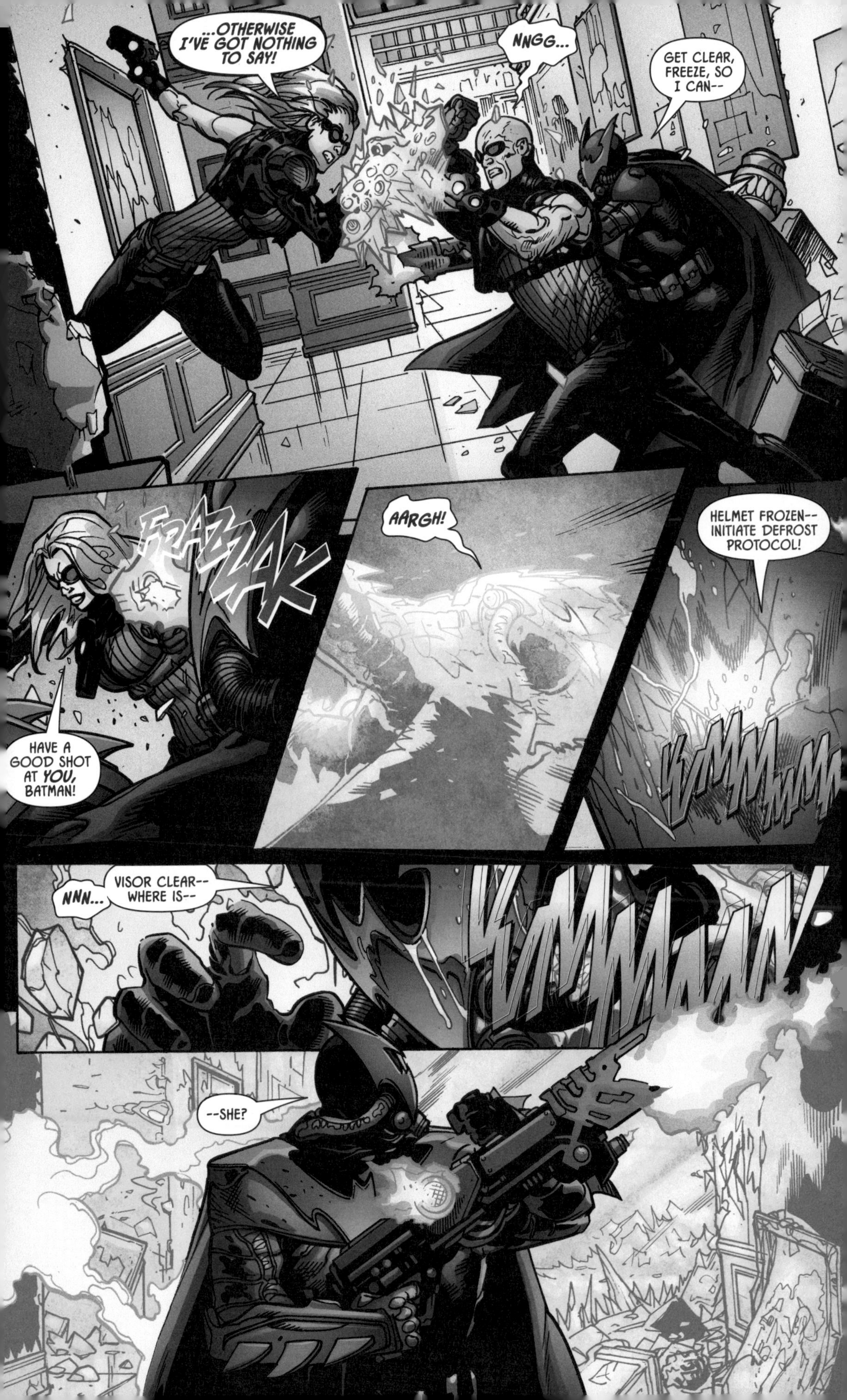
...OTHERWISE I'VE GOT NOTHING TO SAY!
NNGG...
GET CLEAR, FREEZE, SO I CAN--
FRAZZAK
HAVE A GOOD SHOT AT YOU, BATMAN!
AARGH!
HELMET FROZEN-- INITIATE DEFROST PROTOCOL!
VMMMMMM
NNN...
VISOR CLEAR-- WHERE IS--
--SHE?

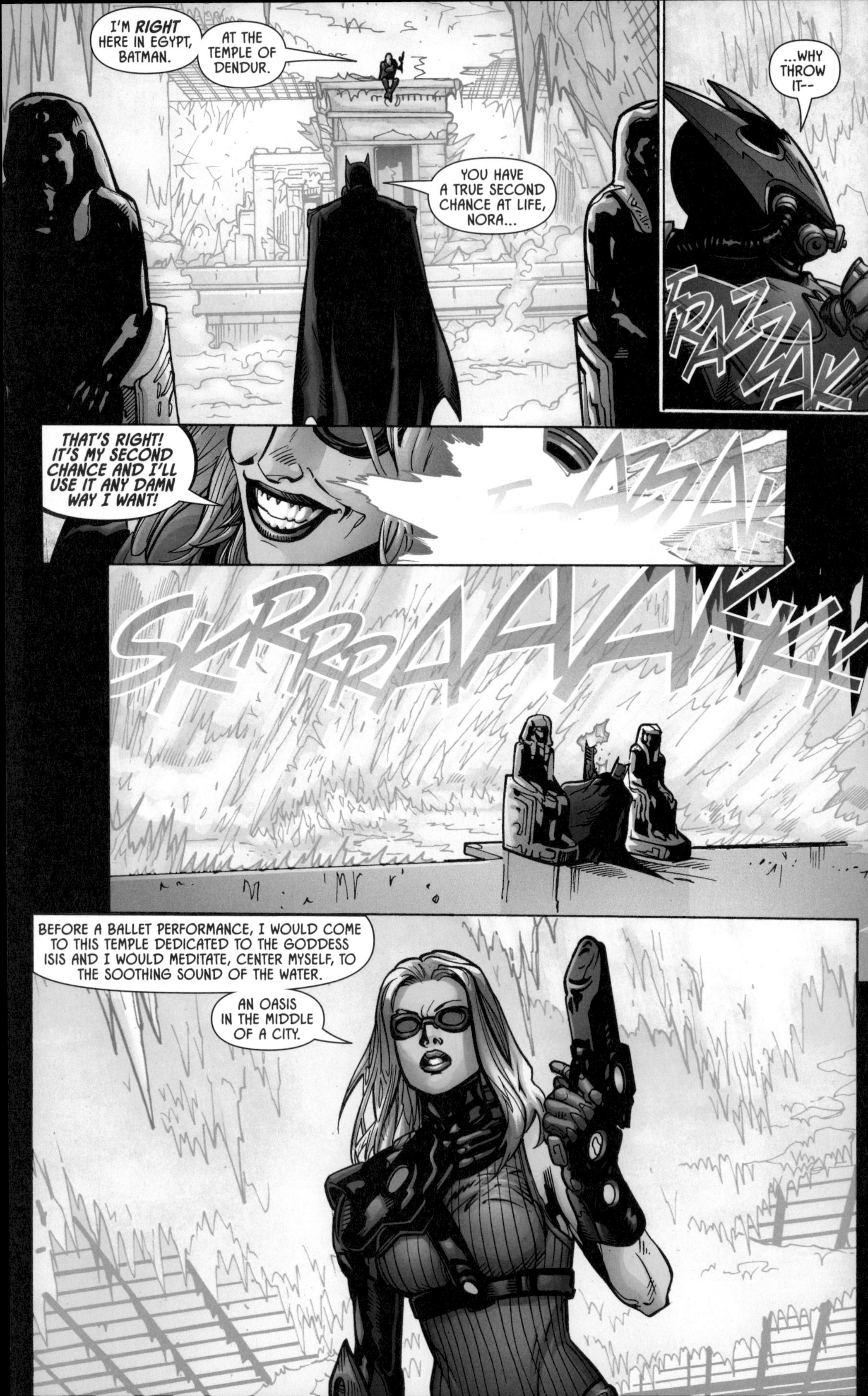

I'M RIGHT HERE IN EGYPT, BATMAN.
AT THE TEMPLE OF DENDUR.
YOU HAVE A TRUE SECOND CHANCE AT LIFE, NORA...
...WHY THROW IT--
FRAZZAK
THAT'S RIGHT! IT'S MY SECOND CHANCE AND I'LL USE IT ANY DAMN WAY I WANT!
SKRRRAAAAKK
BEFORE A BALLET PERFORMANCE, I WOULD COME TO THIS TEMPLE DEDICATED TO THE GODDESS ISIS AND I WOULD MEDITATE, CENTER MYSELF, TO THE SOOTHING SOUND OF THE WATER.
AN OASIS IN THE MIDDLE OF A CITY.

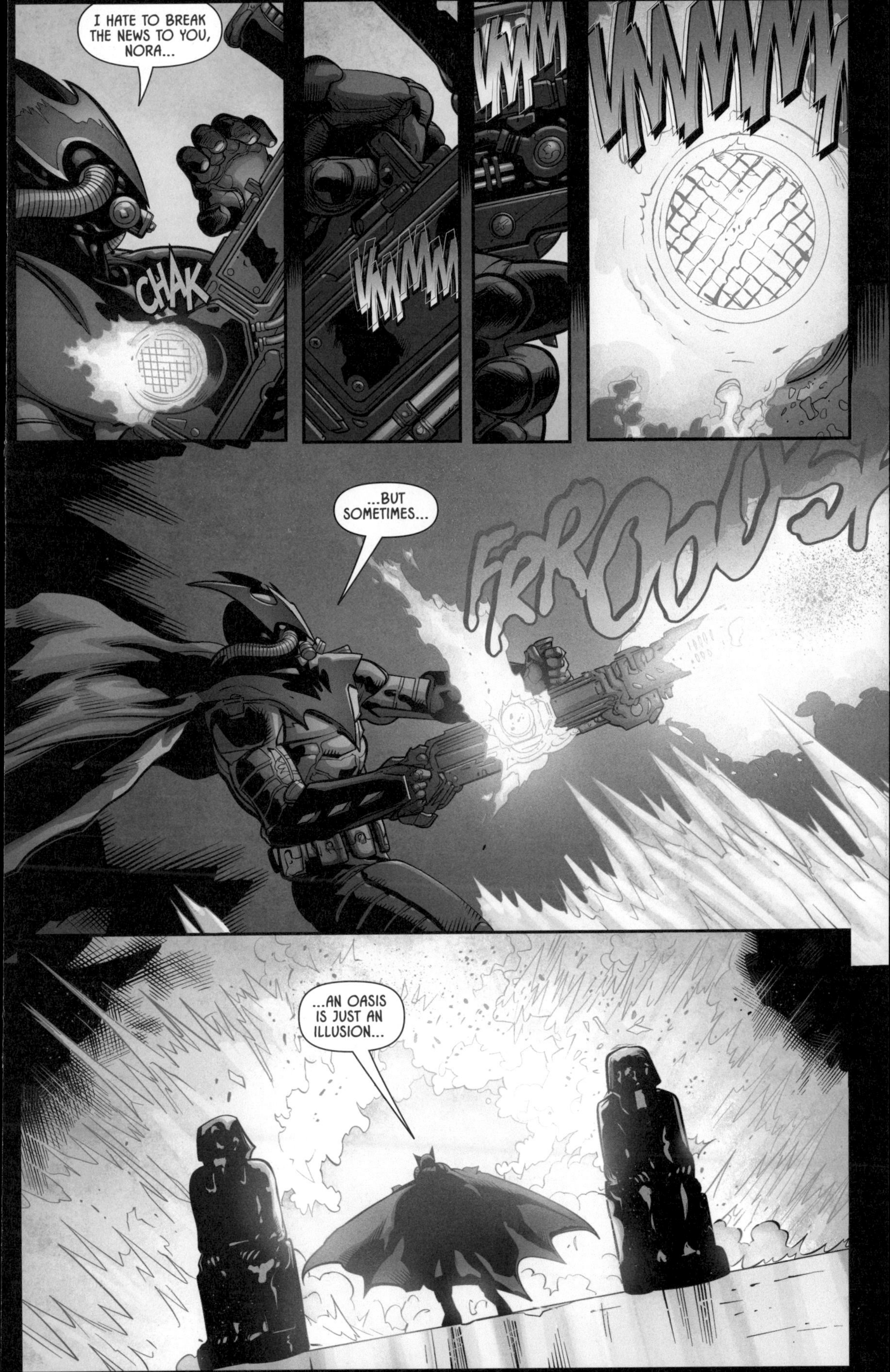
I HATE TO BREAK THE NEWS TO YOU, NORA...
CHAK
VMMM
VMMM
VMMMM
...BUT SOMETIMES...
FRROOOSH
...AN OASIS IS JUST AN ILLUSION...

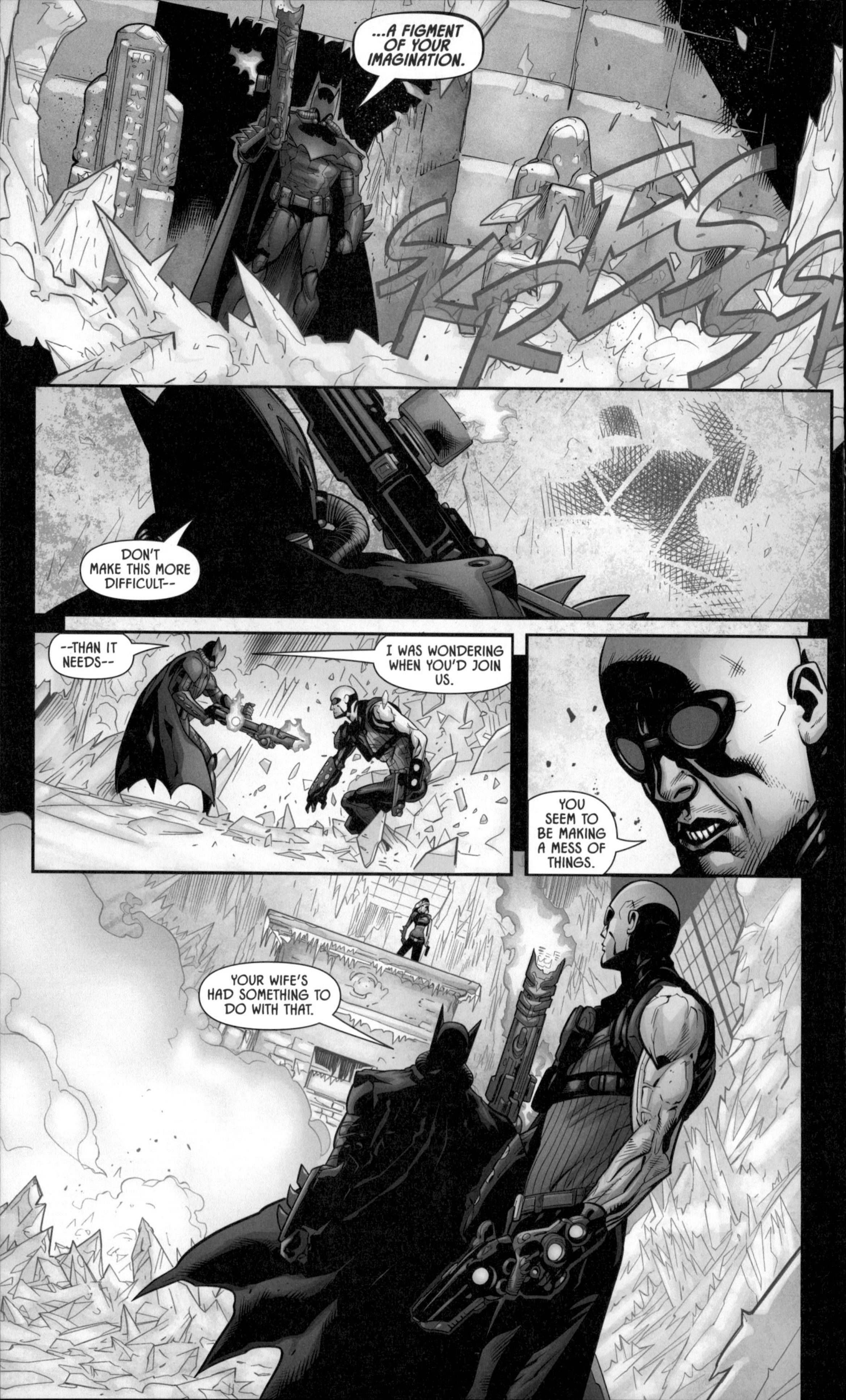
...A FIGMENT OF YOUR IMAGINATION.
SKRESSH
DON'T MAKE THIS MORE DIFFICULT--
--THAN IT NEEDS--
I WAS WONDERING WHEN YOU'D JOIN US.
YOU SEEM TO BE MAKING A MESS OF THINGS.
YOUR WIFE'S HAD SOMETHING TO DO WITH THAT.

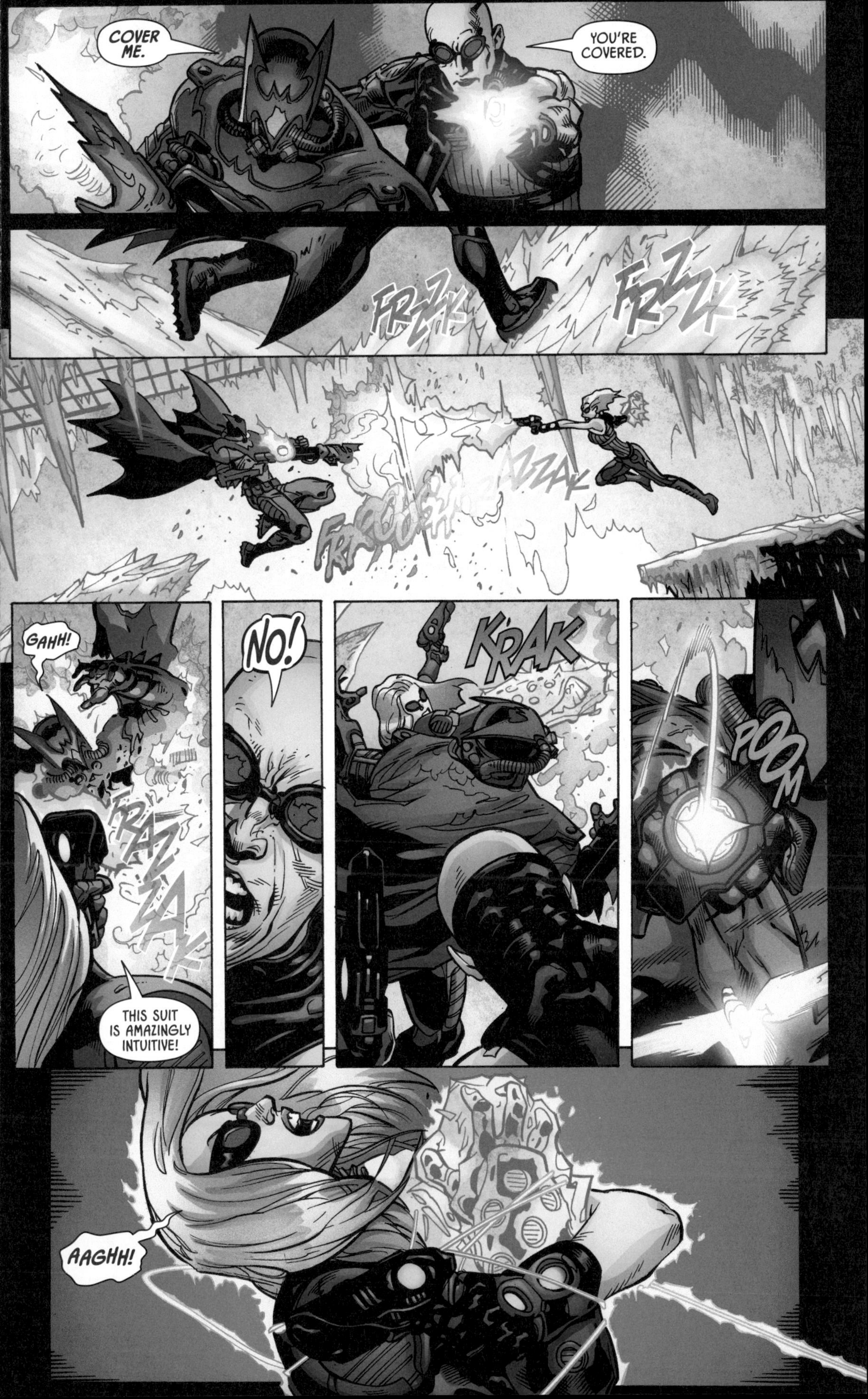
COVER ME.
YOU'RE COVERED.
FRZZZK
FRZZZK
FRZOOSH
FRAZZAK
GAHH!
FRAZZAK
THIS SUIT IS AMAZINGLY INTUITIVE!
NO!
KRAK
POOM
AAGHH!

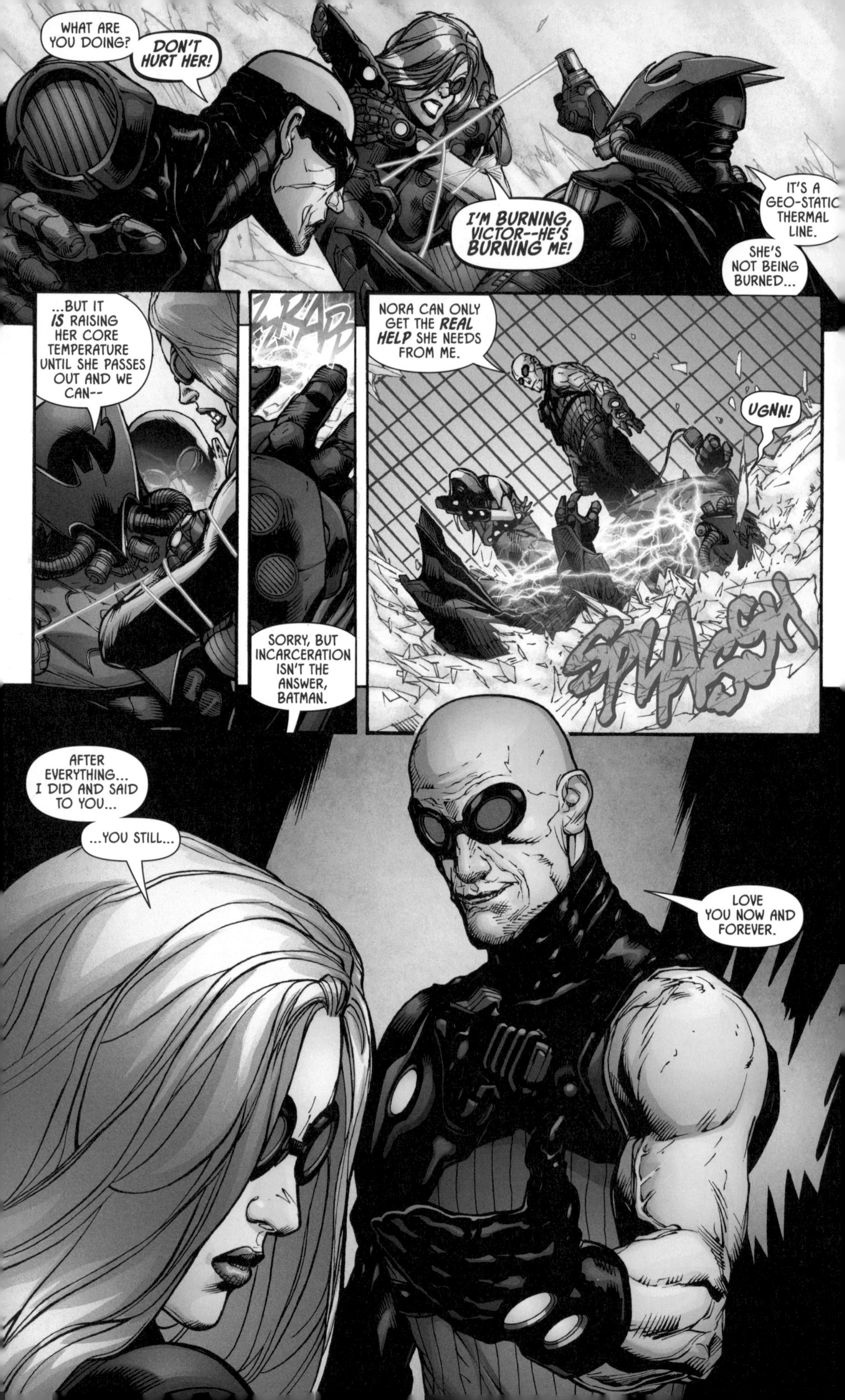

WHAT ARE YOU DOING? DON'T HURT HER!
I'M BURNING, VICTOR--HE'S BURNING ME!
IT'S A GEO-STATIC THERMAL LINE.
SHE'S NOT BEING BURNED...
...BUT IT IS RAISING HER CORE TEMPERATURE UNTIL SHE PASSES OUT AND WE CAN--
SORRY, BUT INCARCERATION ISN'T THE ANSWER, BATMAN.
NORA CAN ONLY GET THE REAL HELP SHE NEEDS FROM ME.
UGNN!
SPLASH
AFTER EVERYTHING... I DID AND SAID TO YOU...
...YOU STILL...
LOVE YOU NOW AND FOREVER.

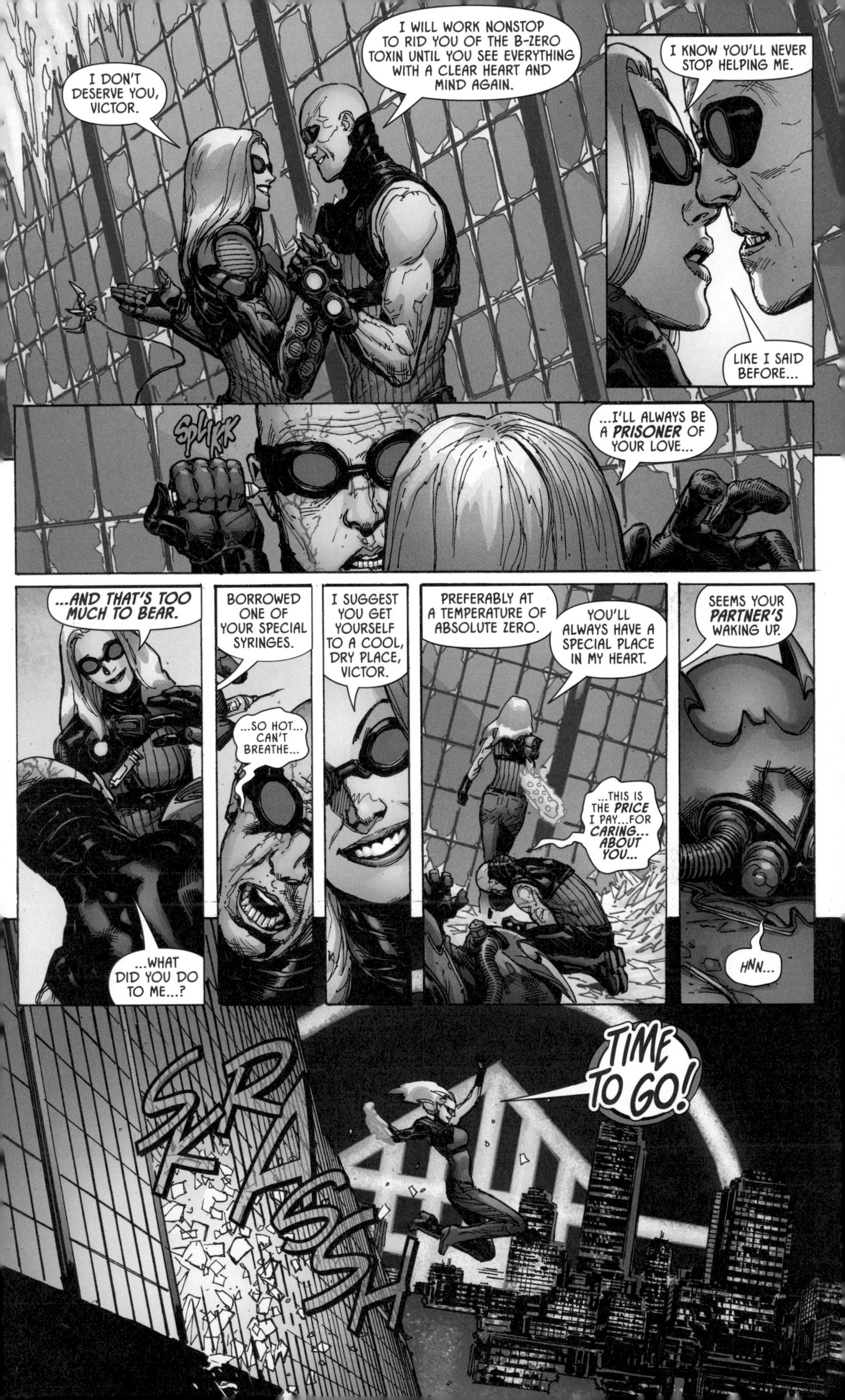
I DON'T DESERVE YOU, VICTOR.
I WILL WORK NONSTOP TO RID YOU OF THE B-ZERO TOXIN UNTIL YOU SEE EVERYTHING WITH A CLEAR HEART AND MIND AGAIN.
I KNOW YOU'LL NEVER STOP HELPING ME.
LIKE I SAID BEFORE...
SPLIKK
...I'LL ALWAYS BE A PRISONER OF YOUR LOVE...
...AND THAT'S TOO MUCH TO BEAR.
...WHAT DID YOU DO TO ME...?
BORROWED ONE OF YOUR SPECIAL SYRINGES.
...SO HOT... CAN'T BREATHE...
I SUGGEST YOU GET YOURSELF TO A COOL, DRY PLACE, VICTOR.
PREFERABLY AT A TEMPERATURE OF ABSOLUTE ZERO.
YOU'LL ALWAYS HAVE A SPECIAL PLACE IN MY HEART.
...THIS IS THE PRICE I PAY...FOR CARING... ABOUT YOU...
SEEMS YOUR PARTNER'S WAKING UP.
HNN...
SPLASSH
TIME TO GO!

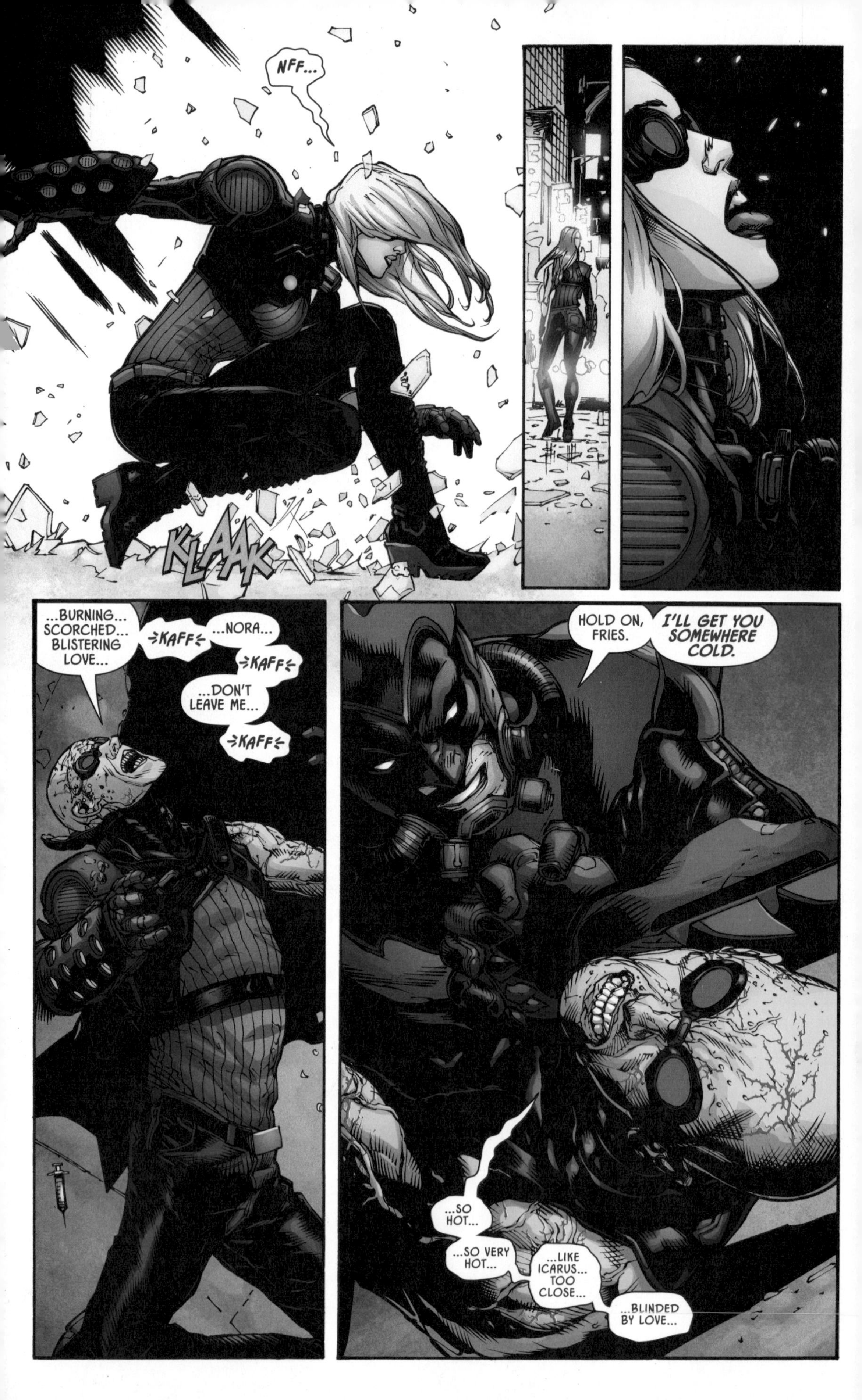
NFF...
KLAAK
...BURNING... SCORCHED... BLISTERING LOVE...
KAFF
...NORA...
KAFF
...DON'T LEAVE ME...
KAFF
HOLD ON, FRIES.
I'LL GET YOU SOMEWHERE COLD.
...SO HOT...
...SO VERY HOT...
...LIKE ICARUS... TOO CLOSE...
...BLINDED BY LOVE...

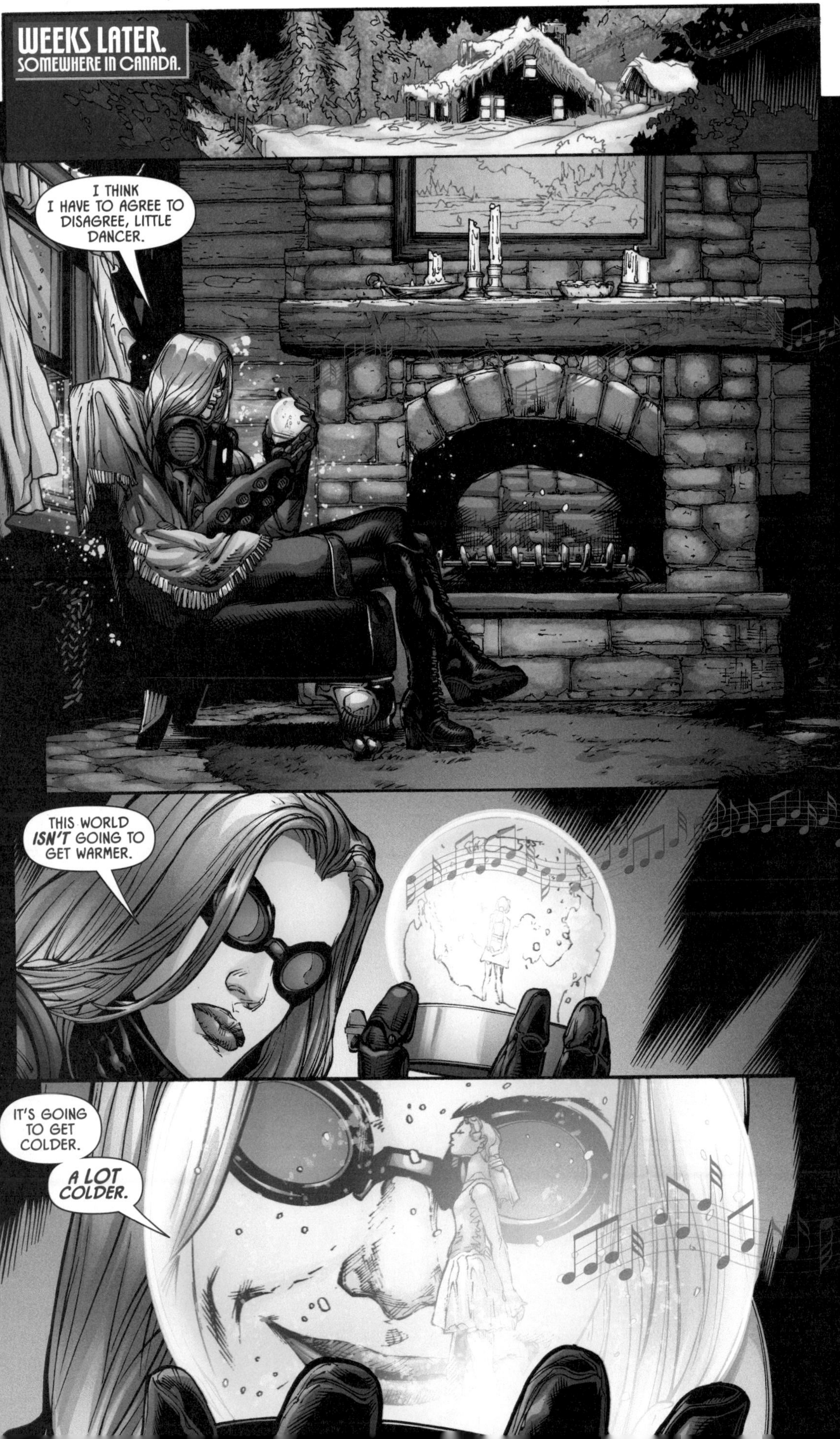
WEEKS LATER.
SOMEWHERE IN CANADA.
I THINK I HAVE TO AGREE TO DISAGREE, LITTLE DANCER.
THIS WORLD *ISN'T* GOING TO GET WARMER.
IT'S GOING TO GET COLDER.
A LOT COLDER.

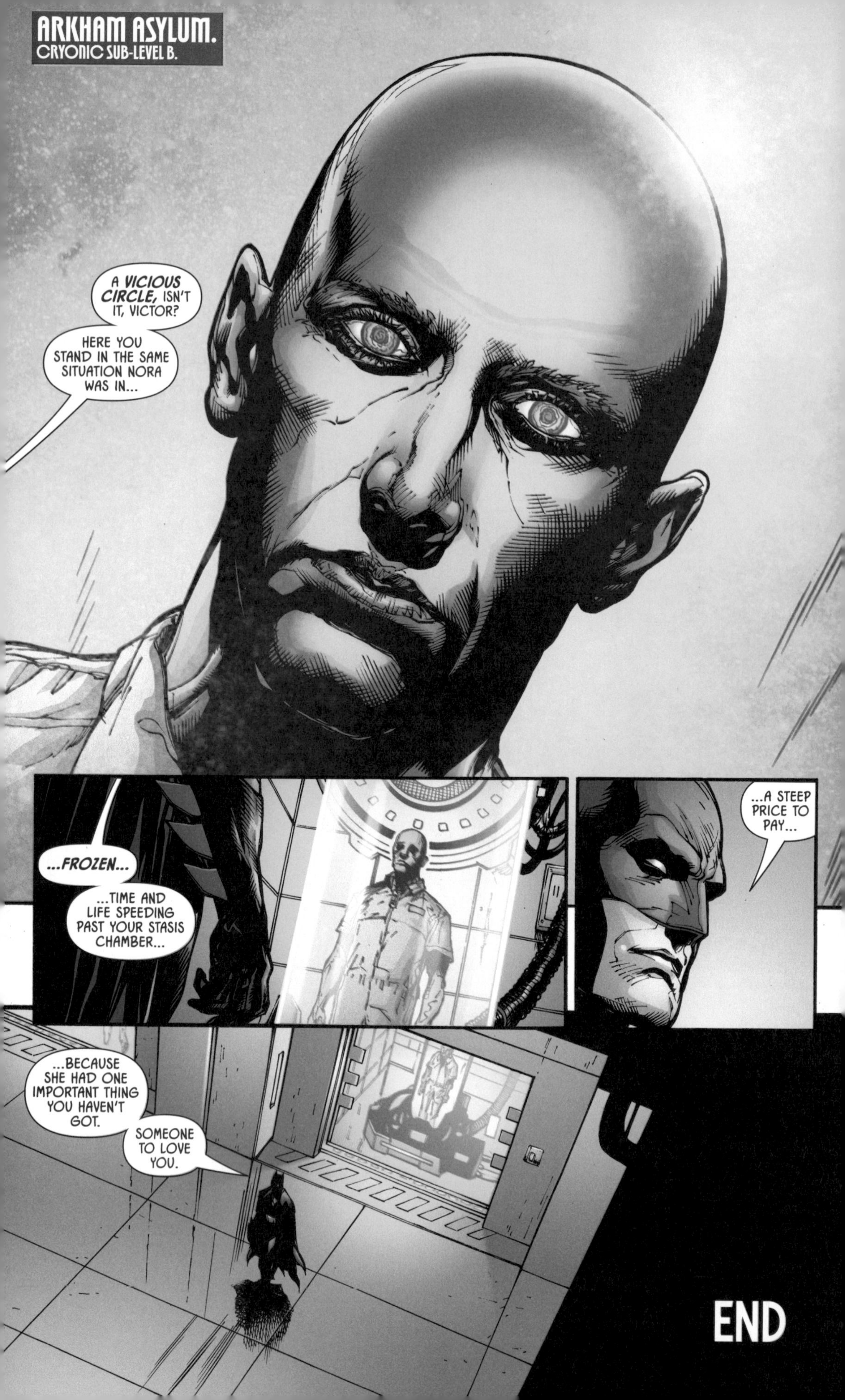
ARKHAM ASYLUM.
CRYONIC SUB-LEVEL B.
A VICIOUS CIRCLE, ISN'T IT, VICTOR?
HERE YOU STAND IN THE SAME SITUATION NORA WAS IN...
...FROZEN...
...TIME AND LIFE SPEEDING PAST YOUR STASIS CHAMBER...
...A STEEP PRICE TO PAY...
...BECAUSE SHE HAD ONE IMPORTANT THING YOU HAVEN'T GOT.
SOMEONE TO LOVE YOU.
END

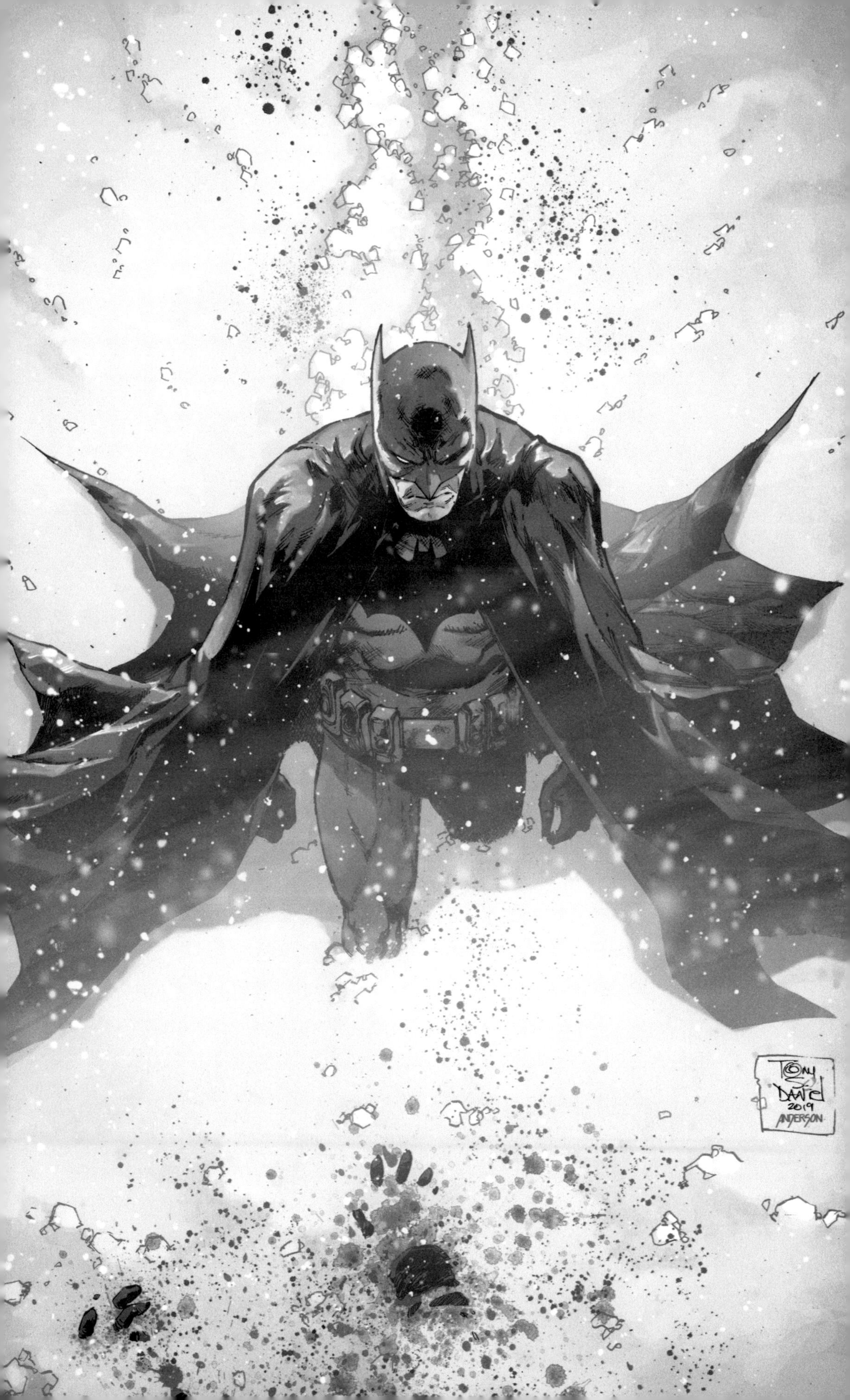
2019
ANDERSON

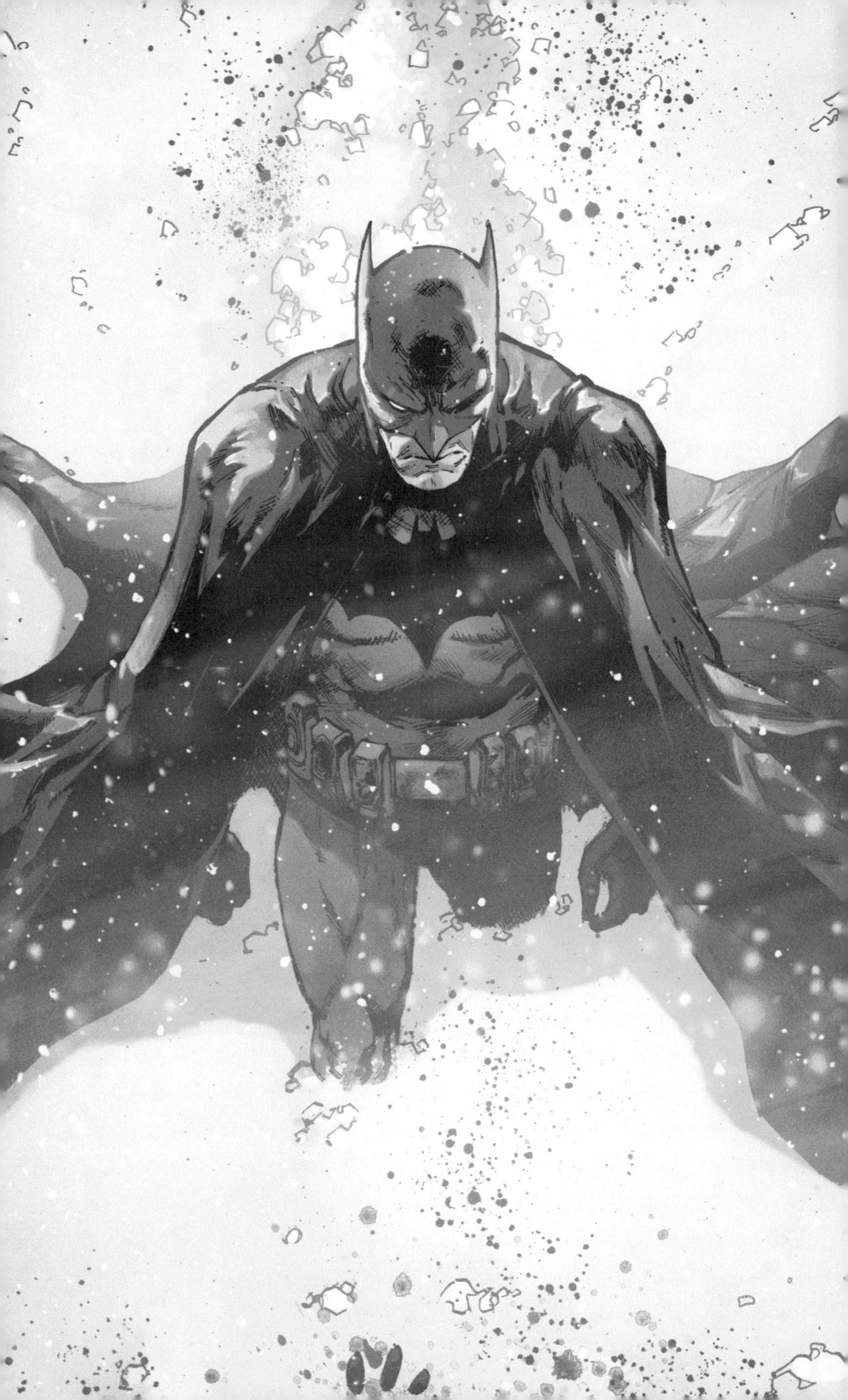

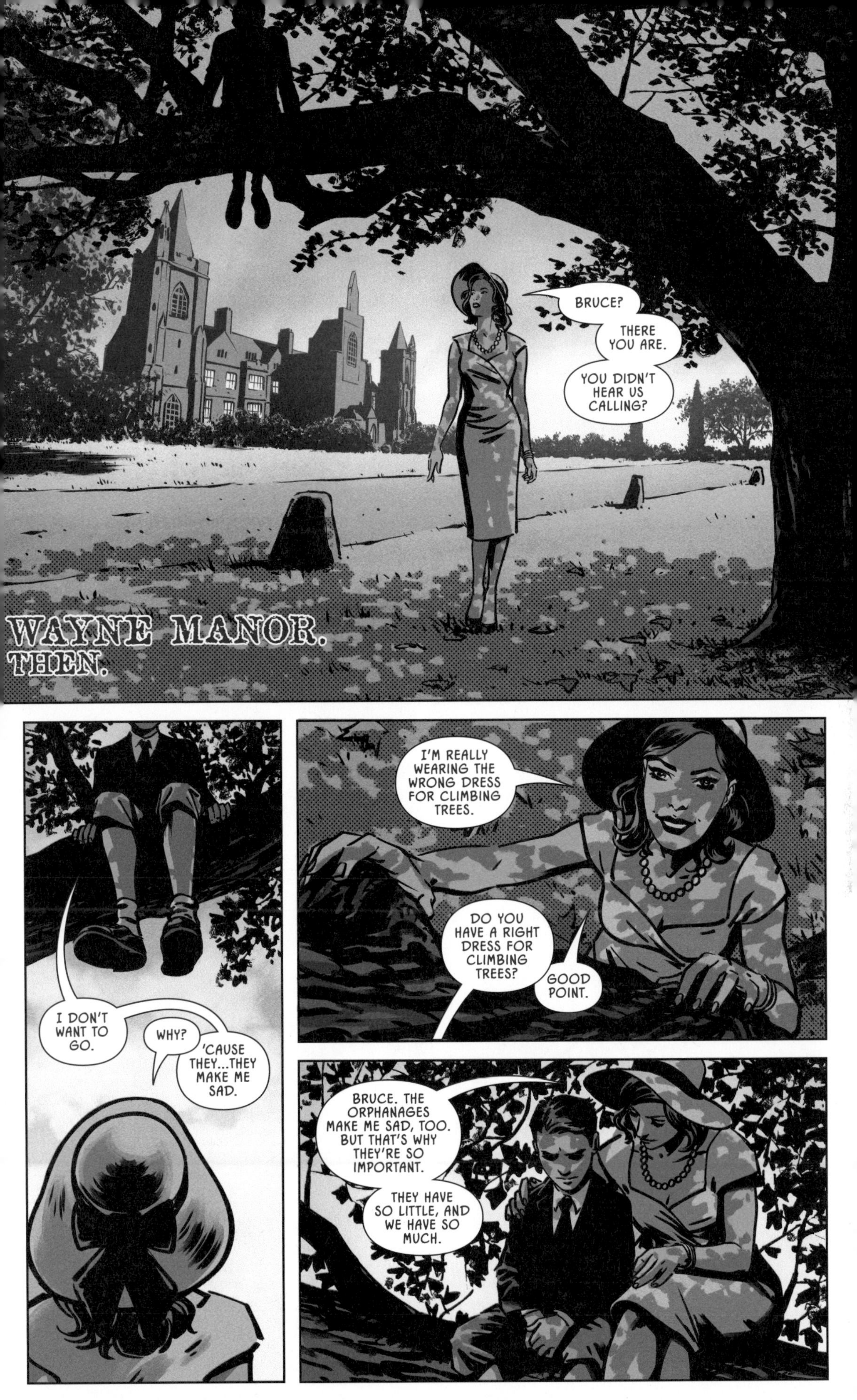
BRUCE?
THERE YOU ARE.
YOU DIDN'T HEAR US CALLING?
WAYNE MANOR. THEN.
I DON'T WANT TO GO.
WHY?
'CAUSE THEY...THEY MAKE ME SAD.
I'M REALLY WEARING THE WRONG DRESS FOR CLIMBING TREES.
DO YOU HAVE A RIGHT DRESS FOR CLIMBING TREES?
GOOD POINT.
BRUCE. THE ORPHANAGES MAKE ME SAD, TOO. BUT THAT'S WHY THEY'RE SO IMPORTANT.
THEY HAVE SO LITTLE, AND WE HAVE SO MUCH.

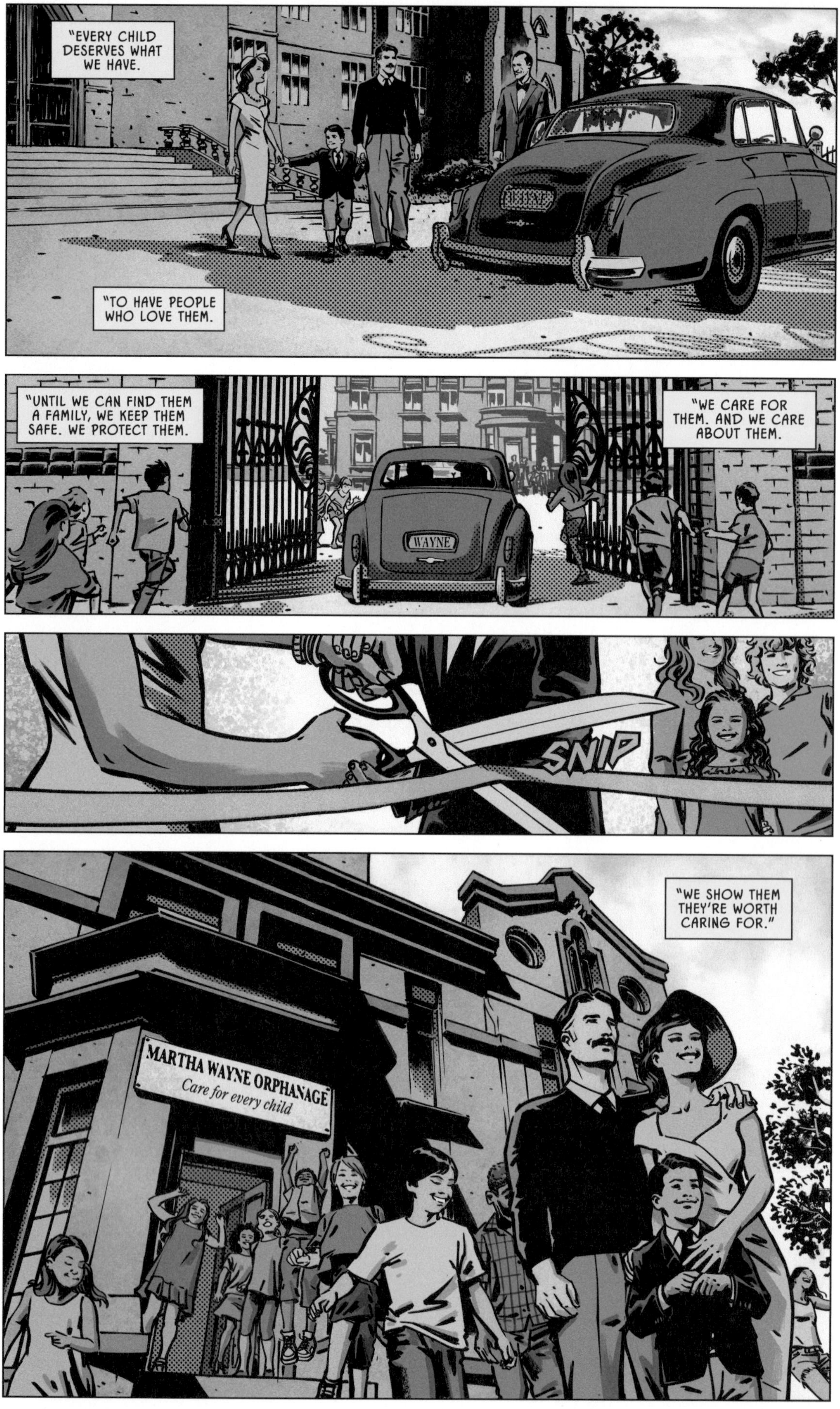
"EVERY CHILD DESERVES WHAT WE HAVE.
"TO HAVE PEOPLE WHO LOVE THEM.
"UNTIL WE CAN FIND THEM A FAMILY, WE KEEP THEM SAFE. WE PROTECT THEM.
WAYNE
"WE CARE FOR THEM. AND WE CARE ABOUT THEM.
SNIP
"WE SHOW THEM THEY'RE WORTH CARING FOR."
MARTHA WAYNE ORPHANAGE
Care for every child

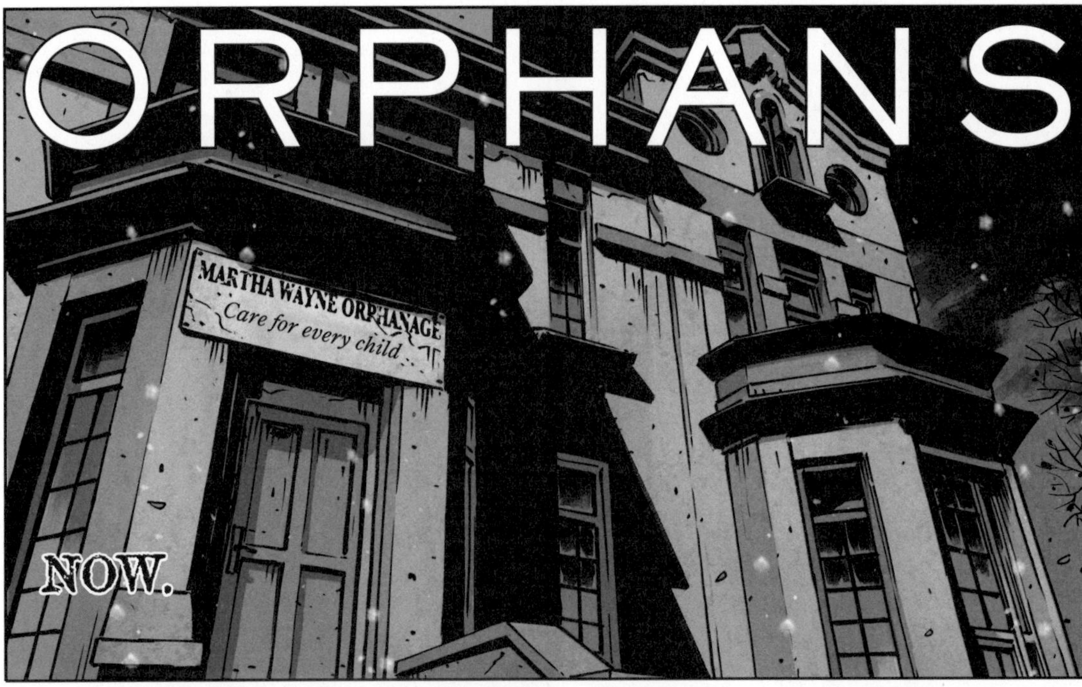
ORPHANS
MARTHA WAYNE ORPHANAGE
Care for every child
NOW.

TOM TAYLOR writer FERNANDO BLANCO artist JOHN KALISZ colorist TRAVIS LANHAM letterer

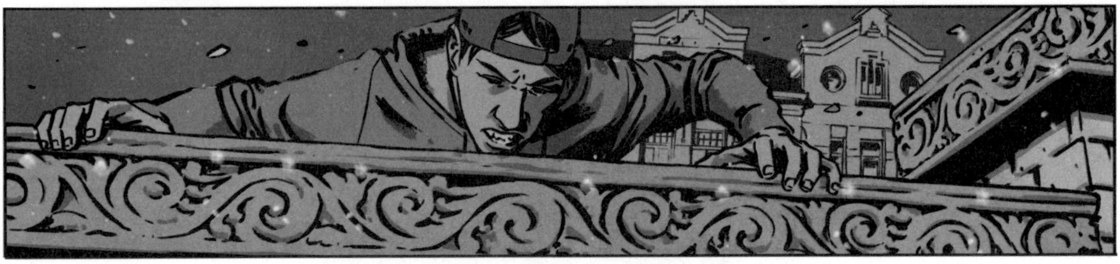

TONY S. DANIEL and BRAD ANDERSON cover
BRITTANY HOLZHERR associate editor JAMIE S. RICH editor

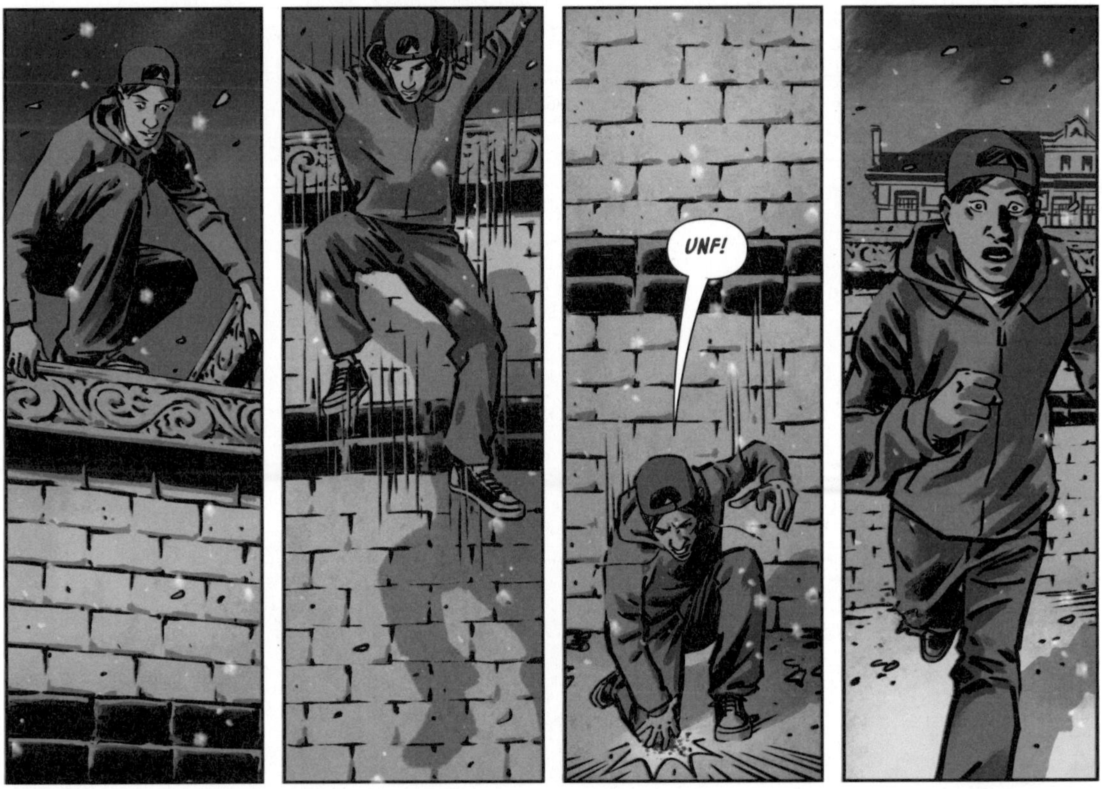
UNF!

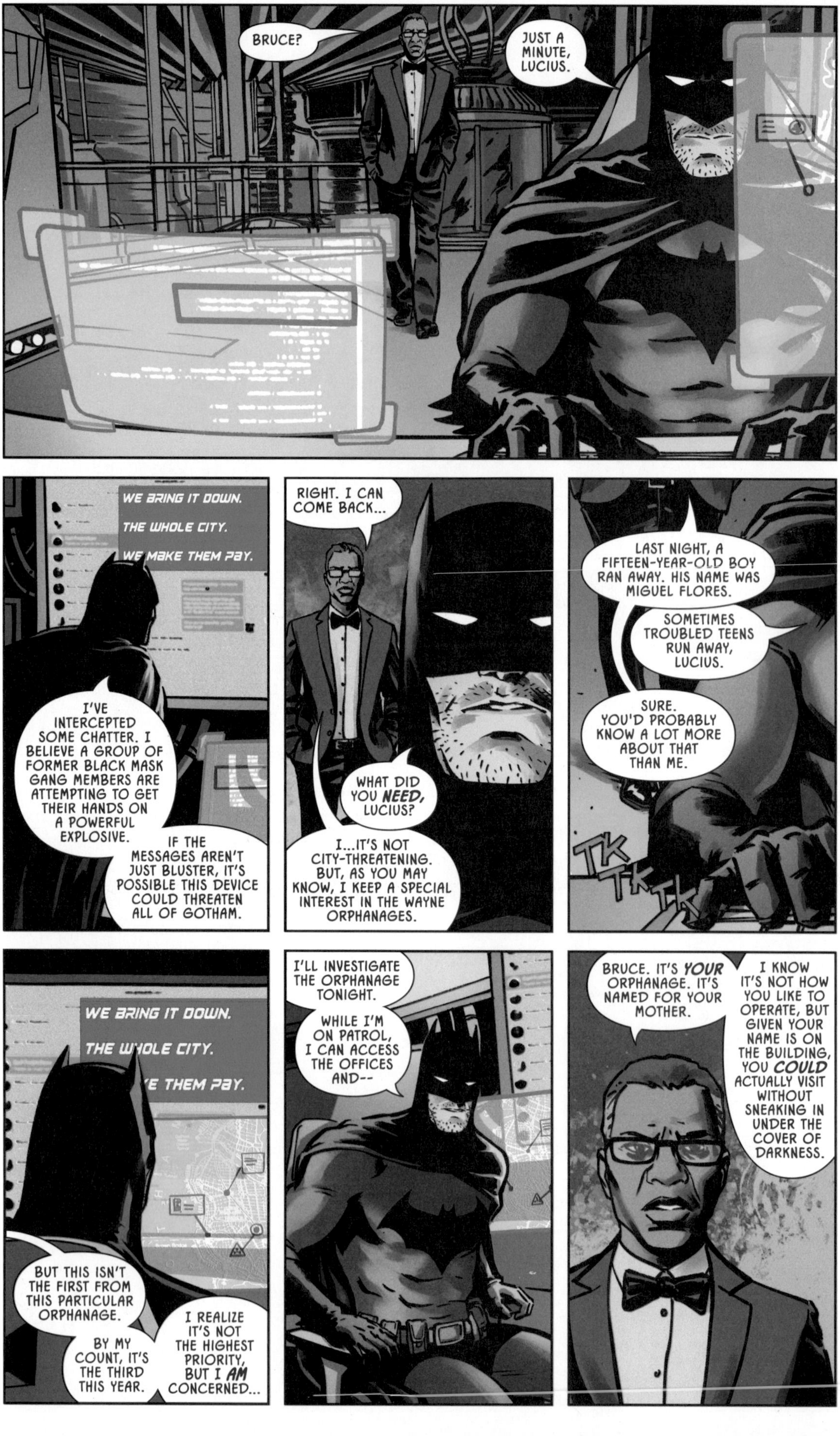
BRUCE?
JUST A MINUTE, LUCIUS.
WE BRING IT DOWN.
THE WHOLE CITY.
WE MAKE THEM PAY.
I'VE INTERCEPTED SOME CHATTER. I BELIEVE A GROUP OF FORMER BLACK MASK GANG MEMBERS ARE ATTEMPTING TO GET THEIR HANDS ON A POWERFUL EXPLOSIVE.
IF THE MESSAGES AREN'T JUST BLUSTER, IT'S POSSIBLE THIS DEVICE COULD THREATEN ALL OF GOTHAM.
RIGHT. I CAN COME BACK...
WHAT DID YOU NEED, LUCIUS?
I...IT'S NOT CITY-THREATENING. BUT, AS YOU MAY KNOW, I KEEP A SPECIAL INTEREST IN THE WAYNE ORPHANAGES.
LAST NIGHT, A FIFTEEN-YEAR-OLD BOY RAN AWAY. HIS NAME WAS MIGUEL FLORES.
SOMETIMES TROUBLED TEENS RUN AWAY, LUCIUS.
SURE. YOU'D PROBABLY KNOW A LOT MORE ABOUT THAT THAN ME.
TK TK TK
WE BRING IT DOWN.
BUT THIS ISN'T THE FIRST FROM THIS PARTICULAR ORPHANAGE.
BY MY COUNT, IT'S THE THIRD THIS YEAR.
I REALIZE IT'S NOT THE HIGHEST PRIORITY, BUT I AM CONCERNED...
I'LL INVESTIGATE THE ORPHANAGE TONIGHT.
WHILE I'M ON PATROL, I CAN ACCESS THE OFFICES AND--
BRUCE. IT'S YOUR ORPHANAGE. IT'S NAMED FOR YOUR MOTHER.
I KNOW IT'S NOT HOW YOU LIKE TO OPERATE, BUT GIVEN YOUR NAME IS ON THE BUILDING, YOU COULD ACTUALLY VISIT WITHOUT SNEAKING IN UNDER THE COVER OF DARKNESS.

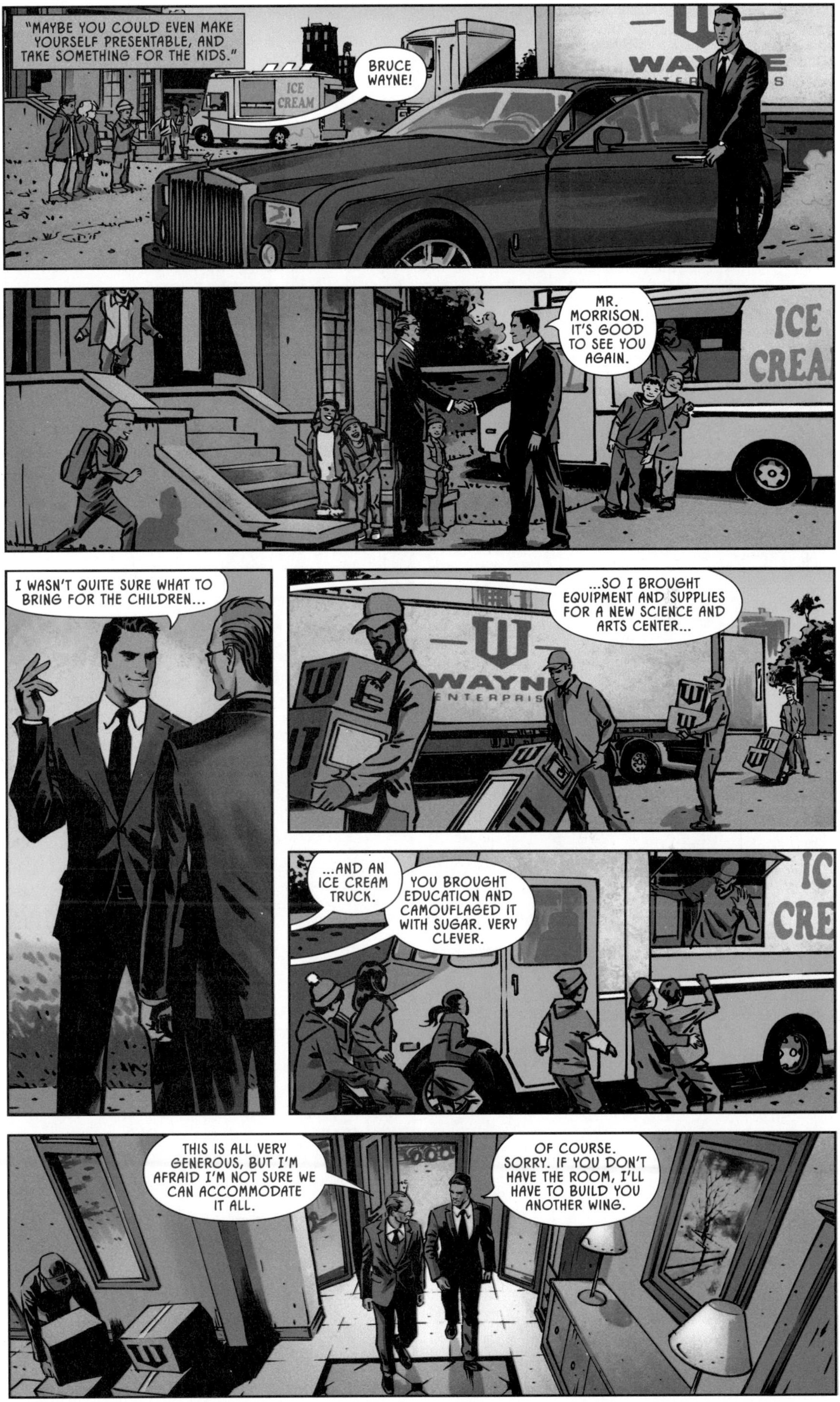
"MAYBE YOU COULD EVEN MAKE YOURSELF PRESENTABLE, AND TAKE SOMETHING FOR THE KIDS."
ICE CREAM
BRUCE WAYNE!
WAYNE ENTERPRISES
MR. MORRISON. IT'S GOOD TO SEE YOU AGAIN.
ICE CREAM
I WASN'T QUITE SURE WHAT TO BRING FOR THE CHILDREN...
...SO I BROUGHT EQUIPMENT AND SUPPLIES FOR A NEW SCIENCE AND ARTS CENTER...
...AND AN ICE CREAM TRUCK.
YOU BROUGHT EDUCATION AND CAMOUFLAGED IT WITH SUGAR. VERY CLEVER.
THIS IS ALL VERY GENEROUS, BUT I'M AFRAID I'M NOT SURE WE CAN ACCOMMODATE IT ALL.
OF COURSE. SORRY. IF YOU DON'T HAVE THE ROOM, I'LL HAVE TO BUILD YOU ANOTHER WING.

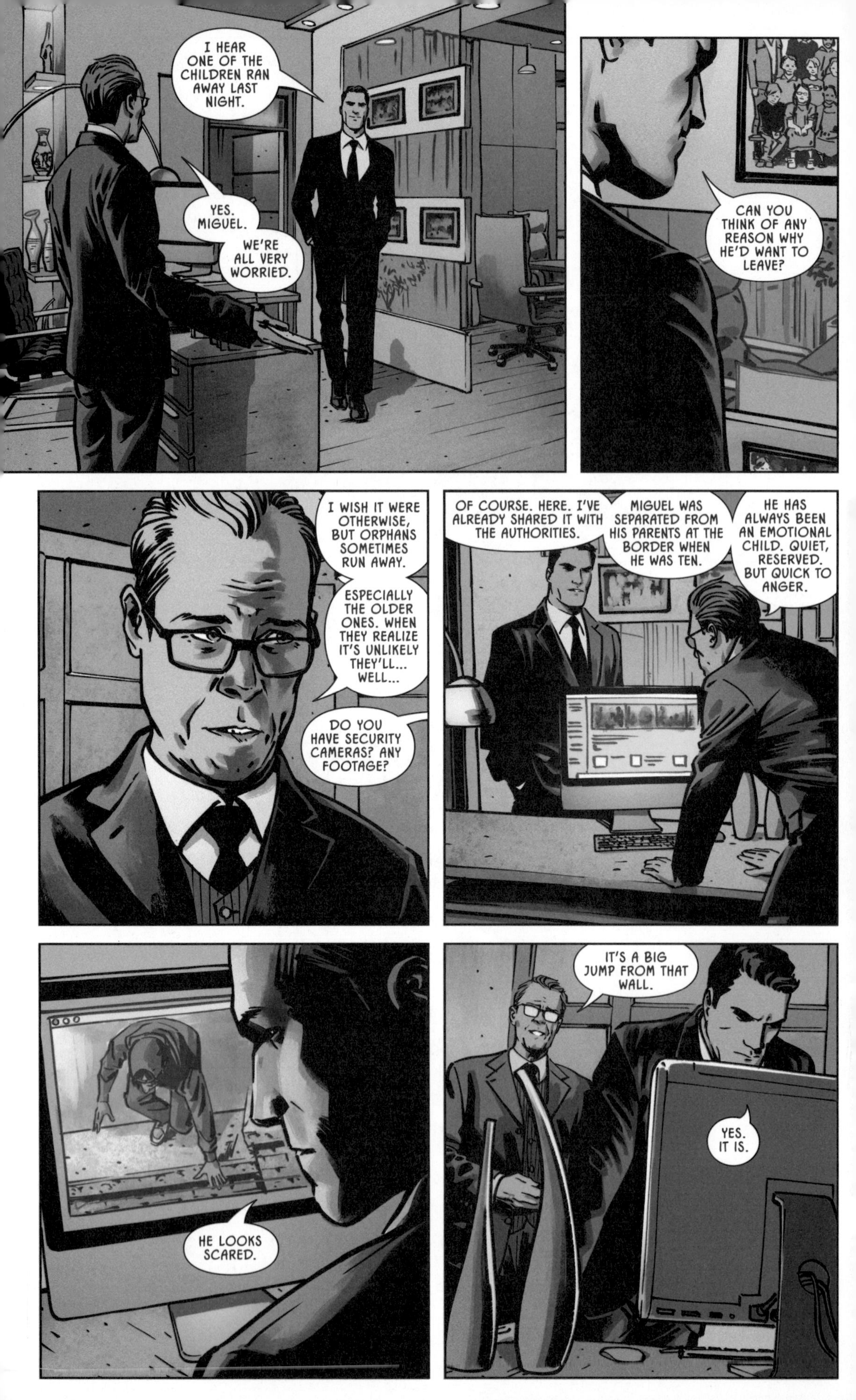
I HEAR ONE OF THE CHILDREN RAN AWAY LAST NIGHT.
YES. MIGUEL.
WE'RE ALL VERY WORRIED.
CAN YOU THINK OF ANY REASON WHY HE'D WANT TO LEAVE?
I WISH IT WERE OTHERWISE, BUT ORPHANS SOMETIMES RUN AWAY.
ESPECIALLY THE OLDER ONES. WHEN THEY REALIZE IT'S UNLIKELY THEY'LL... WELL...
DO YOU HAVE SECURITY CAMERAS? ANY FOOTAGE?
OF COURSE. HERE. I'VE ALREADY SHARED IT WITH THE AUTHORITIES.
MIGUEL WAS SEPARATED FROM HIS PARENTS AT THE BORDER WHEN HE WAS TEN.
HE HAS ALWAYS BEEN AN EMOTIONAL CHILD. QUIET, RESERVED. BUT QUICK TO ANGER.
HE LOOKS SCARED.
IT'S A BIG JUMP FROM THAT WALL.
YES. IT IS.

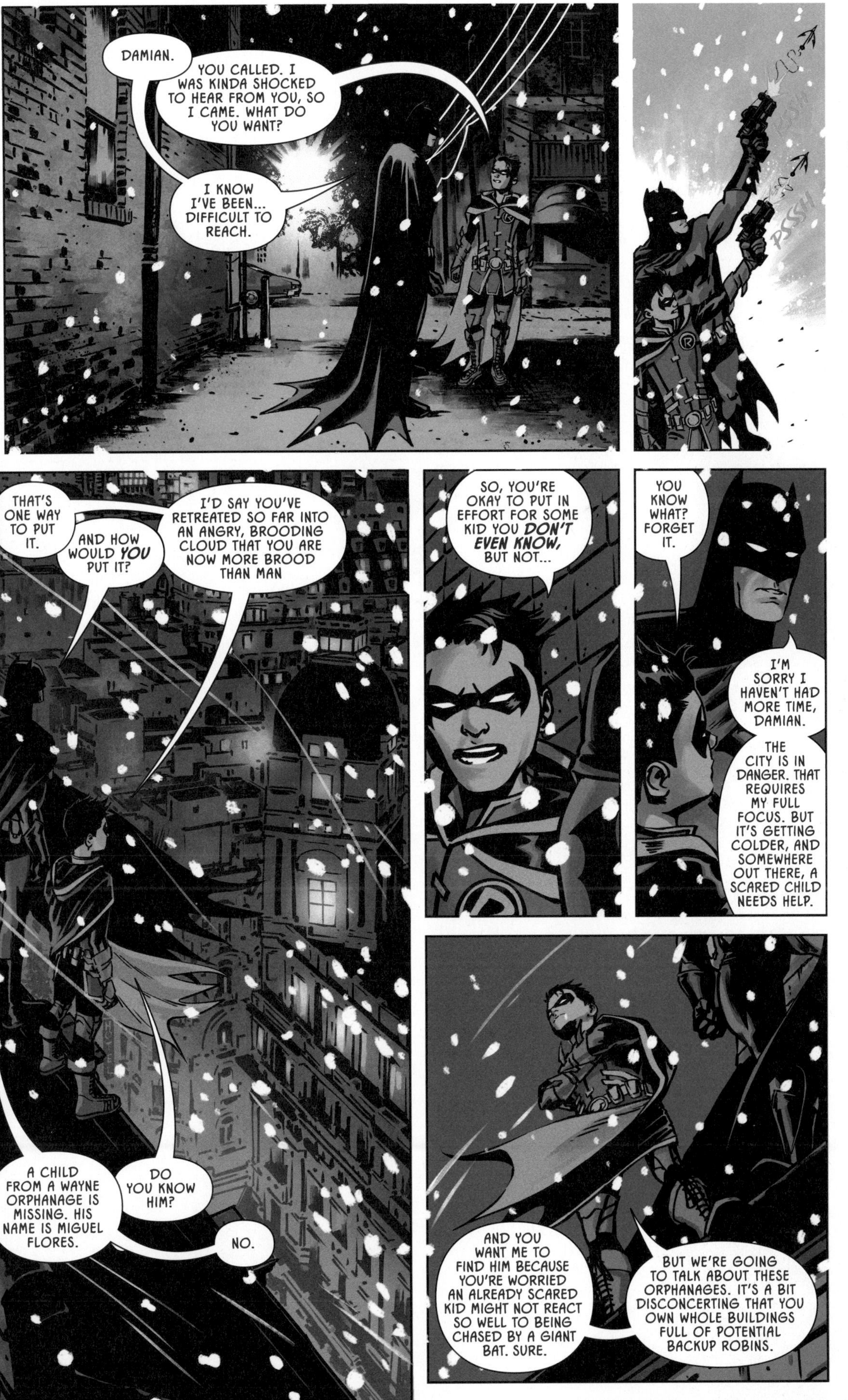
DAMIAN.
YOU CALLED. I WAS KINDA SHOCKED TO HEAR FROM YOU, SO I CAME. WHAT DO YOU WANT?
I KNOW I'VE BEEN... DIFFICULT TO REACH.
PSSSH
PSSSH
THAT'S ONE WAY TO PUT IT.
AND HOW WOULD *YOU* PUT IT?
I'D SAY YOU'VE RETREATED SO FAR INTO AN ANGRY, BROODING CLOUD THAT YOU ARE NOW MORE BROOD THAN MAN
A CHILD FROM A WAYNE ORPHANAGE IS MISSING. HIS NAME IS MIGUEL FLORES.
DO YOU KNOW HIM?
NO.
SO, YOU'RE OKAY TO PUT IN EFFORT FOR SOME KID YOU ***DON'T EVEN KNOW,*** BUT NOT...
YOU KNOW WHAT? FORGET IT.
I'M SORRY I HAVEN'T HAD MORE TIME, DAMIAN.
THE CITY IS IN DANGER. THAT REQUIRES MY FULL FOCUS. BUT IT'S GETTING COLDER, AND SOMEWHERE OUT THERE, A SCARED CHILD NEEDS HELP.
AND YOU WANT ME TO FIND HIM BECAUSE YOU'RE WORRIED AN ALREADY SCARED KID MIGHT NOT REACT SO WELL TO BEING CHASED BY A GIANT BAT. SURE.
BUT WE'RE GOING TO TALK ABOUT THESE ORPHANAGES. IT'S A BIT DISCONCERTING THAT YOU OWN WHOLE BUILDINGS FULL OF POTENTIAL BACKUP ROBINS.

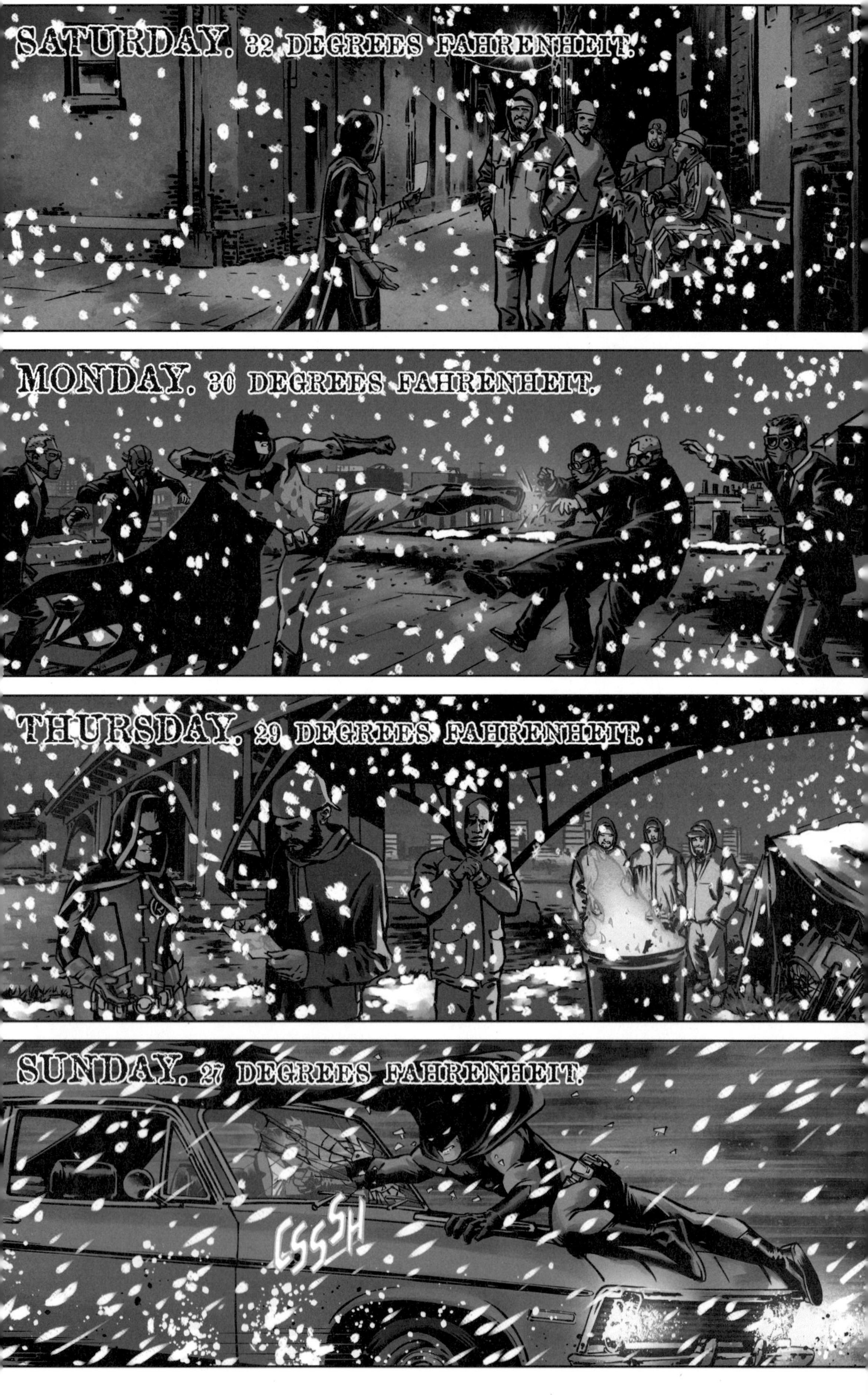
SATURDAY. 32 DEGREES FAHRENHEIT.
MONDAY. 30 DEGREES FAHRENHEIT.
THURSDAY. 29 DEGREES FAHRENHEIT.
SUNDAY. 27 DEGREES FAHRENHEIT.
CSSSH

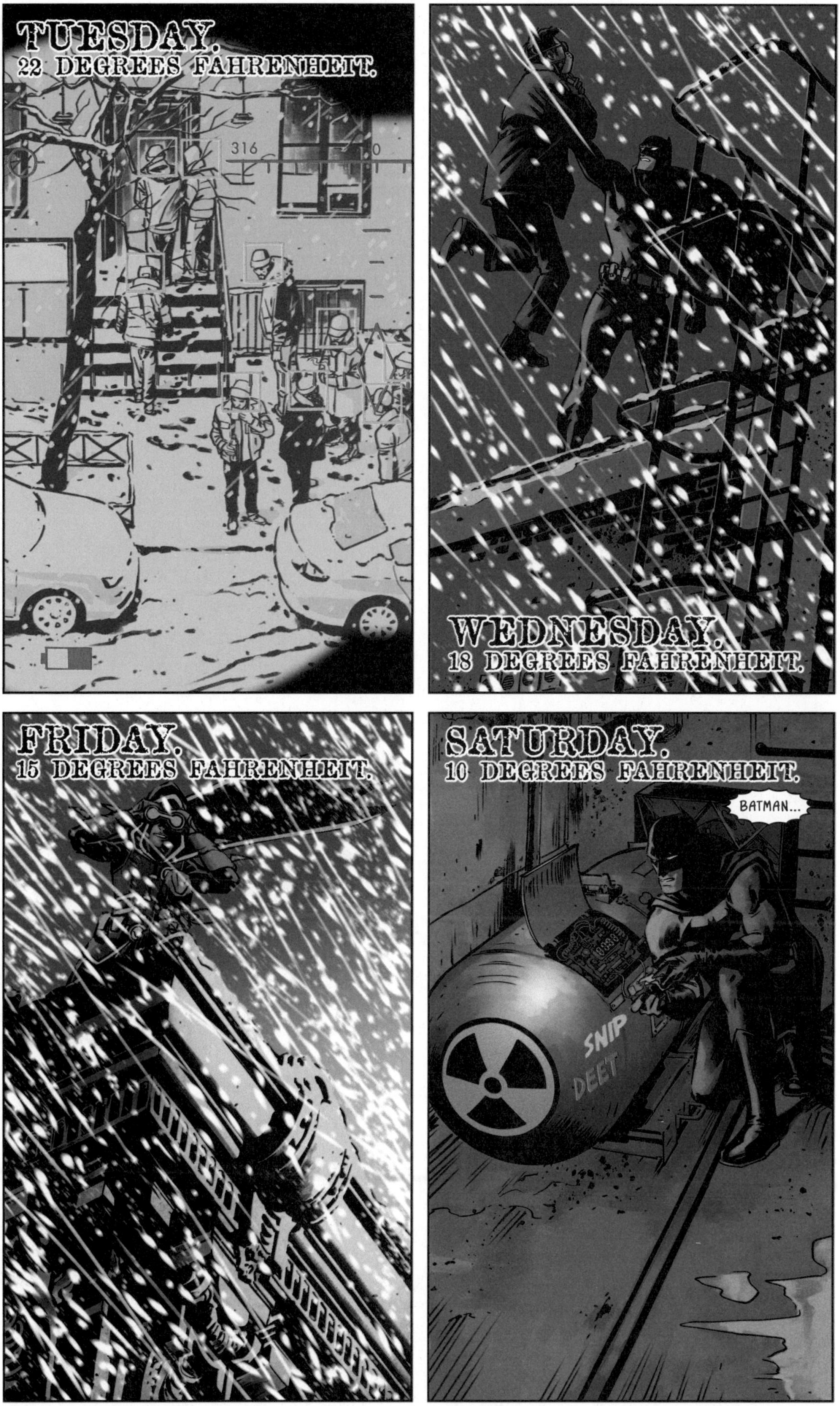
TUESDAY.
22 DEGREES FAHRENHEIT.
316
WEDNESDAY.
18 DEGREES FAHRENHEIT.
FRIDAY.
15 DEGREES FAHRENHEIT.
SATURDAY.
10 DEGREES FAHRENHEIT.
BATMAN...
SNIP
DEET

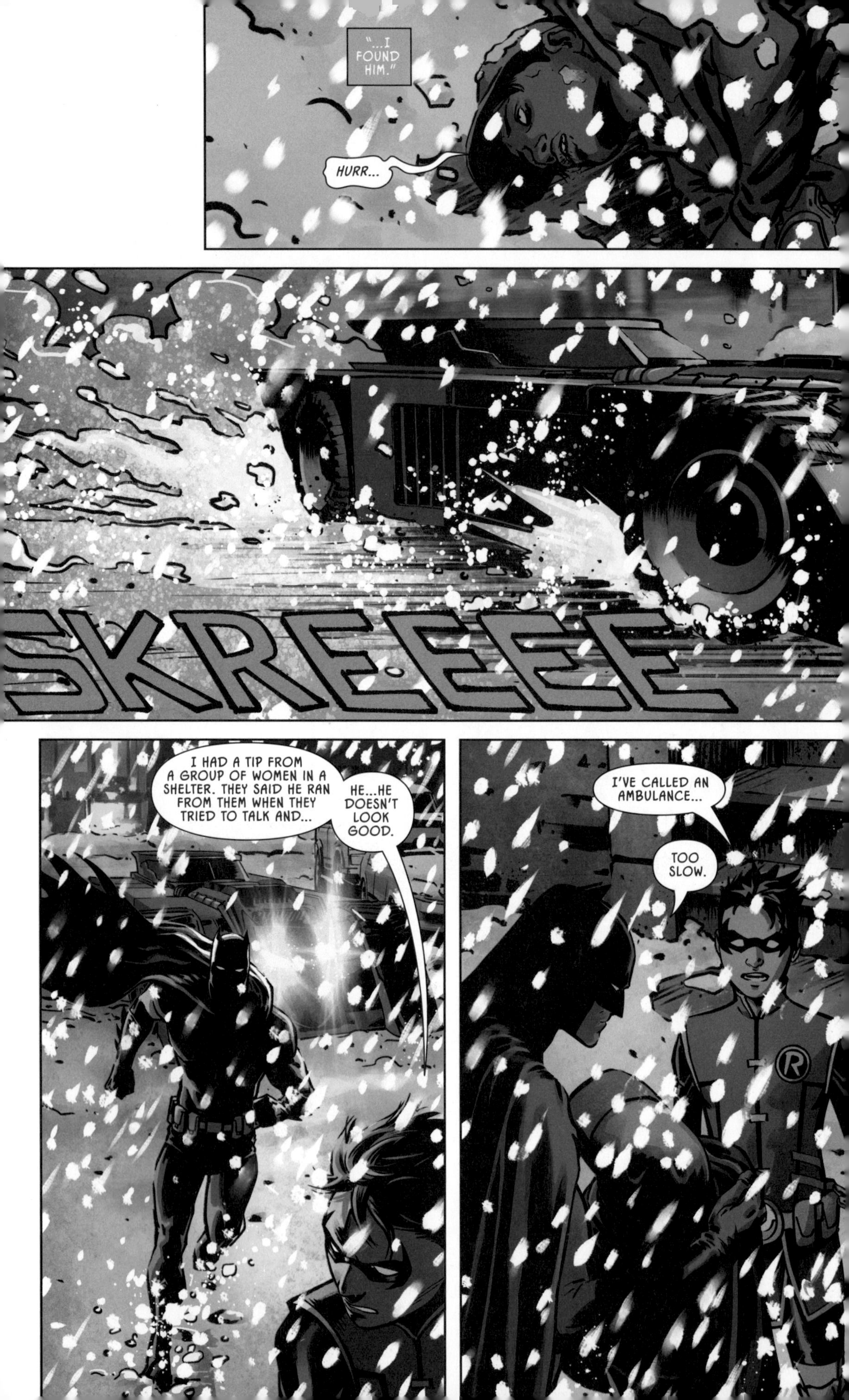
"...I FOUND HIM."
HURR...
SKREEEE
I HAD A TIP FROM A GROUP OF WOMEN IN A SHELTER. THEY SAID HE RAN FROM THEM WHEN THEY TRIED TO TALK AND...
HE...HE DOESN'T LOOK GOOD.
I'VE CALLED AN AMBULANCE...
TOO SLOW.

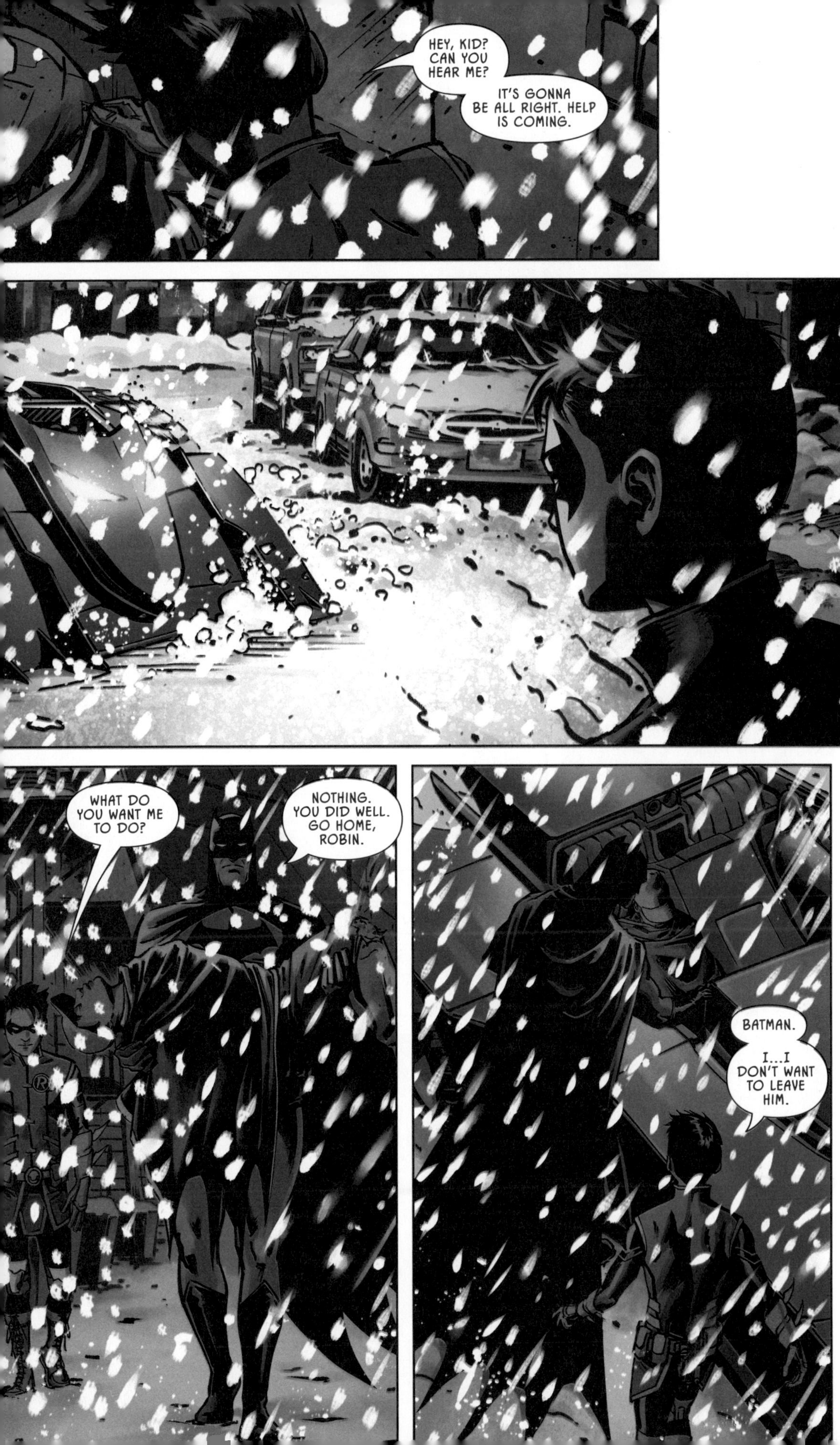
HEY, KID? CAN YOU HEAR ME?
IT'S GONNA BE ALL RIGHT. HELP IS COMING.
WHAT DO YOU WANT ME TO DO?
NOTHING. YOU DID WELL. GO HOME, ROBIN.
BATMAN.
I...I DON'T WANT TO LEAVE HIM.

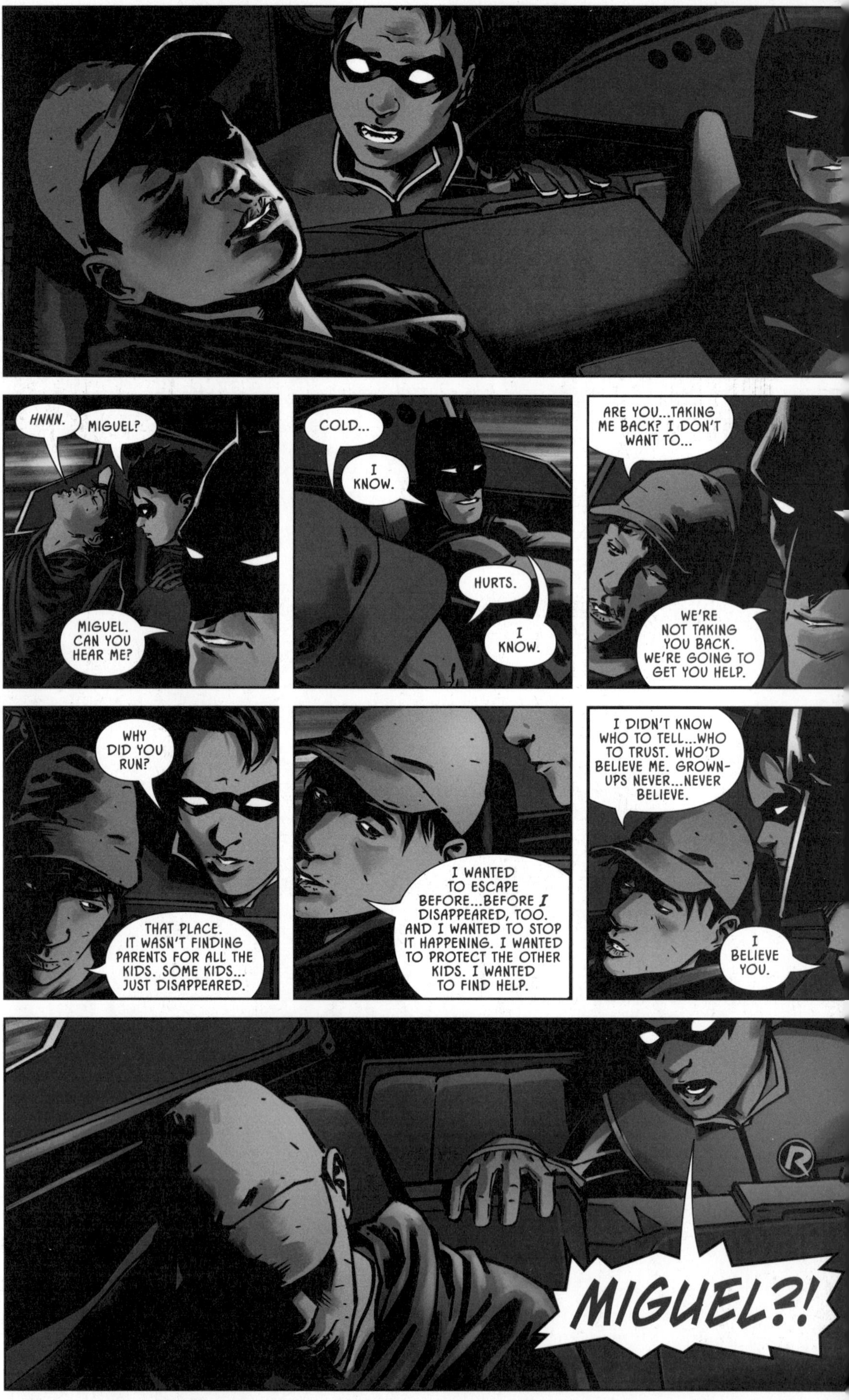
HNNN.
MIGUEL?
MIGUEL. CAN YOU HEAR ME?
COLD...
I KNOW.
HURTS.
I KNOW.
ARE YOU...TAKING ME BACK? I DON'T WANT TO...
WE'RE NOT TAKING YOU BACK. WE'RE GOING TO GET YOU HELP.
WHY DID YOU RUN?
THAT PLACE. IT WASN'T FINDING PARENTS FOR ALL THE KIDS. SOME KIDS... JUST DISAPPEARED.
I WANTED TO ESCAPE BEFORE...BEFORE *I* DISAPPEARED, TOO. AND I WANTED TO STOP IT HAPPENING. I WANTED TO PROTECT THE OTHER KIDS. I WANTED TO FIND HELP.
I DIDN'T KNOW WHO TO TELL...WHO TO TRUST. WHO'D BELIEVE ME. GROWN-UPS NEVER...NEVER BELIEVE.
I BELIEVE YOU.
MIGUEL?!

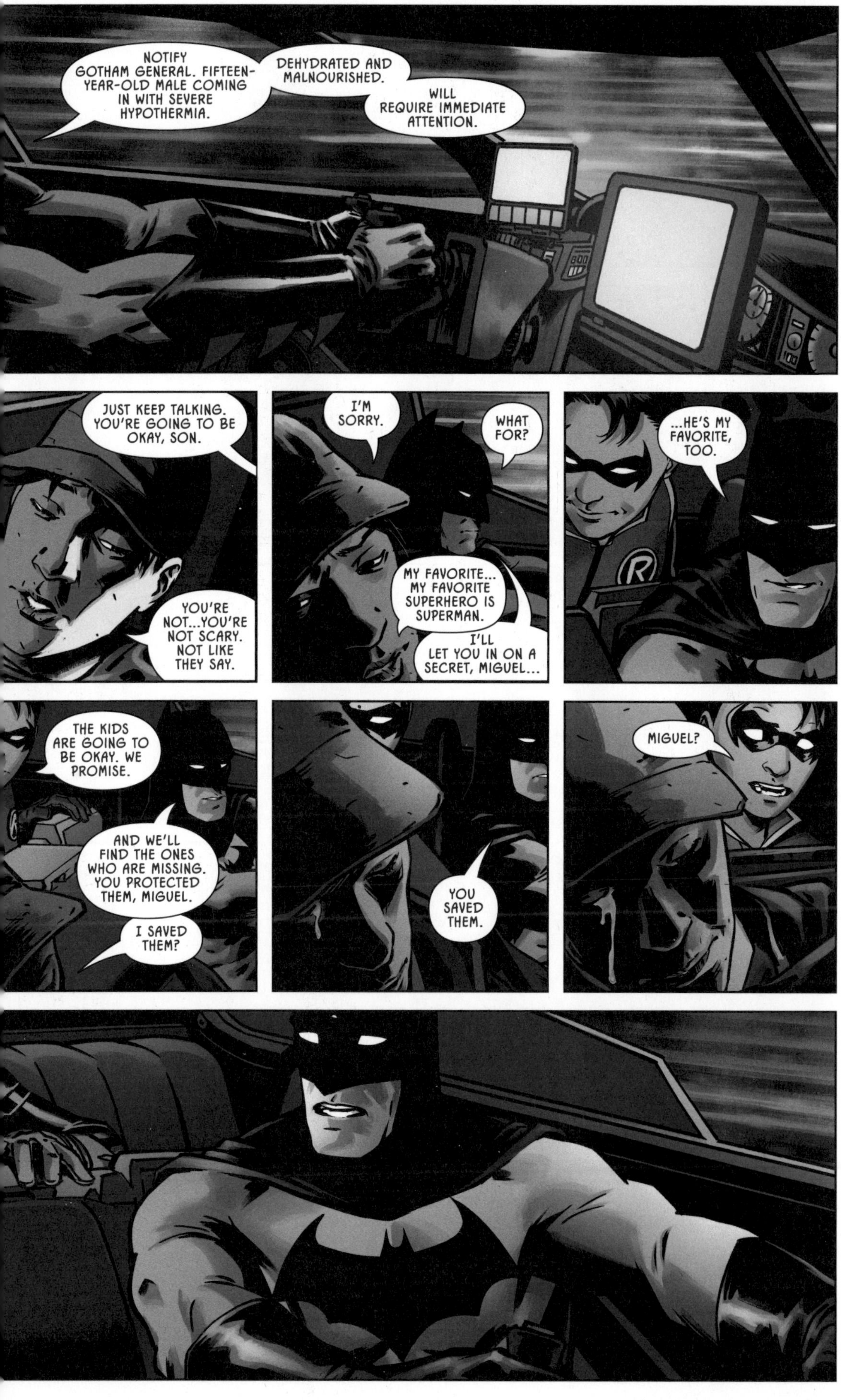
NOTIFY GOTHAM GENERAL. FIFTEEN-YEAR-OLD MALE COMING IN WITH SEVERE HYPOTHERMIA.
DEHYDRATED AND MALNOURISHED.
WILL REQUIRE IMMEDIATE ATTENTION.
JUST KEEP TALKING. YOU'RE GOING TO BE OKAY, SON.
YOU'RE NOT...YOU'RE NOT SCARY. NOT LIKE THEY SAY.
I'M SORRY.
WHAT FOR?
MY FAVORITE... MY FAVORITE SUPERHERO IS SUPERMAN.
I'LL LET YOU IN ON A SECRET, MIGUEL...
...HE'S MY FAVORITE, TOO.
THE KIDS ARE GOING TO BE OKAY. WE PROMISE.
AND WE'LL FIND THE ONES WHO ARE MISSING. YOU PROTECTED THEM, MIGUEL.
I SAVED THEM?
YOU SAVED THEM.
MIGUEL?

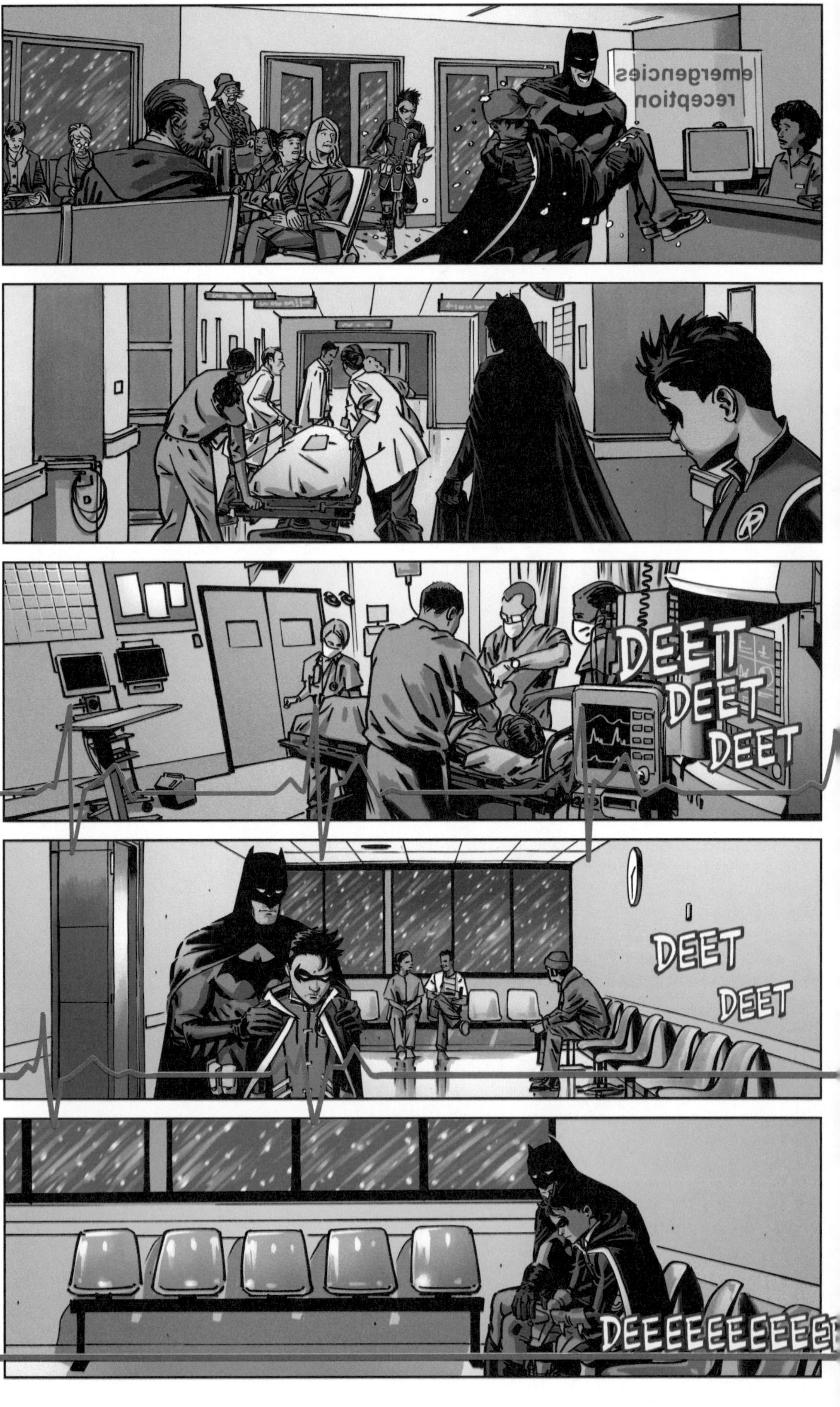
emergencies
reception
DEET
DEET
DEET
DEET
DEET
DEEEEEEEEEEE

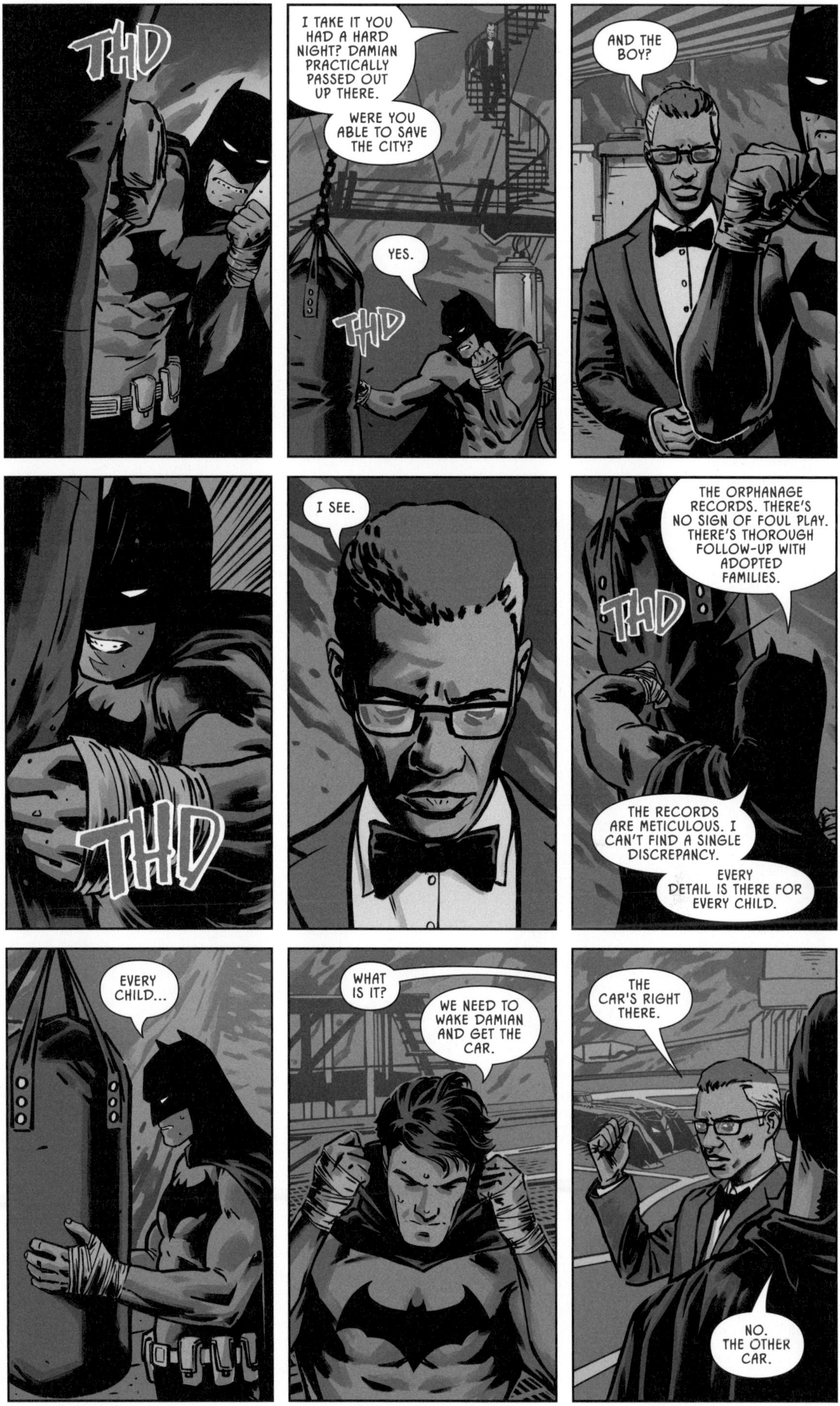
THD
I TAKE IT YOU HAD A HARD NIGHT? DAMIAN PRACTICALLY PASSED OUT UP THERE.
WERE YOU ABLE TO SAVE THE CITY?
YES.
THD
AND THE BOY?
THD
I SEE.
THE ORPHANAGE RECORDS. THERE'S NO SIGN OF FOUL PLAY. THERE'S THOROUGH FOLLOW-UP WITH ADOPTED FAMILIES.
THD
THE RECORDS ARE METICULOUS. I CAN'T FIND A SINGLE DISCREPANCY.
EVERY DETAIL IS THERE FOR EVERY CHILD.
EVERY CHILD...
WHAT IS IT?
WE NEED TO WAKE DAMIAN AND GET THE CAR.
THE CAR'S RIGHT THERE.
NO. THE OTHER CAR.

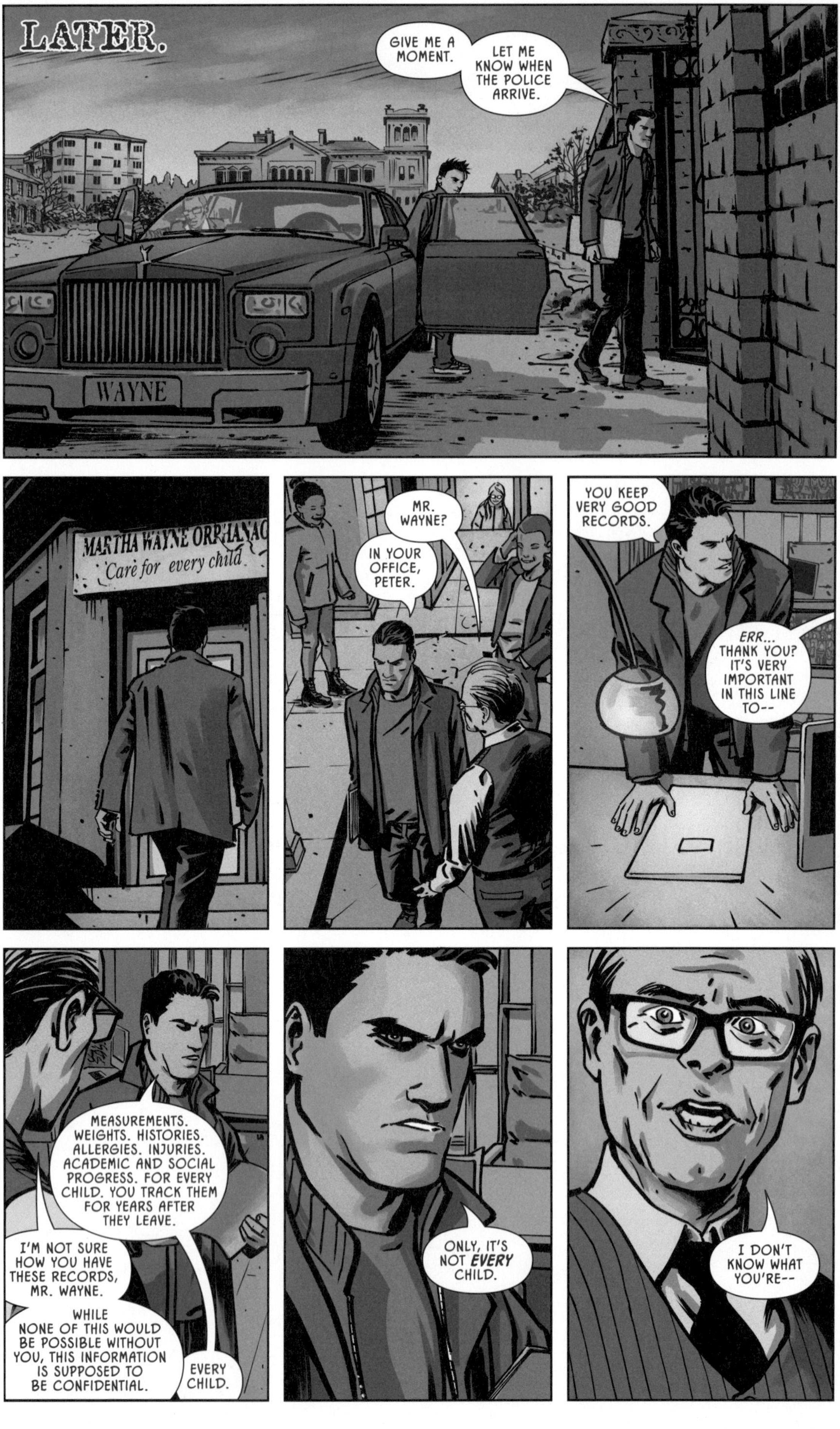
LATER.
GIVE ME A MOMENT.
LET ME KNOW WHEN THE POLICE ARRIVE.
WAYNE
MARTHA WAYNE ORPHANAG
Care for every child
MR. WAYNE?
IN YOUR OFFICE, PETER.
YOU KEEP VERY GOOD RECORDS.
ERR... THANK YOU? IT'S VERY IMPORTANT IN THIS LINE TO--
MEASUREMENTS. WEIGHTS. HISTORIES. ALLERGIES. INJURIES. ACADEMIC AND SOCIAL PROGRESS. FOR EVERY CHILD. YOU TRACK THEM FOR YEARS AFTER THEY LEAVE.
I'M NOT SURE HOW YOU HAVE THESE RECORDS, MR. WAYNE.
WHILE NONE OF THIS WOULD BE POSSIBLE WITHOUT YOU, THIS INFORMATION IS SUPPOSED TO BE CONFIDENTIAL.
EVERY CHILD.
ONLY, IT'S NOT *EVERY* CHILD.
I DON'T KNOW WHAT YOU'RE--

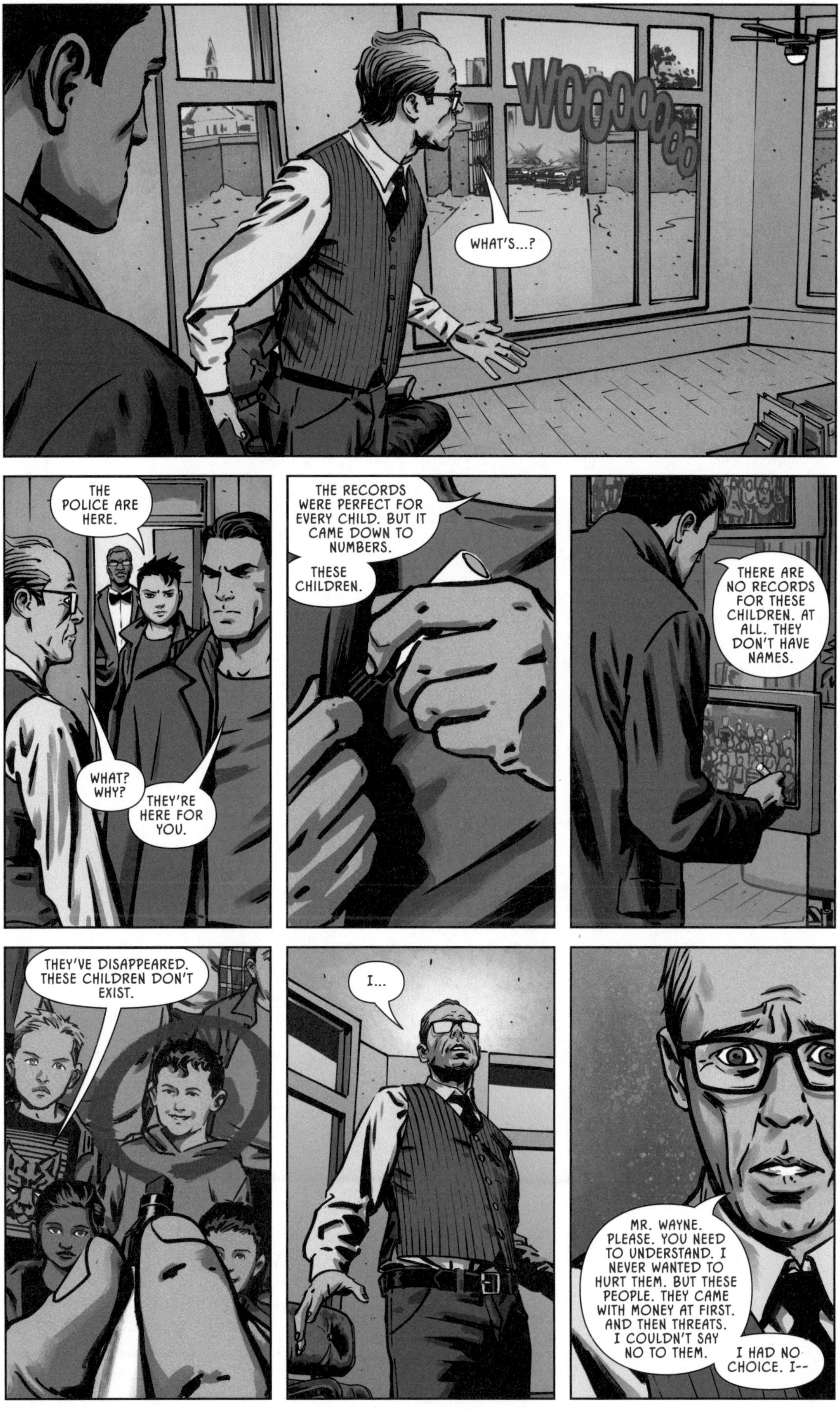
WOOOOOOO
WHAT'S...?
THE POLICE ARE HERE.
WHAT? WHY?
THEY'RE HERE FOR YOU.
THE RECORDS WERE PERFECT FOR EVERY CHILD. BUT IT CAME DOWN TO NUMBERS.
THESE CHILDREN.
THERE ARE NO RECORDS FOR THESE CHILDREN. AT ALL. THEY DON'T HAVE NAMES.
THEY'VE DISAPPEARED. THESE CHILDREN DON'T EXIST.
I...
MR. WAYNE. PLEASE. YOU NEED TO UNDERSTAND. I NEVER WANTED TO HURT THEM. BUT THESE PEOPLE. THEY CAME WITH MONEY AT FIRST. AND THEN THREATS. I COULDN'T SAY NO TO THEM.
I HAD NO CHOICE. I--

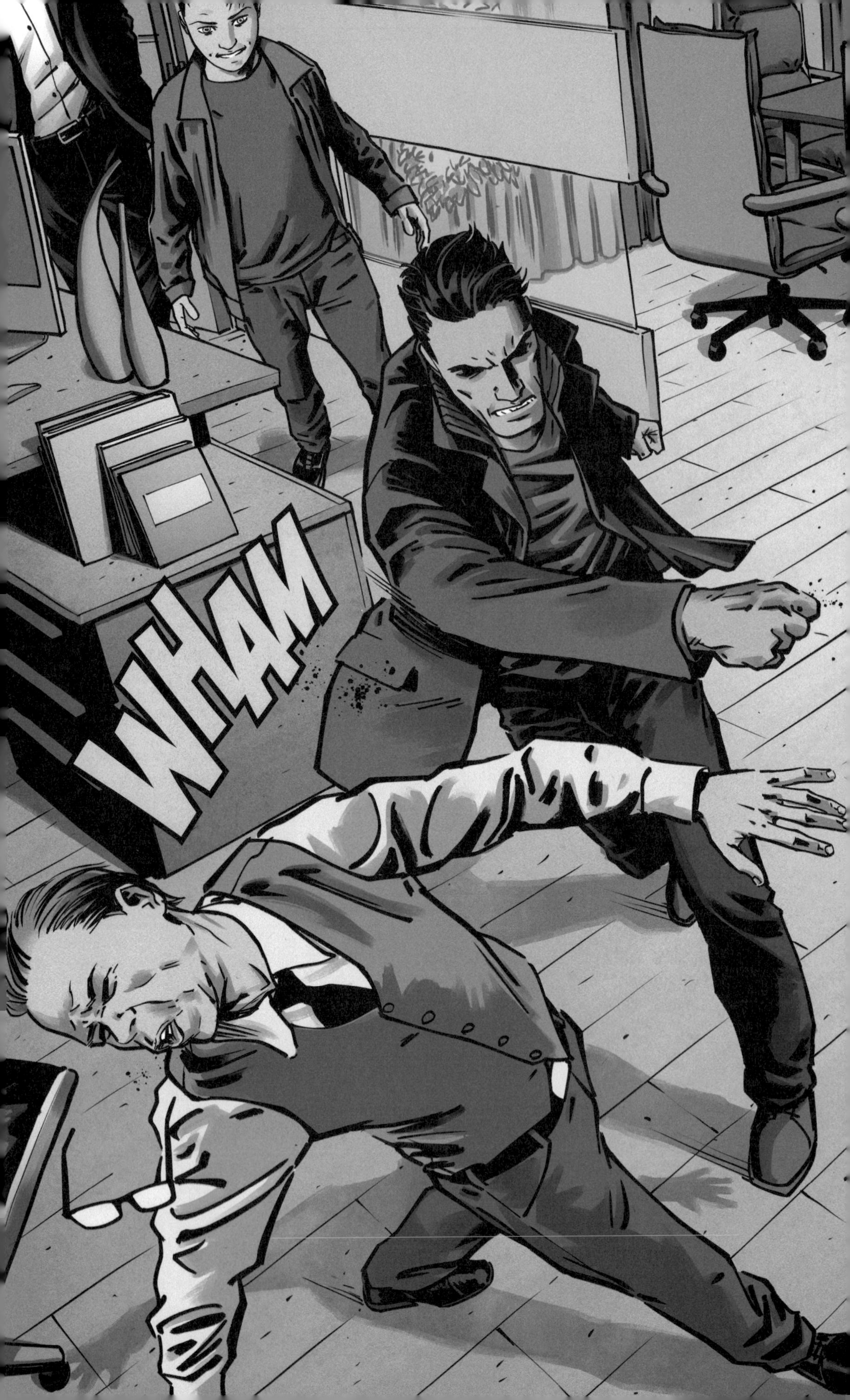
WHAM

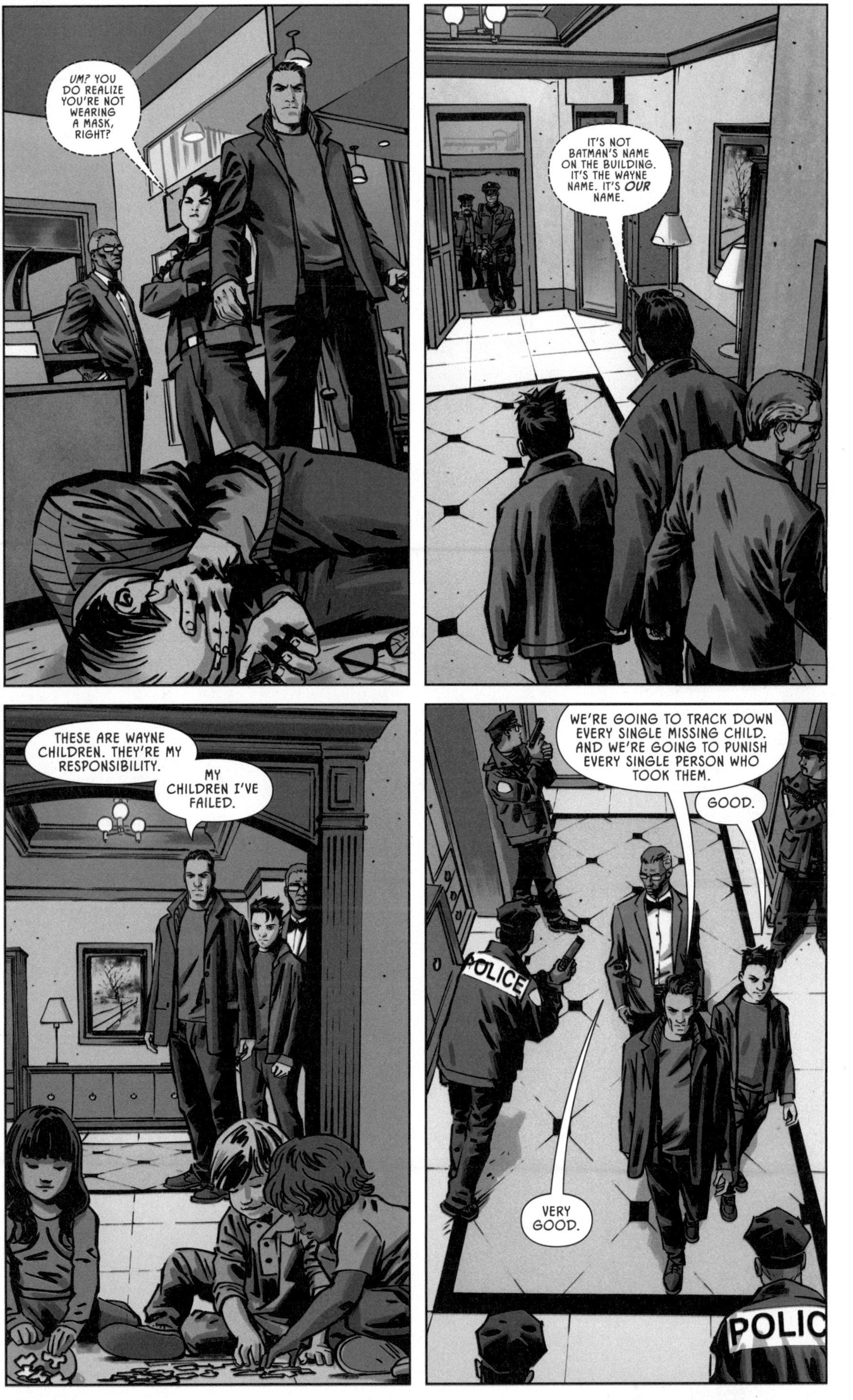
UM? YOU DO REALIZE YOU'RE NOT WEARING A MASK, RIGHT?
IT'S NOT BATMAN'S NAME ON THE BUILDING. IT'S THE WAYNE NAME. IT'S OUR NAME.
THESE ARE WAYNE CHILDREN. THEY'RE MY RESPONSIBILITY.
MY CHILDREN I'VE FAILED.
WE'RE GOING TO TRACK DOWN EVERY SINGLE MISSING CHILD. AND WE'RE GOING TO PUNISH EVERY SINGLE PERSON WHO TOOK THEM.
GOOD.
VERY GOOD.
POLICE
POLIC

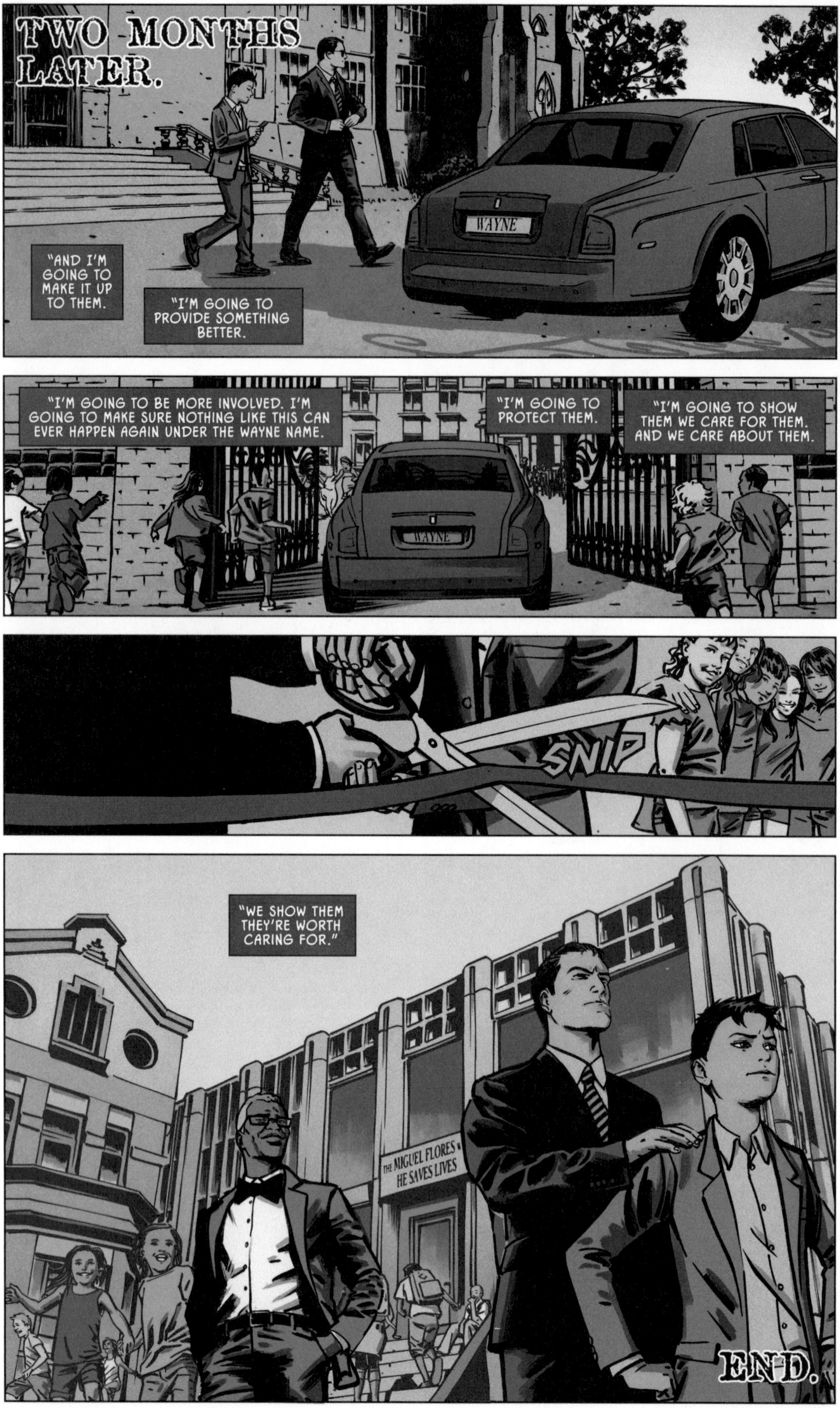

TWO MONTHS LATER.
WAYNE
"AND I'M GOING TO MAKE IT UP TO THEM.
"I'M GOING TO PROVIDE SOMETHING BETTER.
"I'M GOING TO BE MORE INVOLVED. I'M GOING TO MAKE SURE NOTHING LIKE THIS CAN EVER HAPPEN AGAIN UNDER THE WAYNE NAME.
"I'M GOING TO PROTECT THEM.
"I'M GOING TO SHOW THEM WE CARE FOR THEM. AND WE CARE ABOUT THEM.
WAYNE
SNIP
"WE SHOW THEM THEY'RE WORTH CARING FOR."
THE MIGUEL FLORES
HE SAVES LIVES
END.

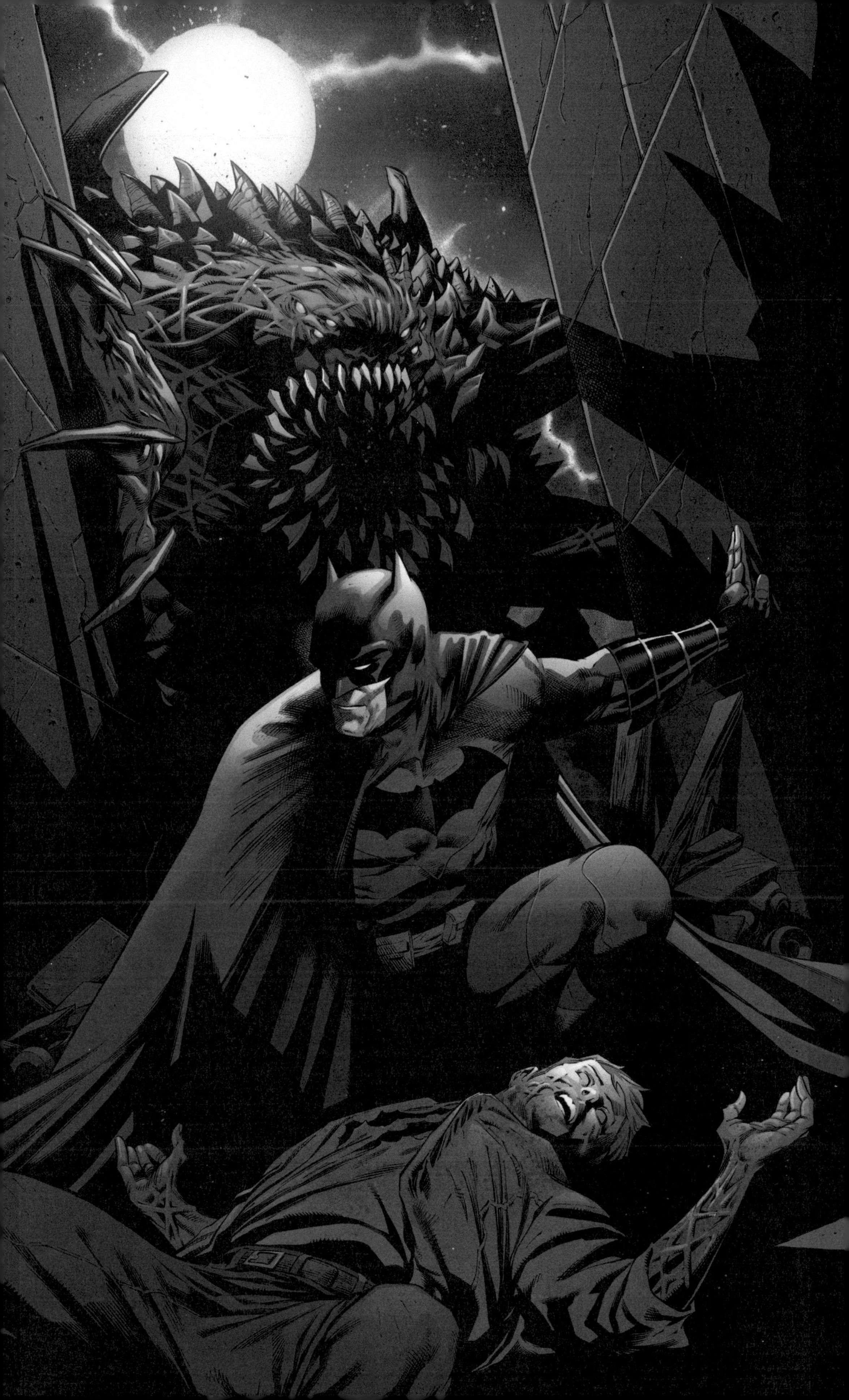

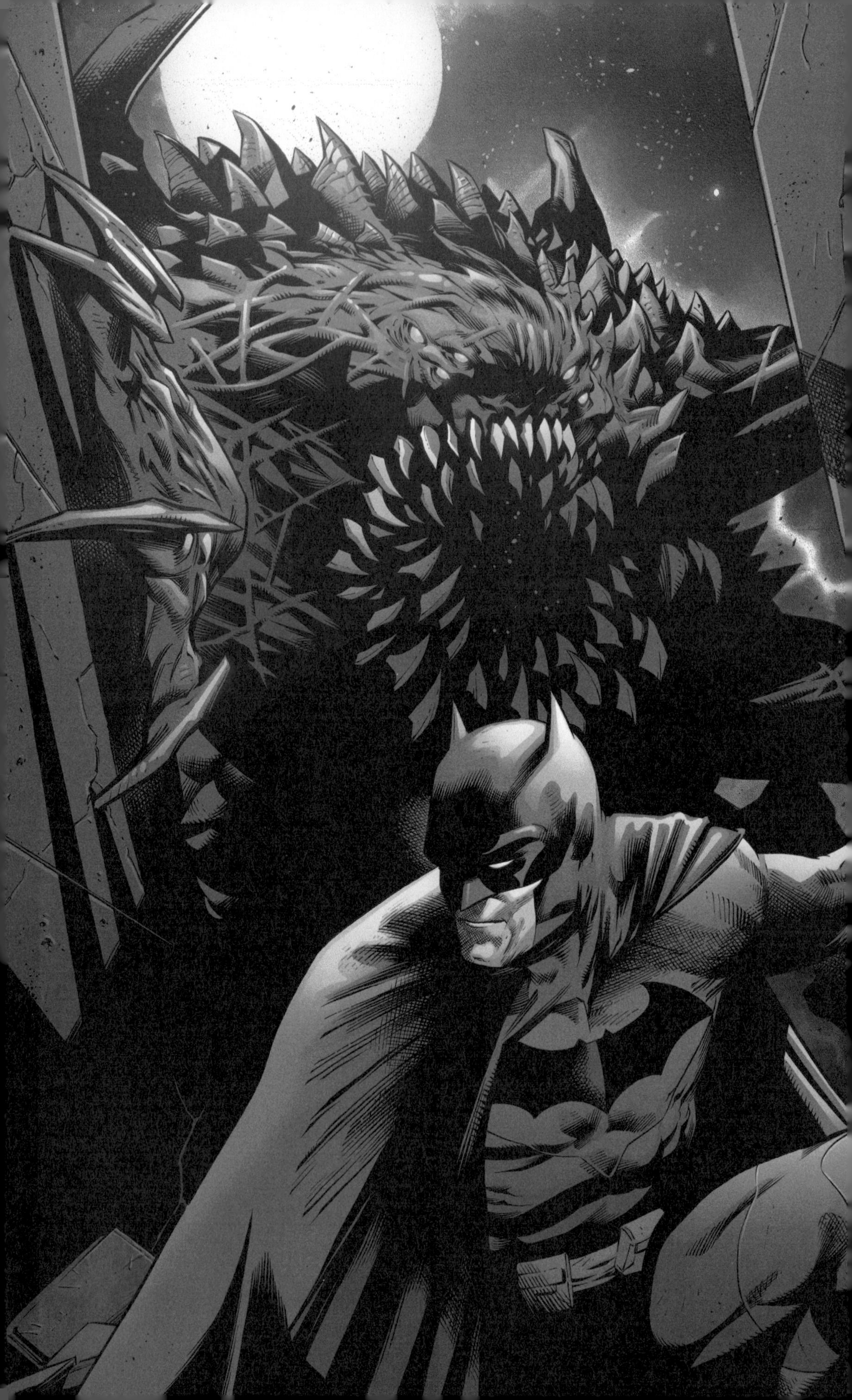

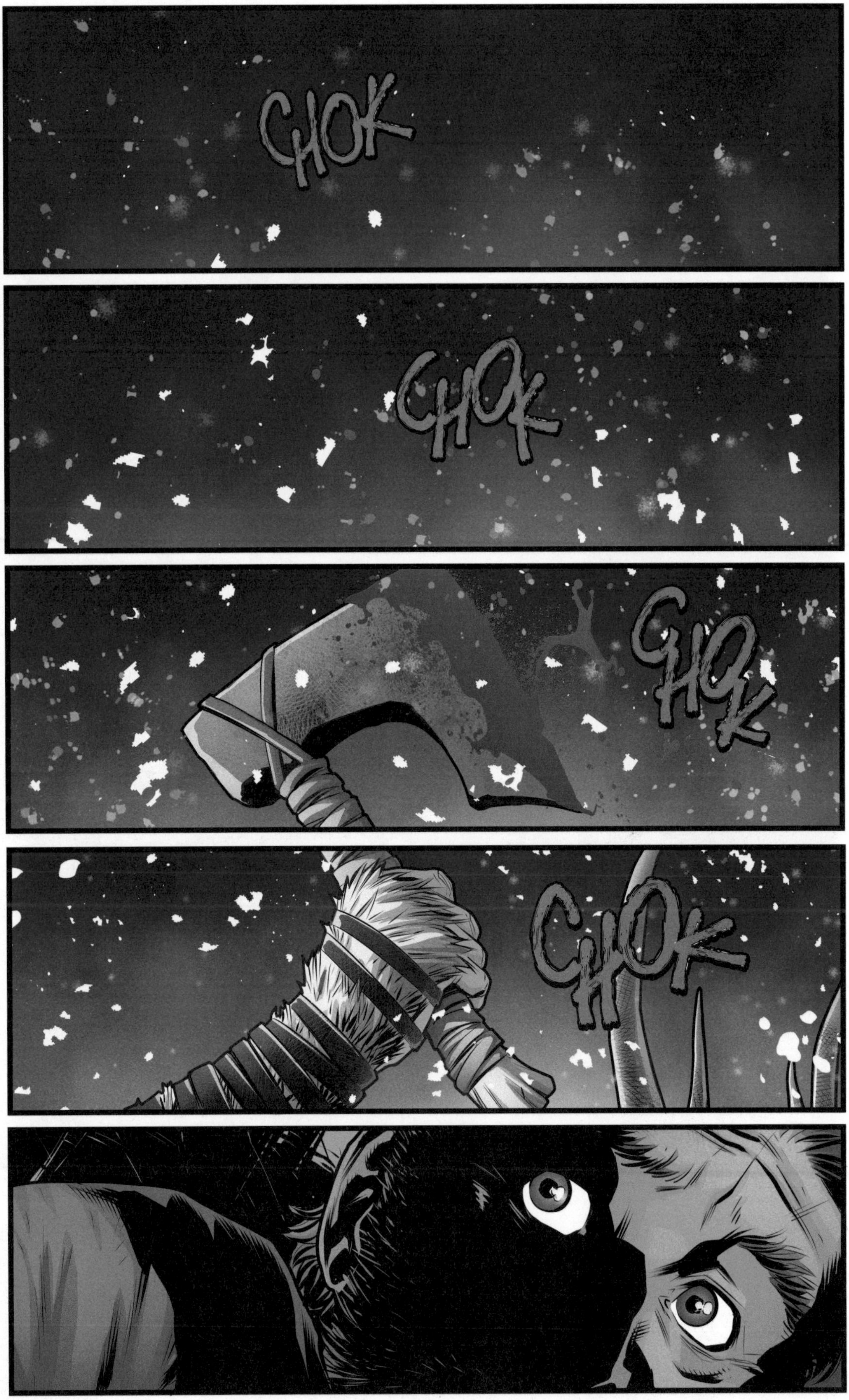
CHOK
CHOK
CHOK
CHOK

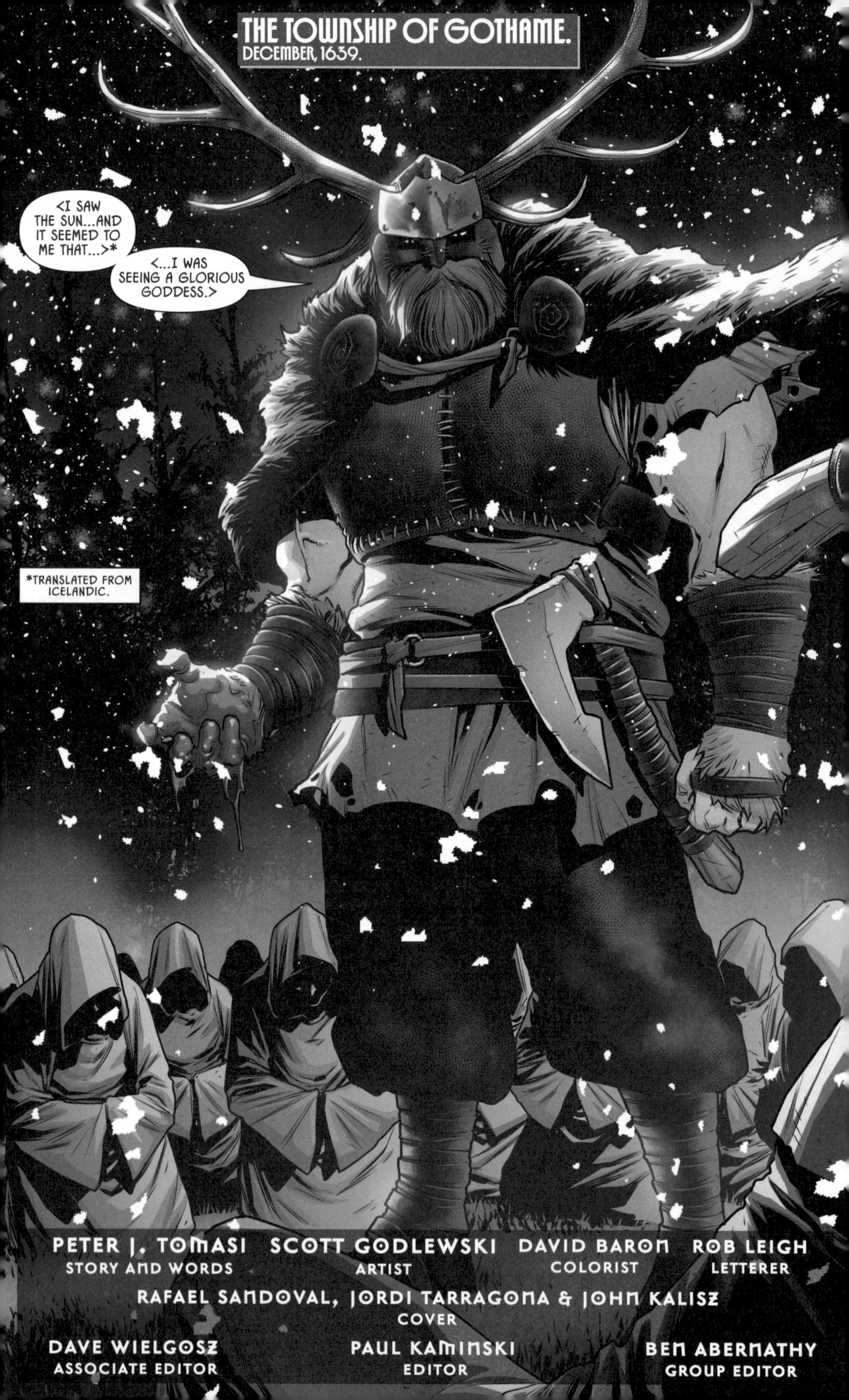

THE TOWNSHIP OF GOTHAME.
DECEMBER, 1639.
<I SAW THE SUN...AND IT SEEMED TO ME THAT...>*
<...I WAS SEEING A GLORIOUS GODDESS.>
*TRANSLATED FROM ICELANDIC.
PETER J. TOMASI STORY AND WORDS
SCOTT GODLEWSKI ARTIST
DAVID BARON COLORIST
ROB LEIGH LETTERER
RAFAEL SANDOVAL, JORDI TARRAGONA & JOHN KALISZ COVER
DAVE WIELGOSZ ASSOCIATE EDITOR
PAUL KAMINSKI EDITOR
BEN ABERNATHY GROUP EDITOR

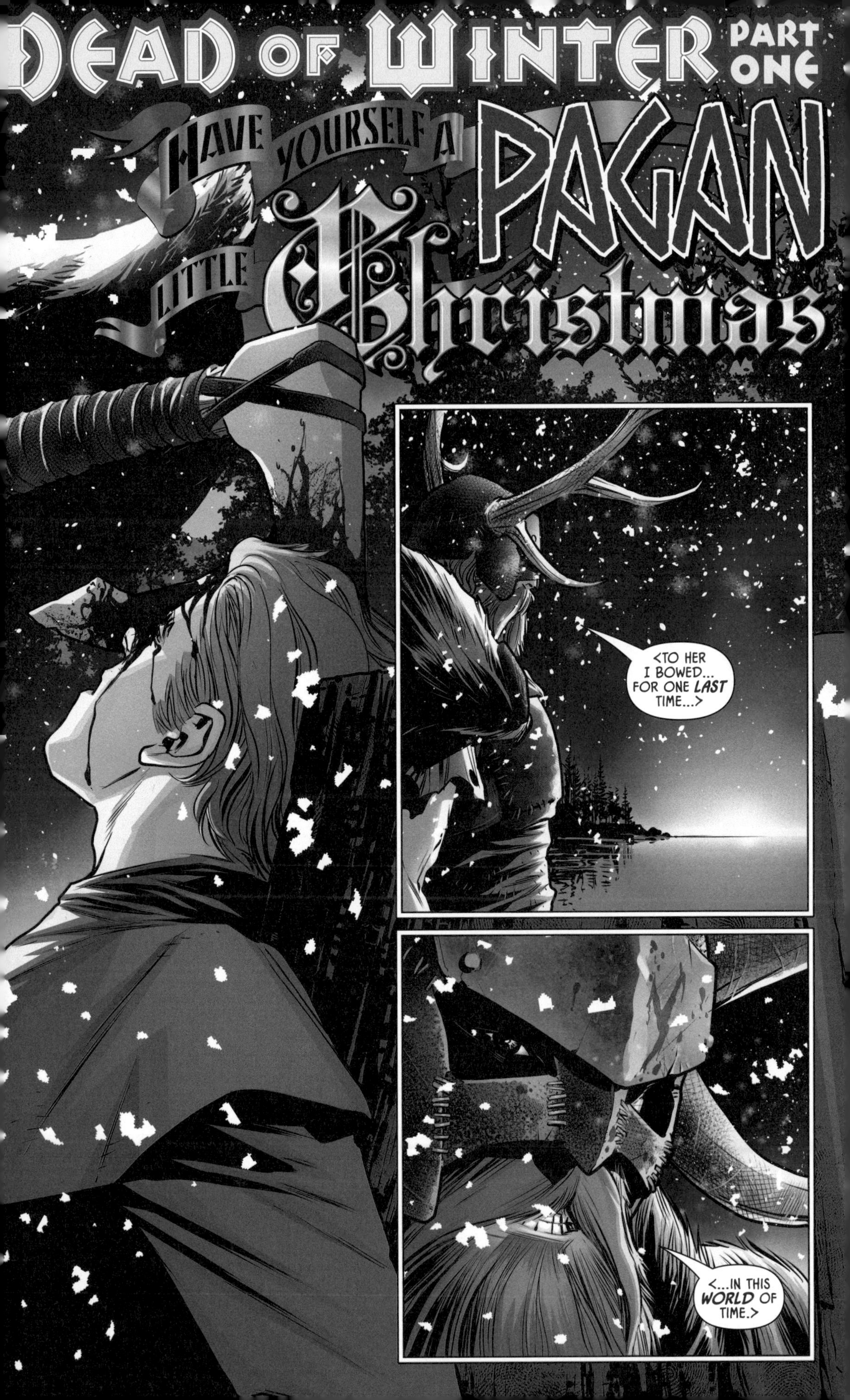
DEAD OF WINTER PART ONE
HAVE YOURSELF A LITTLE PAGAN Christmas
<TO HER I BOWED... FOR ONE LAST TIME...>
<...IN THIS WORLD OF TIME.>

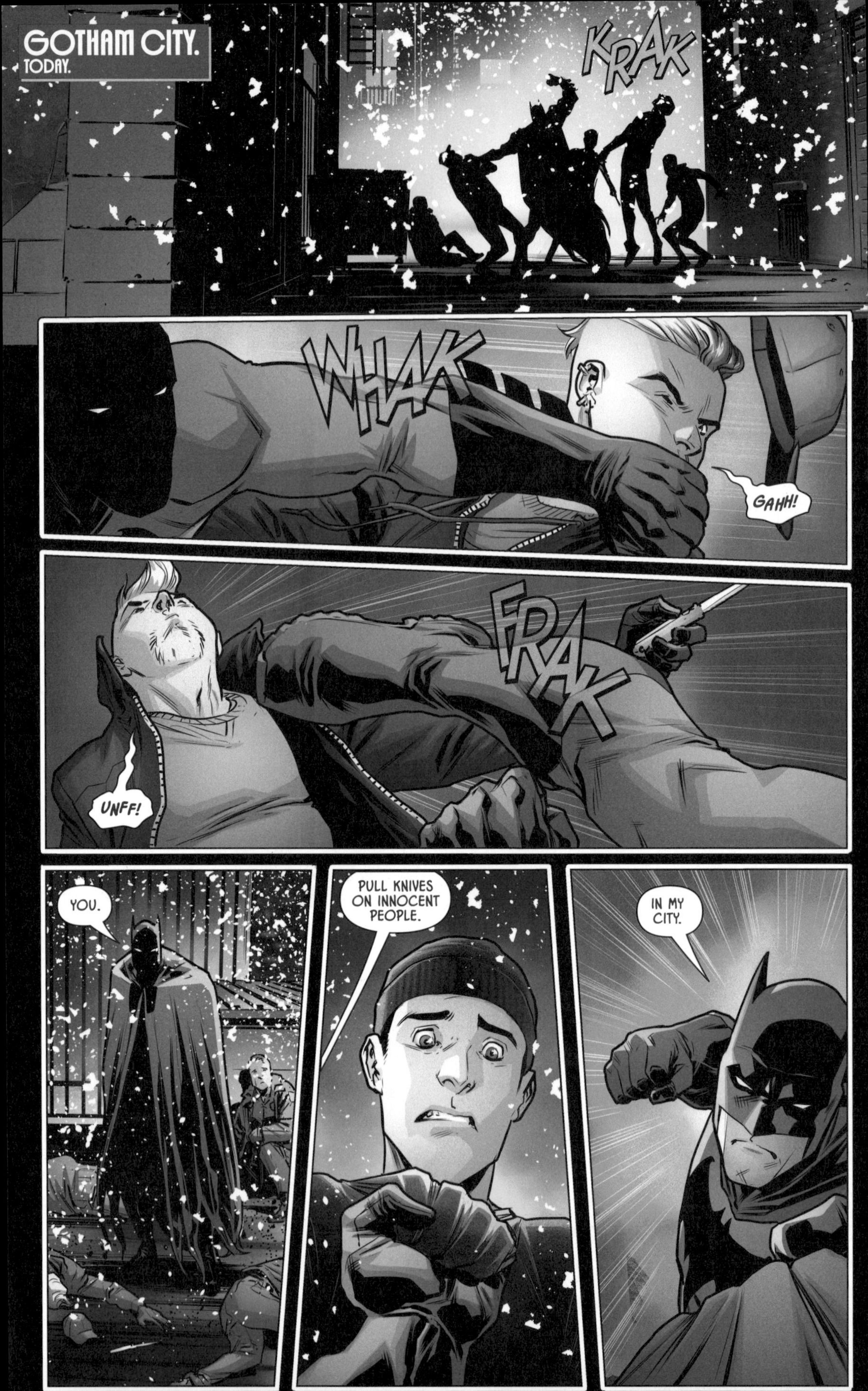
GOTHAM CITY.
TODAY.
KRAK
WHAK
GAHH!
FRAK
UNFF!
YOU.
PULL KNIVES ON INNOCENT PEOPLE.
IN MY CITY.

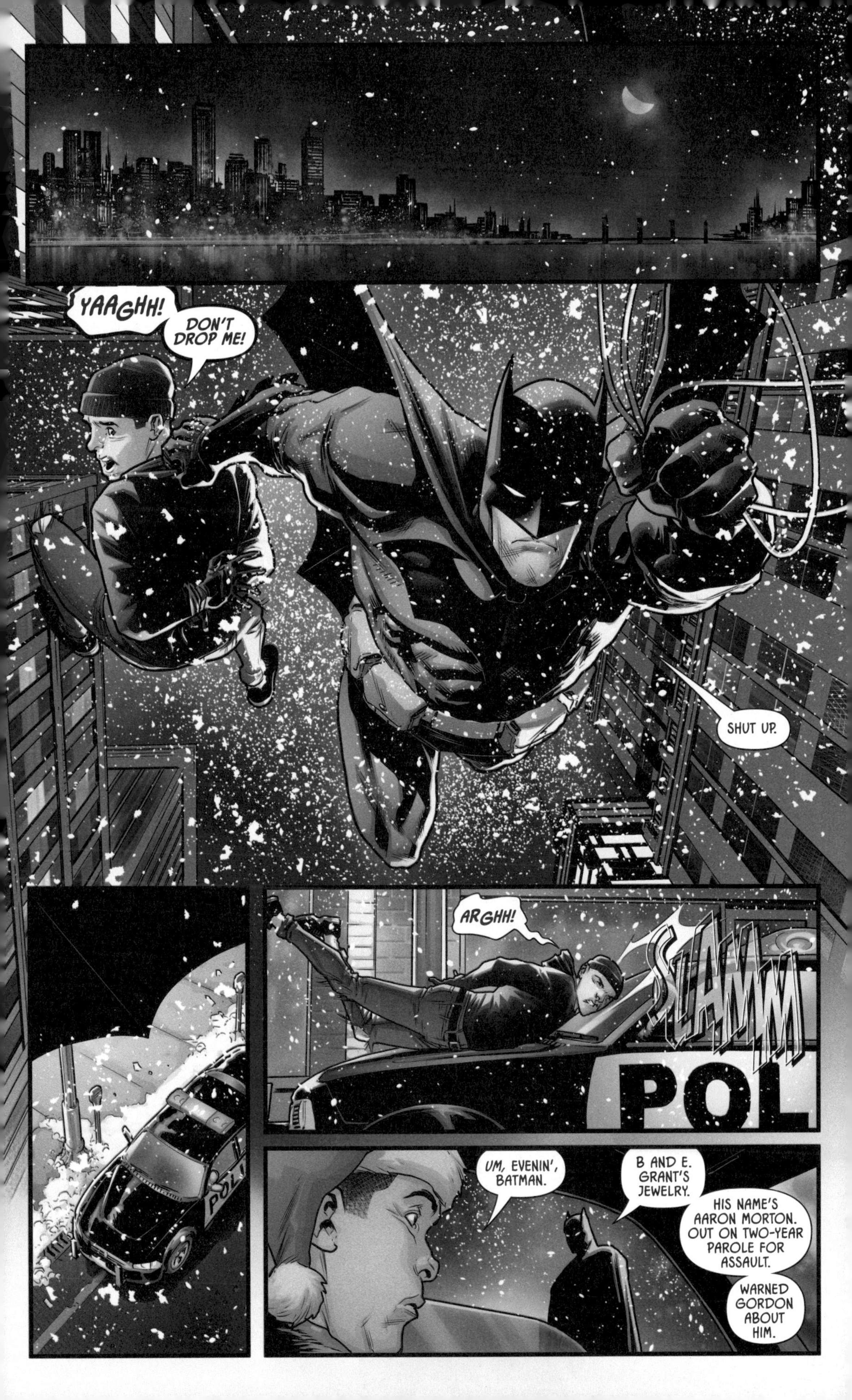
YAAGHH!
DON'T DROP ME!
SHUT UP.
ARGHH!
SLAMM
POL
UM, EVENIN', BATMAN.
B AND E. GRANT'S JEWELRY.
HIS NAME'S AARON MORTON. OUT ON TWO-YEAR PAROLE FOR ASSAULT.
WARNED GORDON ABOUT HIM.

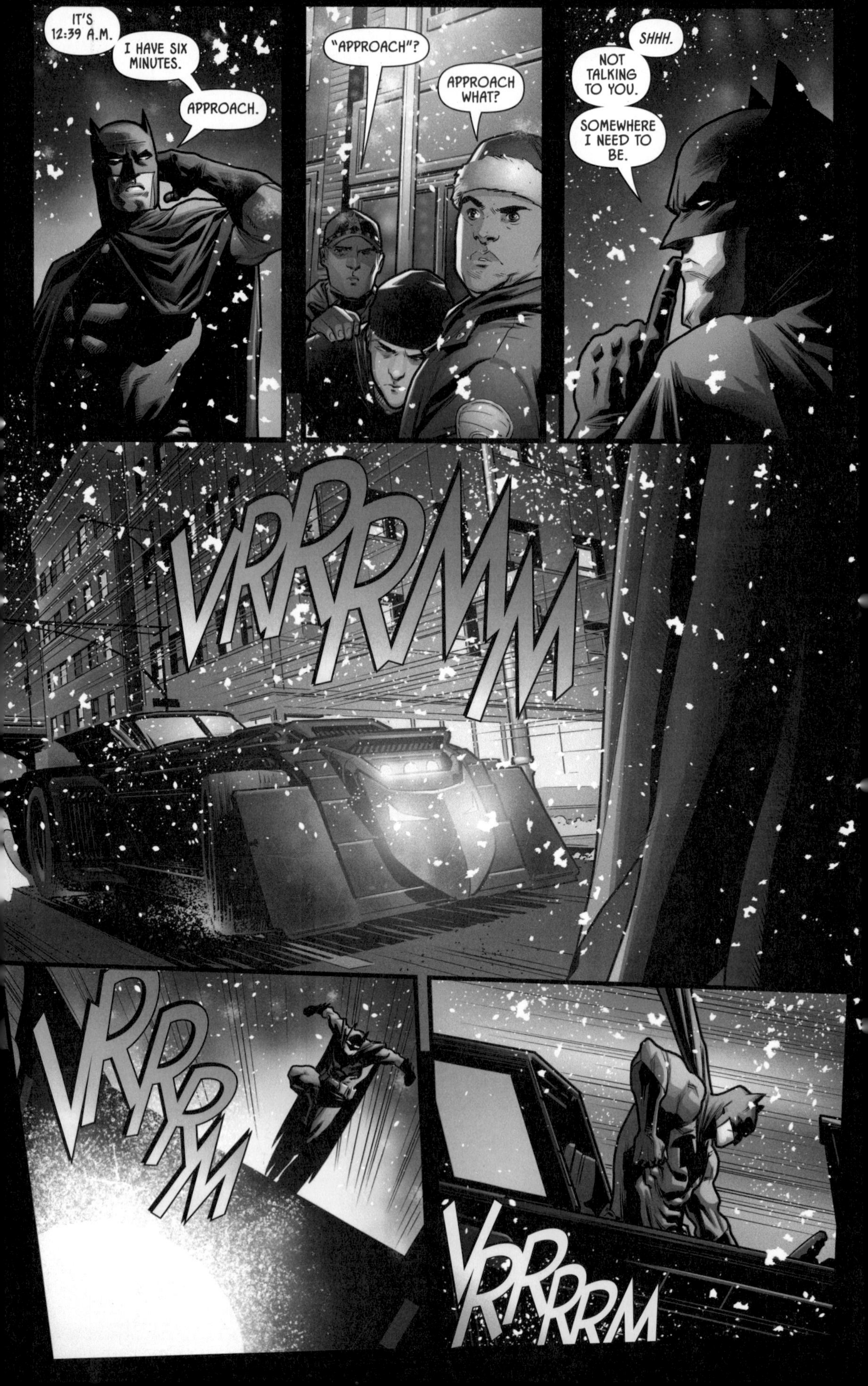
IT'S 12:39 A.M.
I HAVE SIX MINUTES.
APPROACH.
"APPROACH"?
APPROACH WHAT?
SHHH.
NOT TALKING TO YOU.
SOMEWHERE I NEED TO BE.
VRRRMMM
VRRRM
VRRRRM

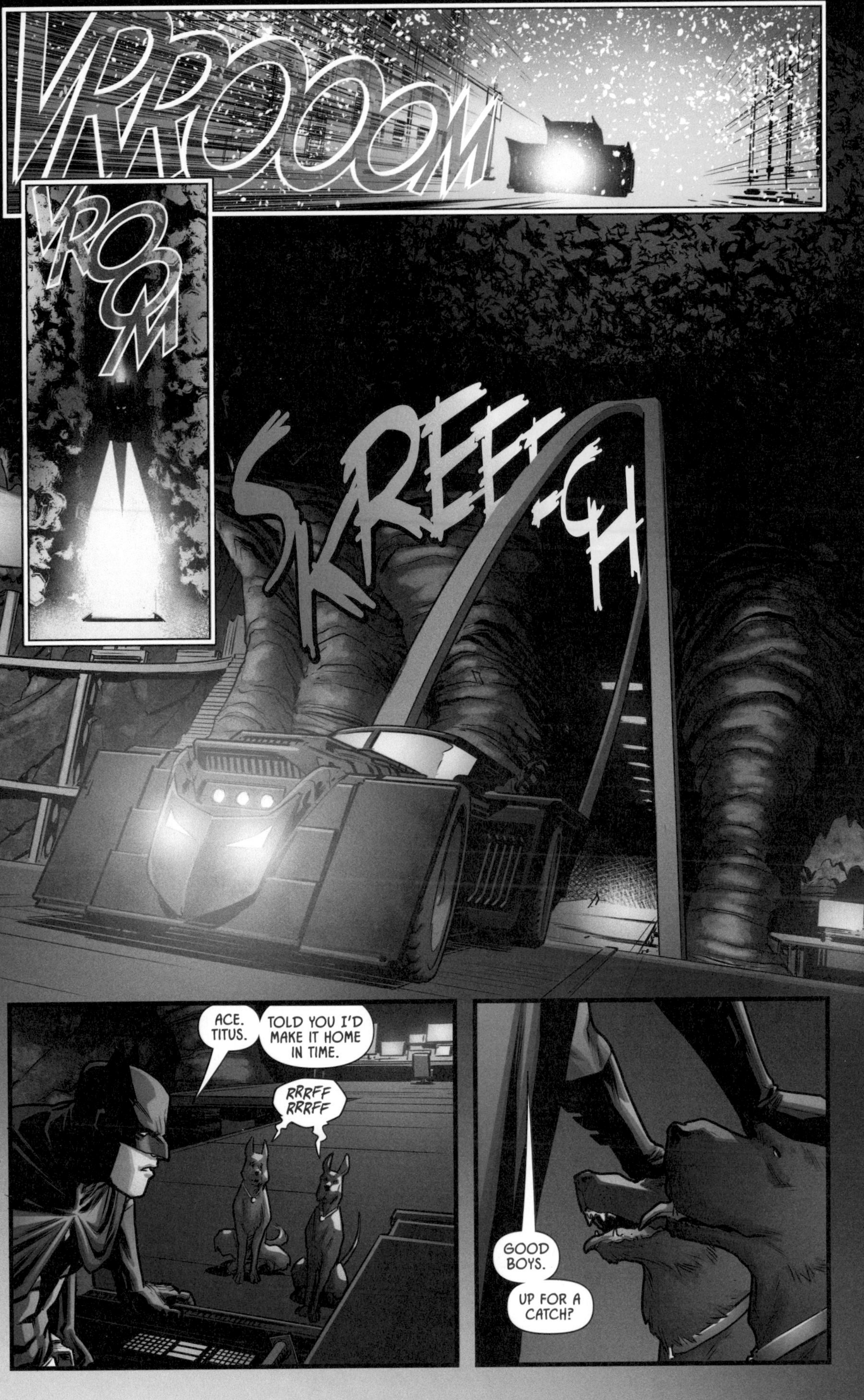
VRROOOOM
VROOM
SKREE-CH
ACE. TITUS.
TOLD YOU I'D MAKE IT HOME IN TIME.
RRRFF RRRFF
GOOD BOYS.
UP FOR A CATCH?

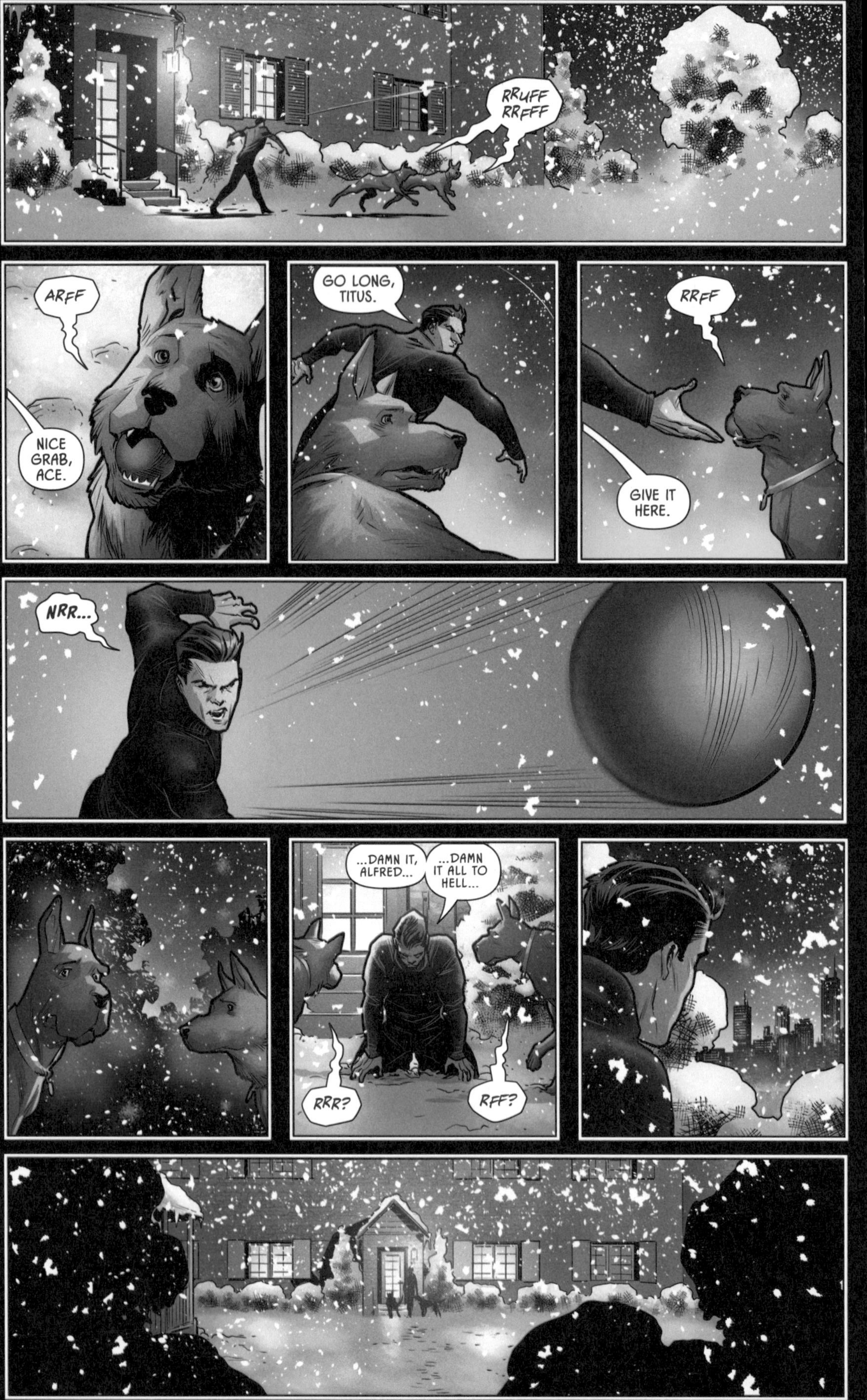
RRUFF
RRFFF
ARFF
NICE GRAB, ACE.
GO LONG, TITUS.
RRFF
GIVE IT HERE.
NRR...
...DAMN IT, ALFRED...
...DAMN IT ALL TO HELL...
RRR?
RFF?

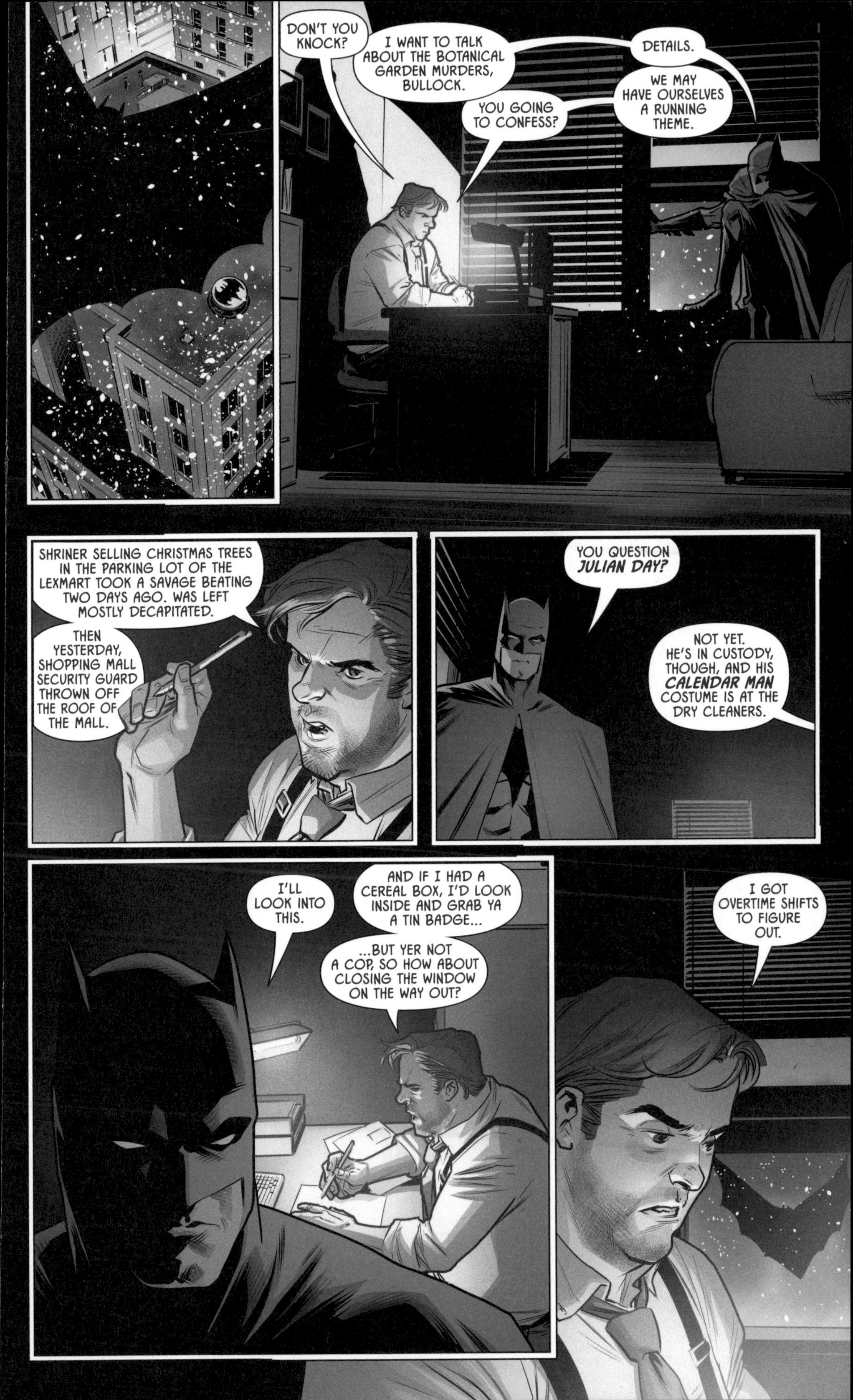
DON'T YOU KNOCK?
I WANT TO TALK ABOUT THE BOTANICAL GARDEN MURDERS, BULLOCK.
YOU GOING TO CONFESS?
DETAILS.
WE MAY HAVE OURSELVES A RUNNING THEME.
SHRINER SELLING CHRISTMAS TREES IN THE PARKING LOT OF THE LEXMART TOOK A SAVAGE BEATING TWO DAYS AGO. WAS LEFT MOSTLY DECAPITATED.
THEN YESTERDAY, SHOPPING MALL SECURITY GUARD THROWN OFF THE ROOF OF THE MALL.
YOU QUESTION JULIAN DAY?
NOT YET. HE'S IN CUSTODY, THOUGH, AND HIS CALENDAR MAN COSTUME IS AT THE DRY CLEANERS.
I'LL LOOK INTO THIS.
AND IF I HAD A CEREAL BOX, I'D LOOK INSIDE AND GRAB YA A TIN BADGE...
...BUT YER NOT A COP, SO HOW ABOUT CLOSING THE WINDOW ON THE WAY OUT?
I GOT OVERTIME SHIFTS TO FIGURE OUT.

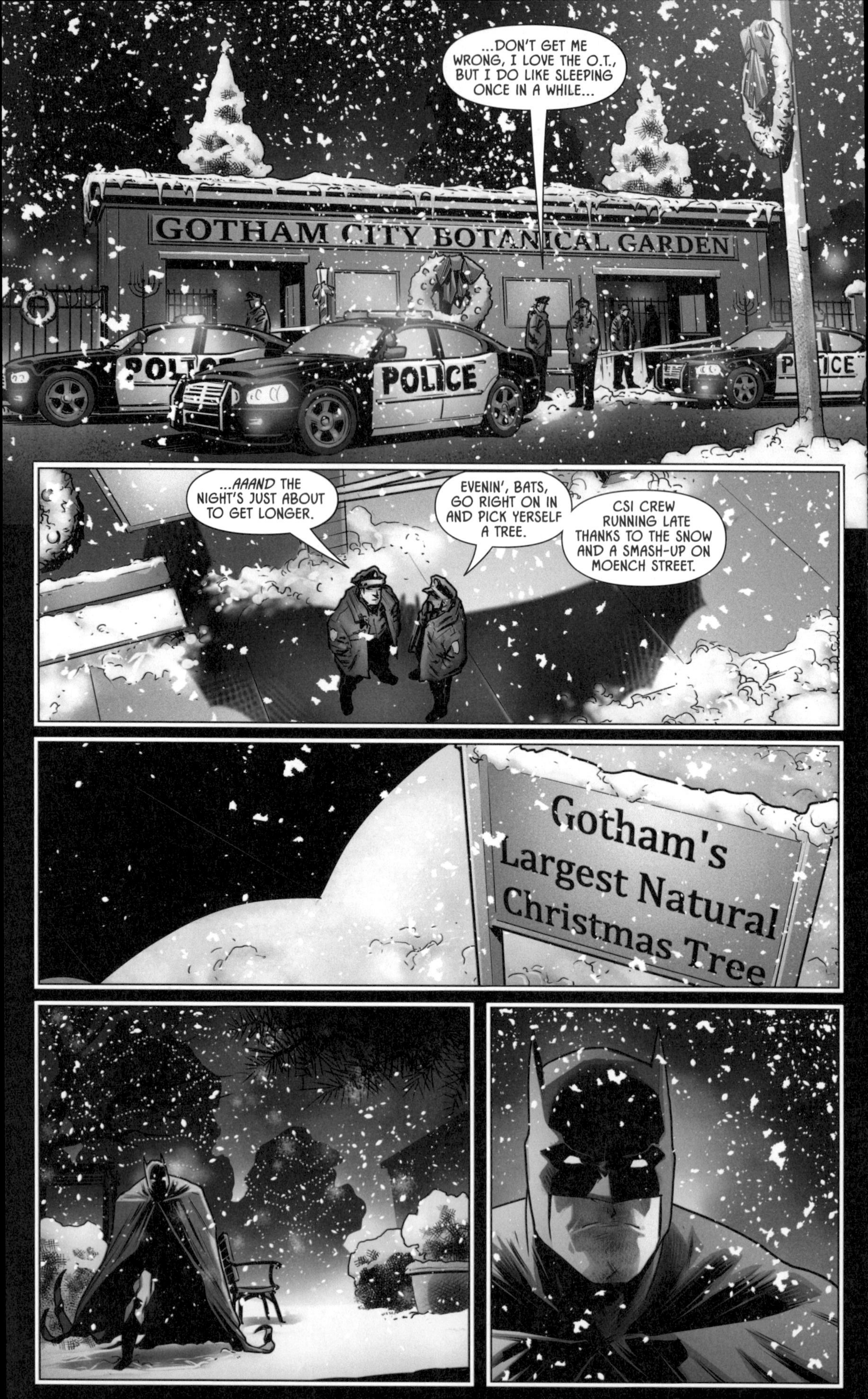
...DON'T GET ME WRONG, I LOVE THE O.T., BUT I DO LIKE SLEEPING ONCE IN A WHILE...
GOTHAM CITY BOTANICAL GARDEN
POLICE
POLICE
POLICE
...AAAND THE NIGHT'S JUST ABOUT TO GET LONGER.
EVENIN', BATS, GO RIGHT ON IN AND PICK YERSELF A TREE.
CSI CREW RUNNING LATE THANKS TO THE SNOW AND A SMASH-UP ON MOENCH STREET.
Gotham's Largest Natural Christmas Tree

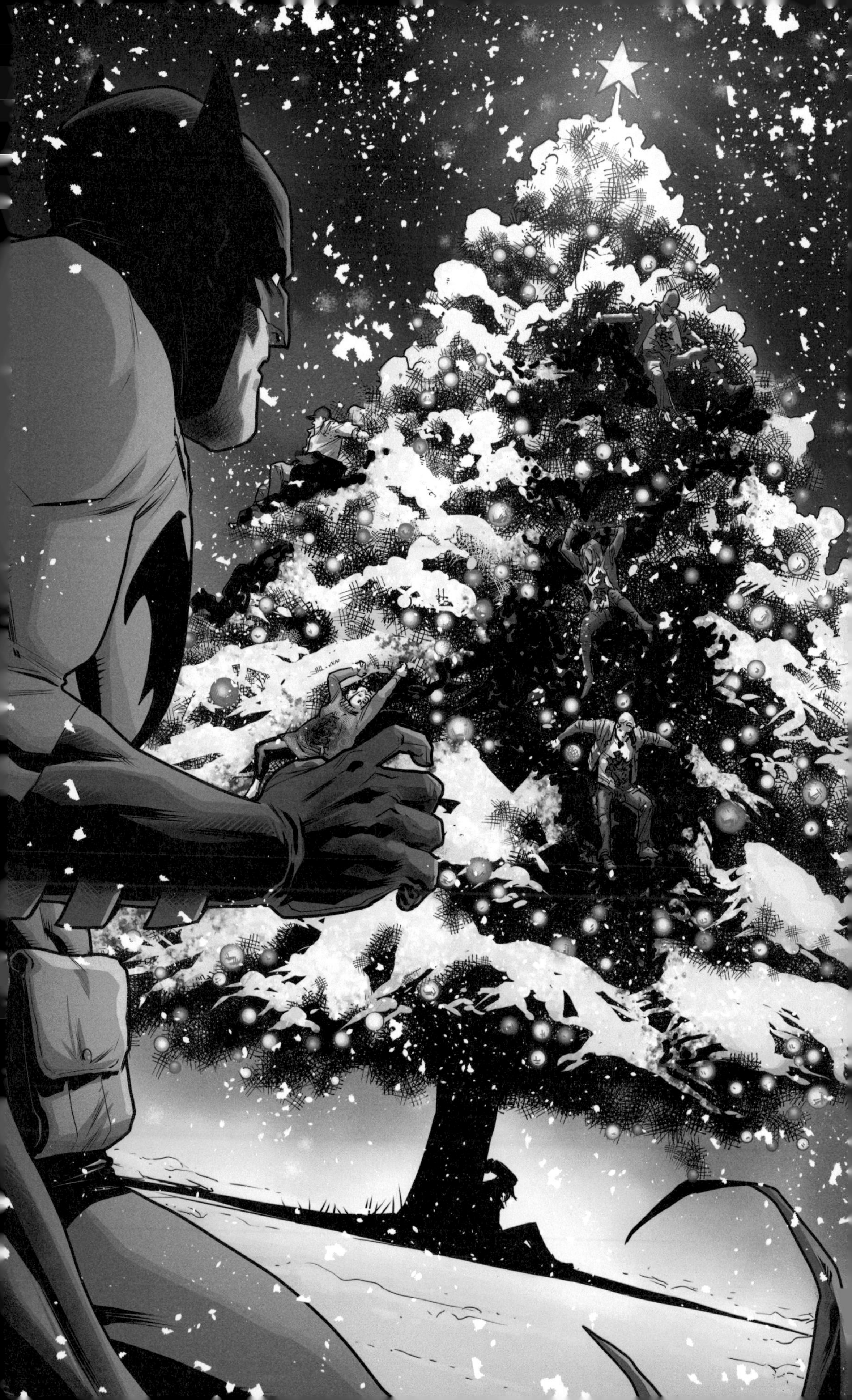

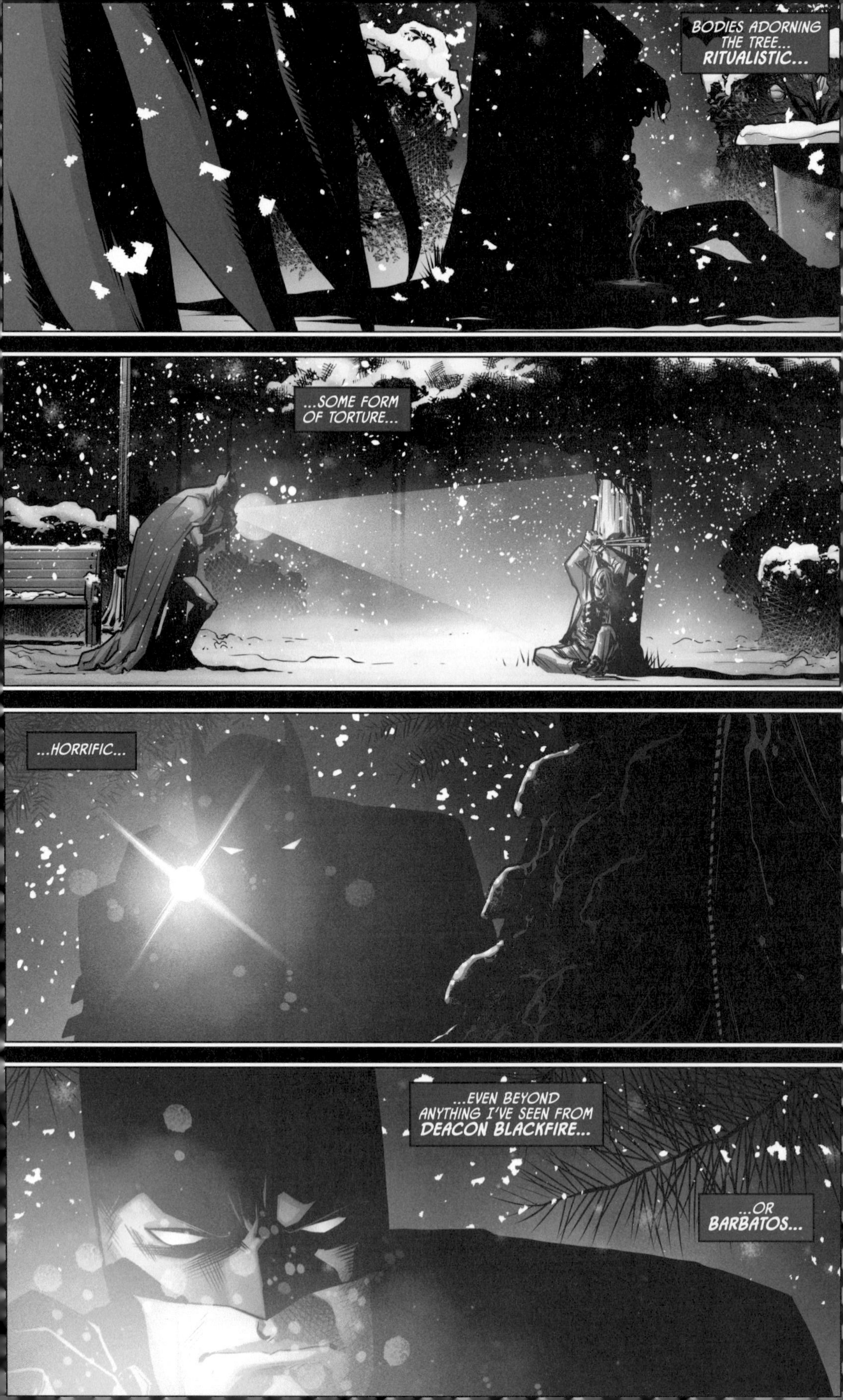
BODIES ADORNING THE TREE... RITUALISTIC...
...SOME FORM OF TORTURE...
...HORRIFIC...
...EVEN BEYOND ANYTHING I'VE SEEN FROM DEACON BLACKFIRE...
...OR BARBATOS...

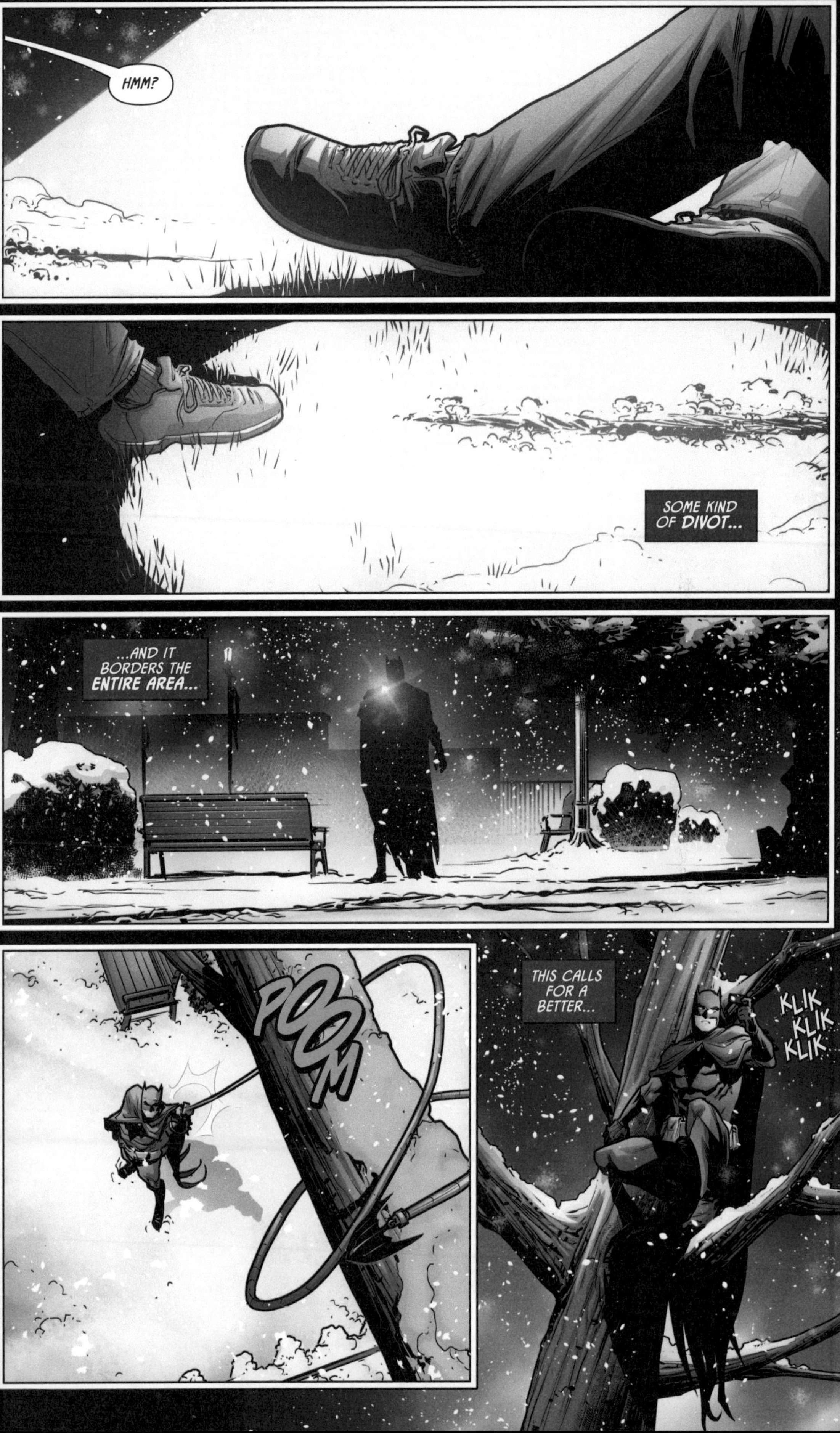
HMM?
SOME KIND OF DIVOT...
...AND IT BORDERS THE ENTIRE AREA...
POOM
THIS CALLS FOR A BETTER...
KLIK KLIK KLIK

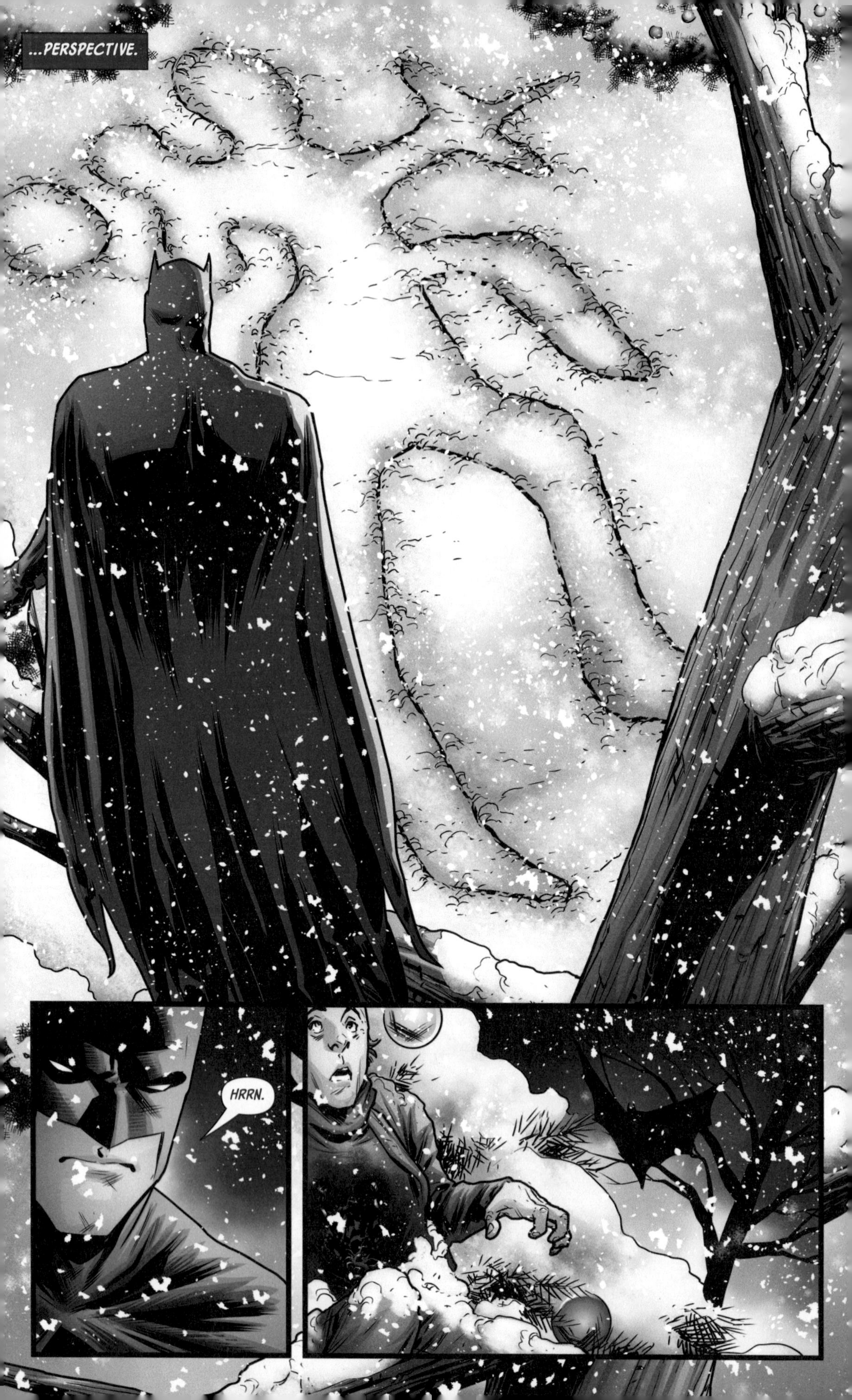
...PERSPECTIVE.
HRRN.

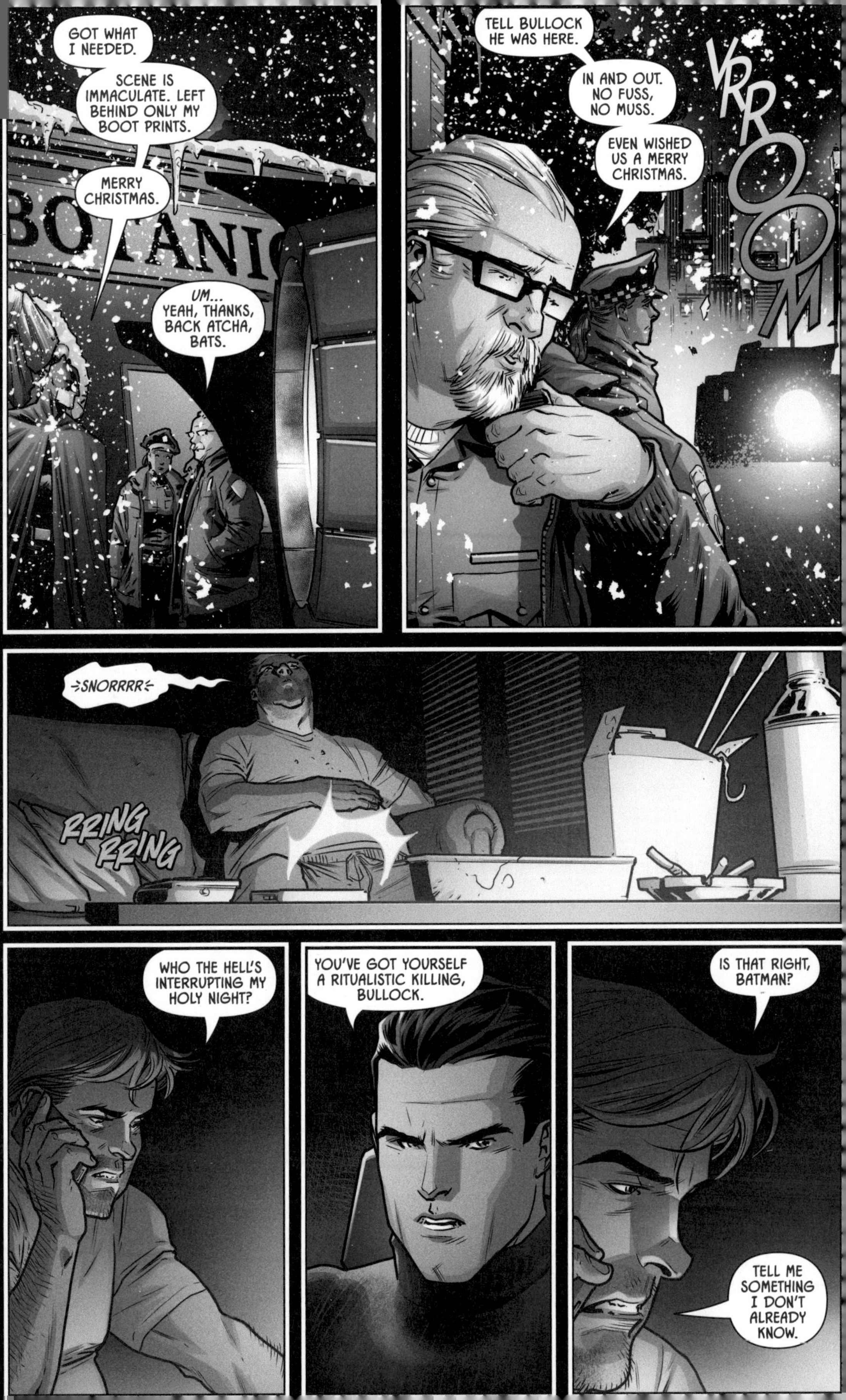
GOT WHAT I NEEDED.
SCENE IS IMMACULATE. LEFT BEHIND ONLY MY BOOT PRINTS.
MERRY CHRISTMAS.
BOTANIC
UM... YEAH, THANKS, BACK ATCHA, BATS.
TELL BULLOCK HE WAS HERE.
IN AND OUT. NO FUSS, NO MUSS.
EVEN WISHED US A MERRY CHRISTMAS.
VRROOOM
SNORRRR
RRING RRING
WHO THE HELL'S INTERRUPTING MY HOLY NIGHT?
YOU'VE GOT YOURSELF A RITUALISTIC KILLING, BULLOCK.
IS THAT RIGHT, BATMAN?
TELL ME SOMETHING I DON'T ALREADY KNOW.

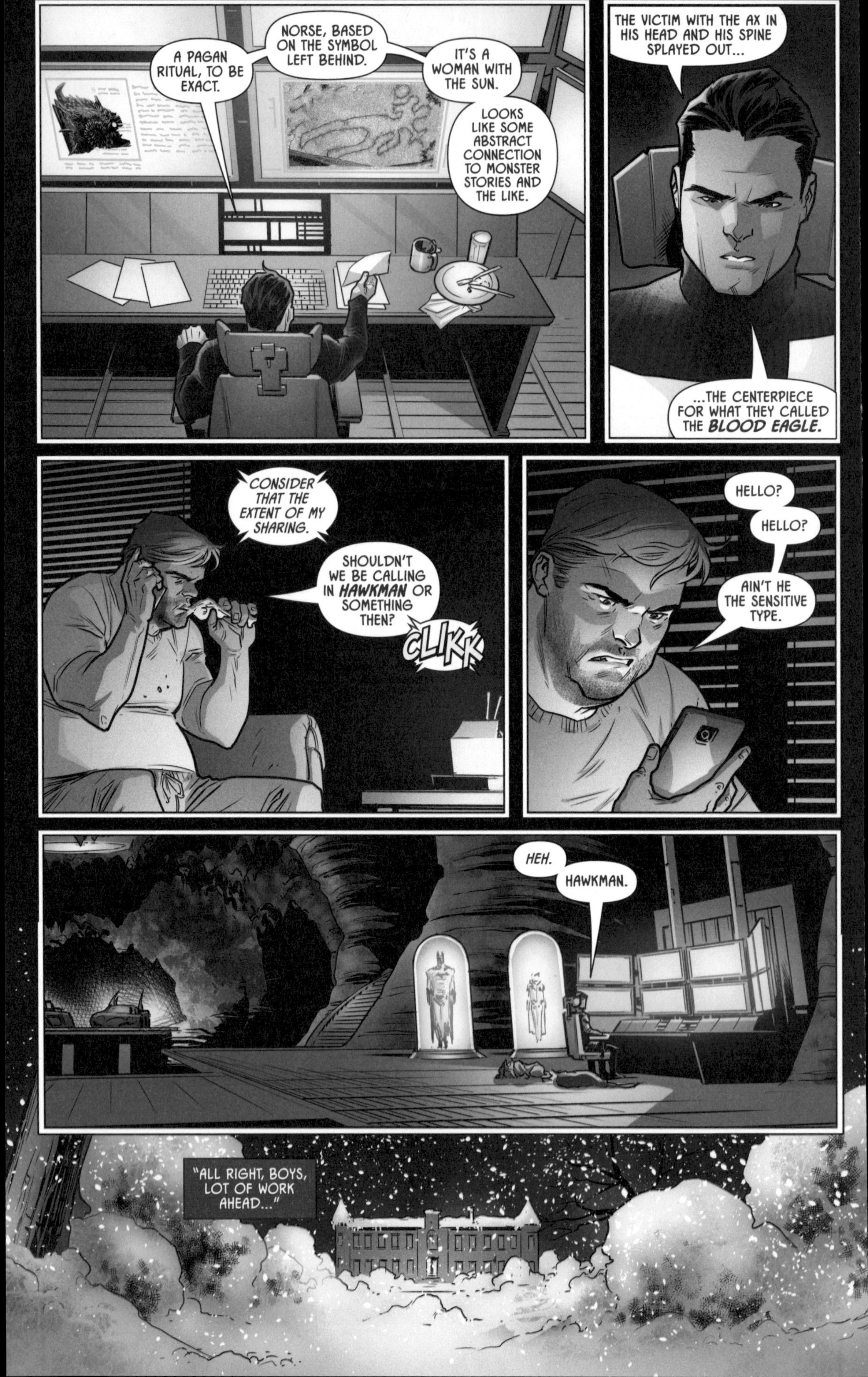
A PAGAN RITUAL, TO BE EXACT.
NORSE, BASED ON THE SYMBOL LEFT BEHIND.
IT'S A WOMAN WITH THE SUN.
LOOKS LIKE SOME ABSTRACT CONNECTION TO MONSTER STORIES AND THE LIKE.
THE VICTIM WITH THE AX IN HIS HEAD AND HIS SPINE SPLAYED OUT...
...THE CENTERPIECE FOR WHAT THEY CALLED THE *BLOOD EAGLE.*
CONSIDER THAT THE EXTENT OF MY SHARING.
SHOULDN'T WE BE CALLING IN *HAWKMAN* OR SOMETHING THEN?
CLIKK
HELLO?
HELLO?
AIN'T HE THE SENSITIVE TYPE.
HEH.
HAWKMAN.
"ALL RIGHT, BOYS, LOT OF WORK AHEAD..."

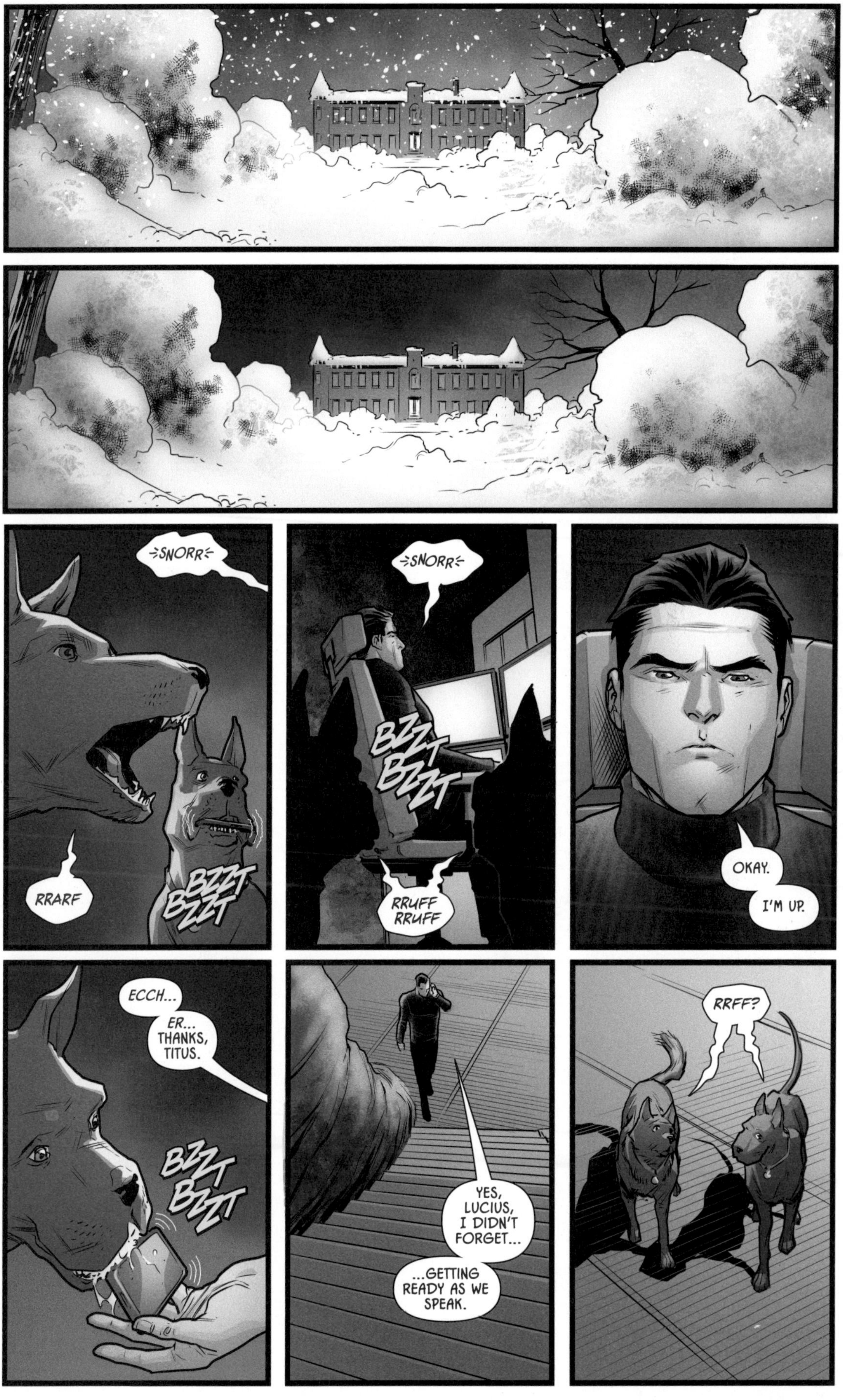

SNORR
RRARF
BZZT BZZT
SNORR
BZZT BZZT
RRUFF RRUFF
OKAY.
I'M UP.
ECCH...
ER... THANKS, TITUS.
BZZT BZZT
YES, LUCIUS, I DIDN'T FORGET...
...GETTING READY AS WE SPEAK.
RRFF?

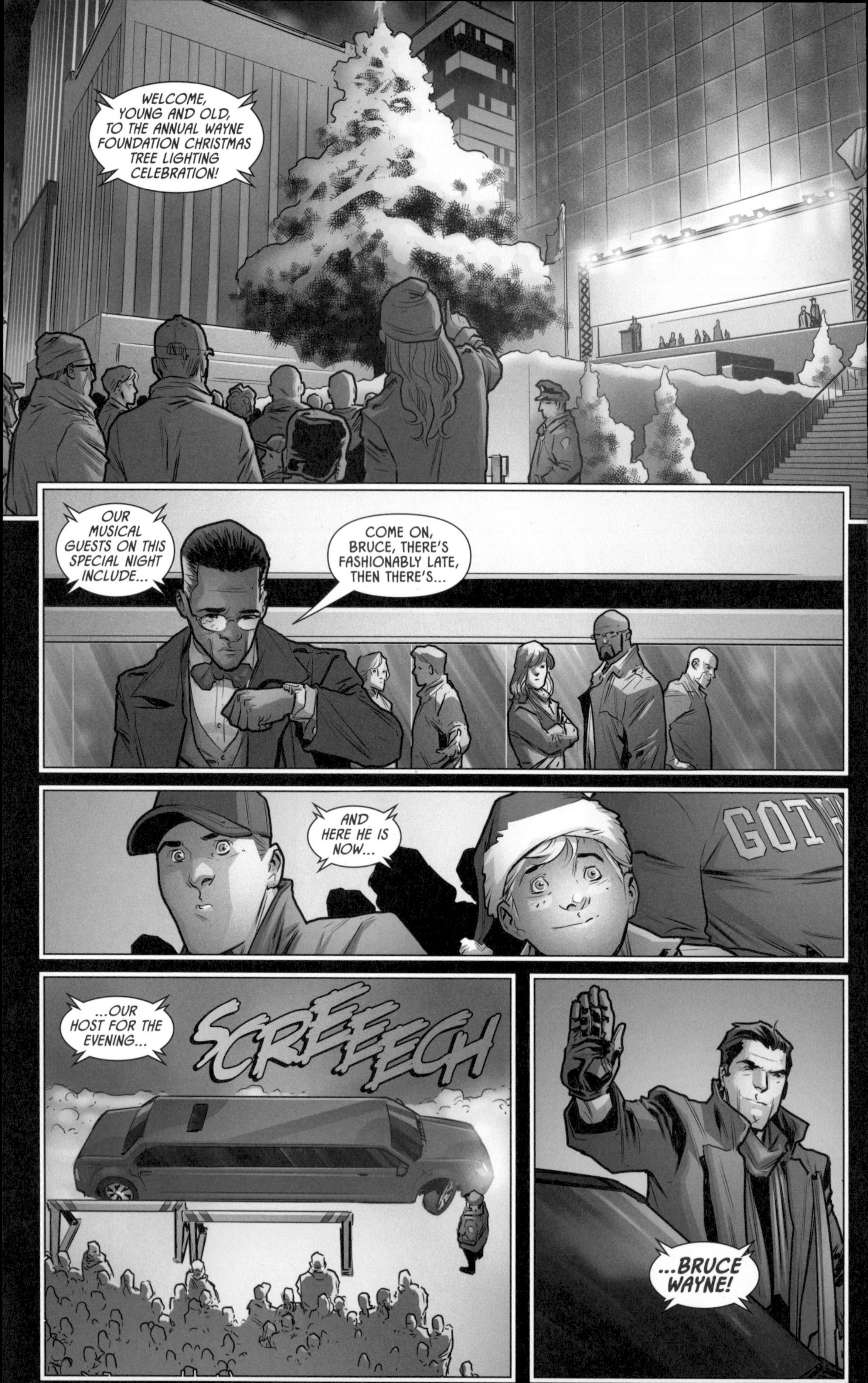
WELCOME, YOUNG AND OLD, TO THE ANNUAL WAYNE FOUNDATION CHRISTMAS TREE LIGHTING CELEBRATION!
OUR MUSICAL GUESTS ON THIS SPECIAL NIGHT INCLUDE...
COME ON, BRUCE, THERE'S FASHIONABLY LATE, THEN THERE'S...
AND HERE HE IS NOW...
...OUR HOST FOR THE EVENING...
SCREEECH
...BRUCE WAYNE!

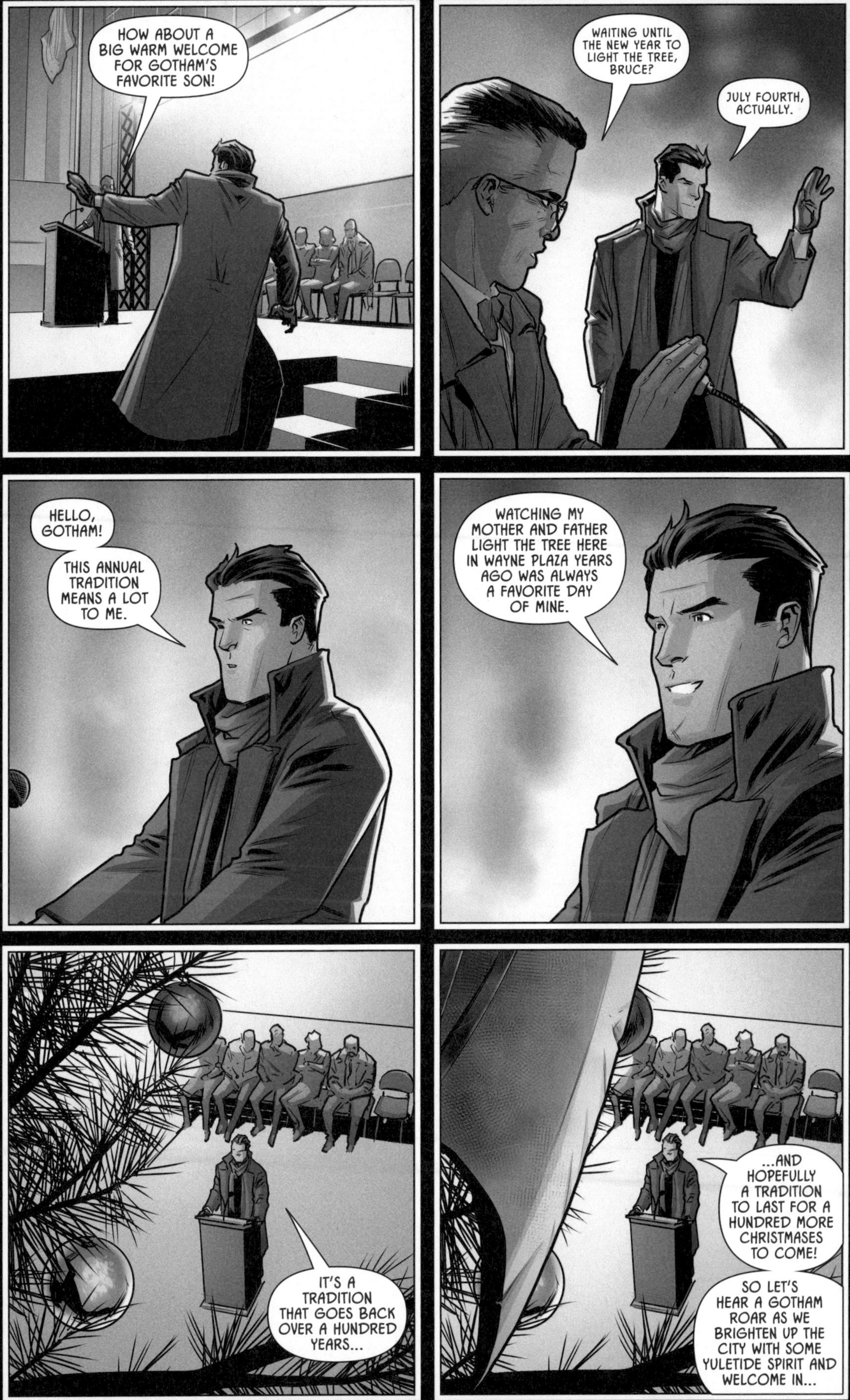
HOW ABOUT A BIG WARM WELCOME FOR GOTHAM'S FAVORITE SON!
WAITING UNTIL THE NEW YEAR TO LIGHT THE TREE, BRUCE?
JULY FOURTH, ACTUALLY.
HELLO, GOTHAM!
THIS ANNUAL TRADITION MEANS A LOT TO ME.
WATCHING MY MOTHER AND FATHER LIGHT THE TREE HERE IN WAYNE PLAZA YEARS AGO WAS ALWAYS A FAVORITE DAY OF MINE.
IT'S A TRADITION THAT GOES BACK OVER A HUNDRED YEARS...
...AND HOPEFULLY A TRADITION TO LAST FOR A HUNDRED MORE CHRISTMASES TO COME!
SO LET'S HEAR A GOTHAM ROAR AS WE BRIGHTEN UP THE CITY WITH SOME YULETIDE SPIRIT AND WELCOME IN...

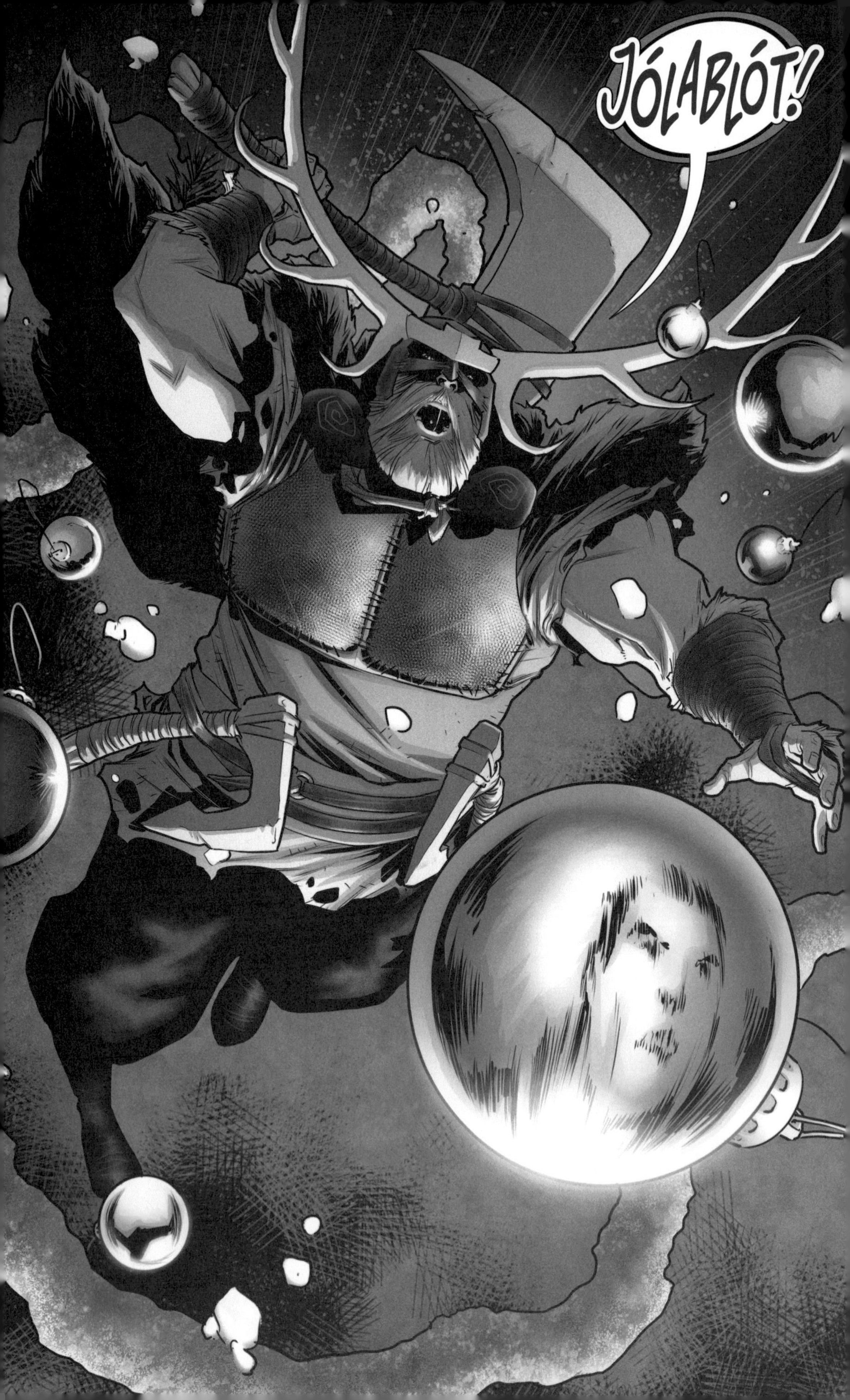
JÓLABLÓT!

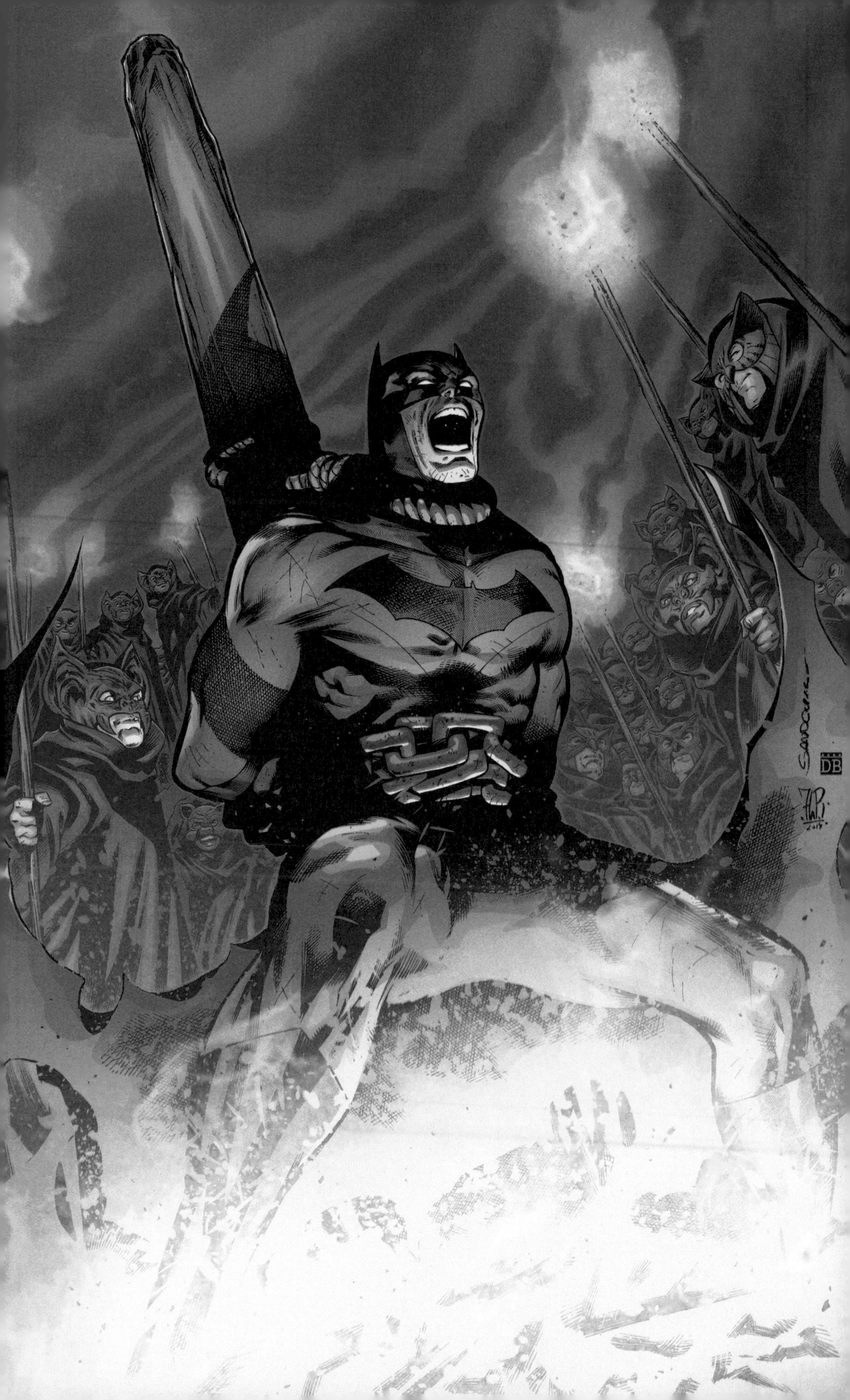

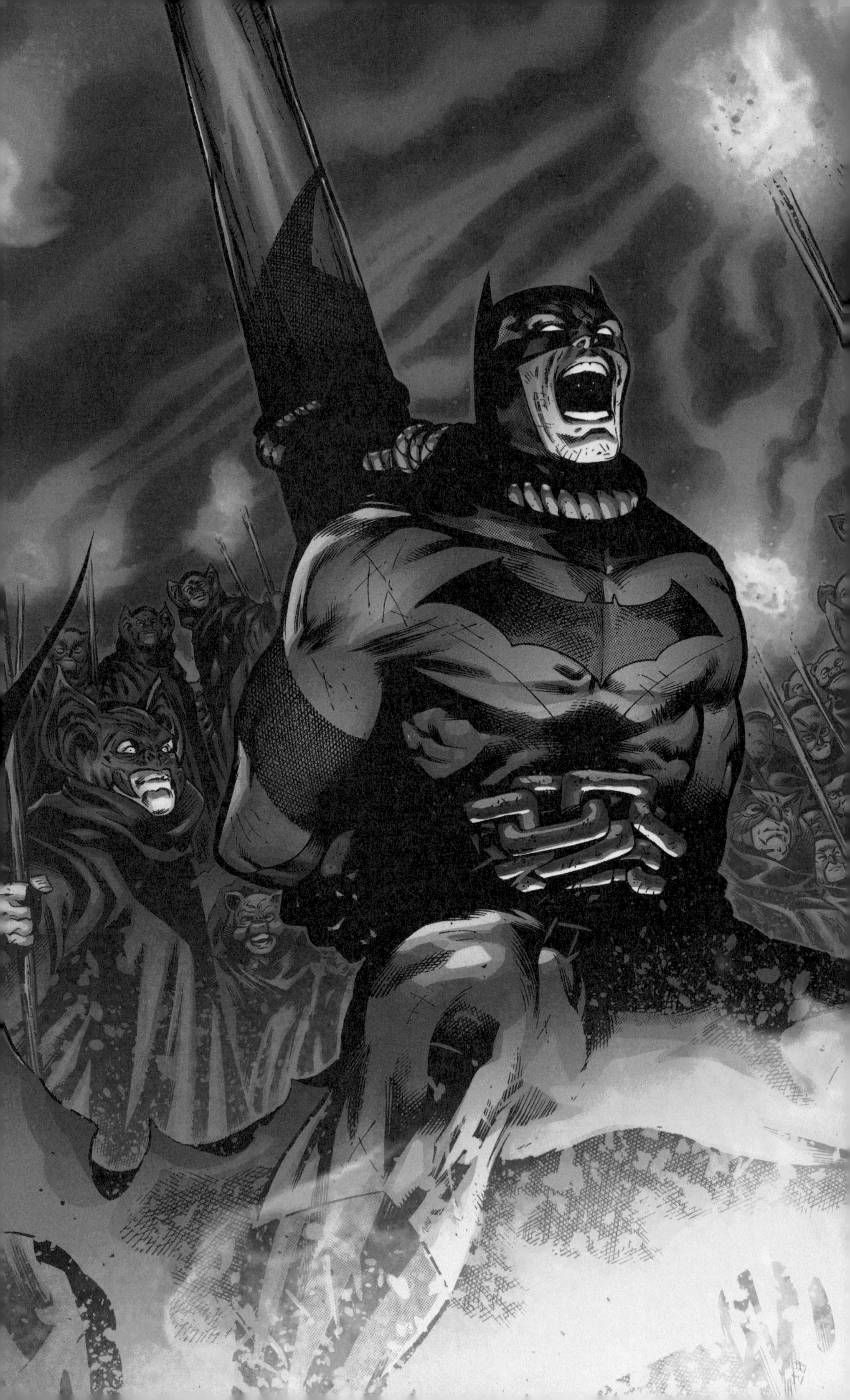

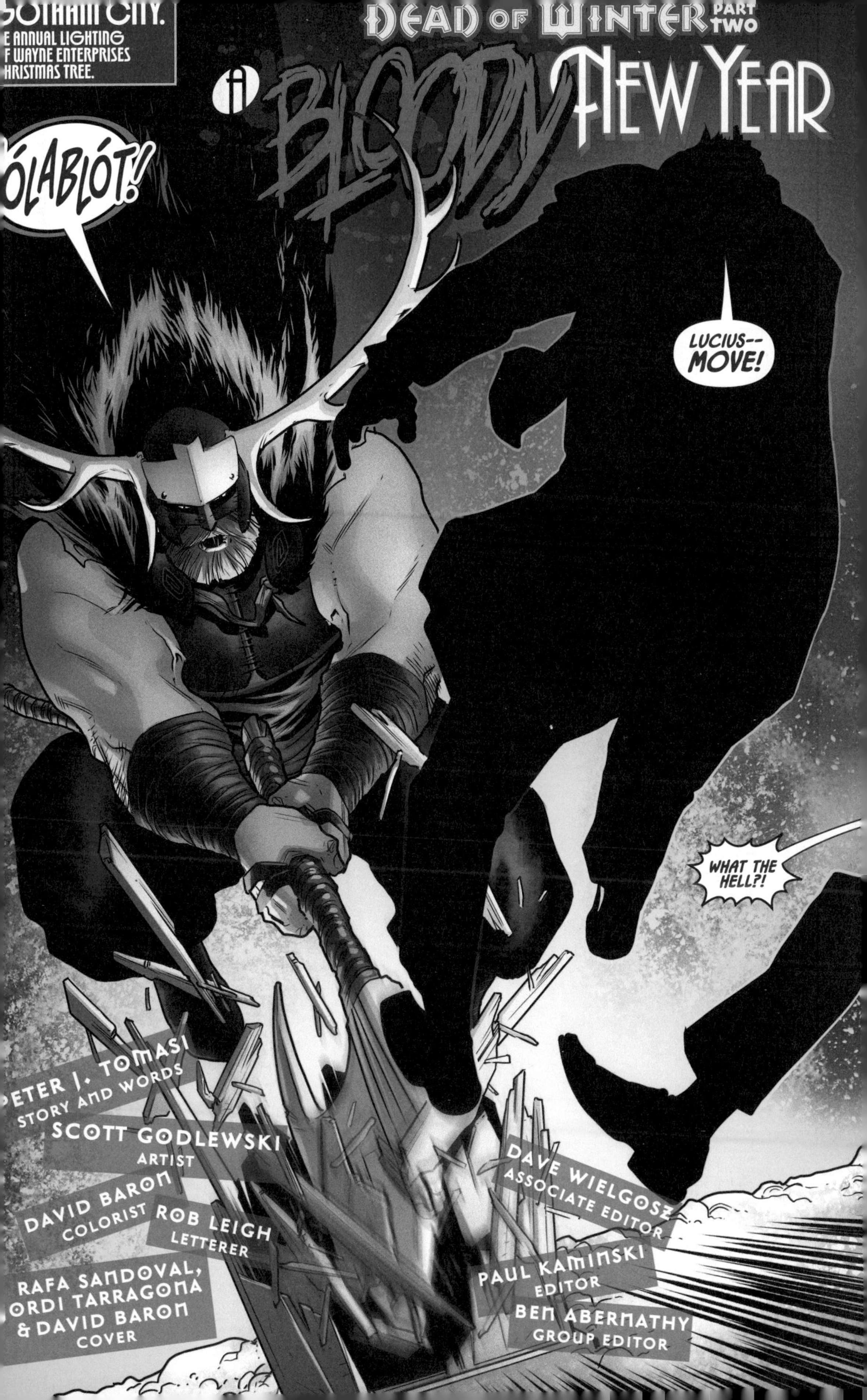

GOTHAM CITY.
E ANNUAL LIGHTING
F WAYNE ENTERPRISES
HRISTMAS TREE.
DEAD OF WINTER PART TWO
A BLOODY NEW YEAR
ÓLABLÓT!
LUCIUS-- MOVE!
WHAT THE HELL?!
ETER J. TOMASI STORY AND WORDS
SCOTT GODLEWSKI ARTIST
DAVID BARON COLORIST
ROB LEIGH LETTERER
RAFA SANDOVAL, ORDI TARRAGONA & DAVID BARON COVER
DAVE WIELGOSZ ASSOCIATE EDITOR
PAUL KAMINSKI EDITOR
BEN ABERNATHY GROUP EDITOR

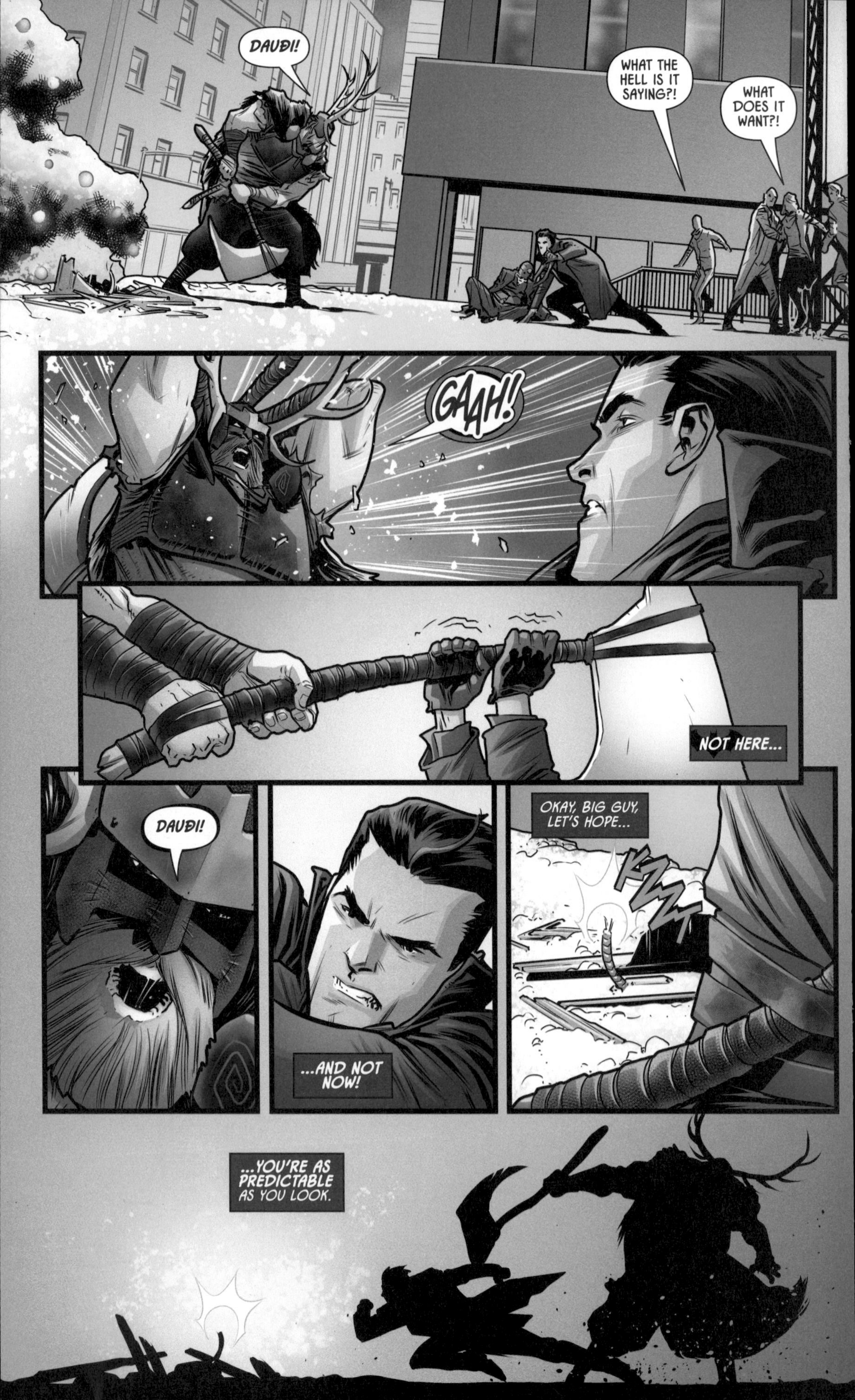
DAUÐI!
WHAT THE HELL IS IT SAYING?!
WHAT DOES IT WANT?!
GAAH!
NOT HERE...
DAUÐI!
...AND NOT NOW!
OKAY, BIG GUY, LET'S HOPE...
KZZT
...YOU'RE AS PREDICTABLE AS YOU LOOK.

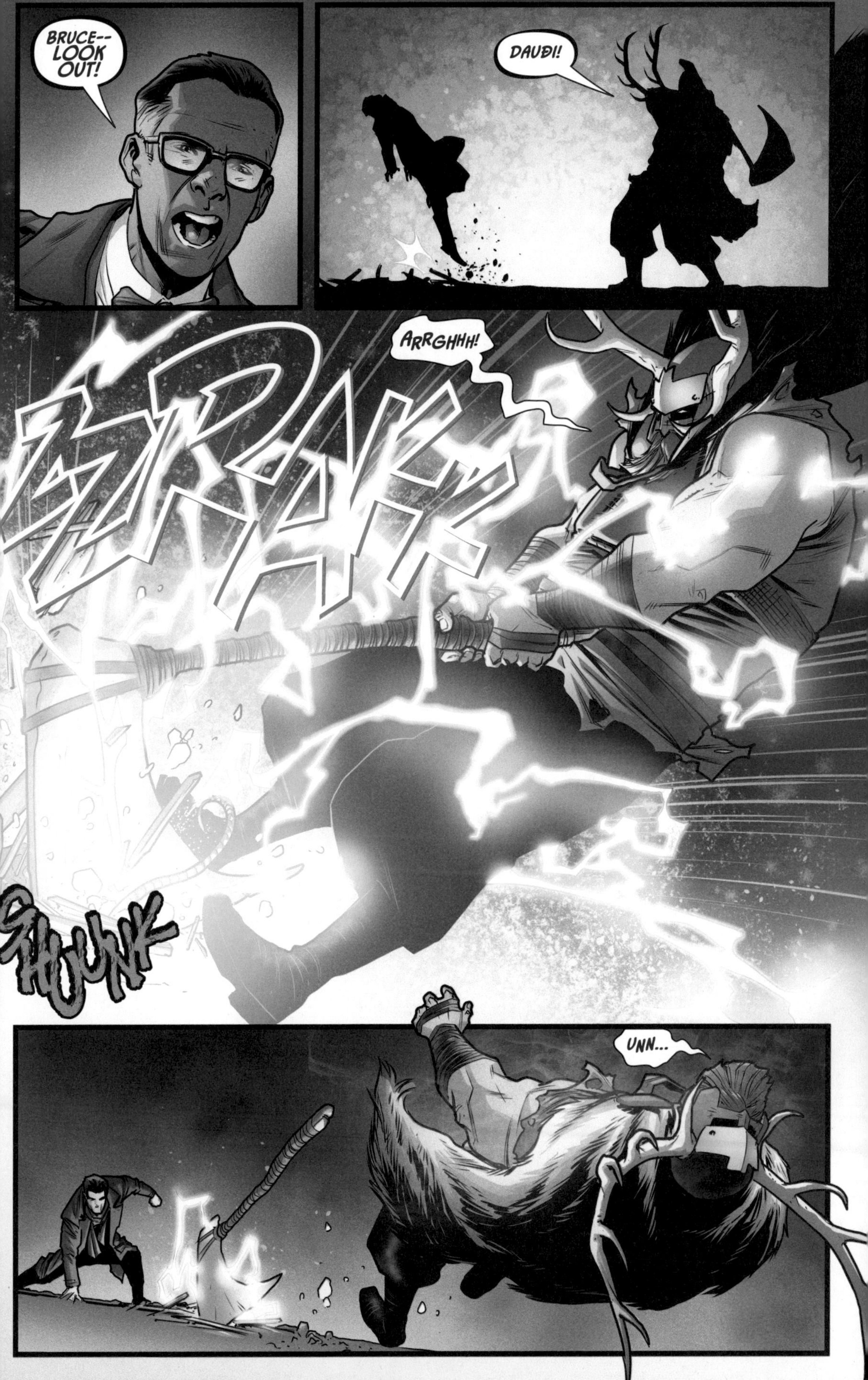
BRUCE-- LOOK OUT!
DAUÐI!
ARRGHHH!
THUNK
UNN...

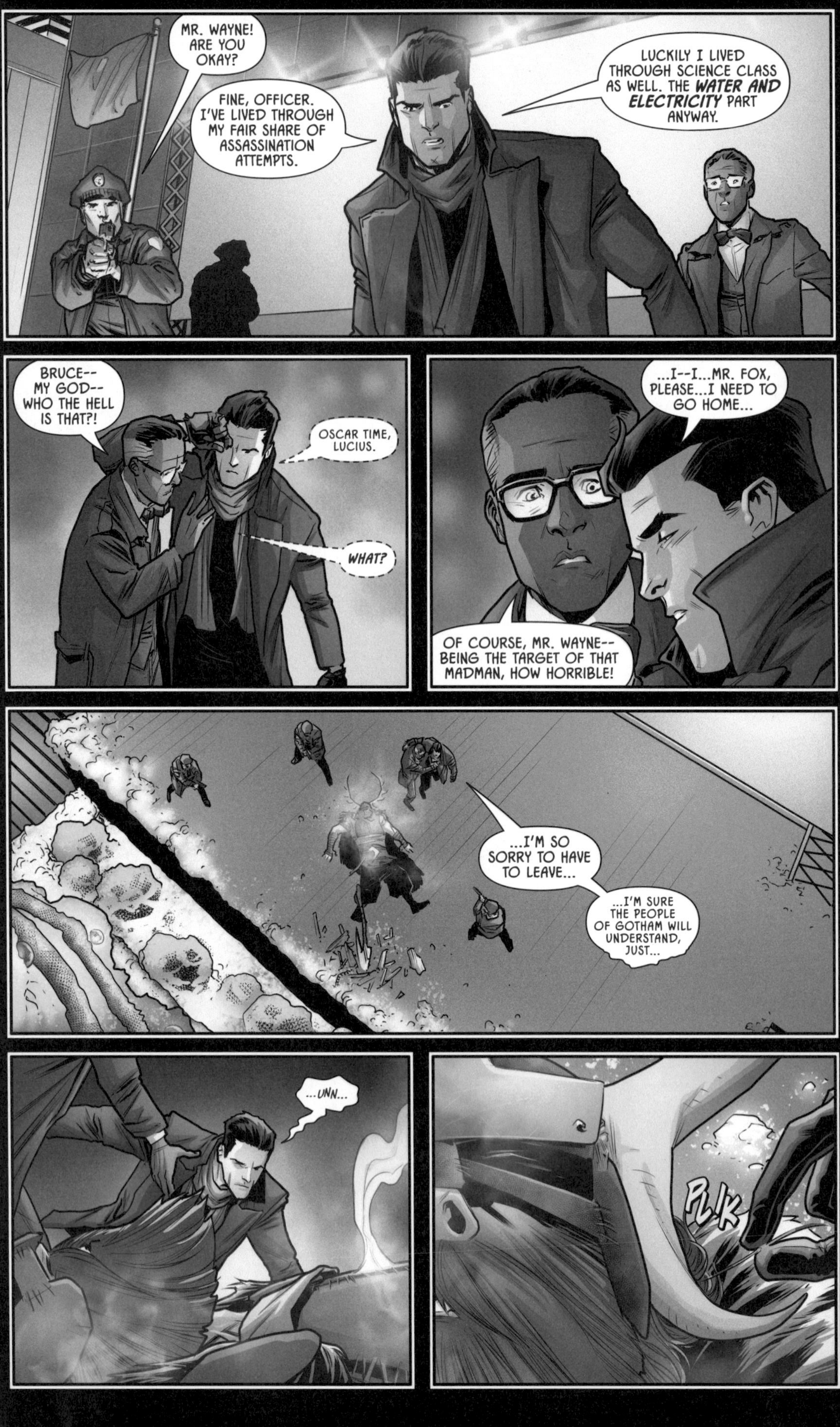
MR. WAYNE! ARE YOU OKAY?
FINE, OFFICER. I'VE LIVED THROUGH MY FAIR SHARE OF ASSASSINATION ATTEMPTS.
LUCKILY I LIVED THROUGH SCIENCE CLASS AS WELL. THE ***WATER AND ELECTRICITY*** PART ANYWAY.
BRUCE-- MY GOD-- WHO THE HELL IS THAT?!
OSCAR TIME, LUCIUS.
WHAT?
...I--I...MR. FOX, PLEASE...I NEED TO GO HOME...
OF COURSE, MR. WAYNE-- BEING THE TARGET OF THAT MADMAN, HOW HORRIBLE!
...I'M SO SORRY TO HAVE TO LEAVE...
...I'M SURE THE PEOPLE OF GOTHAM WILL UNDERSTAND, JUST...
...UNN...
PLIK

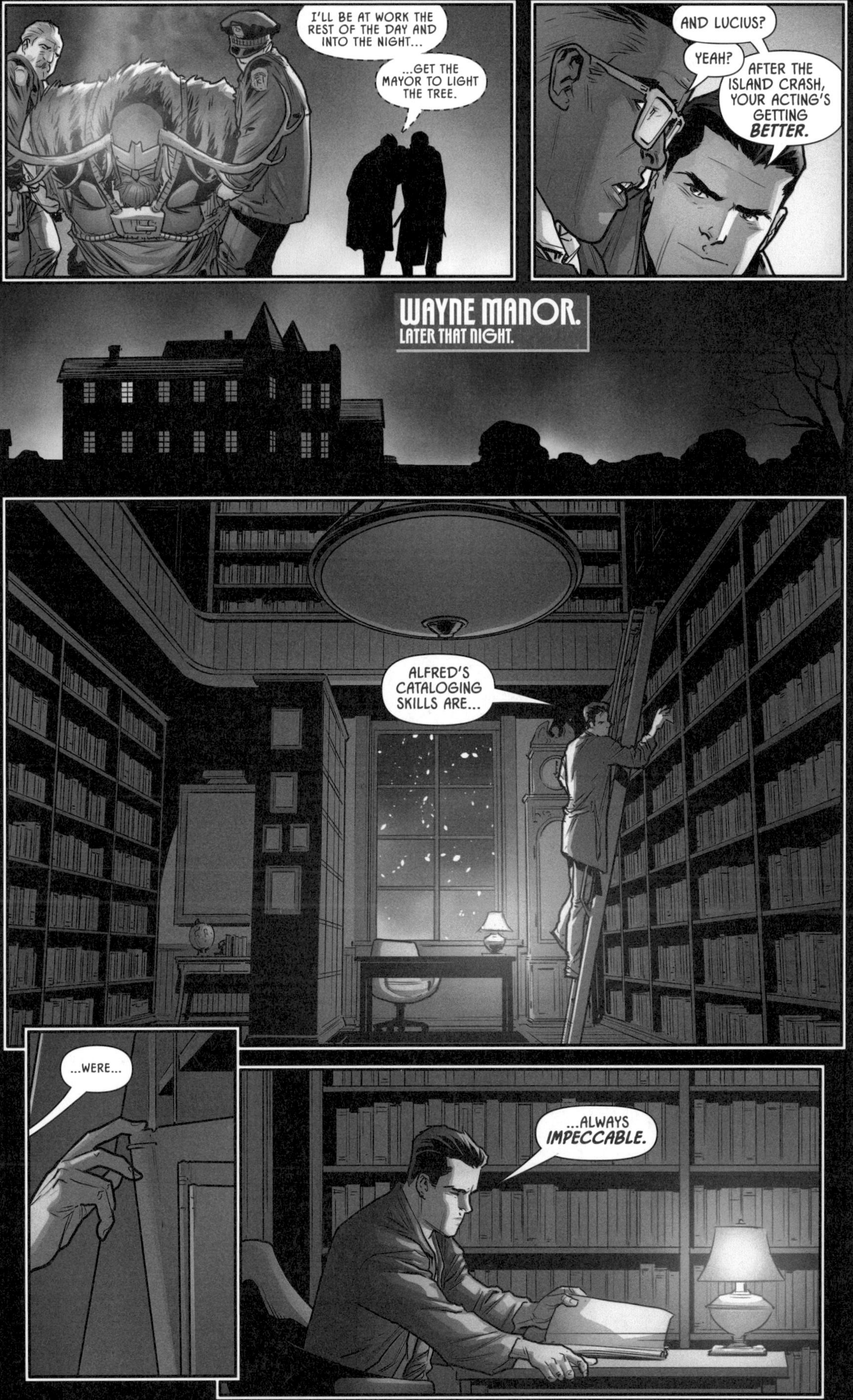
I'LL BE AT WORK THE REST OF THE DAY AND INTO THE NIGHT...
...GET THE MAYOR TO LIGHT THE TREE.
AND LUCIUS?
YEAH?
AFTER THE ISLAND CRASH, YOUR ACTING'S GETTING *BETTER.*
WAYNE MANOR.
LATER THAT NIGHT.
ALFRED'S CATALOGING SKILLS ARE...
...WERE...
...ALWAYS *IMPECCABLE.*

OPEN *VOICE LOG.* SCRAMBLED ENCRYPTION.

MEMO RECORDING. ORIGINAL FILE.

ATTACKER SPOKE IN BROKEN OLD ENGLISH DIALECT.

SOUNDED NORSE...

...WHICH LINES UP WITH THE *GROUND CARVING* I SAW AT THE BOTANICAL GARDEN.

KNEW IT LOOKED *FAMILIAR.*

RELATED TO ANNUAL PAGAN YULE RITUALS AT THE END OF THE SUN'S CYCLE. WINTER SOLSTICE.

MYSTERIES SURROUND THESE CELEBRATIONS.

WERE THEY HONORING A *SUN GODDESS?* FREEDOM FROM *DEATH GODS?* PRAISING THE CYCLE OF *REBIRTH...*

...WHATEVER IT WAS, THERE WAS CERTAINLY NO WRAPPING PAPER OR JINGLE BELLS INVOLVED.

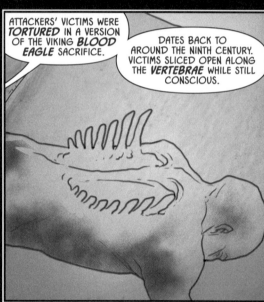

ATTACKERS' VICTIMS WERE *TORTURED* IN A VERSION OF THE VIKING *BLOOD EAGLE* SACRIFICE.

DATES BACK TO AROUND THE NINTH CENTURY. VICTIMS SLICED OPEN ALONG THE *VERTEBRAE* WHILE STILL CONSCIOUS.

THEIR BONES AND MUSCLES PULLED AWAY FROM THE BODY TO REPRESENT WINGS.

...THE THINGS HUMANS DO TO EACH OTHER...

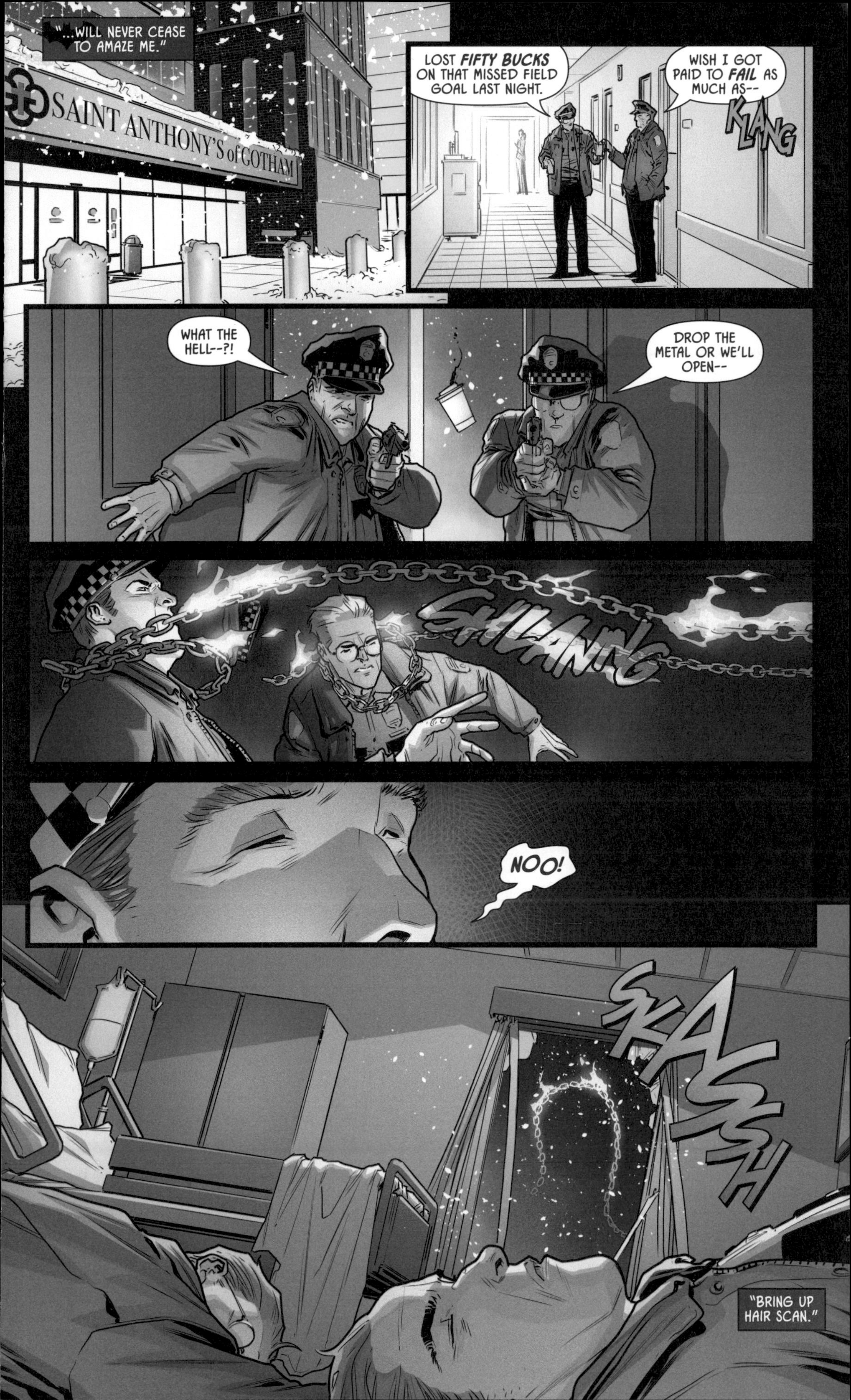
"...WILL NEVER CEASE TO AMAZE ME."
SAINT ANTHONY'S of GOTHAM
LOST FIFTY BUCKS ON THAT MISSED FIELD GOAL LAST NIGHT.
WISH I GOT PAID TO FAIL AS MUCH AS--
KLANG
WHAT THE HELL--?!
DROP THE METAL OR WE'LL OPEN--
SHHANNG
NOO!
SKASSH
"BRING UP HAIR SCAN."

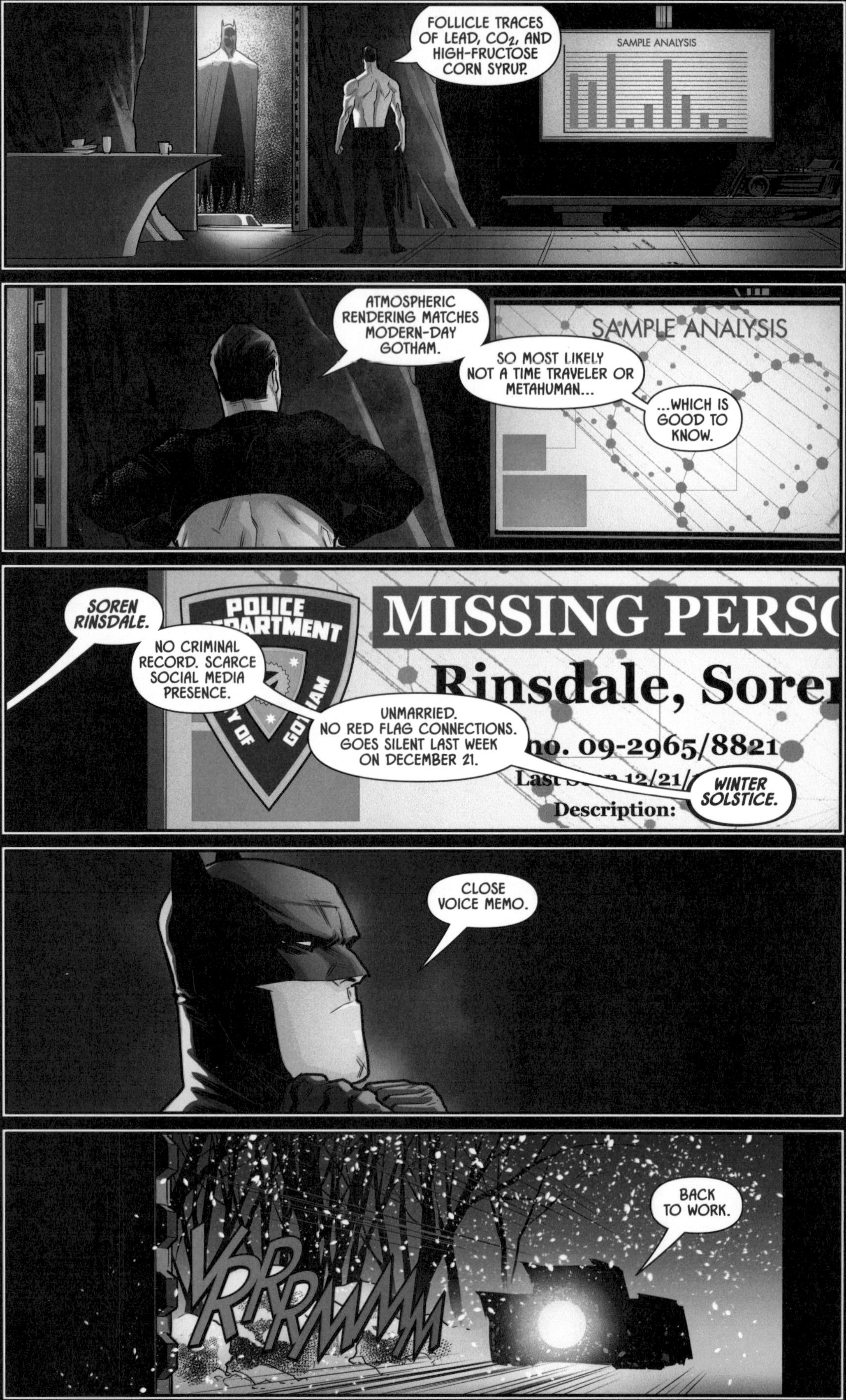
FOLLICLE TRACES OF LEAD, CO_2, AND HIGH-FRUCTOSE CORN SYRUP.
SAMPLE ANALYSIS
ATMOSPHERIC RENDERING MATCHES MODERN-DAY GOTHAM.
SAMPLE ANALYSIS
SO MOST LIKELY NOT A TIME TRAVELER OR METAHUMAN...
...WHICH IS GOOD TO KNOW.
SOREN RINSDALE.
MISSING PERSO
Rinsdale, Soren
NO CRIMINAL RECORD. SCARCE SOCIAL MEDIA PRESENCE.
UNMARRIED. NO RED FLAG CONNECTIONS. GOES SILENT LAST WEEK ON DECEMBER 21.
no. 09-2965/8821
WINTER SOLSTICE.
Description:
CLOSE VOICE MEMO.
VRRRMMM
BACK TO WORK.

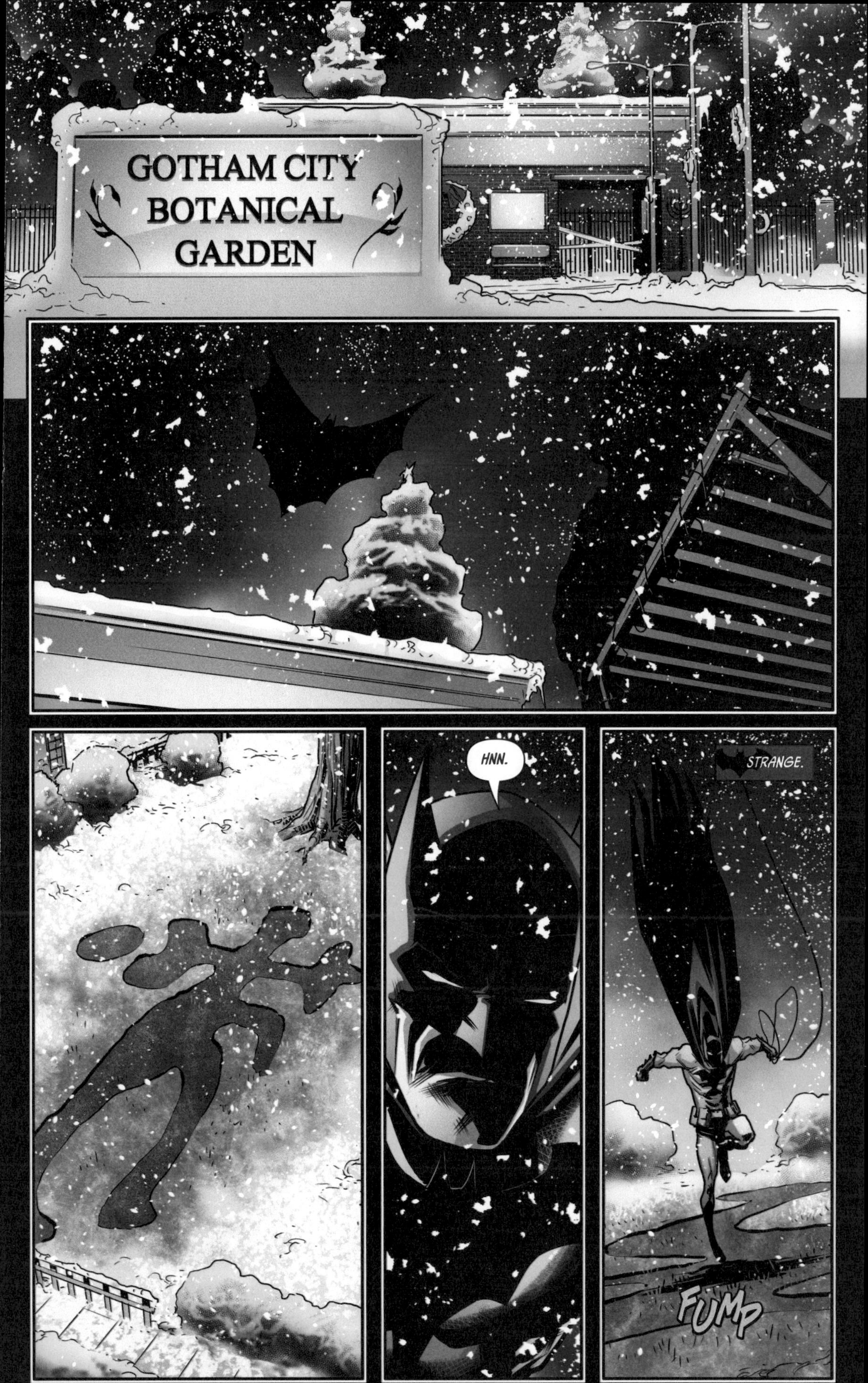
GOTHAM CITY
BOTANICAL
GARDEN
HNN.
STRANGE.
FUMP

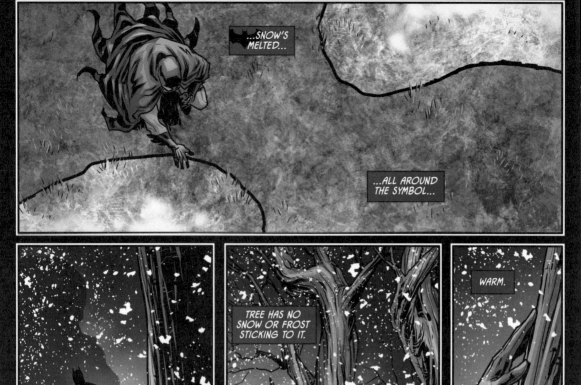

...SNOW'S MELTED...

...ALL AROUND THE SYMBOL...

TREE HAS NO SNOW OR FROST STICKING TO IT.

WARM.

ARGHH!

CHANNG

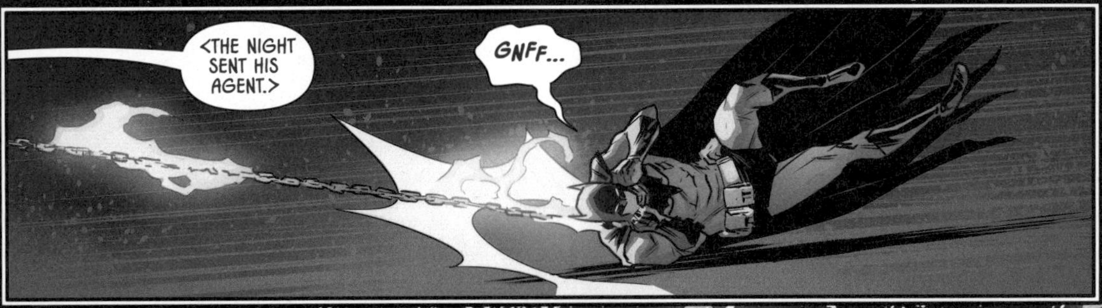
<THE NIGHT SENT HIS AGENT.>
GNFF...

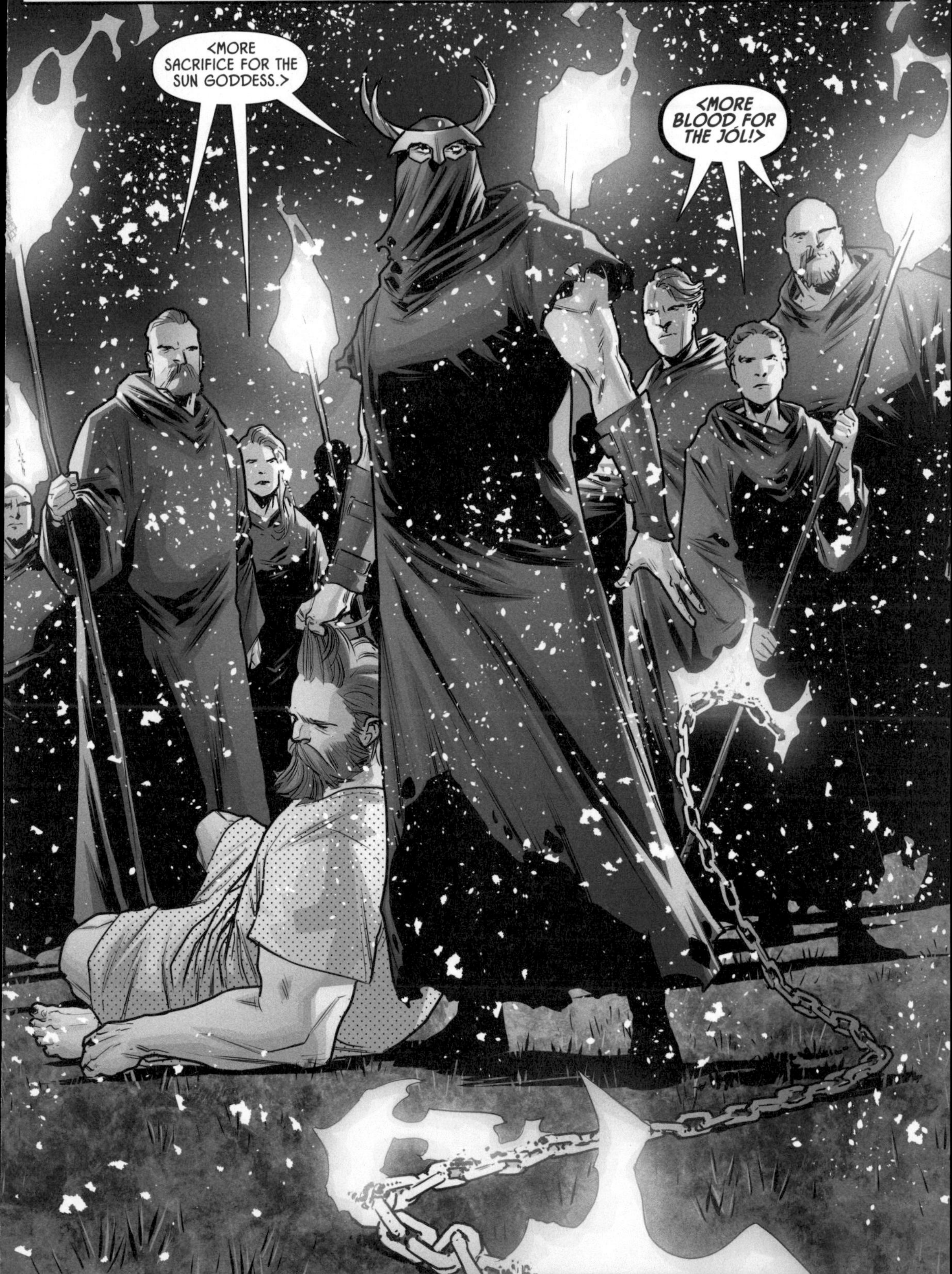
<MORE SACRIFICE FOR THE SUN GODDESS.>
<MORE BLOOD FOR THE JÓL!>

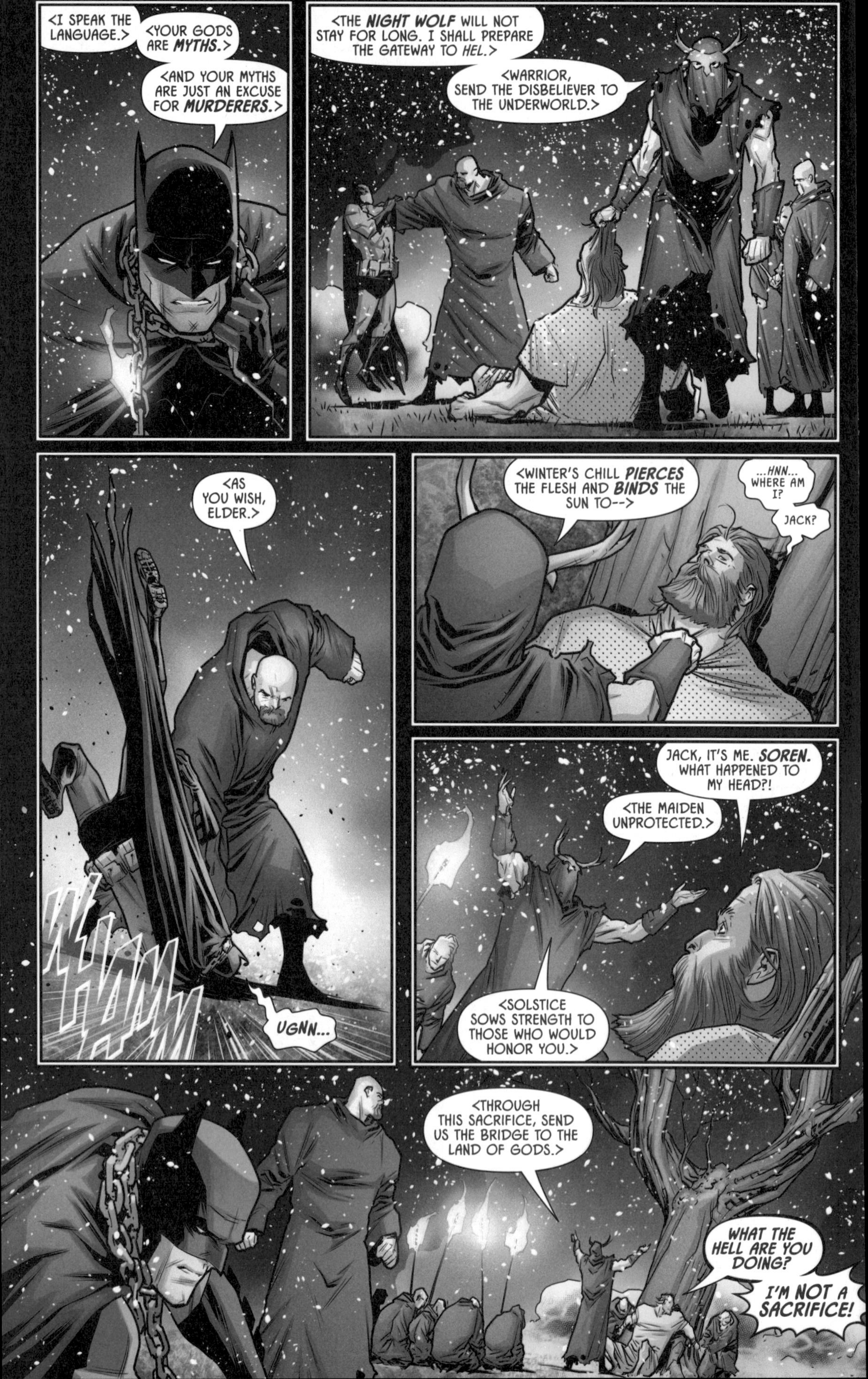

<I SPEAK THE LANGUAGE.>
<YOUR GODS ARE MYTHS.>
<AND YOUR MYTHS ARE JUST AN EXCUSE FOR MURDERERS.>
<THE NIGHT WOLF WILL NOT STAY FOR LONG. I SHALL PREPARE THE GATEWAY TO HEL.>
<WARRIOR, SEND THE DISBELIEVER TO THE UNDERWORLD.>
<AS YOU WISH, ELDER.>
WHAM
UGNN...
<WINTER'S CHILL PIERCES THE FLESH AND BINDS THE SUN TO-->
...HNN... WHERE AM I?
JACK?
JACK, IT'S ME. SOREN. WHAT HAPPENED TO MY HEAD?!
<THE MAIDEN UNPROTECTED.>
<SOLSTICE SOWS STRENGTH TO THOSE WHO WOULD HONOR YOU.>
<THROUGH THIS SACRIFICE, SEND US THE BRIDGE TO THE LAND OF GODS.>
WHAT THE HELL ARE YOU DOING?
I'M NOT A SACRIFICE!

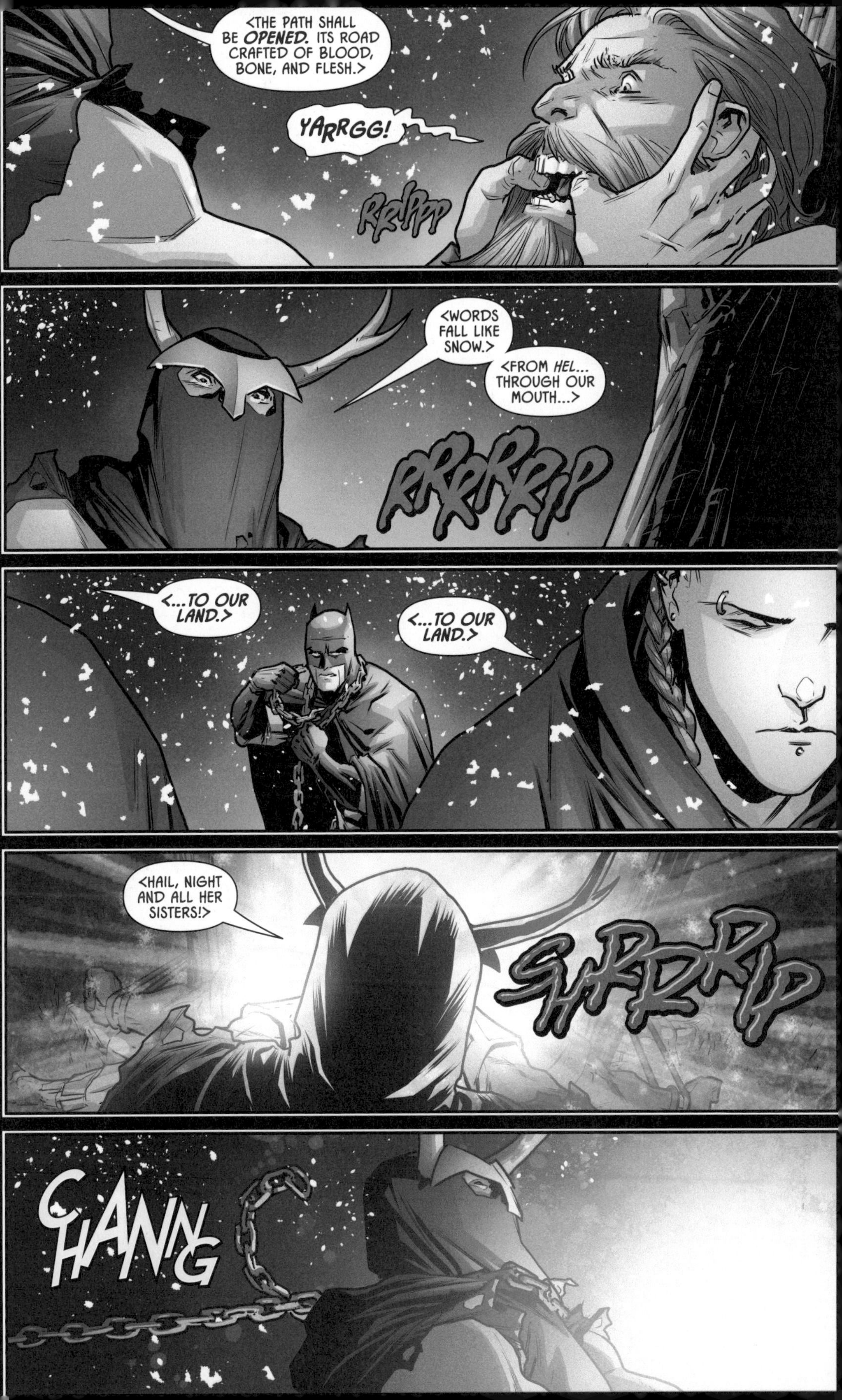
<THE PATH SHALL BE OPENED. ITS ROAD CRAFTED OF BLOOD, BONE, AND FLESH.>
YARRGG!
RRIPPP
<WORDS FALL LIKE SNOW.>
<FROM HEL... THROUGH OUR MOUTH...>
RRRRRIP
<...TO OUR LAND.>
<...TO OUR LAND.>
<HAIL, NIGHT AND ALL HER SISTERS!>
SHRRRIP
CHANNG

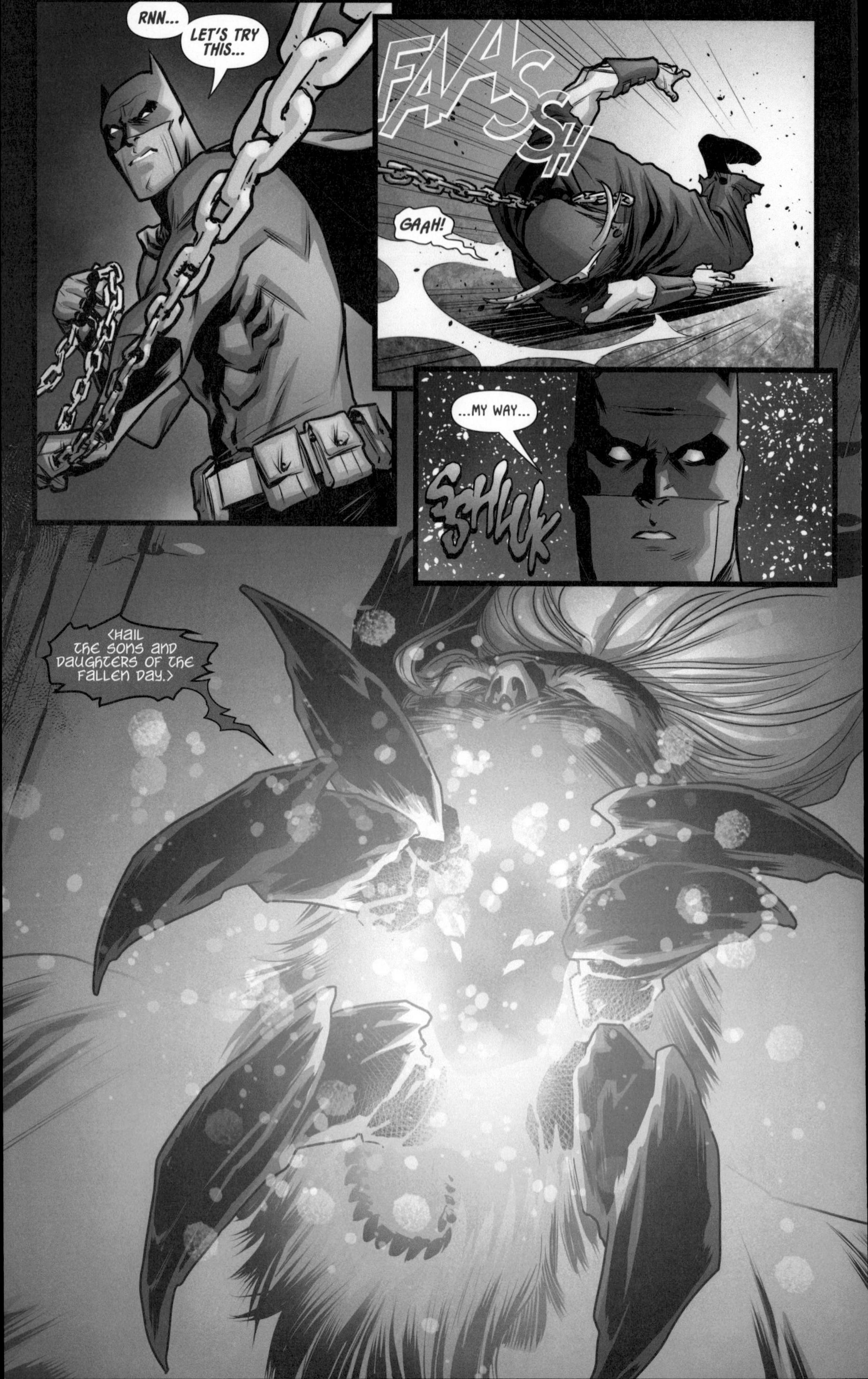
RNN...
LET'S TRY THIS...
FAASSH
GAAH!
...MY WAY...
SSHLUK
<HAIL THE SONS AND DAUGHTERS OF THE FALLEN DAY.>

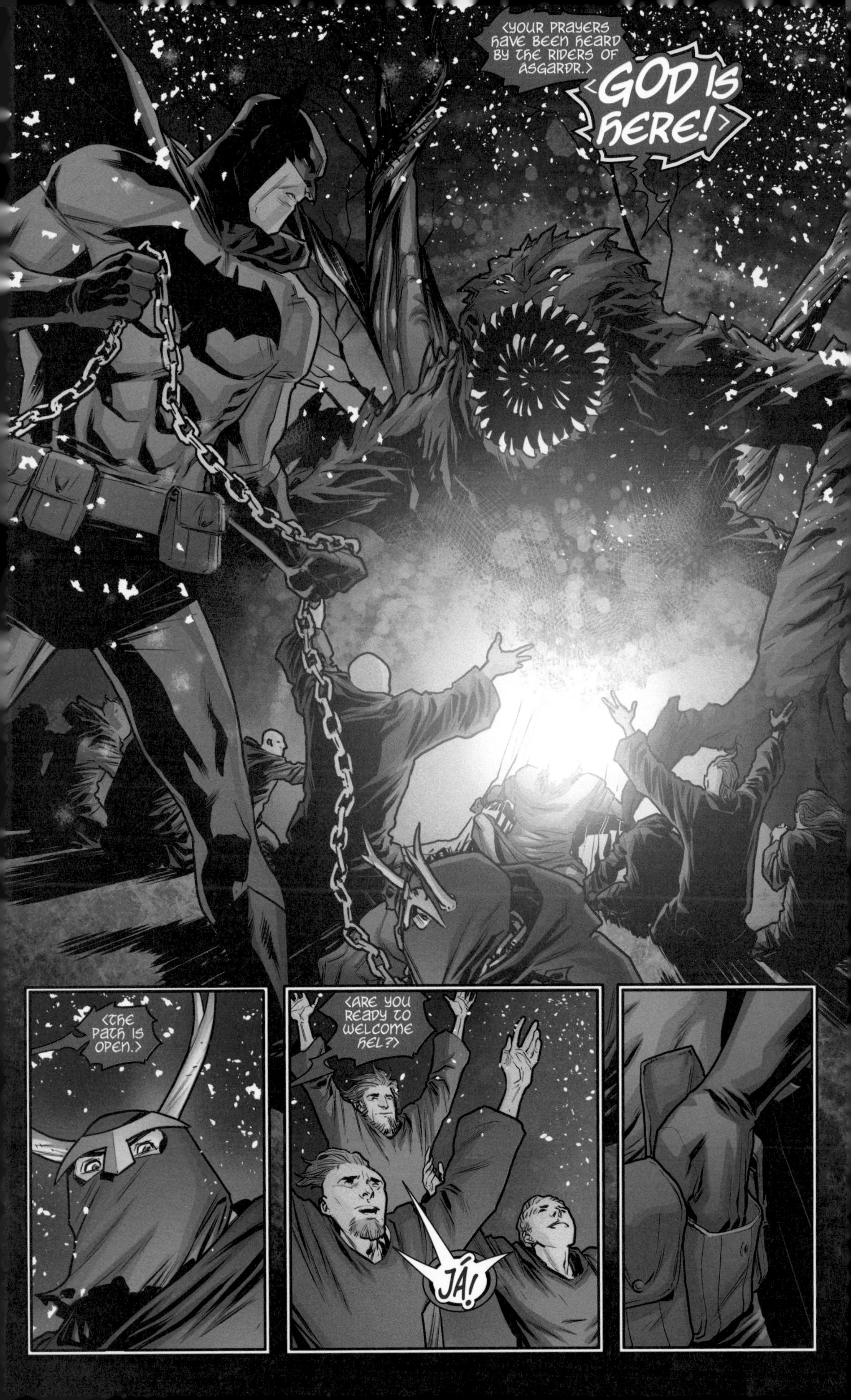
<YOUR PRAYERS HAVE BEEN HEARD BY THE RIDERS OF ASGARDR.>
<GOD IS HERE!>
<THE PATH IS OPEN.>
<ARE YOU READY TO WELCOME HEL?>
JÁ!

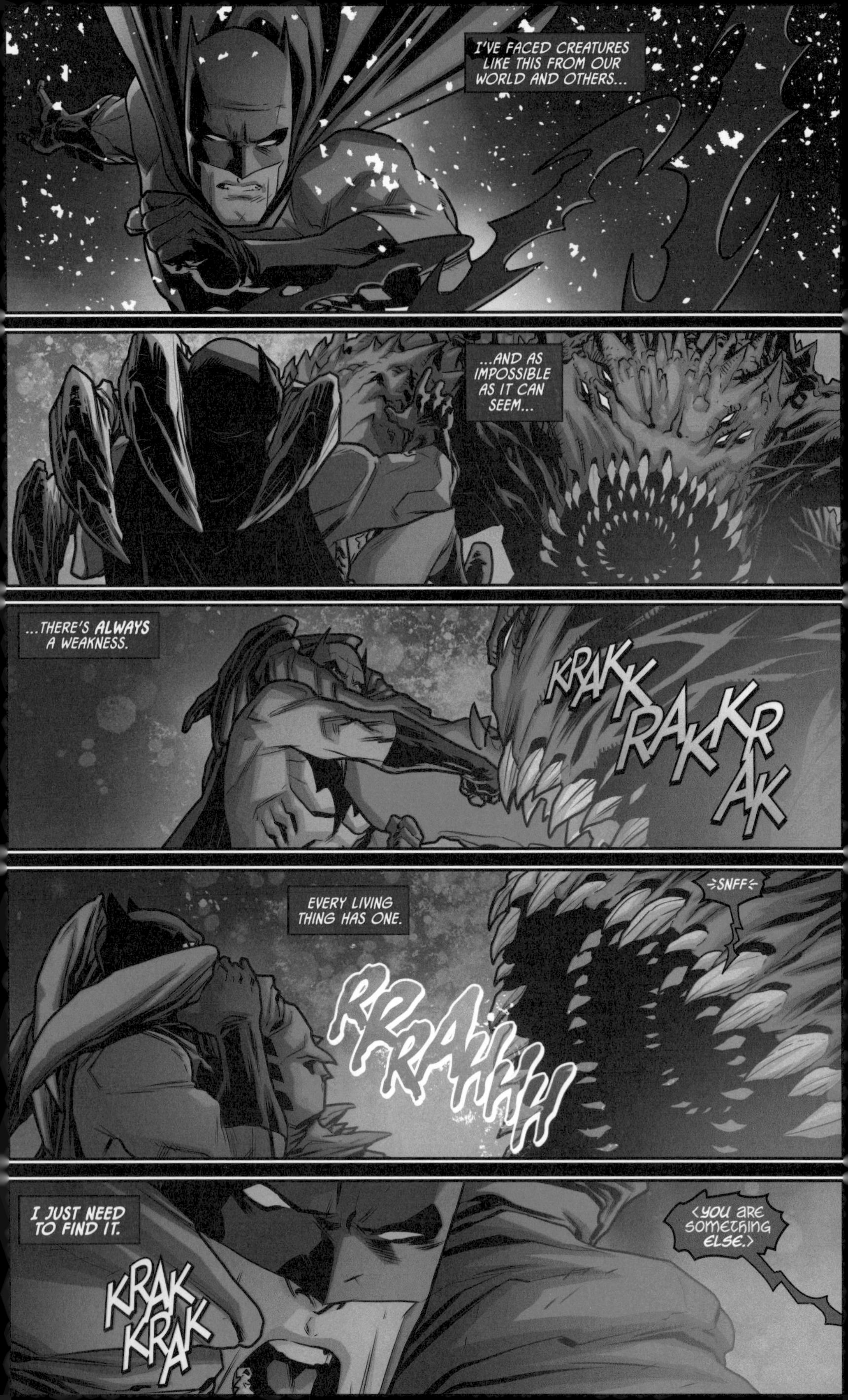
I'VE FACED CREATURES LIKE THIS FROM OUR WORLD AND OTHERS...
...AND AS IMPOSSIBLE AS IT CAN SEEM...
...THERE'S **ALWAYS** A WEAKNESS.
KRAKKRAKKRAK
EVERY LIVING THING HAS ONE.
SNFF
RRRAAHHH
I JUST NEED TO FIND IT.
KRAK KRAK
<YOU ARE SOMETHING ELSE.>

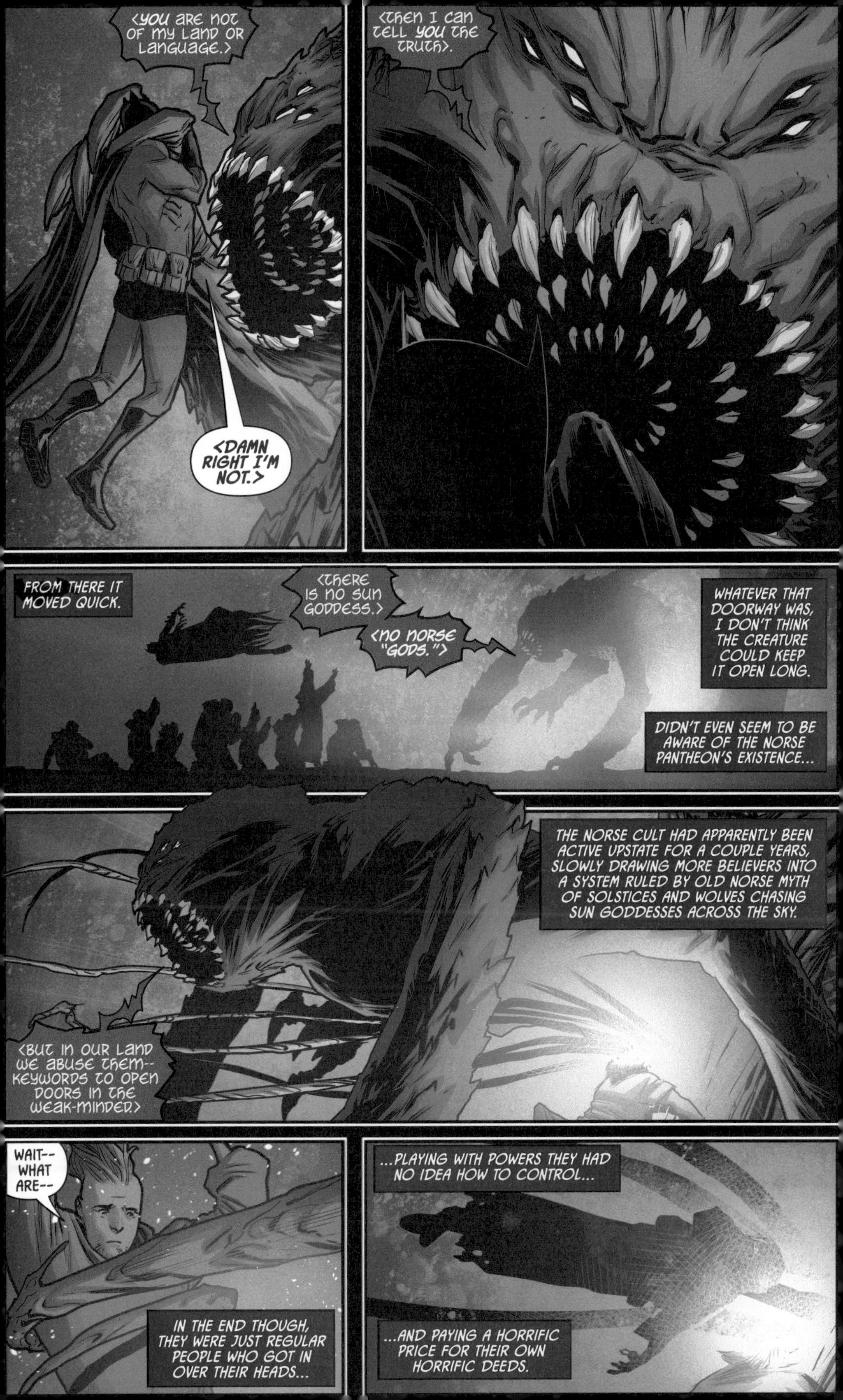

<YOU ARE NOT OF MY LAND OR LANGUAGE.>
<DAMN RIGHT I'M NOT.>
<THEN I CAN TELL YOU THE TRUTH>.
FROM THERE IT MOVED QUICK.
<THERE IS NO SUN GODDESS.>
<NO NORSE "GODS.">
WHATEVER THAT DOORWAY WAS, I DON'T THINK THE CREATURE COULD KEEP IT OPEN LONG.
DIDN'T EVEN SEEM TO BE AWARE OF THE NORSE PANTHEON'S EXISTENCE...
THE NORSE CULT HAD APPARENTLY BEEN ACTIVE UPSTATE FOR A COUPLE YEARS, SLOWLY DRAWING MORE BELIEVERS INTO A SYSTEM RULED BY OLD NORSE MYTH OF SOLSTICES AND WOLVES CHASING SUN GODDESSES ACROSS THE SKY.
<BUT IN OUR LAND WE ABUSE THEM-- KEYWORDS TO OPEN DOORS IN THE WEAK-MINDED>
WAIT-- WHAT ARE--
IN THE END THOUGH, THEY WERE JUST REGULAR PEOPLE WHO GOT IN OVER THEIR HEADS...
...PLAYING WITH POWERS THEY HAD NO IDEA HOW TO CONTROL...
...AND PAYING A HORRIFIC PRICE FOR THEIR OWN HORRIFIC DEEDS.

THEIR LEADER WAS AN OUT-OF-WORK ACTOR NAMED JACK ELDER.

MY RESEARCH SAYS HE FORMED THIS **NORSEMEN RISING** GROUP AS A WAY TO RAISE MONEY FOR HIS TAX DEBT.

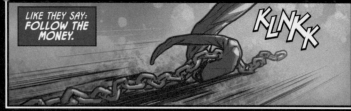

LIKE THEY SAY: FOLLOW THE MONEY.

KLNKK

GHANNK

AGGH!

<NO!>

<I AM READY TO FACE THE NIGHT, GODDESS SUN!>

<ENOUGH-- STOP!>

<YES! I SEE HER!>

THE CREATURE'S POWER-- WHEREVER IT COMES FROM--WAS TOO MUCH.

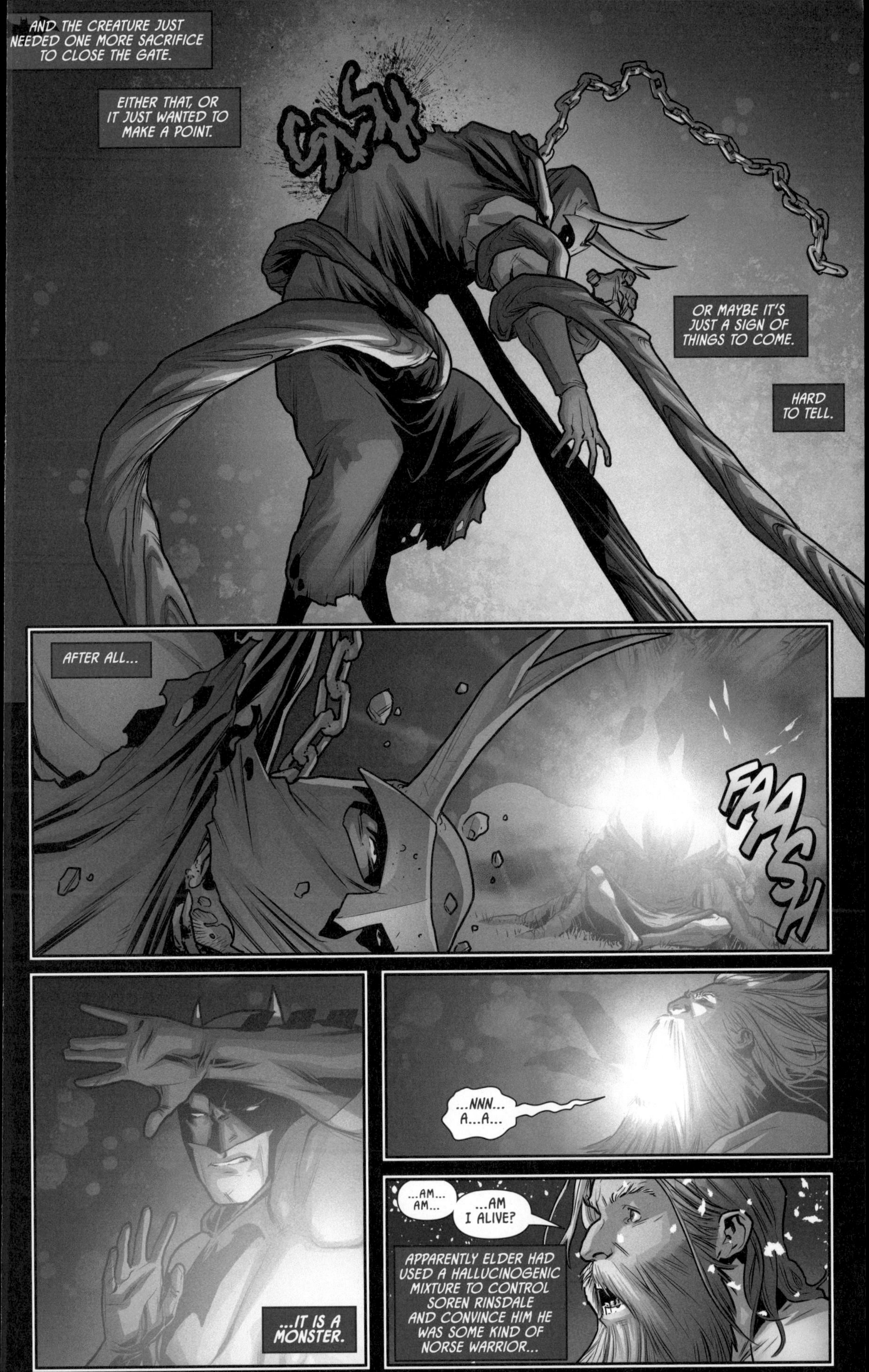
AND THE CREATURE JUST NEEDED ONE MORE SACRIFICE TO CLOSE THE GATE.
EITHER THAT, OR IT JUST WANTED TO MAKE A POINT.
GASH
OR MAYBE IT'S JUST A SIGN OF THINGS TO COME.
HARD TO TELL.
AFTER ALL...
FAASH
...IT IS A MONSTER.
...NNN... A...A...
...AM... AM...
...AM I ALIVE?
APPARENTLY ELDER HAD USED A HALLUCINOGENIC MIXTURE TO CONTROL SOREN RINSDALE AND CONVINCE HIM HE WAS SOME KIND OF NORSE WARRIOR...

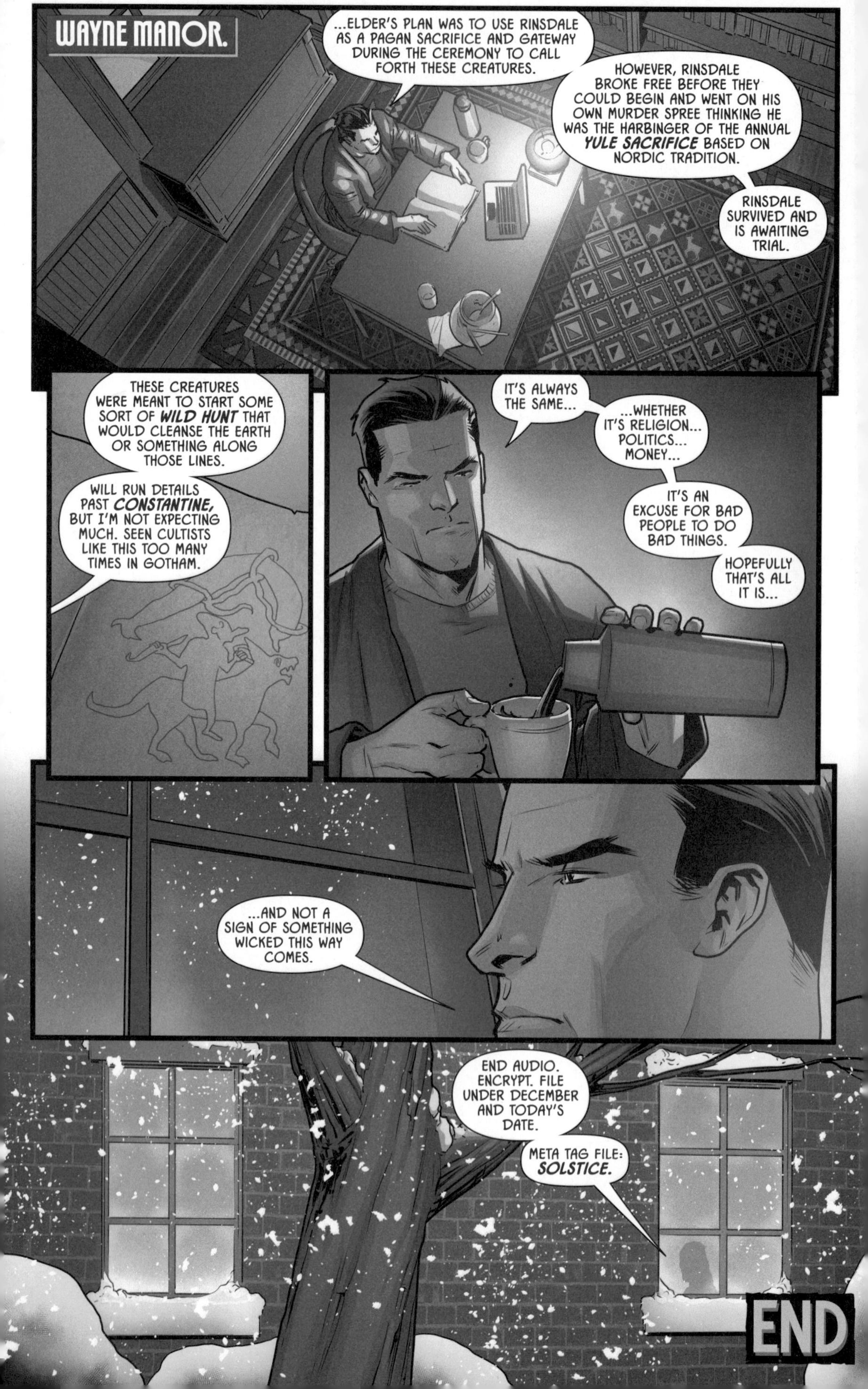
WAYNE MANOR.
...ELDER'S PLAN WAS TO USE RINSDALE AS A PAGAN SACRIFICE AND GATEWAY DURING THE CEREMONY TO CALL FORTH THESE CREATURES.
HOWEVER, RINSDALE BROKE FREE BEFORE THEY COULD BEGIN AND WENT ON HIS OWN MURDER SPREE THINKING HE WAS THE HARBINGER OF THE ANNUAL YULE SACRIFICE BASED ON NORDIC TRADITION.
RINSDALE SURVIVED AND IS AWAITING TRIAL.
THESE CREATURES WERE MEANT TO START SOME SORT OF WILD HUNT THAT WOULD CLEANSE THE EARTH OR SOMETHING ALONG THOSE LINES.
WILL RUN DETAILS PAST CONSTANTINE, BUT I'M NOT EXPECTING MUCH. SEEN CULTISTS LIKE THIS TOO MANY TIMES IN GOTHAM.
IT'S ALWAYS THE SAME...
...WHETHER IT'S RELIGION... POLITICS... MONEY...
IT'S AN EXCUSE FOR BAD PEOPLE TO DO BAD THINGS.
HOPEFULLY THAT'S ALL IT IS...
...AND NOT A SIGN OF SOMETHING WICKED THIS WAY COMES.
END AUDIO. ENCRYPT. FILE UNDER DECEMBER AND TODAY'S DATE.
META TAG FILE: SOLSTICE.
END

VARIANT COVER GALLERY

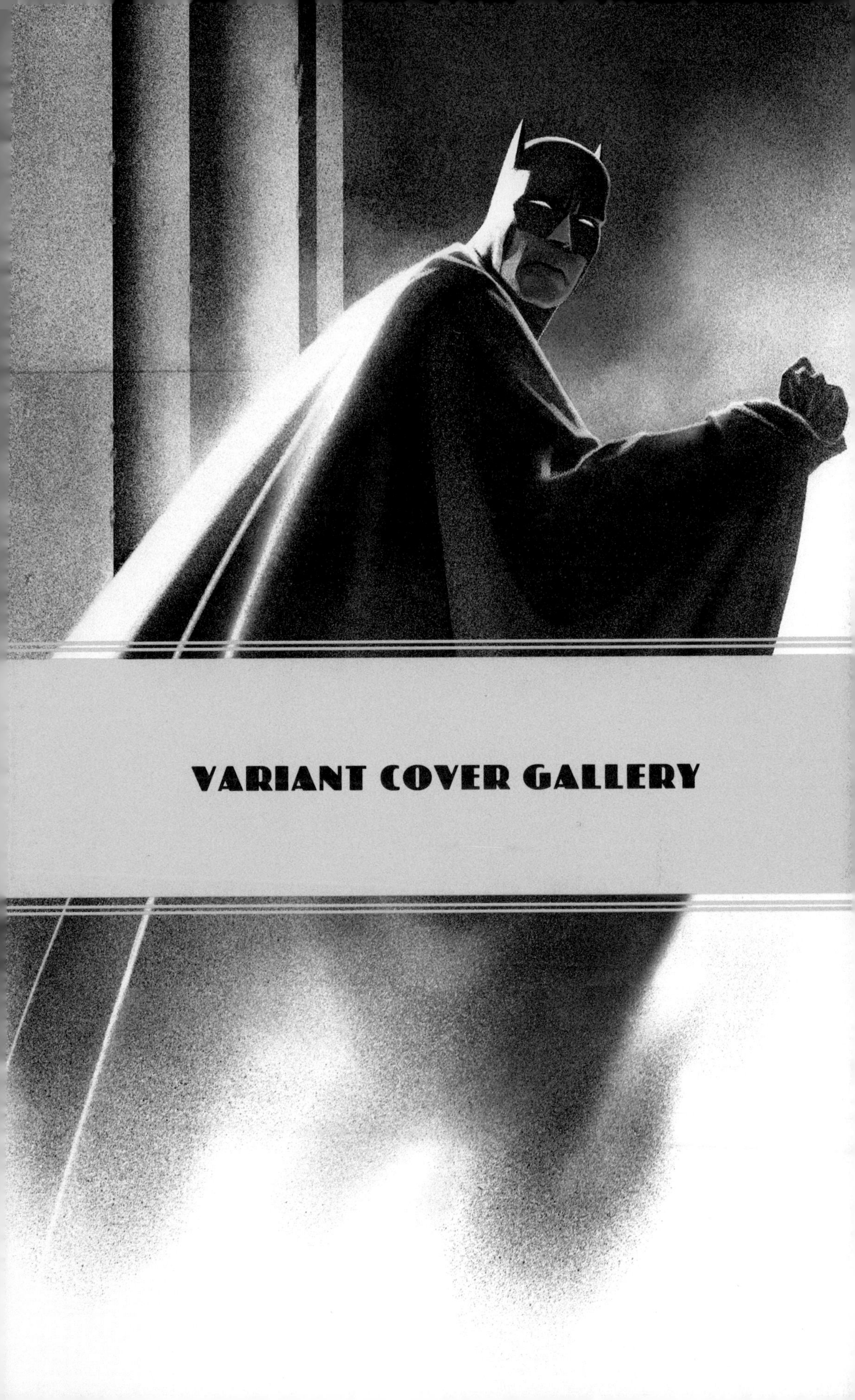

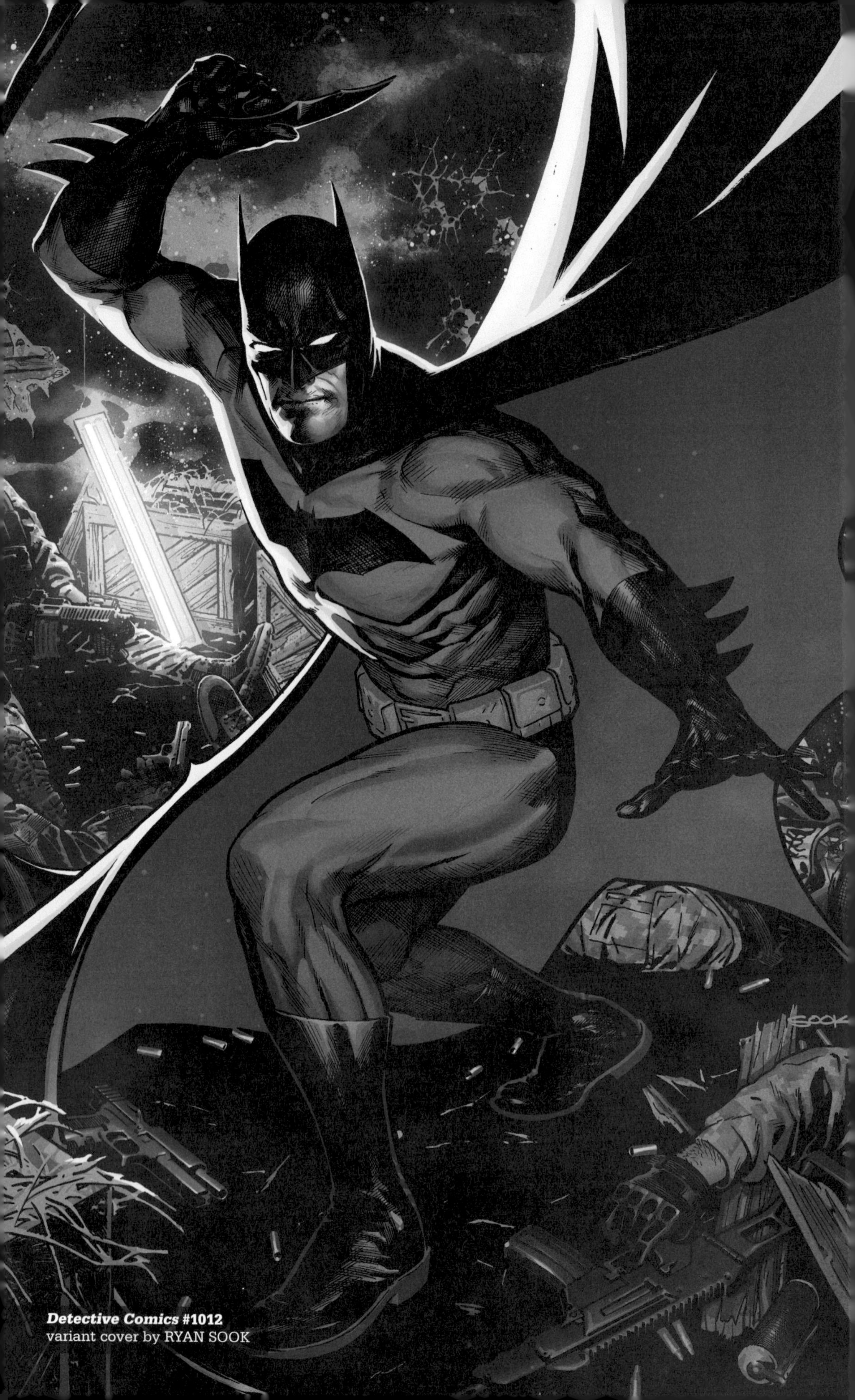
SOOK

***Detective Comics* #1012**
variant cover by RYAN SOOK

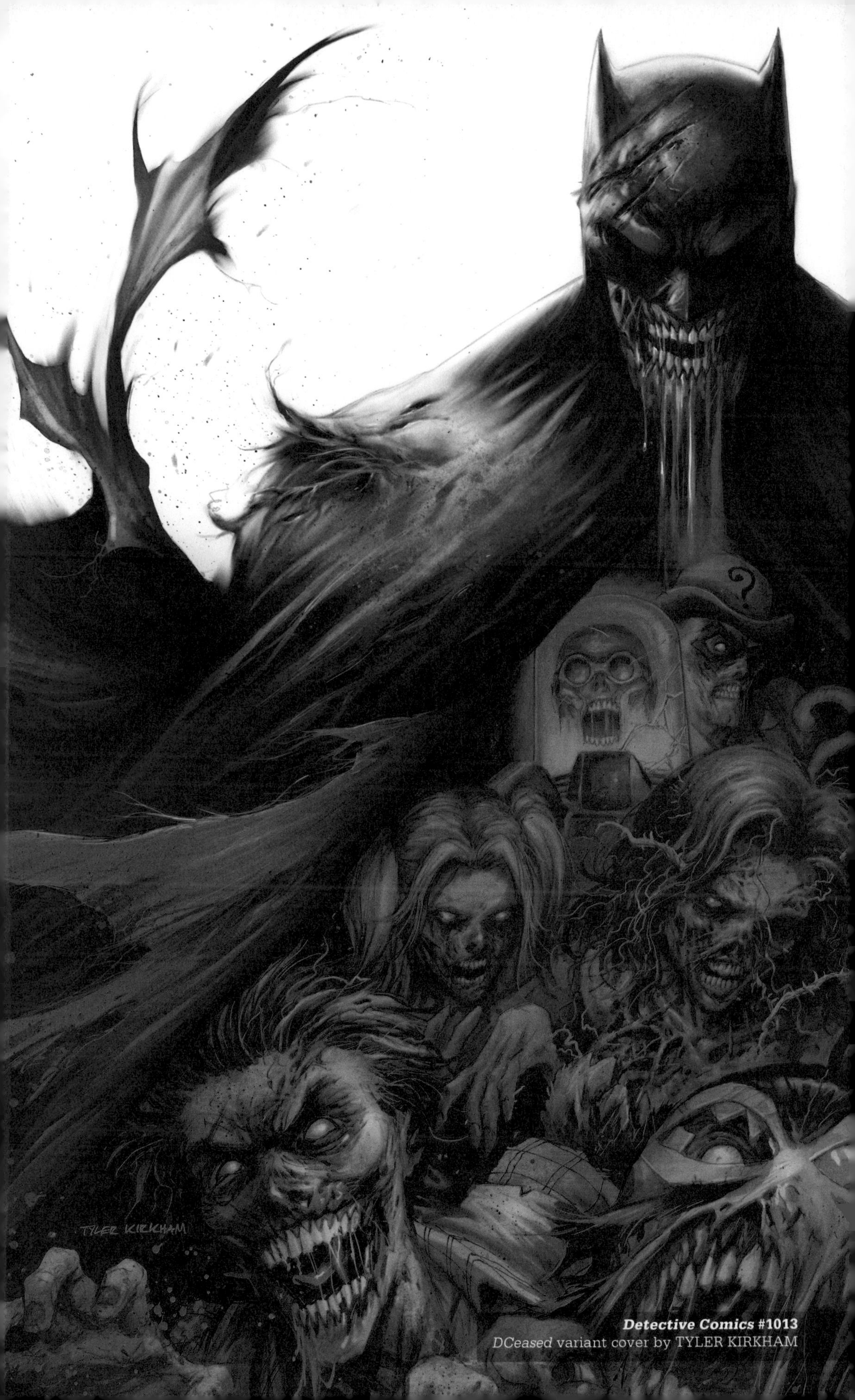
TYLER KIRKHAM

***Detective Comics* #1013**
DCeased variant cover by TYLER KIRKHAM

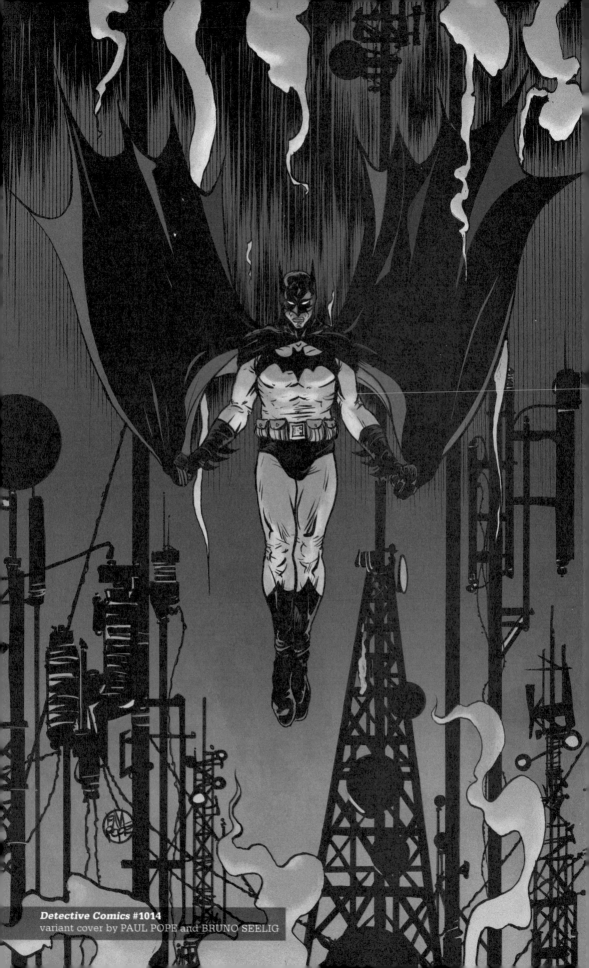

Detective Comics #1014
variant cover by PAUL POPE and BRUNO SEELIG

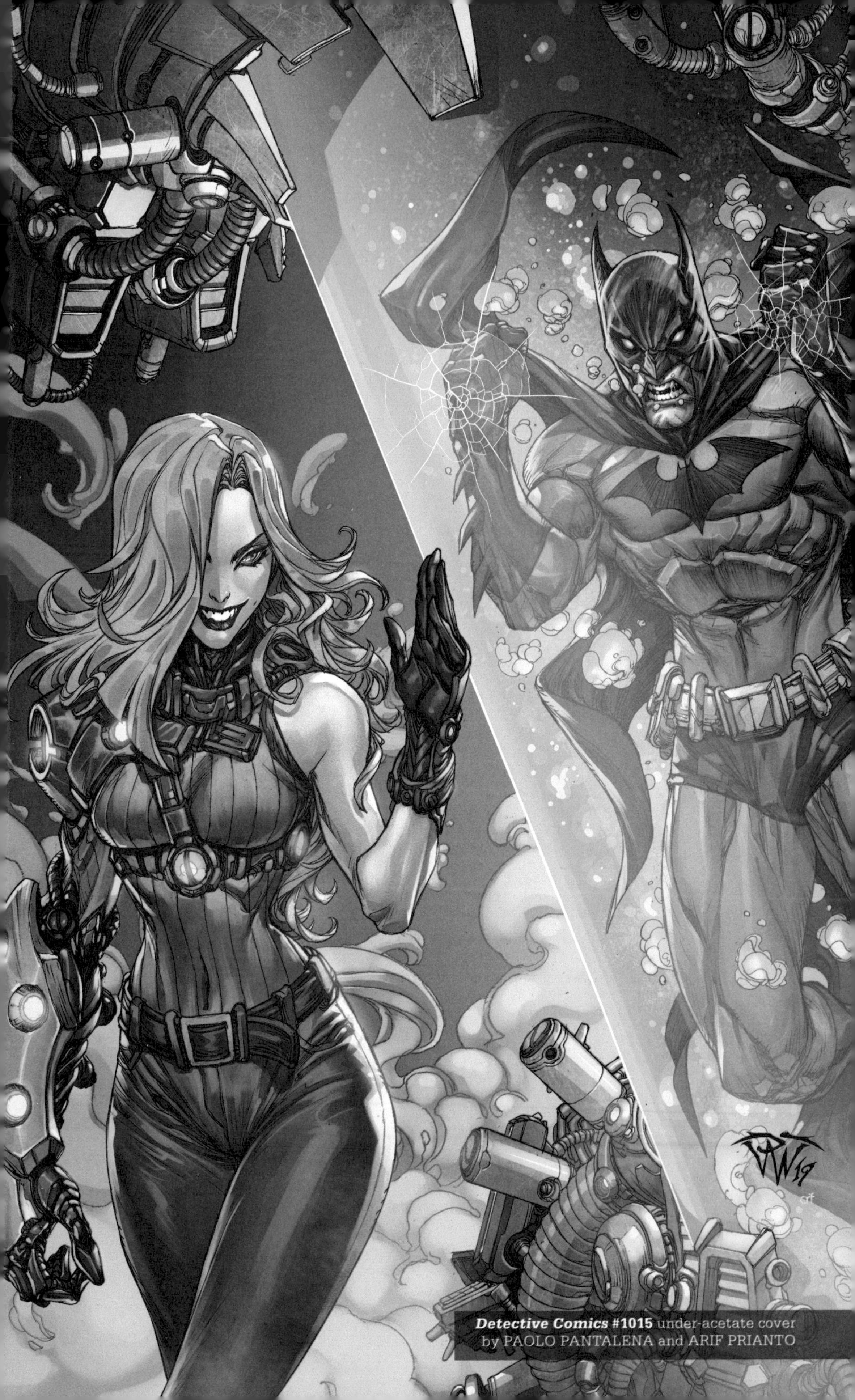

***Detective Comics* #1015** under-acetate cover
by PAOLO PANTALENA and ARIF PRIANTO

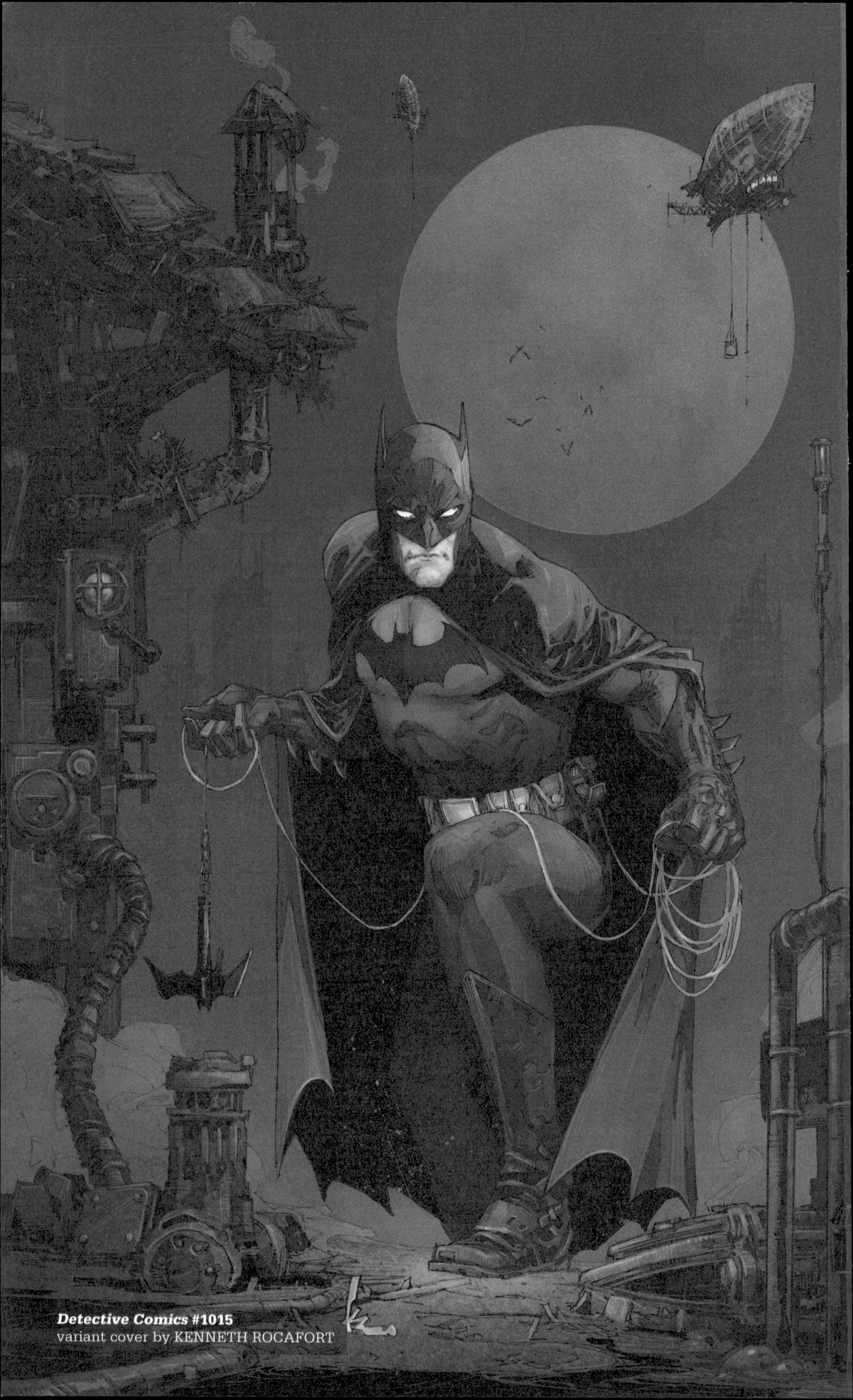

***Detective Comics* #1015**
variant cover by KENNETH ROCAFORT

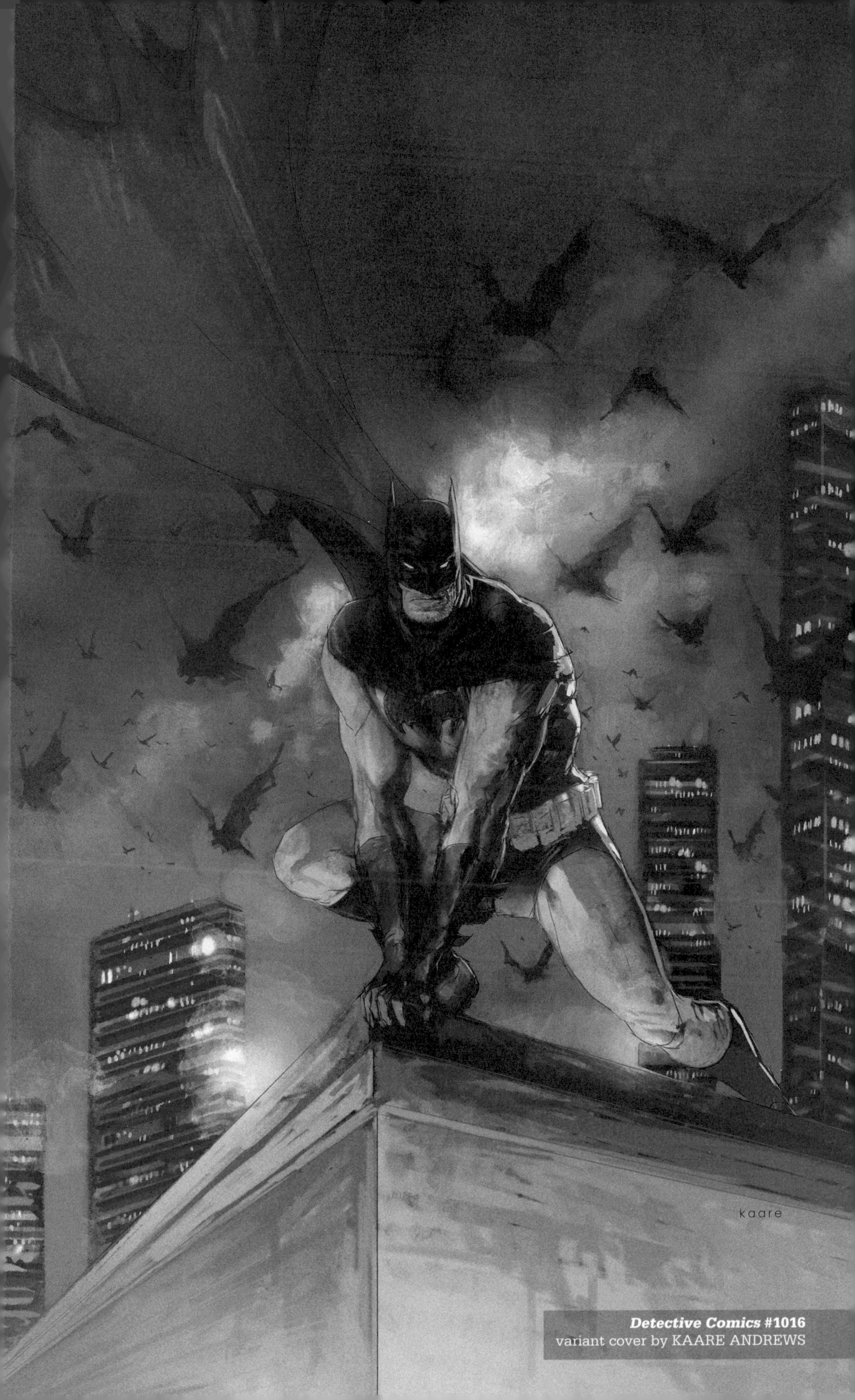
kaare

***Detective Comics* #1016**
variant cover by KAARE ANDREWS

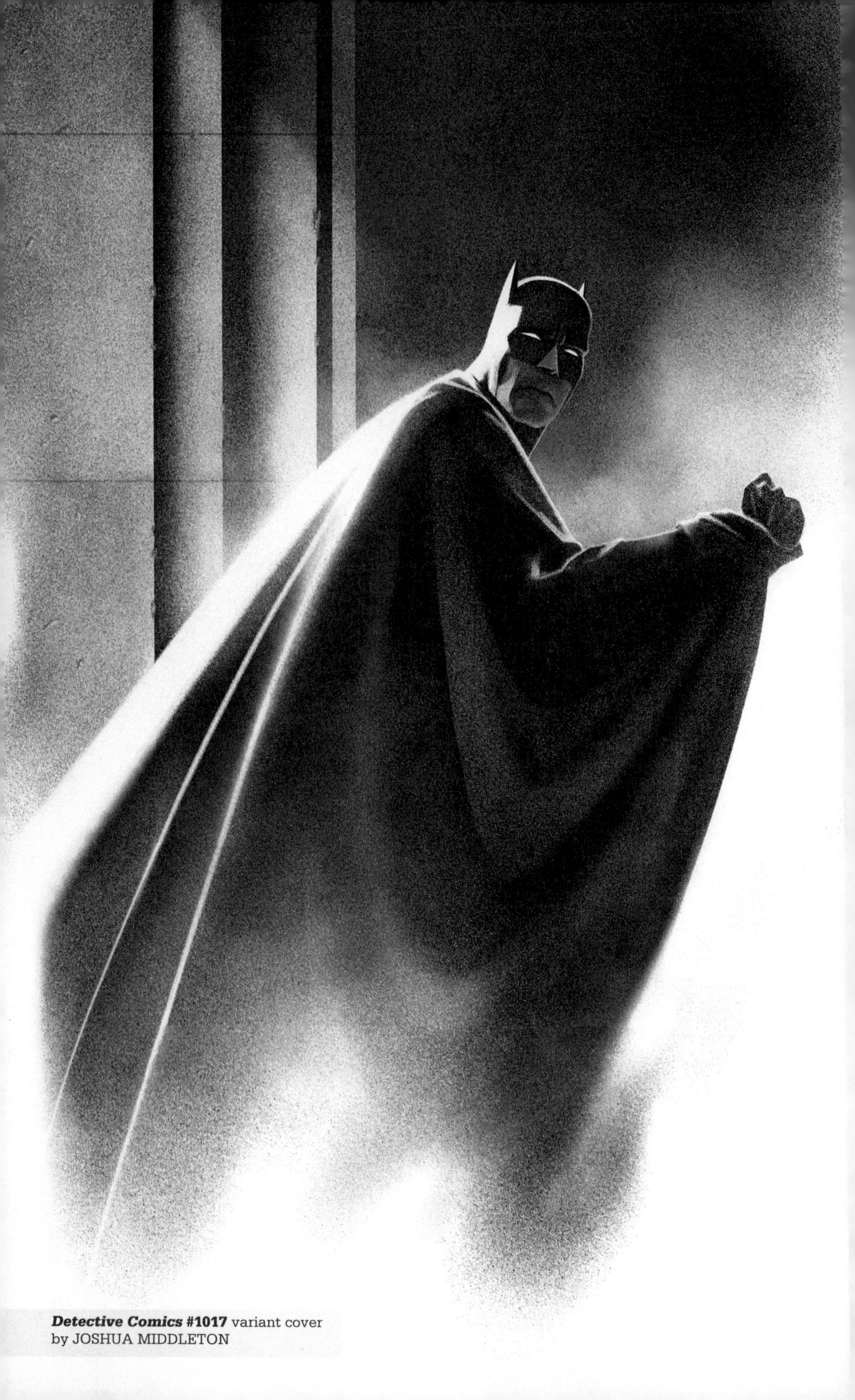

***Detective Comics* #1017** variant cover
by JOSHUA MIDDLETON

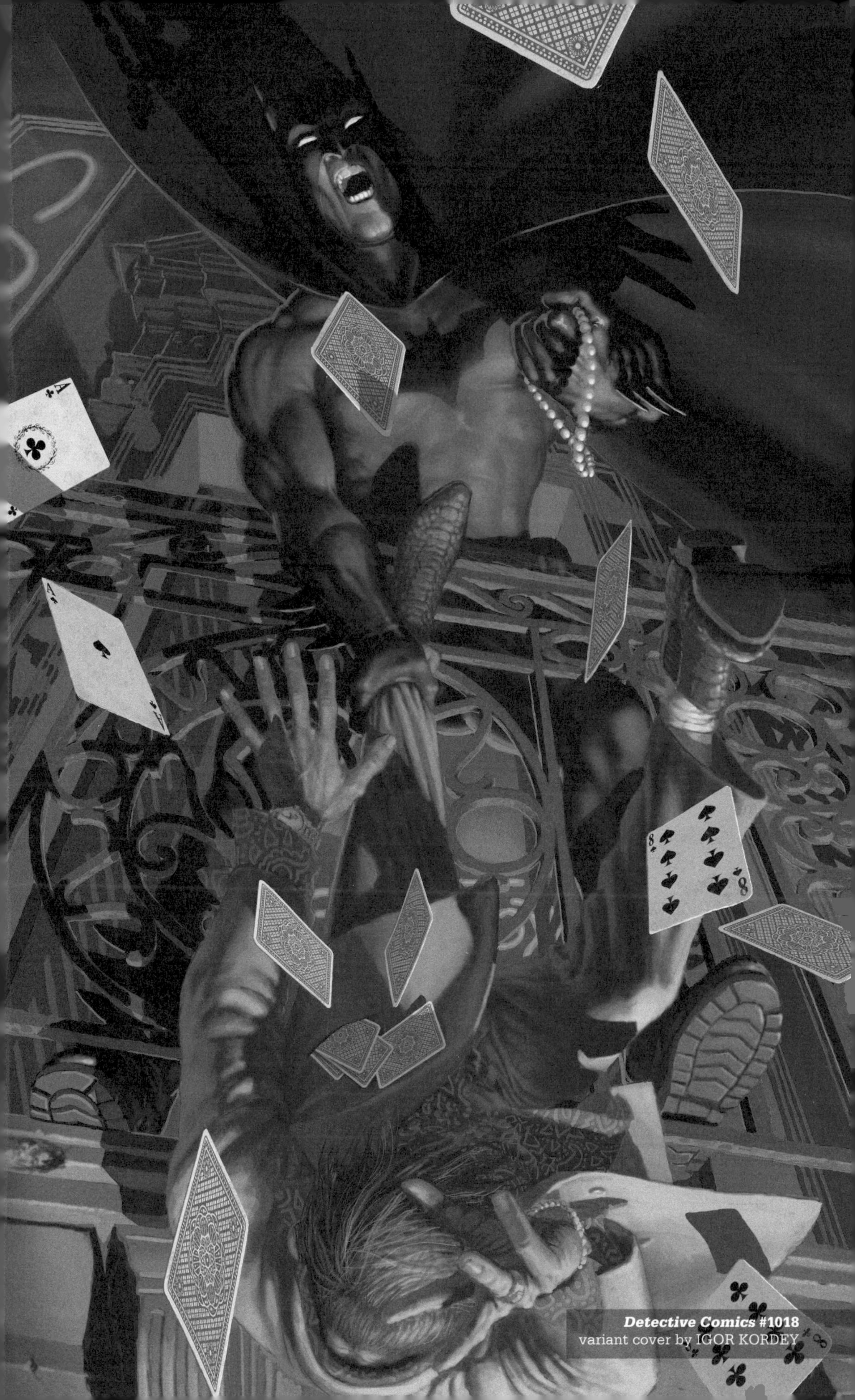

***Detective Comics* #1018**
variant cover by IGOR KORDEY

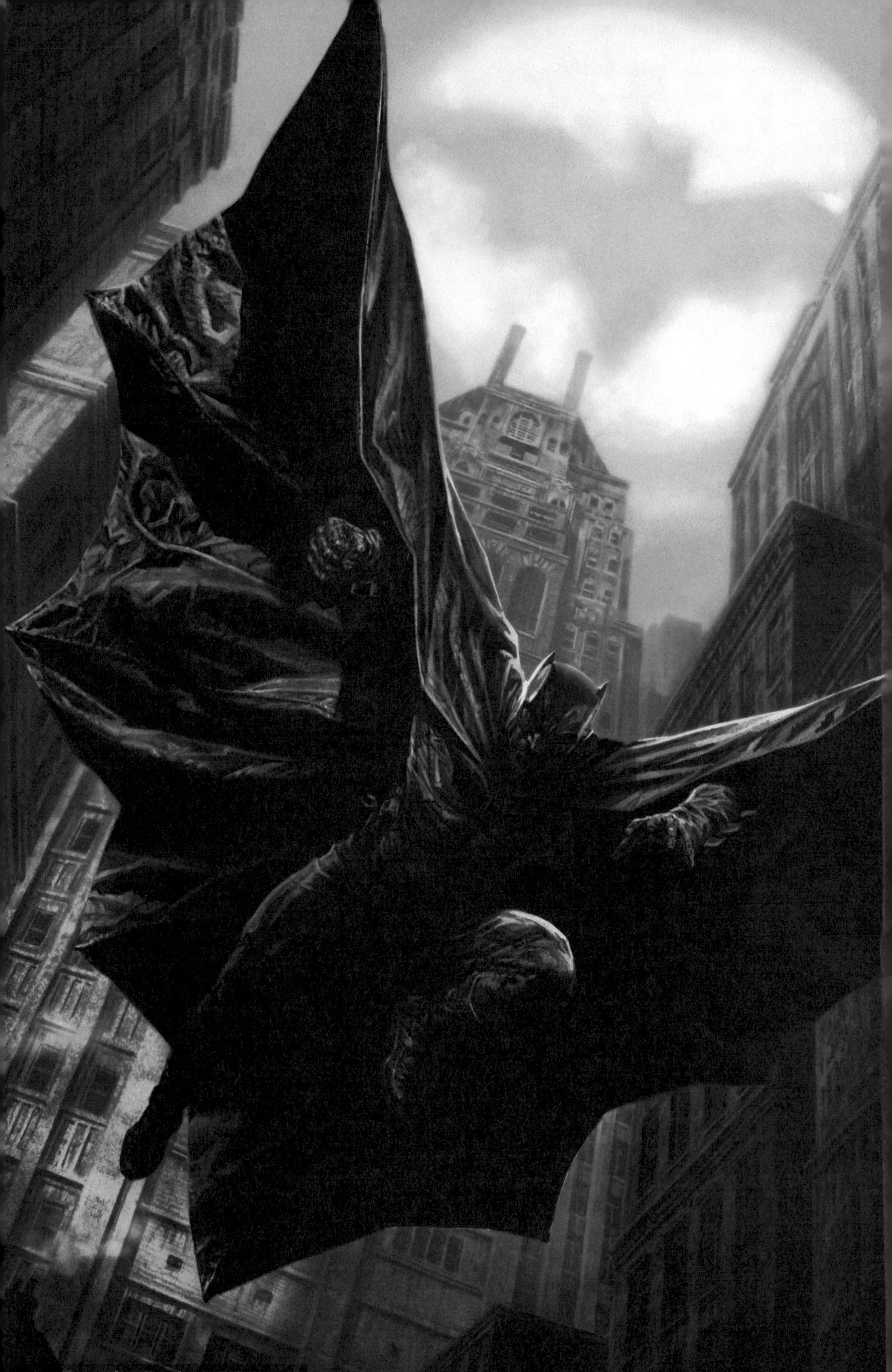

***Detective Comics* #1019**
variant cover by LEE BERMEJO

***Detective Comics* #1014**
page 2 pencils by DOUG MAHNKE

***Detective Comics* #1014**
page 6 pencils by DOUG MAHNKE

***Detective Comics* #1018**
cover pencils by RAFA SANDOVAL

***Detective Comics* #1018**
cover inks by JORDI TARRAGONA